DIRTY GOLD

DIRTY
GOLD

THE RISE AND FALL OF AN
INTERNATIONAL SMUGGLING RING

JAY WEAVER,
NICHOLAS NEHAMAS,
JIM WYSS AND KYRA GURNEY

PUBLICAFFAIRS

New York

PublicAffairs
Hachette Book Group
1290 Avenue of the Americas, New York, NY 10104
www.publicaffairsbooks.com
@Public_Affairs

Printed in the United States of America

First Edition: March 2021

Published by PublicAffairs, an imprint of Perseus Books, LLC, a subsidiary of Hachette Book Group, Inc. The PublicAffairs name and logo is a trademark of the Hachette Book Group.

The Hachette Speakers Bureau provides a wide range of authors for speaking events. To find out more, go to www.hachettespeakersbureau.com or call (866) 376-6591.

The publisher is not responsible for websites (or their content) that are not owned by the publisher.

Print book interior design by Jeff Williams

Library of Congress Cataloging-in-Publication Data

Names: Weaver, Jay (Journalist) author. | Nehamas, Nicholas, author. | Wyss, Jim, author. Gurney, Kyra, author.

Title: Dirty gold : the rise and fall of an international smuggling ring / Jay Weaver, Nicholas Nehamas, Jim Wyss, Kyra Gurney.

Description: New York : PublicAffairs, 2021. | Includes bibliographical references and index.

Identifiers: LCCN 2020038458 | ISBN 9781541762909 (hardcover) | ISBN 9781541762916 (ebook)

Subjects: LCSH: Gold smuggling—Peru. | Gold mines and mining—Peru. | International trade. | Smugglers—Peru—Biography.

Classification: LCC HD9536.A2 W383 2021 | DDC 364.1/336—dc23

LC record available at https://lccn.loc.gov/2020038458

ISBNs: 978-1-5417-6290-9 (hardcover), 978-1-5417-6291-6 (ebook)

LSC-C

Printing 1, 2021

This book is dedicated to Ana, Daniel, Danielle, and Marta. Without your love and support it would not have been possible.

Dirty Gold *also owes an enormous debt to the tireless staff of the* Miami Herald *and* el Nuevo Herald, *who cover America's most interesting city without fear or favor. We are honored to have worked with them.*

Contents

PART II

PART III

Cast of Characters

NTR Metals

Samer Barrage, *NTR Metals vice president for Latin America*
Juan Pablo Granda, *NTR Metals trader*
Renato Rodriguez, *NTR Metals trader*

Elemetal

John and Steve Loftus, *cofounders of Elemetal, NTR's parent company*
Bill LeRoy, *Elemetal CEO*
Alan Stockmeister, *Elemetal chairman*
Steve Crogan, *Elemetal compliance officer*

US Investigators

Drug Enforcement Administration

Timothy Schoonmaker, *DEA special agent, Lima*
Steve Fischer, *DEA special agent, Lima*

Federal Bureau of Investigation

Refina Willis, *FBI special agent, Miami*

Homeland Security Investigations

Cole Almeida, *HSI special agent, Miami*
Danielle DiLeo, *HSI forensic accountant, Miami*

US Attorney's Office for the Southern District of Florida

Frank Maderal, *federal prosecutor, Miami*
Michael Sherwin, *federal prosecutor, Miami*

Perú
Peter Ferrari's Crew

Pedro David Pérez Miranda, aka Peter Ferrari, *Peruvian gold exporter and NTR supplier*
Peter Davis Pérez Gutierrez, *one of Peter Ferrari's twin sons*
Gian Piere Pérez Gutierrez, *one of Peter Ferrari's twin sons*
Joseph Cesar Leyva Miyashiro, *Peter Ferrari's driver*
Rolando Madueño Chocano, *one of Peter Ferrari's associates and alleged straw men*
Andrés Tejeda, *a customs broker*

Peruvian Investigators

Ramón Barboza Montes, aka Pequeño, *Peruvian police sergeant*
Jorge Domínguez Grandez, *Peruvian National Police supervisor*

Peruvian Prosecutor

Lizardo Pantoja, *Peruvian prosecutor investigating Peter Ferrari*

Ecuador
MVP Imports

Jeffrey Himmel, *president*
Paul Borja, *consultant*

Chile

Harold Vilches's Crew

Harold Vilches Pizarro, *NTR's main gold supplier in Chile*
Javier Concha Montes, *Vilches's employee*
Carlos Rivas Araya, *Vilches's father-in-law and employee*

Chilean Investigators

Juan Figueroa, *Investigations Police of Chile (PDI) supervisor*
Juan Pablo Sandoval Valencia, *Investigations Police of Chile (PDI) case agent*

Chilean Prosecutors

Pablo Alonso Godoy, *prosecutor on the Vilches case*
Emiliano Arias Madariaga, *lead prosecutor on the Vilches case until mid-2016*
Tufit Bufadel Godoy, *lead prosecutor on the Vilches case starting in mid-2016*
José Luis Pérez Calaf, *regional prosecutor overseeing the Vilches case*
Nicolás Rodríguez Videla, *prosecutor on the Vilches case*

PART I

Prologue

JUAN PABLO GRANDA STEPPED INTO A SMALL OFFICE IN A MIDDLE-CLASS neighborhood in the permanently foggy city of Lima, Perú, on February 18, 2013.[1]

The lights were off.

He couldn't see.

As his eyes adjusted to the darkness, Granda began to make out menacing shapes: two men, short and squat, with handguns strapped to their hips. Behind them, their boss sat at a desk. A single-barreled shotgun leaned against the wall.

Granda, a thirty-one-year-old Florida State University graduate with degrees in international business and management, wasn't there to buy cocaine or weapons, as the room's bristling tension might suggest.

He was there to buy gold, the metal that has mystified, entranced, and led human beings to destroy themselves since the dawn of time.

The office belonged to one of the biggest gold exporters in Perú, a developing South American nation where precious-metals brokers sometimes operate more like drug dealers than suit-and-tie commodities traders. Where Africa has its "blood diamonds," Perú and its neighbors in South America have "dirty gold"—and much of it ends up in jewelry and electronic goods purchased by unsuspecting consumers in the United States.

The metal Granda sought is produced by a little known and incredibly destructive criminal economy fueled by the cocaine trade. Under the nose of governments and law enforcement agencies around the world, dirty gold has infiltrated the global precious-metals industry.

Deep in Perú's Amazon rain forest, tens of thousands of struggling wildcat miners use backhoes, pickaxes, and high-powered hoses to rip the metal from pristine jungle riverbanks and toxic mercury to strip it from rock. Violent drug traffickers and other criminal gangs control many of the mines and smuggling routes. Mining camps are overrun by vermin and disease. Women and children are coerced into the sex trade to serve the hard-living miners, who travel from Perú's mountains and coasts to find some of the most lucrative work available in this country of 32.5 million people. Nearly half of the people who live in Perú's rural highlands, along its jungle rivers, or on the edges of its subtropical deserts do so in poverty, many without running water, electricity, or basic healthcare.[2] Illegal gold mining is one of the best ways out.

The miners have turned an area in Perú's southeastern rain forest known as La Pampa into one of the hemisphere's largest illegal gold mines, a giant tear-drop-shaped desert that stretches more than forty-two square miles. In La Pampa, anywhere from thirty thousand to forty thousand men, women, and children dig through the muck day and night in search of the elusive metal. While the rain forests of the surrounding province, Madre de Dios (Mother of God), support some of the richest wildlife found anywhere on Earth, La Pampa has been transformed into a hostile, alien planet. For every ounce of gold the miners extract, researchers estimate that they leave behind nine tons of waste, amid giant craters filled with chemical-tainted water colored in unearthly shades of electric blue and metallic orange.[3]

Thanks in part to mines like La Pampa, South America's old-growth rain forest is being turned into a desolate wasteland. After fossil fuel combustion, deforestation is believed to be the second-leading driver of climate change. In Perú alone, an area bigger than all five boroughs of New York City has been stripped to bare, mottled earth.[4] The story is the same across much of the Amazon. Although loggers and cattle ranchers tear down far more jungle than miners, the mercury used in illicit gold mining can poison the rain forest and local peoples for generations.

For Perú's government, La Pampa became something even more sinister than an environmental catastrophe: a toxic stew of poverty and criminality, where police dared not tread and international and Peruvian laws were mere conjecture. If miners wanted to sleep with underage girls, there was a price for that. If they needed to settle a score, La Pampa's mining pits were ready-made graves with no undertaker to ask questions.

"You can find everything in there . . . abuses of every kind," Peruvian defense minister José Huerta Torres said. "And that's not to mention the ecological barbarities that are being committed against the Amazon."[5]

Although solutions do exist—including less destructive forms of mining that would actually increase gold yields—there is little will to solve the problems as long as the gold keeps flowing. And the rush of gold won't stop as long as there are men like Granda who come from overseas to buy it.

By the time he stepped into that dark Lima office, Granda knew all about the evils of illegal mining—he just didn't care. His job was to acquire gold for NTR Metals, the Miami subsidiary of Dallas-based Elemetal, one of the largest international gold-trading companies in the United States. As much gold as he could possibly find.

For Granda, convincing the Peruvian gold dealer to agree to an exclusive relationship with NTR could jump-start his new career, one that followed jobs in South Florida selling subprime mortgages and classes for an online university.

Granda launched into a carefully crafted pitch. NTR had the best prices, Granda told the gold dealer—and could pay faster than any of its competitors. He had seen how rival American firms operating in Perú misweighed and undervalued the gold that suppliers brought in to sell.

"You're getting ripped off," Granda said.

The Peruvian gold dealer was impressed. He was the second in command in his office—which, it turned out, was dark not for purposes of intimidation but because of one of Lima's frequent power outages. He invited Granda and his fellow NTR salesman, Renato Rodriguez, to join his boss for dinner that evening.

Over a meal of ceviche, Perú's signature citrus-cured raw fish dish, they closed the deal. The rookie trader had won his first client for NTR.

It wouldn't be his last.

Over the next few years, Granda, Rodriguez, and their boss, a savvy British-born salesman named Samer Barrage, would help NTR's parent company, Elemetal, dominate Latin America's often dangerous and corrupt gold market, going from importing a few bars per month to doing $1 billion worth of business in a single year. By the end of their run, they had traded $3.6 billion of gold.

The three NTR gold traders thrived on cutting deals with a roguish cast of precious-metals suppliers, customs officials, and money men. Their bosses in Dallas turned around and sold that dirty gold to some of the biggest corporations in the United States, including nearly seventy Fortune 500 clients.[6] Apple, Google, Lockheed Martin, Macy's, and many more—unaware of the gold's tainted origin— bought Elemetal's product, turning the metal into watches, jewelry, and smartphones for millions of Americans.

NTR's success wouldn't go unnoticed.

US federal law enforcement agents had been sniffing around the gold industry for years. They suspected the trade in Latin America had ties to narco-trafficking. But they didn't know just how destructive illegal mining was—or why the United States should care. To contend with NTR, it would take an ambitious, bow-tie-wearing Miami prosecutor and a team of federal investigators from three different agencies more used to battling each other for turf than collaborating against international criminal syndicates. The feds would christen themselves "The Fellowship of the Ring"— named after the fractious crew of J. R. R. Tolkien characters tasked with destroying Sauron's evil golden ring of power. By the end of their investigation, the prosecutors and agents would come to see dirty gold as one of the most serious environmental and human rights catastrophes of the twenty-first century.

Perhaps no one has described the crisis with the searing moral clarity of Pope Francis, who visited Madre de Dios in 2018 and witnessed what he called unadulterated cruelty.

Addressing thousands of people who had traveled for days by canoe, foot, and minibus to hear him speak, Francis described the gold industry as a clash between two worlds. On one side were the rapacious miners and multinationals who were feeding the vanity of unwitting consumers in places like New York, Miami, Paris, and Hong Kong. On the other side were the locals, who were forced by economic circumstances to participate in the destruction of their own ecosystem and health.

Gold, Francis told his audience, was a pernicious and corrupting idol.[7]

It was, he said, a "false god that demands human sacrifice."

CHAPTER 1

The Party

THREE DAYS AFTER CLINCHING HIS FIRST GOLD DEAL, JUAN PABLO GRANDA clutched a toilet in the bathroom of Lima's trendy beachside restaurant Costa Verde, vomiting uncontrollably.

A torrent of bitter stomach acid mixed with pisco sours—Perú's supersweet, deadly strong national drink—rained down into the porcelain bowl.

It had been a hell of a birthday party for his company's biggest supplier, Pedro David Pérez Miranda, a muscular playboy with a thick mane of curly black hair who had been dubbed "Peter Ferrari" by the local press for his love of European sports cars, tight shirts, and beautiful women. Rumors of his fondness for plastic surgery abounded, including speculation that his tight buttocks were aided by implants. Ferrari spared no expense on his fifty-third birthday. A bottle of Johnnie Walker stood on each table. Gold Label, of course. Models and expensively suited men danced to the rhythms of a live salsa band. The room screamed money—and not necessarily the legitimate kind. In Perú, the world's second-leading producer of cocaine, the flashy Pérez Miranda had been dodging allegations for two decades that he dealt in stronger stuff than gold.

Granda was starting his new job traveling Latin America and the Caribbean as a gold buyer for Miami-based NTR Metals. His boss, Samer Barrage, and the more experienced salesman Renato Rodriguez had brought him to the party on February 21, 2013.

The three men had known each other in Miami for nearly a decade before going to work for NTR. Now, twenty-six hundred miles south in Perú, they were embarking on a grand adventure.

Granda, short and round-faced with jet-black hair, was the baby of the bunch, a hard-working, hard-partying bachelor from the suburbs south of Miami who had recently earned his MBA.[1]

Rodriguez, forty, was a working-class family man born to Ecuadorian immigrants and raised in Brooklyn.[2] He went by "Ronnie." On his arms, he wore three tattoos: his father's signature, his daughter's footprints, and the postmark from the letter that his father had mailed his mother asking her to marry him. He was a big man, six foot one and 280 pounds, sensitive about his weight, and desperate to fit in with Barrage and Granda, both handsome and suave. When the other two called him "Fat Ronnie," as they often did, the nickname stung. But Rodriguez didn't fight back. He yearned to be one of the gang. On their business trips across South America, when Granda and Barrage frequently hired escorts at local hotels, Rodriguez would shed his family-man exterior and join them.

Barrage, thirty-six, was the boss, more worldly and sophisticated than his subordinates.[3] Born in London, he spoke with a posh British accent and owned homes in Nicaragua and Spain. His brother worked at a top law firm in Washington, DC. His son went to an elite Miami prep school that produced half the city's mayors, lawyers, and judges.

They were three amigos, alike in their ambition and disregard for following the rules. They hungered for their vision of the American Dream. And Miami, America's modern-day Casablanca, was the best place to find it. Because of its proximity to Latin America, Miami had become the United States' gold-import capital, the center of a multi-billion-dollar gold industry that sells metal to hundreds of Fortune 500 companies and central banks.

The global supply chain rests on exporters like Pérez Miranda. For a year, Barrage and Rodriguez had cultivated the man better known as Peter Ferrari, finally stealing his business away from a rival Miami gold company in 2012. It was a major coup. Pérez Miranda didn't own any mines himself; rather, he was a "collector" or "aggregator" of metal that he bought from miners and smaller dealers. These brokers—in Spanish called *comercializadoras*—feed jungle metal from places like La Pampa, the giant illegal rain forest mine, into our pockets, through our ears, and around our fingers, wrists, and necks.

When Granda was finally done throwing up at Peter Ferrari's birthday party, Barrage and Rodriguez helped him from the bathroom to a couch in the restaurant's lounge. He took a fifteen-minute nap and then jumped up and started drinking again.

There was no time to rest. With Ferrari as a major client, the Americans believed they had bought a lucrative one-way ticket into the narcotics-fueled netherworld of illegal gold trading in Perú. Drug traffickers, always seeking ways to launder their money and appear to the outside world as legitimate businessmen, had started investing their cocaine cash in South America's informal gold-mining industry. It was a perfect cover.

Trading gold made financial sense, too. Between 1999 and 2011, the price of a single, fourteen-pound gold bar skyrocketed from $51,000 to $390,000, driven by terrorist attacks, financial insecurity, and a searing hunger for jewelry and electronics in the consumer markets of India, China, and the United States.[4] In America, the boom was helped by bullish gold bugs like Fox News host Glenn Beck, who produced fear-mongering advertisements urging listeners to invest in the reliable metal.

Most of the world's gold comes from mines controlled by multinational conglomerates. Just five countries produce half the world's annual gold supply: China (roughly 400 tons per year), Australia (300 tons per year), Russia (295 tons per year), the United States (210 tons per year), and Canada (180 tons per year).[5]

Those big mines have a host of problems: They destroy mountains, ravage landscapes, and contaminate the air, water, and soil. In countries with weak labor protections where gold is also mined— like Indonesia, South Africa, and Ghana—the big mines are known to exploit workers. But big mines are generally subject to far more regulations, and are more free from the influence of organized crime, than the industry that has come to be known as informal, or "artisanal," mining. The informal miners work outside the regulated government system.

There is nothing artisanal about how the vast majority of them mine; they are not craft cheese makers or country vintners. Rather, they are people desperately trying to earn a living through subsistence mining, with little education or access to financing and safe equipment. Because of their crude methods, the small-scale miners have become the world's largest source of mercury pollution, releasing an estimated 1,400 tons of the dangerous chemical into the earth's environment every year. As big mines and traditional sources of gold tap out, the growth in the small-scale mining industry has been tremendous. Twenty-five years ago, an estimated six million people worked in small-scale mines. Today, the World Bank estimates a hundred million artisanal miners worldwide are active in eighty countries, producing 20 percent of the global gold supply. At least a third of them are believed to be women and children. They abound in remote areas of underdeveloped countries in Latin America, Africa, and Southeast Asia.[6]

Elemetal, NTR's parent company, saw the small-scale miners as an opportunity. Before the Great Recession caused prices to spike, Elemetal only bought gold domestically, operating a chain of "We Buy Gold" stores across the United States. The storefronts took in metal from pawnshops, antique stores, and people looking to junk their heirlooms and old coins. But in 2012, the company expanded its operations abroad, to Latin America, where the legion of artisanal miners was carving a valuable new supply of gold out of the jungle.[7] Elemetal quickly surpassed its competitors as the largest buyer of South American gold. The rapid expansion brought the American company into contact with unsavory characters like Ferrari, particularly in the major gold-producing nations of Perú, Colombia, and Bolivia, which supply 40 percent of raw gold exports to the United States—and all of its cocaine. Thanks to the three amigos' aggressive sales tactics and see-no-evil approach, NTR Metals would buy nearly $1 billion worth of Peruvian gold by the end of 2013, or one of every two ounces of Peruvian metal heading for Miami.[8]

Granda, Barrage, and Rodriguez were far from the only traders buying dirty gold in Latin America.

They were simply the best at it.

∞∞∞∞∞∞

Even as a kid growing up in the flat, sprawling suburbs south of Miami, Juan Pablo Granda was fascinated by gold.

When his parents took him to visit his native Ecuador, which he'd left as a small child, Granda begged them to buy him one of the gold chains hanging in Quito's outdoor markets. "Gold is in my blood," Granda told his friends after joining NTR Metals in late 2012. "The Incas worshipped gold. It's in the water down there."

Named after Pope John Paul II, the Quito-born Granda became the man of the house as a young teen, when his parents split up and his father and older brother moved back to Ecuador. His mother, who worked in sales for wholesale flower companies, needed support—and Granda was clever and hard-working enough to provide it. He brought gum to school to sell to his friends. One winter, he hawked Christmas trees. He enrolled in one of the best high schools in Miami-Dade County, studying business and finance. Even though he stood barely five feet six inches, his tenacity and speed won him a starting spot as a cornerback on the school's football team. His grades were strong enough to earn a scholarship to Florida State University.

In 2004, Granda graduated from FSU with a double major in international business and management. He was so broke he had to borrow twenty dollars from a friend to fill up his car for the eight-hour drive south to Miami, where he moved back into his mother's modest suburban home. Work quickly found him. Thanks to a fraternity brother, Granda landed a job selling subprime loans for home lender Household Finance—a subsidiary of the financial giant HSBC—just as Miami's real estate market was peaking with record-high prices.

During the heady days of the housing bubble, anyone who wanted a loan could walk into a storefront and come out with money for a brand-new home.

Granda made $90,000 in his first year. He leased a Lexus 350. He bought a three-bedroom house on a lakefront in Cutler Bay, close to where he grew up, for $275,000. His down payment? Five bucks.

The job was mostly phone sales. In the office, the bosses showed them movies like *Boiler Room* and *Glengarry Glen Ross*, not as cautionary tales about the pitfalls of unethical salesmanship but as inspiration. The films were required viewing. Alec Baldwin's famous speech from *Glengarry Glen Ross* became a mantra for the testosterone-driven young salesmen.

"Coffee is for closers," they would shout as they sold homes to people who couldn't afford them.[9]

It was in this hothouse that Granda met the two men who would one day bring him on to their team of Miami's top gold dealers. Working in the subprime industry couldn't have been better training.

Renato Rodriguez was the manager at the loan office. Rodriguez and Granda didn't spend time together outside the office, but they did bond over their shared Ecuadorian heritage. At work, Rodriguez certified Granda as a fluent Spanish speaker, allowing him to earn more money.

Samer Barrage managed a branch the next town over. Rodriguez had hired him at a job fair a few years earlier and the talented Barrage rose quickly.

Barrage grew up in England in the 1980s. He was eleven when his parents split up. Two years later, he was packed off to boarding school. When he was seventeen, his mother married an American doctor and the family left for a new life in Macon, Georgia. By 2001, he had graduated from college, moved to Miami, started working for HSBC, gotten married, and had a son. While working full-time, he earned an MBA at the University of Miami.

In South Florida, the Barrage and Rodriguez families grew close, buoyed by successful careers. Selling subprime mortgages was easy money—until suddenly it wasn't. The real estate market didn't just crash in 2007. It imploded, wiping out the savings of a nation and costing many homeowners their heavily mortgaged properties. Soon, Cutler Bay, the city south of Miami where Granda worked and had grown up—with its newly built pool-filled subdivisions that desperate homeowners could no longer afford—boasted the highest foreclosure rate in Miami-Dade County.[10] It seemed to happen so fast. Six months before Granda was laid off, he had been promoted to manager and opened a new branch. Now, with no income, he stopped paying his mortgage so he could short-sell his house, returned his Lexus to buy his mother's Acura, and moved in with a friend in Fort Lauderdale. Barrage's marriage fell apart and he divorced.

Gloom hung over Miami. But the three amigos landed on their feet.

Barrage took a job as a sales manager at Kaplan University, one of the leaders in the booming field of for-profit higher education, which reeled in students who couldn't gain admission at traditional schools. Soon, he was promoted to director of the graduate admissions department. Barrage threw Granda a lifeline, hiring him as a salesman. Instead of selling the dream of a home, Granda was now selling the dream of higher education. The product didn't matter. Granda knew what he was really selling was himself. He was pursuing an MBA at Kaplan, he told prospective students. Why would he pitch them something he didn't believe in himself?

The hustle at Kaplan was lucrative, mainly because of easy-to-get federal government loans for students. But the school and others like it were criticized for offering worthless degrees and for practices like "guerrilla registration" that left students deeply in debt for classes they never signed up to take.[11] The Obama administration pushed to crack down.

Barrage, who by this point had remarried, didn't stick around for Kaplan's decline. In early 2011, he left for a new job. Something to do with gold, he told Granda. He didn't say much. They fell out of touch.

Then, more than a year later, in December of 2012, Barrage called Granda at home out of the blue.

"Unless you're happier than a pig in shit," he said, "I've got the perfect job for you."

CHAPTER 2

Moths to the Flame

GOLD HAS EXERTED A POWERFUL DOMINION OVER HUMANKIND FOR millennia.

Human beings have laid their dead to rest alongside hoards of the lustrous metal as far back as 4600 BCE, when the Neolithic Varna culture of modern-day Bulgaria, known for its skill in metallurgy, began to construct a vast cemetery containing more than three hundred graves.

The Varna necropolis was the first recorded instance of gold being deposited at a burial site.[1] But even then gold was the preserve of only the wealthiest: Just four graves contained more than three-quarters of all the gold that modern-day archaeologists have unearthed across the entire cemetery. One highly revered man, a chieftain presumably, was discovered "adorned with gold bangles, necklaces made from gold beads, heavy gold pendants, and delicate, pierced gold disks that once hung from his clothes," according to *Smithsonian Magazine*. In his hands, the man held a gold-handled axe. Lying next to him was the strangest discovery of all: a penis sheath made entirely of gold.

Later, the powerful pharaohs of Egypt insisted on being entombed clothed in gold, which they called the "flesh of the gods." In Greek mythology, a golden apple sparked the Trojan War of Homeric lore roughly twelve hundred years before the birth of Christ. And, millennia later, when the Incas went on the warpath in the fifteenth century—transforming themselves from a small highland tribe into one of the Southern Hemisphere's greatest empires—they absorbed their rivals' miners, artisans, and goldsmiths with religious zeal.

For the Incas, gold and silver held mystical qualities that connected them with the cosmos and their origins. The sun, Inti, was a deity and yellow gold was his earthly manifestation: "the sweat of the sun."

As the Incas scoured their growing empire for precious metals, they went beyond simple panning techniques and began gouging into mountains chasing veins of the sacred substance.

And when Christopher Columbus set sail for the New World, he remarked in his journal: "O, most excellent gold! Who has gold has a treasure [that] even helps souls to paradise."[2]

The arrival of the Spanish radically rewrote the New World's relationship with the metal. Although the Incas and the Aztecs prized gold for its natural attributes and beauty, it wasn't used as currency.

For the Spanish, the golden statues, vessels, and idols they found in the Americas were literal money—as soon as they could be melted down and pressed into coins.

Thanks to Sir Isaac Newton, who, as England's Master of the Mint, in 1717 standardized the price of gold, the metal known by the chemical symbol Au became the basis of modern currencies and the underpinning of the global financial system.

Gold became so precious—and remains so today—because it combines nearly all the qualities sought by craftspeople: virtual indestructibility, luminous beauty, easy workability, and extreme rarity.

Very little gold actually exists in the world.

The metal was formed hundreds of millions of years ago in the fiery furnaces of distant stars bursting into supernovas.[3] Brought to Earth by meteorites crashing into the planet's surface, it was buried deep below the crust, where it has waited for us. Since humanity's dawn, fewer than 200,000 tons of gold have been pulled from the earth, more than two-thirds of that since 1950.[4] All the gold ever mined would fit into roughly three Olympic-size swimming pools.[5] (A great deal of precious metal also resides far out of human reach at the earth's core.) Humans have visited terrible wars and atrocities on one another to possess it.

"Gold has always had this kind of magic," Peter L. Bernstein, author of the book *The Power of Gold*, told *National Geographic* in 2009. "But it's never been clear if we have gold—or gold has us."

◇◇◇◇◇◇◇◇◇

It was Samer Barrage's Nicaragua-born second wife, Iska, who got him into the gold business in Miami.

Like him, she had been working at Kaplan University but left in 2010 when a job as an office manager opened at NTR Metals.[6] The branch was housed near Miami International Airport in a one-story warehouse in the industrial suburb of Doral, about forty-five minutes west of downtown Miami. NTR Metals bought scrap metal like old watches and rings from pawnshops, antique stores, and other gold scavengers. Buying scrap was a booming business, thanks to the long tail of the Great Recession. Many people lucky enough to hold gold were looking to trade it for cash.

As 2010 drew to a close, Iska and her husband flew to Dallas for a Christmas party hosted by NTR's parent company, Elemetal. The couple struck up a conversation about Elemetal's future with the firm's cofounder Steve Loftus. Loftus told the couple about Elemetal's plan to move beyond scrap and expand into Latin America, where gold was more plentiful. But the Texas businessman had drastically underestimated the importance of hiring people who understood Miami's market and culture and spoke Spanish. Loftus was impressed with Barrage's background, his education, and his fluency in Spanish and French. The former subprime salesman was good with numbers and had a proven history of closing sales.

"Do you want to buy gold in Latin America?" Loftus asked Barrage.

Soon after, Loftus flew to Miami to have dinner with Barrage and offer him the job of sales manager for NTR Metals in Latin America. Barrage accepted.

Barrage's first hire was his old buddy Renato Rodriguez. The two men had remained close friends. Rodriguez was even the godfather of Barrage's daughter.

Above all, Rodriguez was a family man. Raised in Brooklyn, he saw his parents struggle every day to provide. His father washed bedsheets and scrubs in the laundry department of a hospital. His mother cleaned houses.[7]

He moved to South Florida after dropping out of high school but was able to earn his GED in Miami. He met his future wife, Miriam, who had a young son from a previous relationship, when they were working at Papa John's Pizza in 1994. Three years later, they married. After a miscarriage and two IVF cycles, they had twin daughters. The girls loved the cheesecake and chocolate chunk cookies their father considered his specialties as a baker.[8] He took them on litter clean-up trips to Key Biscayne and the Everglades. They volunteered at children's shelters and old folks' homes and attended Good Shepherd Catholic Church.[9] They still lived in the same house Rodriguez and his wife had paid less than $200,000 for in 1999. Rodriguez loved talking to his clients about his family and asking them about theirs. Sometimes, he grew to consider them as family, too. He would sulk if they ever decided to take their gold to NTR's competitors. "I can't believe you betrayed me," he would say. "I would never do that to you."

For Barrage, it was strictly business, never personal. And he knew breaking into the coveted Latin American gold market, especially in Perú, would not be easy. Other major gold refineries, including Republic Metals Corporation in Miami, one of the largest gold buyers in the United States, already had a firm foothold in Perú and were better capitalized.

NTR Metals just needed an in. A whale. A big client to sell them gold. That would show their competitors they meant business.

CHAPTER 3

A Gold-Covered Brick

IT WAS THE SUMMER OF 2012 WHEN TROUBLE—AND A MOUTH-WATERING opportunity—came knocking at NTR Metals' office in Doral, Florida.[1]

The representatives of a gold outfit from Lima, Perú, called Business Investments SAC had made a pilgrimage to South Florida with an offer too good to resist. The South American company had access to a river of gold that flowed through southern Perú and was already selling it to NTR's competitors in Florida. With the stroke of a pen, NTR would not only have access to as much gold as it could handle but undercut its rivals too.

Hundreds of small companies in Perú are authorized to buy and sell gold. At first glance Business Investments seemed like just one more of the pack. But even the most cursory digging should have set off alarms. For starters, the company had almost no track record exporting gold; it had been registered in February of that same year—a red flag for regulators.[2] Its headquarters was a tiny storefront tucked between pawnshops and a tourist stand that sold alpaca ponchos and cheap imitations of Peruvian religious art. On paper, the store was registered as "Arianda," but there was no name on the storefront—just a vinyl sign reading "We buy gold at $50 a gram."

If the operation itself was nondescript, the man behind Business Investments was anything but.

Born in Lima on February 21, 1960, Pedro David Pérez Miranda was raised in a family of jewelers and gold merchants.[3] His grandfather had emigrated from Spain and became a miner in the northern state of Trujillo. His father had expanded the family business by setting up a jewelry store and gold-buying operation in downtown Lima. But Pérez Miranda had bigger dreams. When he was ten years old, he informed his parents that he was going to move to Los Angeles and become a movie star.

His Hollywood dreams came to an abrupt halt, however, when he was fifteen and got one of his girlfriends pregnant with twins. The father-to-be had no choice but to start working at the family jewelry store. He found the industry as bright and promising as the metal itself. Checking the trade papers for international spot rates, he was gripped by the thrill of making so much money in so little time. He discovered that gold prices on the streets of Lima fell over the weekend as merchants shut shop and liquidity dried up. So he started buying during the weekend gold dip and selling during the week to maximize profit. Buy low, sell high.

In 1983 his father bought him his own business—a money exchange house and gold-buying shop called Peter's.[4] The place was part business, part party. After long days of trading cash and gold, Pérez Miranda's store would fill up with friends and hangers-on who would go on drinking jags that often lasted until the wee hours of the morning.

If Pérez Miranda had given up on his Hollywood dreams, he nonetheless seemed to be living a movie star lifestyle. Starting in the 1990s, the young gold merchant was increasingly spotted around town with flashy cars, designer clothes, and a rotating cast of beautiful women and gold jewelry—lots and lots of gold jewelry. Even at the beach, wearing nothing but a tiny black Speedo, he flaunted his good fortune. An undated seaside photo shows the muscular businessman with a gold medallion around his neck, a thick gold chain on one wrist, and a gold Rolex on the other.

Asked about his penchant for jewelry, Pérez Miranda said he considered it good marketing. "Maybe people don't like it that I'm well dressed, maybe they don't like that I'm ostentatious," he said. "But if I work with gold all day I can't be wearing silver."[5]

The garish display of wealth was particularly jarring in a country wracked by violence and crushed by poverty. Although modern-day Perú is full of gleaming office buildings, award-winning restaurants, and Inca-obsessed tourists, that wasn't the case just a few decades ago. Starting in the 1970s, the country was staggering from one economic crisis to another. In one year alone—from 1988 to 1989—a quarter of Perú's gross domestic product vanished. Poverty in the capital spiked from 17 percent in 1985 to 54 percent just five years later.[6] Rising up amid the economic chaos was one of the most brutal guerrilla groups to ever have surfaced in Latin America, El Sendero Luminoso, or the Shining Path.

Founded in 1980 by a charismatic philosophy professor named Abimael Guzmán, the Shining Path subscribed to a cruel form of Maoism and class warfare that considered union organizers, politicians, peasants, and innocents valid targets for murder in the name of creating a "dictatorship of the proletariat." Gaudy capitalists like Pérez Miranda were often in the group's crosshairs. By the time the leader of the Shining Path, who went by the nom de guerre Chairman Gonzalo, was finally captured in 1992 and sentenced to life in a specially built prison, his guerrilla army had murdered more than six thousand people.[7] And by the end of that decade, the bloody civil war would leave more than seventy thousand dead.

But Pérez Miranda seemed to be living in another country—on another planet. Throughout the 1990s, as car bombs rocked Lima and locals grimly joked that you could wring blood from the newspapers because of all the violence, Pérez Miranda was hobnobbing with actresses, models, dancers, writers, and politicians, screeching through Lima in the latest sports cars.

In his telling, the clothes, cars, jewelry, and glamorous women were the happy by-product of the family business, the rewards of all his hard work. But authorities weren't convinced. Instead, they wondered how someone so young had amassed so much wealth so quickly. How could this small-time gold merchant have joined the Peruvian jet set?

By the late 1990s, the police thought they had their answer. Pérez Miranda dressed and acted like a drug trafficker because, they believed, he was one. They claimed Pérez Miranda was using his family gold business and his eponymous shop to hide a growing criminal empire.

In June of 1999, authorities announced they had caught "Peter Ferrari," the "czar of fake gold," in southern Perú, on the shores of Lake Titicaca, trying to escape into Bolivia with 1,600 grams of gold and $27,600 in cash.[8] Officials described how Pérez Miranda had conjured up a drug-money machine masquerading as a gold-trading company. According to them, he was covering lead, iron, and zinc bricks in a thin layer of copper or gold and exporting them to Miami as if they were solid gold ingots. The idea was that drug traffickers in the United States would pay for those "gold" bars in cash, and Pérez Miranda would bring the dirty money back to Perú and launder it into the financial system. For that magic trick—allegedly turning illegal drug money into legal gold-trading profits—he charged a 15 to 20 percent commission.

During just two months in 1998, police claimed he had laundered $18 million in narco-cash, pocketing at least $2.7 million.[9] As icing on the cake, they said he was using the fake gold scheme to get a 5 percent tax refund from the government as part of its program to support exporters. When police raided his home and businesses, they said they seized more than $2 million in cash, jewelry, and gold.

The press couldn't get enough of the story of the dashing young businessman fallen on hard times. In what one newspaper called a "spectacle that lasted for weeks," the media went into overdrive delivering increasingly colorful and bizarre details about Pérez Miranda's supposed criminal exploits, leaked by police sources who always remained anonymous. The newspapers said he was swimming in so much dirty lucre that it wasn't uncommon for him to drop $2,000 to $10,000 a day on meals, and "one time he gave his driver a $1,800 tip."[10] His wife, María del Rosario Untiveros, was arrested while she was in Lima cashing five checks worth $2.6 million.[11]

Authorities told the press that "Peter Ferrari" had confessed to laundering money since at least 1994 and, not content with that line of work, was also muscling into the drug trade. According to these anonymous sources, Pérez Miranda was engaged in a fantastic bit of double deception. Not only was he shipping lead bricks disguised as gold to Miami, but sometimes there was cocaine hidden inside the metal—a veritable turducken of smuggling. Other times, they said, he hid cocaine in bottles of fine wine that were shipped to Ecuador and then to Spain.[12] There was also the time in 1991 that he allegedly sent 26 kilos of cocaine to South Florida in a fake Chilean diplomatic pouch mixed in with packets of mustard and pepper to disguise the smell.

Over the ensuing weeks, a picture emerged of Pérez Miranda as an underworld kingpin with global ties to organized crime. Peruvian authorities said he orchestrated at least four flights to Colombia during 1989 and 1990 to carry two tons of coca paste—a precursor of cocaine. During one of those trips, the police's star witness said, Pérez Miranda had been held hostage in Cali, Colombia, by the notorious North Valley Cartel as a "guarantee" the deal would go through. He was also tied to a Peruvian narco-trafficking group called Los Colochos that was accused of moving at least ten tons of cocaine. Then there were the details of a murderous shootout at Pérez Miranda's currency exchange house.[13]

As the breathless stories about Pérez Miranda grew so did the number of people sucked into his web of suspicion by association. Models, dancers, authors, and a congresswoman were among the people accused of partying and perhaps doing business with Peter Ferrari, the "king of fake gold."

On July 11, 1999, Pérez Miranda was transferred to the notoriously violent Miguel Castro Castro prison, a hotbed for guerrillas and gangs, as he faced charges of money laundering, tax evasion, and drug trafficking. It was the sort of prison habitually rocked by riots and mayhem. In 1992, police had killed at least forty-two inmates and tortured more than three hundred others as they tried to regain control of the prison.

Though things at the prison had settled some by the time Pérez Miranda arrived, it was still considered a hellhole where a brief detention could quickly become a death sentence if the right thugs weren't appeased.

From the beginning, Pérez Miranda claimed he was innocent. But his version of events was even more colorful and bizarre than what the police claimed. In his telling, he was being framed by Vladimiro Montesinos, the right-hand man of President Alberto Fujimori and the head of Perú's notorious National Intelligence Service, known as the SIN.[14] According to the jailed magnate, Montesinos had a sideline gig extorting successful businessmen. When Montesinos had wanted a cut of his gold business, Pérez Miranda had resisted. That's when his troubles began. Pérez Miranda claimed Montesinos used his national intelligence operatives to spy on people's bank accounts and therefore knew exactly how much he could extort from them.

"They would jail businessmen and as soon as they'd pay they would let them go," Pérez Miranda said. "I didn't pay and I got screwed."

The gold merchant said he'd been detained by the police in February 1999, blindfolded in a basement, and asked for $1 million. Rather than pay, he went on the run. When the police caught him four months later on the shores of Lake Titicaca, he wasn't fleeing justice, he said, but desperately trying to escape Montesinos's extortion goons.

Pérez Miranda's Kafkaesque tale would have been easy to dismiss as the ravings of a criminal trying to get off. But time would prove that the acronym of Montesinos's SIN security apparatus was grimly appropriate. From his headquarters in Lima, Montesinos ran a network of spooks, informants, and paramilitary enforcers that was credited with helping dismantle two guerrilla groups—the Shining Path and the smaller Túpac Amaru Revolutionary Movement—and bringing a semblance of stability to the country. But the SIN and Montesinos were also violent and corrupt to the core.

In 2000, while Pérez Miranda was still in prison awaiting trial, videotapes emerged showing Montesinos bribing lawmakers, military officials, and media organizations to support the government. The ensuing "Vladivideo" scandal forced Montesinos to flee to Venezuela and his boss, President Fujimori, to catch a flight to Japan and fax in his resignation. Both men were eventually hauled back to Perú to face justice. Montesinos, who had always been suspected of being on the CIA's payroll, was accused of more than thirty crimes, including murder, drug trafficking, embezzlement, and the sale of ten thousand AK-47 rifles to Colombia's Marxist rebels.[15] Fujimori would ultimately be sentenced to twenty-five years in prison for human rights abuses, including running a death squad.

For Pérez Miranda, this was vindication, proof that he'd been telling the truth about Montesinos. But despite his protestations, in March 2002 he was sentenced to nine years in jail for his alleged crimes. Within weeks, however, the case against him began to unravel, and six months later Perú's Supreme Court absolved him of the drug charges, saying police had found no trace of narcotics at his homes, at his workplace, or in his system.[16] It also dropped money laundering charges against him and more than a dozen family members and friends, saying there was no indication their income came from drug trafficking or terrorism. But Pérez Miranda was not completely innocent. The court said there were clear indications that he'd been involved in gold smuggling—a much less serious crime for which he'd already done his time.

The acquittal was just part of Perú's reckoning with its past.

As part of their political strategy, Montesinos and Fujimori had controlled dozens of Perú's media outlets and co-opted others. Pérez Miranda said it was those government newspapers that had come up with the "Peter Ferrari" moniker as a way to make him out to be a cartoon villain. And when he refused to go along with Montesinos's extortion attempts, the government slapped him with trumped-up drug trafficking and money laundering charges that were amplified through the compliant press.[17]

After writing dozens of articles about "Peter Ferrari"—the drug trafficking playboy—the country's independent media were forced to admit they had been duped by the government. In 2005, the same year that Pérez Miranda was finally absolved of the most serious charges and released from jail, *El Comercio*, one of the nation's most reputable media outlets, admitted that it had played a role in creating the "Peter Ferrari" persona and destroying Pérez Miranda the man. "In 1999, the case of Pérez Miranda was promoted with particular diligence and endeavor by the mafia that governed the country at the time, likely with the objective of covering up other, presumably more serious, acts," the newspaper wrote in its mea culpa. Among the crimes that the "Peter Ferrari" saga helped obscure was an investigation into Los Camellos, a powerful drug trafficking gang that had ties to the upper ranks of the army, the Peruvian National Police, and Montesinos's SIN.[18] In its final ruling, Perú's Supreme Court ordered the state to return $2.5 million in property it had seized from Pérez Miranda—the largest asset reimbursement in the country's history at the time.[19]

Although the courts may have found Pérez Miranda innocent, many in law enforcement weren't convinced. The national police department, the attorney general's office, and the Ministry of Interior all appealed the drug charges, but the Supreme Court shot them down. It was as if Montesinos, his henchmen, and an unbridled press—now besmirched for their smear campaign against him—had muddied the waters so much that the truth was unknowable.

Society was also less than forgiving. Even as Pérez Miranda tried to rebuild his business and his life, he lived under the cloud of money laundering and drug charges. To many in Lima's tight-knit business circle, Pérez Miranda was little more than a drug trafficker who, through luck, and likely some well-placed bribes, had beaten the charges.

And even though Pérez Miranda had initially groused at being called "Peter Ferrari," he later seemed to embrace the flamboyant persona. At bars and clubs—as he tried to pick up women—he would often introduce himself by his alias. And he started using pictures of the sports car on his social media accounts.[20]

When Business Investments SAC approached NTR Metals in Miami that steamy summer day in 2012, it was coming in the name of Pedro David Pérez Miranda, the son of a long line of gold merchants and a survivor of one of Latin America's most abusive and corrupt regimes. But authorities believed that hiding just beneath the surface—like a lead brick covered in gold—was Peter Ferrari.

CHAPTER 4

Hand of God

BY THE TIME HE APPROACHED NTR METALS, PETER FERRARI WAS RUNNING A finely tuned gold-exporting machine. He and his small staff of long-time friends and family members would buy gold from anyone willing to sell it and sell it to anyone willing to buy it.

Facing stiff competition and razor-thin margins, gold aggregators like Ferrari asked their sellers few questions. It didn't matter exactly where the jewelry, watches, coins, and bars were coming from as long as they were made of gold. Almost daily, weathered workers from the Peruvian jungles and highlands would carry in small backpacks stuffed with pounds of rough gold and walk out with wads of cash.[1]

Ferrari's storefront was tucked in with dozens of other gold-buying outfits along a three-block stretch of shops on La Paz Avenue in Lima's underwhelming gold-buying district. Most of the aggregators had sideline gigs such as changing money or buying and selling antiques, giving the street the look of an upscale pawnshop. But by all accounts, the sleepy little storefronts on La Paz Avenue were moving thousands of pounds of gold per week and had become a critical link in the global commodity trade. Whereas most of Lima's gold merchants tended to be low-key and discreet (one of the best ways to protect themselves from extortion and kidnapping), Ferrari was the polar opposite.

Despite his previous run-ins with the law, the businessman was still flaunting his wealth—rubbing his good fortune in the faces of his competitors and Lima's high society. Frequently, he'd post videos of himself on social media partying with kids half his age as they tore through town in SUVs and posed on beaches draped in gold chains. Out on the town, or at the gym, he'd always have bodyguards in tow, more conspicuous than they should be, as if they, too, were a status symbol.

Peruvian police weren't the only ones watching. Ferrari's flamboyance had attracted the attention of American law enforcement officers stationed at the US Embassy in Lima. In their cramped office, they knew him by his nickname—and watched. "Ferrari flaunted his wealth. He thought he was untouchable," said one US official. "He thought of himself as a celebrity."[2]

Everything about Ferrari seemed larger than life, even his family. He had ten children with five different women and made no secret of his weak spot, beautiful ladies.

But maintaining that lifestyle was expensive, and Ferrari needed to find new pipelines for his gold. Though his company, Business Investments SAC, was already exporting to NTR's competitors in Florida, the buyers weren't paying him fast enough—and speed was critical. Perú's gold business is largely done in cash, and Ferrari and his men constantly needed bags full of dollars and Peruvian *soles* to pay their suppliers. He would often empty all of his accounts to buy new batches of gold and then have to wait for the money to slosh back into the accounts via bank transfers. Just as quickly, he'd empty the accounts again to start the cycle over.

The faster he could get paid by his buyers in the United States and Europe, the more gold he could buy and the more money he would make. It was the kind of business that financial institutions hated. "The banks felt like they were getting used," one of Ferrari's lawyers said. "He wasn't even leaving enough money in the accounts for the bankers to buy a cup of tea."[3]

In July of 2012, Ferrari dispatched two people to South Florida to speed up the cash flow.

The two men visited at least three South Florida gold buyers, PMXG, Atomic Gold, and NTR Metals.

It was NTR that seemed the most eager to please. The two Peruvians met with NTR's Samer Barrage and quickly hammered out the broad details of their arrangement. NTR would buy all the gold that Ferrari could ship at the price of 92.2 percent of the daily spot rate—or a 7.8 percent discount. In return NTR would wire money back to Perú within twenty-four hours—faster than other gold importers in South Florida.[4]

There was just one last step before the gold and cash could start flowing: the new account had to pass muster with the compliance office at NTR's parent company, Elemetal.

Whereas Barrage may have been eager to do business with Ferrari and his crew, Elemetal's compliance team was not. All they had to do was Google their prospective customer's name. Alarm bells started ringing. "We need to be extremely careful going forward," the compliance office, led by retired US Customs Service agent Steven Crogan, told Barrage and his Elemetal bosses in an email after reviewing Ferrari's file.[5]

Crogan, a former assistant special agent in charge for Customs at the Boston field office, had deep experience investigating gold.[6] During his time in Boston, Customs had investigated the American arm of Swiss gold giant Metalor, a major competitor of Elemetal. In 2004, Metalor pleaded guilty to federal charges that it helped South American criminals launder $4.5 million through smuggled gold.[7] The scheme involved metal being hidden and transported in shampoo bottles. Metalor paid a $2.7 million fine and was placed on probation for five years. Crogan retired in 2007—and was hired by Metalor to make sure it never experienced such a scandal again. In 2012, he became Elemetal's compliance chief.

Crogan had final say over who Elemetal bought gold from. His job was to make sure Elemetal didn't do business with criminals who were laundering money. There were two reasons for this. One was that the USA Patriot Act—passed after the terrorist attacks of September 11, 2001—required precious-metals companies to do business with legitimate suppliers. The second—and perhaps the more important—was that Elemetal's bankers demanded the same thing, because the Patriot Act's "know your customer" provisions applied to banks, too. Elemetal's business depended on the short-term bank credit used to buy gold. If the banks lost faith in Elemetal's ability to weed out criminals from its supply chain, the money would dry up fast—and the company would go under.

Crogan took one look at Barrage's application for Pedro David Pérez Miranda and immediately rejected it.[8] According to news accounts dating back to the 1990s, Peter Ferrari was known for one thing: allegations that he laundered money for drug traffickers through gold. The compliance officer put Barrage and other Elemetal executives on notice that Ferrari was radioactive. NTR Metals could not buy metal from him.

Crogan understood how dangerous Perú could be for an American gold company looking to make money while keeping its nose clean. "Perú is a HIGH RISK venue for obvious reasons," he wrote to Elemetal executives, as well as Barrage and Rodriguez, after visiting Lima in 2012.[9] But he also knew it was a bonanza.

"We have the potential to become a major player in the Peruvian market (larger than Colombia), as long as we build a sound foundation," he said. "With proper planning, we have infinite opportunities."

A sound foundation, Crogan explained, meant shunning customers like Peter Ferrari. But the gold merchant was used to the fact that the mere mention of his name would shut doors. He had a solution.

According to Perú's Supreme Court, in November 2012, just a few months after their first visit, Ferrari's representatives were back in Miami with a brand-new company, this one called Lern United Mines Corporation—created three months earlier.[10] The men assured NTR Metals that Ferrari's name was nowhere on any of the corporate documents. But they also sweetened the deal, telling Barrage about the rivers of gold that were being extracted from Madre de Dios, the region in southern Perú that had become synonymous with illegal mining, brothels, child labor, and ecological devastation.[11]

(Ferrari and people involved in that sales trip say the Peruvian courts were lying, that they never had a business called Lern, and that they never told NTR—a potential client they were trying to woo—that they were buying illegal gold. "Why would we tell them we had access to illegal gold if we were trying to win their business?" a man involved in those conversations explained. "It's bullshit.")

Either way, the Peruvian courts say Elemetal executives in Dallas realized the firm was a front company and once again blocked the transaction.[12] Crogan issued another warning on doing any gold deals with Ferrari in Perú, sending Barrage and his NTR colleague,

Rodriguez, an alarming blurb from a Peruvian newspaper. It reported that Ferrari was under investigation for money laundering and narco-trafficking.

Whatever the difficulties of doing business, NTR and Ferrari needed each other. The Peruvian wanted a large reliable partner that could handle his gold and pay quickly; Barrage and his men were working as salaried employees but also pocketed commission-like bonuses based on volume—so they needed as much Peruvian gold as possible.

A few days after Elemetal rejected Lern United Mines, the duo from Perú presented Barrage with a third company: Minerales la Mano de Dios, or Hand of God Minerals. The company was a perfect cutout. Established in 2009 and registered in an industrial area of Lima surrounded by textile mills and car repair shops, Hand of God had a history of legitimate business, buying and selling copper, silver, and lead. On paper, the company was owned by a mother and her daughter, but it was the woman's husband who had negotiated the deal to sell the company to Ferrari's representatives.

On October 13, 2012, in a Lima restaurant that served the Chinese-Peruvian fusion cuisine known as *chifa*—pioneered by waves of East Asian immigrants to Perú in the nineteenth and early twentieth centuries—they had handed the woman $20,000 in cash for the company.[13] Two of Ferrari's employees were named the general manager and assistant manager of the business. His name stayed off the forms.

The alleged deceit worked, and Hand of God finally passed muster with Elemetal's compliance department.

It was time to get rich.

CHAPTER 5

Mr. Third Rail

DESPITE DOING BUSINESS WITH PERÚ'S MOST NOTORIOUS GOLD DEALER, Samer Barrage and Renato Rodriguez didn't consider themselves hardened criminals plotting to break the law. They simply rationalized away their crimes.

After all, NTR Metals' competitors were also buying gold from traders like Peter Ferrari, Barrage and Rodriguez told each other. What NTR was doing wasn't any worse. And don't forget Elemetal's compliance office was signing off on their deals. That meant the gold was legitimate, right? Rodriguez and Barrage were just looking the other way when a lucrative client like Ferrari came along and maybe sometimes withholding information that might discomfit their bosses. That wasn't against the law, they reasoned. They were businessmen, family men, not gangsters. Illegal mining was a tragedy, but it was happening, and Perú's government wasn't stopping it and there was nothing they could do about that. Anyway, if they didn't buy the gold, someone else would.

A few months later, after Hand of God was approved, Barrage and Rodriguez came up with a new way for Elemetal to buy more gold from Ferrari. The ease with which they snookered compliance officer Steve Crogan—who called Ferrari "Mr. Third Rail" in internal emails—showed how lax Elemetal's anti–money laundering procedures really were.

On February 15, 2013, just a few days before he and Barrage would travel to Lima for Ferrari's beachside birthday bash, Rodriguez wrote to Crogan with an application for a new gold supplier called Minerales Gold MPP. He said the company was currently doing business through an intermediary with Elemetal's rival, Miami-based Republic Metals, but its owners weren't happy with how they were being paid. "They have aspirations to grow with NTR," he explained.[1]

Rodriguez named the company's two principals as Gian Piere Pérez Gutierrez and Miguel Ángel Rivero Pérez. Unbeknownst to Crogan, Pérez Gutierrez was one of Ferrari's twin sons; Rivero Pérez was his nephew. (MPP are the initials for Pedro Pérez Miranda spelled backward.)

In the email, Rodriguez described the men simply as "artisanal miners." But he knew exactly who they were: cutouts, and not very convincing ones, for Ferrari. The next day, Crogan replied with a few questions. Minerales Gold MPP had just been established that month, Crogan pointed out, appearing to have formed from thin air. Moreover, he couldn't help but notice that both men shared a surname with Pedro David Pérez Miranda.

"Obviously Pérez is a common name like Smith," Crogan wrote. "However, as they say in Boston, the only stupid question is the one you don't ask. Please reach out to the applicants and ensure they are not relatives or any relation to Mr. Third Rail."

He added, "Please keep your sense of humor as we navigate the deep end of the pool together."

Rodriguez was quick to respond with a lie, telling Crogan that the applicants "do not know of Peter Ferrari." Later, he would describe the men as "extremely humble people who are looking to work with a reputable refiner that will not nickel-and-dime them."

Crogan signed off. He trusted Rodriguez and Barrage—far more than his training as a customs agent and seasoned anti–money laundering expert suggested he should. The foxes were in charge of the henhouse. "Please approve," Crogan wrote to another company executive.

Mr. Third Rail was now NTR's biggest supplier.

CHAPTER 6

The Gold Rush

LA PAMPA COMES FROM THE QUECHUA WORD FOR "PLAINS," AND IT OFTEN conjures up images of the fertile lowlands and cow pastures of South America.

La Pampa in Madre de Dios, however, makes a mockery of its name.

In a few short decades, first a trickle and then a flood of wildcat gold miners transformed once-verdant grasslands and forests into a barren moonscape of toxic mud pits and trash-littered dunes. When a police foot patrol ventured into the area in 2015, two officers died of heat stroke and thirst. The men were surrounded by pools of water. But the liquid was undrinkable, tainted with cyanide and mercury.[1]

"To get to one of the main mining areas called Mega 16 you have to walk for five hours," explained Commander Dante Gallardo, a member of the Madre de Dios environmental police. "All you see back there are motorcycle tracks going in every direction as far as the eye can see. But you have no idea where you are or where they go."

Most people driving by La Pampa—usually making the pilgrimage from Cusco to the nature reserves in Madre de Dios—never see the devastation. It's blocked off by a sprawling shantytown that has formed at the edge of the highway, a long, thin city built out of spare lumber, corrugated tin, and pilfered vinyl road signs turned into makeshift walls.

Until recently there was no running water or electricity in La Pampa. Open-air sewers ran in front of the bars and cantinas that line the street. As the sun dips, women in short skirts and rubber work boots stand by the road trying to separate lonely workers from their money and gold.

As one recent visitor put it: "There's nothing there but miners, brothels, and garbage."[2]

For years Perú's central government refused to shut down the illegal mining, even as it became an international embarrassment. It was simply generating too much money for almost everyone: the collectors, the mine owners, the equipment sellers, the pimps, the drug dealers, even the dirty politicians and police officers who took bribes. Some people were not getting rich—the sex workers, for one, and the miners themselves, for another. But as long as those people continued to work, other parties could profit handsomely.

Even those who hated what was going on in the gold mines admitted that it was the economic engine of Madre de Dios—representing 60 to 80 percent of the economy.[3]

Perú is riddled with gold deposits and rich veins of the metal. Any number of spots in the country have enough gold to merit a crush of miners.

So why did La Pampa become ground zero for Perú's illegal gold trade? It was a perfect storm of geology, corruption, globalization, greed, and decades of neglect.

Gold deposits come in two forms: lodes and placers.[4]

Lode deposits are concentrations of gold embedded in solid rock, often in veins, that usually require heavy machinery, tunneling, and the resources of a major corporation to tap. Placer deposits, however, occur in sand, gravel, and sediment associated with streams and rivers.

Historically, most gold rushes have been sparked by placer discoveries, where the metal sits near the surface and is accessible to thousands of low-tech miners. The California Gold Rush of 1848 was a placer deposit.[5]

Millennia ago, gold from lodes in the Andes eroded, washed into the Amazon through mountain waterways, and settled along the banks of lush jungle rivers in the form of placer deposits. The Incas had traded for rain forest gold and over the years even sent armies to seize it. The Spanish were convinced the region hid a wealthy El Dorado–like civilization called Paitití.

It was in the late 1960s and early 1970s that Germán Ríos, a local historian, first started seeing gold miners stumble into Madre de Dios fleeing the crushing poverty of the Peruvian highlands.[6] Now seventy-four, Ríos said these were men who had left behind alpaca herds and potato farms, lured by tales of the riches of Madre de Dios.

It was hard and harmless work. These were subsistence miners who panned for gold along riverbanks and whose ability to disrupt nature was limited by their tools: little more than a wheelbarrow and a shovel.

But things changed rapidly in the 1970s, as this first wave of miners was joined by Brazilians and Bolivians coming upstream with a long history of riverside, or alluvial, mining and new tools.

A longtime miner in Madre de Dios remembers Brazilians hauling car motors on barges and using them to run a series of pumps and hoses to suck up the mineral-rich riverbed.[7] Another recalls the first time he saw a Brazilian diver—gripping an air hose between his teeth—dip beneath the murky river to drag a suction tube along the basin.

The new tools were eagerly adopted, increasing profits but also exponentially increasing damage to the fragile ecosystem.

Around that same time a story began circulating about a tree deep in the forest that had been blown over in a storm. Its roots—so the story went—were caked in mud laced with gold. The place was dubbed *La Fortuna*, the Fortune.

That story metastasized the industry, Ríos said, by luring miners off the riverbanks and into the jungle, where they had to clear virgin forests to get to the riches below.

Gold mining in the jungle is a brutally simple process. Once miners have identified a good spot, they start digging holes, often diverting rivers and streams to fill the depressions with water to loosen the soil. As the holes become water-clogged pits, the miners make rafts—planks of wood lashed to empty oil drums.

Using a combination of high-pressure water hoses and suction pumps called *tracas* or *carancheras* that run off of automobile engines, they blast sediment off the walls of the pits and pump out the muck, pouring it over large wooden ramps, or sluices, that are covered in something akin to industrial carpeting. The heavy gold particles get trapped in the fibers, and at the end of a shift the miners shake out the fabric to isolate the gold.

This is where things get ugly. To trap those tiny gold particles, workers douse the sediment with liquid mercury, which binds with the metal particles to form a lumpy amalgam called *torta*, or cake.[8]

If the process is done carefully, it doesn't necessarily have to be damaging to the environment. But in the wild west of La Pampa, laws, rules, and regulations are flouted. Researchers have estimated that anywhere from 40 tons to 180 tons of mercury are dumped into the environment every year in and around the region.

The health effects of mercury—like the fluid metal itself—are hard to pin down. The most common form of mercury, the silvery liquid in thermometers, is elemental mercury that, though still a health risk, is difficult for the body to absorb.

Once that mercury is dumped into a river, stream, or pit, however, naturally occurring bacteria turn it into methylmercury, a powerful neurotoxin that can wreak havoc on nervous systems, particularly those of babies and adolescents.

As bottom-feeding fish suck up contaminated sediment and are then eaten by larger fish, methylmercury content is magnified up the food chain until it accumulates in dangerously high doses in fish like the *mota punetada* and catfish—dietary staples for many rural villagers.

The way mercury travels through the food chain makes it an unpredictable enemy. Around Madre de Dios, researchers have found idyllic-looking riverside communities have far higher mercury exposure than debris-riddled mining towns, in part because miners often have access to other sources of protein such as chicken and beef.

Rural indigenous communities in this part of Perú have about three times higher mercury levels than "nonnative" city dwellers, according to investigators. And the children in those villages have mercury levels 3.5 times higher than average.[9]

But in the early years, the Peruvian government encouraged the gold rush. The nation had been mining gold long before the Spanish arrived, and it was seen as one of the few ways people could dig themselves out of poverty.

The state-run Banco Minero, or Mining Bank, established in 1940, became an important pillar of life in Madre de Dios, giving miners loans to buy wheelbarrows and shovels and more sophisticated tools.[10]

The business in those early years was extremely lucrative. There's the story of one gold miner who took out a $50,000 loan to buy a front-end loader—and paid it back within a week.[11] That's how rich the goldfields were.

But Madre de Dios was rich in other ways the miners rarely appreciated. This swath of the Amazon basin is also one of the most biologically diverse places on the planet, teeming with pumas, jaguars, giant anacondas, woolly monkeys, and other rare wildlife.

Biologists have recognized the value of the region for decades, but it wasn't until 2000 that they finally convinced the government to protect a massive extent of the rain forest and create the Tambopata National Reserve. It's a sprawling 1,060-square-mile habitat that's home to more than a thousand butterfly species, a hundred mammal species, and about six hundred species of birds.[12]

The northern perimeter of Tambopata is delineated by the Malinowski River, which forms the southern edge of La Pampa. The battle lines could not be more starkly drawn. On one bank of the river is one of the world's premier tropical reserves. On the other side is a wasteland of mercury- and cyanide-filled pools, but also a place that more than thirty thousand people depend on to scrape out a livelihood.

If the creation of Tambopata set the stage for a confrontation, the next move was the first shot. In 2005, authorities created a buffer zone—almost as large as the park itself—that incorporated La Pampa.[13] The buffer was an area where traditional communities could live and where sustainable agriculture could be practiced, but where gold mining was strictly forbidden.

For environmentalists, the buffer zone was an ecological imperative to save the park. For miners, the buffer zone, overnight, made them outlaws. If they had been considered "informal" miners before—working without permits or titles—now they were working in an area explicitly off-limits to prospectors. They were officially illegal miners.

And yet poverty, greed, and the hidden hand of global economics proved stronger than any new law or bureaucratic line drawn on a map. Defying police and park rangers, the miners stayed in La Pampa, and often punched into the natural reserve seeking gold.

"It would be the equivalent of having thousands of acres of illegal strip mines in Yellowstone National Park—and the government not being able to stop it," said Luis Fernandez, a tropical ecologist at Wake Forest University's Center for Amazonian Scientific Innovation, who has worked in the area for years.

∞∞∞∞∞∞

The 2007–2008 US financial crisis that began in real estate quickly spread across the globe, sparking a rush toward safe-haven assets. And nothing was safer than gold.

As the world's jittery markets demanded more of the shiny metal, the number of people willing to risk life and limb to find it in La Pampa multiplied.

The global crash also coincided with one of the most ambitious construction projects in South American history. After decades of planning and false starts, in 2010 Perú and Brazil inaugurated the Interoceanic Highway, a 1,600-mile-long road that slices through South America's thick belly, connecting the Brazilian Atlantic with the Peruvian ports on the Pacific.

It was also a freeway through La Pampa.

Every other road that cut through virgin territory had brought a host of ills, including logging, mining, hunting, and clear-cutting for cattle ranching. This project was even more problematic because it encroached on the territory of some of the world's last uncontacted tribes, including the Mashco Piro.[14]

Not surprisingly, the new road acted like an anabolic steroid for the mining industry. Before the completion of the Interoceanic Highway, often it could take days or weeks to drive the three hundred miles from Cusco to the goldfields of Madre de Dios. The new road shortened the journey to less than a day. The pace of deforestation caused by mining has grown fourfold since the highway construction began, according to satellite data analyzed by the Center for Amazonian Scientific Innovation.[15]

Because of the very nature of illegal gold mining, no one knows for sure how much metal comes out of La Pampa. But the Ministry of Energy and Mines says more than 12 million grams of gold, some 13 tons, were extracted from Madre de Dios in 2017.[16] Industry sources say that's most likely an undercount, and the real amount could be as much as double.

Ríos, the local historian, acknowledges that the road has been a huge economic boost for Madre de Dios. But it's also become the main artery for outsiders to keep siphoning the wealth from his province, a long historical grievance.

In the nineteenth century, rubber barons enslaved native tribes, forcing them to walk through the jungle lugging 120 pounds of rubber on their backs. Many died of exhaustion and European diseases. Poaching, cattle ranching, and logging followed.

"Historically, Madre de Dios has been linked to pillaging," Ríos said. "First they took the rubber, then they took the animals, then they took the wood, and now they're taking the gold."

∞∞∞∞∞∞∞

At first, Peruvian authorities tried to stop the growth of the mining town forming around La Pampa through strategic neglect. By denying the area public services—including electricity, water, schools, health centers, and sewage—they hoped to starve it to death.

Instead, the shanty became self-sufficient. Generators provided power, water was trucked in, resourceful locals started day care centers and crude health clinics. Several transportation companies—running motorcycle taxi services for the miners—built their own roads into the mining area and charged tolls.

And though the area was certainly lawless—and largely off-limits even to police—it was by no means defenseless. When criminal gangs moved in to rip off miners, the mining community created its own security force, Los Guardianes de la Trocha, the Guardians of the Trail, who were both effective and brutal.[17]

By the time NTR Metals began buying gold in Perú in 2012, the illegal miners of La Pampa had created their own world, governed by their own laws. And they had powerful friends.

One congressman from the region, a miner named Amado Romero, sported the nickname Come Oro, the Gold Eater. In 2014, Luis Otsuka, the president of the Mining Federation of Madre de Dios, was elected to the governor's office for the 2015–2018 term.

Although the federation represented legitimate mining interests, Otsuka had been accused by government officials of supporting illegal mining operations—allegations he always denied.[18]

But once in office, he went to war with organizations he saw as antagonistic to the mining industry: environmental groups, nonprofits, and the central government in Lima. He argued that it was immoral for international organizations to worry about birds and trees when people in Madre de Dios were suffering from malnutrition and poverty. In his view, foreign activists were using an ever-shifting array of excuses to stop small miners.

Whether it was groups advocating for the environment, warning about mercury contamination, defending tribes living in voluntary isolation, or raising alarms about sex trafficking, they all had the same goal: to shut down small Peruvian miners. "They come here and tell us that we can't touch a tree or eat the fish because they won't allow it," Otsuka said of environmental groups. "They're the ones who should be starving to death, not the people from these communities."[19]

∞∞∞∞∞∞

The chaos and complicity of La Pampa made it the perfect hunting ground for gold buyers. Merchants from Lima and abroad could buy the illegal gold from local aggregators or from the miners themselves with little fear of police interference.

Ferrari always denied he'd ever been in Madre de Dios. But locals there remember him vividly, flashing wads of money, weighed down by jewelry, and hungry for pretty young locals and more gold to ship to his clients abroad.[20]

Ironically, or predictably, depending on whom you asked, by making mining illegal in La Pampa, the government laid the foundations for a criminal empire. Because the gold was off the books and unaccounted for, the profits went directly into the pockets of the powerful gangs that controlled the area.

The police were mostly powerless. Although they were being told they had to crack down on La Pampa, they didn't have the manpower or resources to do so. Instead, a well-choreographed dance developed. The police and military would occasionally conduct high-profile raids on the area that looked great in the press but that didn't make a dent in the mining industry. Miners were almost always tipped off and found ways to limit the damage, burying their machinery in the sand or even sinking it in the water to keep it from being seized. Once the police retreated (as they always did), the machinery could be put out to dry, tweaked, and up and running within a day or two.

When the miners weren't given fair notice, things would get ugly. In 2017, a police convoy that ventured into La Pampa was ambushed. One officer died and three were wounded.[21]

Walter, a thirty-four-year-old illegal gold miner, said workers in La Pampa also died regularly. Some were killed for trying to cheat their bosses, others drowned on the job or were buried alive as the walls of the mining pits gave way.

The government doesn't know how many people have worked, died, or disappeared in La Pampa, but stories abound about death, murder, and retribution in the goldfields.

Almost every family in the region seems to know someone who had a son, uncle, or nephew who went to work in La Pampa and never came out. Old-timers swap stories of the Guardians of the Trail killing criminals en masse. The government says it has never uncovered a mass grave in the area, but locals are convinced the bodies are out there, beneath the sands, beside the gold.

CHAPTER 7

The Fed

SPECIAL AGENT TIMOTHY SCHOONMAKER ARRIVED IN LIMA ON DECEMBER 30, 2012, just a few weeks before Juan Pablo Granda struck his first gold deal in the dark Lima office.[1]

Lima was Schoonmaker's final assignment for the US Drug Enforcement Administration. The tour of duty would see the veteran agent, who had served as a Pararescue jumper in the US Air Force Reserves and once worked as a rodeo cowboy, through his scheduled retirement in 2017.

Schoonmaker's mission in Perú could not have been more different from Granda and his bosses' at NTR Metals. They were on a collision course that would transform the US government's role in this cocaine-producing country, where criminal networks large and small were suspected of washing billions in illicit profits through the exploding gold trade.

The reach of US law enforcement is not confined to US borders. Like the Federal Bureau of Investigation and the Department of Homeland Security, the DEA has offices around the world, ninety-three of them in sixty-nine foreign countries, making it the federal law enforcement agency with the largest presence overseas.[2] Schoonmaker, fifty-one, was once again joining the ranks of federal agents stationed abroad. He was a well-decorated agent, fluent in Spanish. Over his twenty-five years in the DEA, he had chased fishing boats stuffed with hashish off the coast of Oregon, gone undercover to infiltrate syndicates pushing "China White" heroin in Thailand, and busted cocaine lords in Bolivia and pill-pushing doctors in Salt

43

Lake City. DEA agents overseas are tasked with helping local law enforcement agencies bring down drug cartels while steering clear of messy internal politics. They are constantly reminded that they are guests in a foreign land. They must respect local rules and customs and forge partnerships with police and prosecutors—to make cases that can ultimately be tried in American courts by the US Department of Justice.

Perú was a major office for the DEA, which worked out of the US Embassy in Lima. Together, Colombia, Perú, and Bolivia produce almost all of the world's cocaine.[3]

Fighting the cocaine trade meant the United States had to know what was happening at its source on the ground in Perú. Schoonmaker's supervisor told him his first detail would be with DEA-Perú's money laundering team. The squad worked with the intelligence units of local police around the country, including one group in Puerto Maldonado, capital of the Madre de Dios region and Perú's illegal gold-mining industry. The city had grown tremendously as the illegal gold rush boomed. "Picture the Alaska gold rush set in the jungle to the tune of electronic cumbia music," a correspondent for the *New Yorker* wrote around the time Schoonmaker visited.[4]

Traveling from Puerto Maldonado out to the mines sent Schoonmaker straight into the hell of "human sacrifice" later described by Pope Francis. The DEA agent and the Peruvian cops had to drive ninety minutes in heavily armed convoys to get to the camps around La Pampa, then drive back to Puerto Maldonado before darkness fell. There was no place to stay in the camps, and their snooping was not welcome. Journalists and aid workers were shunned. No one wanted the outside world to see what was happening there.

Later, Schoonmaker and the local cops would get a chilling bird's-eye view of the devastation after commandeering a DEA plane. Looking down at a pitted hell that extended farther than their eyes could see, the men fell completely silent. The vista of destruction in La Pampa reminded Schoonmaker of photographs he'd seen of the Battle of Verdun. His grandfather had fought in the United States Army during the World War I battle in which artillery shells and chemical weapons left the French ground poisoned and scarred. Today, immense swaths of Perú's jungle resemble the largest and longest battle of the war to end all wars.

Schoonmaker first began to understand the scale of the problem—and why it should matter to the DEA—when he met with an informant in Lima who owned a legally titled mine. The informant told him a shocking statistic: one ton of illegal gold was leaving Perú every single day.

"Are you sure?" Schoonmaker asked. "That's a lot of gold." It was 2,200 pounds, the equivalent in weight of a male walrus or subcompact car, worth about $40 million.[5] Per day.

"I'm sure of it," said the informant, a gold mine owner who had worked in the industry for three decades. "I've been in this business. I know everything going on."

The informant said narcotics traffickers were snapping up mines across the country to seize a piece of the booming gold business. Some of the metal was flown out of Lima's airport. Some was smuggled across the border to Bolivia, Ecuador, and Chile. Many of the mines didn't even produce gold. Instead, the criminals would buy metal off the street with drug money and, to make it look legitimate, forge paperwork claiming it had been dug out of the ground at their new holdings. When they sold the gold, they ended up with "clean" cash. Classic money laundering. In the end, almost all of the gold was shipped to the United States, Switzerland, Dubai, and India, where major refineries melted it down for sale and entry into the global financial and manufacturing systems.

Schoonmaker drove back to the DEA office at the US Embassy. He sat down in his tiny cubicle in the crowded bullpen and pulled out a pen and paper. Then he reached for his calculator.

If what the informant said was true and Perú was exporting $40 million worth of illegal gold every day, well, that would mean . . . He typed in the numbers. "Holy shit," he thought, his fingers working over his strong jaw. "That's $15 billion a year."

Schoonmaker kept scribbling. The informant said the profit margin for gold sales was about 4 percent. That meant Peruvian criminal groups earned about $600 million in pure profit from selling illegal gold, $600 million they used to buy houses and acquire legitimate businesses, to bribe politicians and pay for the assassination of rivals—in short, the money they used to destabilize Perú.

Compared to gold, the profit margin for Perú's other major illegal export, cocaine, was far less impressive. The foreign cartels and mafias were the real moneymakers in that business, not the Peruvian gangs that grew coca, turned it into one of the world's favorite drugs, and then sold it to organized crime syndicates from Mexico, Colombia, and Eastern Europe, which smuggled the coke abroad and resold it in wealthy nations at a steep markup. Most of the illicit money in the narcotics trade went to foreigners. According to Schoonmaker's math, Peruvian gangs made only about $117 million per year in cocaine profits.[6] Gold yielded five times as much cash. For Peruvian criminals, gold had become far more lucrative than cocaine.

Illegal gold mining was not just a crime against the environment and human rights, offenses the DEA was duty-bound to stop. Because the criminal gangs invested drug profits into the mines, the trade in illegal gold was also enriching the criminals and traffickers spreading corruption and violence in Perú and around the world, Schoonmaker realized. Street gangs in Chicago. Cartels in Mexico. The Russian mob. They were all getting rich, one way or another, by a criminal alchemy that turned drug money into glistening gold—gold that ended up around the necks and in the pockets of oblivious American consumers.

The conversation also illuminated another trend Schoonmaker hadn't been able to figure out. US Federal Reserve data showed Perú's banking system was awash in unexplained cash. His colleagues in Lima and counterparts in the United States assumed the money came from cocaine trafficking. But the DEA agent was beginning to realize it all traced back to gold. The business was so profitable, his informant had said, that many traffickers were abandoning drugs for gold.

The cocaine trade was no longer the biggest problem in Perú—dirty gold was. And if Schoonmaker had anything to say about it, dirty gold would now be the DEA's problem, too. But the slow-moving wheels of American law enforcement had only just begun to turn.

∞∞∞∞∞

Organized criminal enterprises produce massive amounts of money. The criminals can't just spend it freely. Try walking into a bank with $50,000 cash. Bankers won't risk depositing the money without knowing where it came from. They are legally obligated to ask how it was earned. So instead of taking their dirty money to banks, many criminals use the cash to buy high-value investments like real estate. Developers and real estate agents are notorious for asking no questions about the source of their clients' wealth. Other scofflaws invest in luxury goods like yachts, cars, and jewelry, but buying fancy things can only use up so much dirty cash.

The rest has to be laundered.

Money laundering—a phrase often used but rarely explained—is the act of taking money earned by breaking the law and disguising it as revenue generated by a seemingly legitimate business. Money laundering can be as simple as buying a restaurant and claiming to sell 100 meals a day, when in fact only 50 patrons came in. The other 50 "meals" are really just drug dollars layered into the restaurant's cash flow.

For South American drug lords and their syndicates, gold became the perfect vehicle for laundering billions from cocaine sales in the United States, Europe, and other consumer drug markets. Gold is inherently valuable. It is accepted as currency around the world. It is always in high demand. And it can be melted down, making it impossible to trace.

As Latin America's gold-mining industry took off, cartels and guerrilla groups saw the perfect opportunity. They could sell cocaine and use the dirty profits to buy gold. Selling the precious metal to refineries in the United States gave them a cover. They could tell banks they weren't criminals; they were gold dealers. Their money, they claimed, came from the international trade in precious metals, not drugs. The new nexus between criminals and gold helped fuel Latin America's destructive illegal mining boom. Some of the organized gangs began devoting more time and resources to gold than to cocaine. It was far safer: If you're caught carrying gold, all you need to do is pull out some forged papers saying it was mined legally. If you're caught carrying cocaine, no documents in the world can save you from prison.

Experts believe the illegal mining industry has surpassed the cocaine trade in overall profitability, confirming Schoonmaker's calculation. And not just in Perú. Take Colombia, for instance, where illicit mining generates about $2.4 billion a year in criminal cash—three times more than the country's notorious cocaine industry, according to some intelligence estimates. "Today, criminal mining brings more money to criminal groups, to guerrilla groups, to mafias . . . than drug trafficking," Colombia's then-president Juan Manuel Santos warned in 2015.[7]

As gold prices took off, Miami International Airport became the strategic gateway for huge amounts of precious metal from Latin America—worth billions and billions of dollars—to enter international markets.[8] The best thing about Miami, Latin American business executives like to joke, is how close it is to the United States.

In 2007, the city imported 27 tons of gold worth $436 million. By 2011, it was importing more than five times that amount. Three years later imports peaked at 173.5 tons, valued at more than $6 billion. More than a third of the gold coming into the United States was being flown into Miami, with the rest headed to New York City and Los Angeles. At the front of the pack were experienced exporters of dirty gold, men like Peter Ferrari.

CHAPTER 8

A Well-Oiled Machine

BY 2013, NTR METALS WAS DOMINATING PERÚ'S GOLD TRADE—THANKS IN no small part to the Miami-based importer's biggest client, Pedro David Pérez Miranda, the man better known as Peter Ferrari.

That year, Ferrari's alleged shell companies sold NTR $400 million worth of gold, accounting for more than one-third of its Peruvian business.[1] In total, NTR's dealers purchased fifteen times more Peruvian gold than the $73 million worth they bought in 2012.

They were blowing their competitors away.

But by September 2013, Samer Barrage and Renato Rodriguez realized they needed someone to run NTR's operation on the ground. They both had families in Miami. They didn't like spending weeks away from their wives and kids.

Juan Pablo Granda would solve the problem. He'd already been working for them since February, learning the business as a traveling dealer scooping up gold from across the Caribbean and Central America. He was ready to work full-time in the big leagues: Perú.

Before Granda left Miami, he hosted a barbecue for his friends and family at a waterfront park on Biscayne Bay near his downtown apartment. The green space was framed by soaring high-rise condo towers that symbolized the city's new status as an international business capital. Boosters point to South Florida's luxury buildings—which offer eye-popping amenities such as a Porsche-branded automobile elevator that delivers residents' exotic cars straight up to their "sky garages"—as a sign that Miami has been reborn.[2] Long gone are its days as a playground for murderous "cocaine cowboys" and as the site of searing race riots, an era when *Time* magazine infamously put the city on its cover with the headline "Paradise Lost."[3] Today, the annual number of murders in metropolitan Miami has dropped from 612 in 1981—when the *Time* cover came out—to 202 in 2019, even as the population has shot up by nearly one million people.[4]

Miami may be less violent, but cynics point out that wealthier and more sophisticated criminals have emerged: Many of the buyers fueling the condo boom made their fortunes in less-than-legitimate business overseas. Russian mobsters, corrupt Latin American politicians, and kleptocrats of all stripes show up in South Florida's property rolls, putting cash down for their gleaming homes in the sanctuary of the United States.[5] Making money on the margins of what society deems acceptable is a Miami tradition—and most locals simply accept the inexplicable sources of wealth produced by the thriving underground economy. At one sentencing for an international drug trafficker who owned more than $20 million worth of Ferraris, Bugattis, and Miami-area condos, a federal judge caustically noted the "plethora of funny money" floating around the city.[6]

By the time of his farewell barbecue, Granda had gotten a pretty good idea of how the gold trade worked: the dark rooms with armed bodyguards, the flashy gold traders like Peter Ferrari, the black SUVs full of men holding AR-15s that rolled up to do business deals. He knew there was no point in asking questions: Where was the gold coming from? Who sold it to you? But he didn't fully grasp the degree to which he was signing up to take part in a full-blown criminal conspiracy.

His boss, Samer Barrage, who had engineered sneaking Peter Ferrari's alleged shell companies past Elemetal's compliance program, did understand. Still, that didn't stop him from pulling Granda's mother, Susana, aside at the party.

"Don't worry about your son," Barrage said. "I'm going to take good care of him."

Granda moved to Lima in September 2013—a month in which the city is shrouded in fog and the skies are the color of lead. Visitors often expect Lima, perched over the Pacific and hugging the equator, to be tropical and sweltering. But the city's location in an arid valley and on a coast chilled by the Humboldt Current means it rarely rains; instead, Lima is often enveloped by overcast skies. Even famously foggy San Francisco gets about twice as much direct sunlight as *Lima La Gris*, or Gray Lima, as locals call it.[7]

Its dusty, monochromatic, and often melancholy vibe stands in sharp contrast to the city's colorful culture and cooking. Fusing indigenous, Spanish, and Asian cuisine, Lima has become a gastronomical powerhouse, home to some of the region's top-rated restaurants.

But it's the country's mining industry that powers the city. Since the gold-hungry Spanish founded Lima in 1535, Perú has become Latin America's top producer of gold, lead, zinc, and tin.[8] Only five other countries in the world mine more gold. And much of Perú's metal—whether gouged out by legitimate multinationals, informal miners, or criminal gangs—flows through its capital, Lima. So it was a perfect spot for Granda and NTR Metals.

Granda's first assignment in his new home was to open up an office in the commercial district of Santiago de Surco, where several of the city's main roads pass through, including a major highway that allowed easy access to the airport. He chose a small space for NTR Metals inside the much larger secure facility of an armored-truck carrier and logistics firm called Prosegur, which NTR's parent company, Elemetal, had hired to transport gold shipments. At first, Granda had two local salesmen working for him, but he quickly realized he didn't need them. He became a one-man operation: buying the gold, testing its purity, filling out customs paperwork, and alerting Elemetal's compliance staff to check into the history of new customers.

One Peruvian gold merchant said Granda turned the industry upside down.

"Granda and his people were like lions, hungry for gold, anywhere they could get it," he said.[9]

One of Ferrari's associates had a more risqué metaphor: "They were like prostitutes running around with their legs open, taking gold from anyone who would offer it."[10]

In Perú, the gold trade works like a funnel. Laborers working in desperate conditions deep in the Amazon or high in the Andes dig the metal out of the ground. They sell it in nearby towns and cities to small-time businessmen known as "aggregators" or "collectors." Then those small-timers drive the metal to Lima or other major cities to sell it to the mega gold dealers like Peter Ferrari and his crew, who sell it on to Granda and NTR.

Customers came to Granda's office carrying boxes or briefcases filled with rough-hewn semipure bars of gold mixed with silver known as "doré." Sometimes the bars were small. But they could weigh as much as 29 kilos each, or 64 pounds, right up to the maximum allowed for export.

The customers had to leave their armed security details outside. No guns were allowed. Some of the customers were businessmen; some were street guys from the mountain cities of Cusco and Juliaca, where gold from Madre de Dios was traded on its way to Lima.

Suppliers learned to trust the soft-spoken, even-keeled Granda, who gained a reputation for not cheating on weights and prices—and for charming personal touches. On one client's birthday, Granda sent him a picture of a gold bar topped with a lit candle. Another new client was so smitten with Granda that he made him the godfather of his daughter the first time they met in person, picking him up in a Hummer at the airport in Juliaca and taking him straight to a church ceremony.

Sometimes the customers would even leave Granda's office to have lunch—leaving their gold unsupervised—while he weighed and tested the metal.

His tool for testing, or assaying, doré looked like a handheld price scanner you'd see in Home Depot or Walmart. Technically, it was called an X-ray fluorescence spectrometer. But everyone called it an XRF gun. Its capabilities were impressive: the gun could scan a piece of metal, measure the energy of its electrons, and determine its exact composition.[11] (In Perú, they sold for as much as $22,000. In the United States, Granda could get them for $10,000. So he ran a side business buying them in bulk in Miami and selling them to his Peruvian customers for $15,000.) Gold from Madre de Dios was generally so pure—at the very least 90 percent and sometimes close to 99 percent—that Granda could recognize its shiny luster without even using his XRF gun. Gold from other parts of Perú had a far duller sheen.

Once Granda verified the metal's content, a Prosegur armored truck drove it to Lima's airport. The bars would then be loaded onto an American Airlines plane, accompanied by a courier, and flown to Miami International Airport. After landing, another armored truck would take the gold to NTR's facility in Doral for a fuller assay. At the Doral office, workers would melt the doré bar in a gray ceramic pot called a crucible, extract a pen-sized amount of metal, cut it into three pieces, and test each piece six times to get an average reading of the concentration of gold. The tests determined how much NTR would pay its customers.

After the assay, the bars would be remolded, trucked back to MIA, put on a flight for Ohio, and ferried by armored trucks to parent company Elemetal's refinery in the small town of Jackson, perched in densely wooded hills thirty-five miles from the West Virginia border. There, workers would refine the doré bars into 99.95 percent pure gold, removing the silver through the so-called Miller process, developed at the Sydney Mint by Dr. F. B. Miller in 1867.[12] "[The process] is based upon the fact that chlorine readily combines with silver and any base metals to form chlorides, while gold is unaffected," writes Timothy Green in his book *The Gold Companion*. "Doré is placed in clay pots in a furnace; once it is molten, chlorine is pumped into each pot and is absorbed by the base metals, forming volatile chlorides. After two to three hours, the pot is removed from the furnace and the molten chlorides skimmed off, leaving [pure] gold."[13]

The constant flow of gold from Latin America kept everyone busy at the Jackson refinery. "We were working seven days a week and we couldn't keep up," said one worker at Elemetal's refinery. From Jackson, the precious metal could be sold to banks, investors, and Fortune 500 companies and manufactured into jewelry, electronics, and coins.

The global gold-buying system that brought gold from the Amazon to American wrists and wallets was lubricated by short-term bank credit. To buy metal, Elemetal depended on loans from Scotiabank and its gold-lending division called ScotiaMocatta, which traced its origins to a London bullion house founded in 1671.[14] Without the banks, the whole business would go belly-up.

Back in Lima, Granda had plenty of competition. There were buyers from nearly a dozen Miami-based importers, as well as from Metalor, the Swiss firm with a refinery in North Attleboro, Massachusetts, and a host of traders selling gold to India and China, which are even larger gold markets than the United States is.

But Elemetal's biggest rival was the Miami-based firm Republic Metals Corporation. Founded as a scrap business in 1980 by a Baltimore transplant named Richard Rubin, Republic had helped open up Latin America as a gold market for US companies.[15] The charismatic Rubin was on the cutting edge, traveling to Central and South America and striking deals by the force of his personality as much as with his pocketbook. Capitalizing on Latin American gold, Rubin had built one of the largest gold refineries in North America in an impoverished African American community on the edge of Miami called Opa-locka. The massive facility employed more than two hundred people. It could refine 350 tons of gold per year, nearly equal to the entire output of the mines of China, the world's leading gold producer.[16]

Rubin's search for gold sometimes led Republic into deals with sketchy characters. In 2012, the year before Granda arrived in Perú, one of Republic's biggest customers was Peter Ferrari. Rubin's firm bought $174 million worth of gold from Ferrari that year, despite the Peruvian's well-publicized reputation as an alleged money launderer.[17] But eventually, Republic Metals grew suspicious. Ferrari was sending ever-larger quantities of gold to Miami. That set off alarm bells at Republic. When a compliance officer had visited Ferrari at his pawnshop headquarters in Lima to check out his operation, it seemed he was dealing in moderate amounts of scrap gold. So where was all this new metal coming from? Republic asked Ferrari for an explanation—but he didn't have one. So the company cut him.

It was a smart move and revealed another one of Rubin's talents. In addition to his business savvy, Rubin knew how to stay on the good side of federal law enforcement and regulators. He was one of the DEA's best sources in the precious-metals industry. He understood all the rules—and how people broke them. In the gold trade, he once told a reporter, "there's on the books and there's off the books."[18]

In 2012, when federal prosecutors in New York claimed a Peruvian family of alleged cocaine traffickers was laundering dirty money through gold, they seized tens of millions of dollars held in Republic's bank accounts. Republic, the prosecutors alleged, had done business with drug dealers.

Within a few weeks, Republic had its money back. It was Rubin, it turned out, who had initially tipped off the DEA in Miami about the Peruvian cartel. He had only continued buying its gold at the agency's behest, his lawyers argued. The DEA wanted to continue investigating the drug syndicate and didn't want to tip it off. But somehow the message that Republic was cooperating with the DEA never made it to prosecutors in New York. It was one of several instances where, by helping the feds, Republic got out of a jam.

In June of 2013, Rubin died unexpectedly at an industry conference in Phoenix at the age of sixty-four. His children took over the business. Replacing a titan like their dad wasn't easy. All of a sudden, a vacuum seemed to emerge in Perú's gold industry.

Into the breach stepped NTR Metals.

∞∞∞∞∞∞∞∞

Having Granda open up an office in Lima gave NTR a huge advantage over its previous business model—and helped it challenge competitors like Republic, Metalor, and another major Miami firm, Kaloti Metals & Logistics.

The gold trade is a volume business that depends on quick transactions happening over and over again. Averaging 1 percent or less on every deal, the profit for refineries is in the margins. Opening an office in Lima allowed NTR to pay customers on the spot rather than having to wait hours or days until the gold arrived in Miami. Now the customers could get their cash immediately, go right back out to buy more metal, and then bring it in to NTR to start the whole dance anew.

And in Lima, one guy greased all the wheels: a customs broker and freight-forwarding agent named Andrés Tejeda.[19]

Tejeda worked with Ferrari and Perú's other biggest gold dealers. He and Granda met at Ferrari's birthday party in Lima and quickly became close friends. They were young. They were making money. And they liked to have a good time.

Together, they realized they could move vast quantities of gold out of the Peruvian rain forest and into the lucrative American market. Tejeda knew how to game Perú's customs system. Granda had the weight of a major American gold refiner—and the money of its bankers—behind him.

While much of Ferrari's gold allegedly came from outlaw mines, Tejeda's skill was making it appear that the gold had been mined legally and sold to NTR by legitimate businesspeople. It wasn't that hard. All Tejeda had to do was fill out mining paperwork saying that the gold had come from a licensed mine operated by an upstanding citizen. Perú's overstretched mining agency never went out to the remote jungle to check whether that mine was producing gold—or even existed.

Law enforcement officials said Ferrari's crew would canvass Lima social clubs looking for old-timers who were open to an easy payoff by becoming straw mine owners. All they had to do, in between sips of beer, was sign paperwork saying that they ran a gold-mining operation. That gave Tejeda something to work with: a fake mine, a fake company, and a fake owner, none of which had any connection—on paper at least—to Ferrari. If Peruvian customs officials started asking questions, Ferrari was quick to supply Tejeda with bribe money, according to Granda.

Granda blanched a bit in October 2013 when Tejeda first filled him in on the bribes. That obviously wasn't legal—and it seemed far more serious than fudging paperwork. But Tejeda assured him it was business as usual in Perú. All their competitors were doing it, too, Tejeda said. It was the only way to ensure the metal got out of the country. Besides, the customs broker said, he always told Ferrari he needed twice as much bribe money as he really did—and kept the extra cash for himself.

Away from work, Granda lived the leisurely life of an American expat being paid good money in dollars.[20] He rented a three-bedroom penthouse apartment for $2,000 a month in the upscale neighborhood of Miraflores, where all of Lima's wealthiest families lived. It came with a rooftop pool.

A bachelor, he rarely cooked, instead turning to the work of the food writer and television show host Anthony Bourdain for restaurant recommendations. Most nights would find him ordering omakase at the counter at Mido Sushi, frequenting the award-winning Amazonian-style fusion joint Amaz, or drinking piscos at a nightclub. He had three big-screen TVs in his apartment. On weekends, he traveled around Perú, for pleasure, not work, touring the Amazon jungle and the stunning Inca ruins at Machu Picchu.

During the week, Granda kept a low profile. He wasn't flashy, wanting to blend in so he wouldn't be marked as an easy target for robberies and kidnappings. His standard uniform was a button-down shirt, jeans, and loafers or well-kept sneakers. He left his Rolex and blazers at home.

Once, a good friend came to him with a problem. The guy's socialite girlfriend, a professional model, had a serious weakness for cocaine. The friend was going out of the country and didn't want to leave her alone with their stash. He had a balloon bag stuffed with a hundred grams of cocaine.

"Can you hold it for me?" the friend asked.

Granda, who valued his reputation as a man of his word, kept the powder in his apartment for ten months without taking so much as a sniff.

Life was good because the gold was flowing.

NTR's three amigos were exporting hundreds of millions of dollars' worth of gold to Miami. They were superstars back in the Dallas office of their parent company, Elemetal. Executives there had never seen so much money rolling in, but they didn't ask any questions. And Granda was keeping the whole operation going from his base in Lima, thanks to his new best friend, Tejeda.

But whether he wanted to admit it to himself or not, the young American businessman was now deeply entangled in a criminal conspiracy with Tejeda and his two NTR colleagues, Barrage and Rodriguez. Their principal client was a notorious gold dealer suspected of laundering mountains of cash for drug traffickers who dominated many of the outlaw mines in La Pampa. The three amigos were lying to their bosses at Elemetal about where the gold was coming from, falsifying paperwork to make it appear legally mined, and paying bribes to Peruvian customs officials to ensure all the metal arrived safely in Miami.

And yet the times were changing: The government of Perú had finally woken up to the disaster unfolding in its rain forests. In 2012, a new president imposed a law making it a crime to mine gold without a license, which was previously only a civil violation.[21] Those wildcat mines allegedly supplied a lot of Ferrari's gold.

By the time NTR set up shop in Lima, Peruvian cops, tax agents, and customs officials were all looking for a high-profile scalp. And Ferrari, with his curly black locks, was the most conspicuous target.

CHAPTER 9

Under Ferrari's Hood

BEING A DRIVER FOR PETER FERRARI HAD ITS PERKS. THAT'S WHAT JOSEPH Cesar Leyva Miyashiro was discovering two years into the job.

In October 2012, the gold magnate had taken his girlfriend, his lawyer, his secretary, and two other people to the Dominican Republic for an all-expenses-paid vacation. Leyva got to tag along as the official photographer for the outing.[1]

The trip to the Caribbean island was one of the highlights of his time with the man he sometimes considered his friend. But it turned out it wasn't exactly free.

Leyva and Ferrari had met two years earlier by pure chance. Like many Peruvians, Leyva's family had ties to Japan and he'd grown up there before returning to Perú in 2010.

Low on cash and options, the twenty-three-year-old stumbled into Ferrari's gold-buying shop on La Paz Avenue to see whether he could pawn his Omega wristwatch. But it was a chance incoming call that changed his life. The call came from a friend in Japan and Leyva spoke Japanese fluently. Ferrari overheard and, impressed by his linguistic prowess, asked for his phone number. Within two months, they had struck up a friendship of sorts, with the older gold merchant taking the young man out to bars and discos. He even hired Leyva to be the driver of his Toyota RAV4—just one of his multiple vehicles.

The job was a huge break for the young man, who was trying to find his feet in a country he barely knew. Working Monday through Saturday, he drove his boss around town for ten hours a day, making anywhere from $100 to $200 a week.

Leyva discovered Ferrari was a man of routines. He would begin his day at the BodyTech gym, just a few blocks from the US Embassy, where DEA agents hot on his trail often rubbed shoulders with him. From there, he would go to his store on La Paz Avenue to receive a stream of gold sellers.[2]

"He met with people who came in with backpacks and then left with lots of money in those backpacks," said Leyva, who often watched the gold merchant and his adult twin sons, Peter Jr. and Gian Piere, count stacks of money.

After a long day of shuffling bullion, Ferrari would often go to restaurants and then visit some of his girlfriends.

But there were also things that made Leyva uneasy about the job. Just days after coming back from the Dominican Republic, he was summoned to a notary's office in Lima and asked to sign some papers so that Ferrari could "put him on the payroll."

Not giving it too much thought, he signed the documents without reading them and authenticated them with his thumbprint. Leyva claimed he didn't know it at the time, but with that casual act, investigators said, he became part of Ferrari's growing legion of cutouts and straw men.

It was only about two months later, on December 20, that he suspected something wasn't right. Leyva stumbled across a notice at the office that listed him as a shareholder of a company called Mano de Dios—Hand of God. The other shareholder was Ferrari's bodyguard, a pudgy middle-aged man everyone called Galleta, or Cookie.

When Leyva asked Ferrari about it, his boss told him not to worry, that it was simply a formality. And he promised he'd buy him a car for his troubles. But the following month, the company's accountant let it slip that Mano de Dios—which traded millions of dollars in bullion—wasn't paying its taxes.

Worried, Leyva went to an outside accountant who warned him he was at risk of being declared a tax cheat.

Leyva also discovered that he and Galleta weren't the only employees that Ferrari had roped into his gold-buying scheme. There was also Luis Rolando Madueño Chocano, a retiree in his late seventies, who had come to Ferrari looking for a job in 2013. Madueño's last job had been as a forklift operator at a beer company and he was living in abject poverty. He received a pension of $194 a month but was spending almost all of it—$133 a month—on a rented room.

Madueño's son was part of Ferrari's security staff, so the father likely had some insight into the gold magnate's operation. But he told police that he had no idea what he was getting into when his new boss put him to work signing documents and opening bank accounts.

What's clear is that he seemed to be in awe of his patron, who helped him in myriad ways.

When Madueño's ATM card got blocked by the bank, Ferrari made some phone calls and had a card reissued. It was likely a routine problem, but Madueño was impressed.

"See how I can fix problems?" Ferrari told him. "It's because I can talk to the owner of the circus and not just the clowns."[3]

Leyva would eventually become suspicious and try to warn the banks that something fishy was going on with Ferrari's accounts. But by then it was too late for him and the old man.

CHAPTER 10

"Flight of Last Resort"

NTR METALS STARTED OUT MELTING DOWN JEWELRY, GOLD COINS, AND even gold teeth when brothers John and Steve Loftus launched the precious-metals business in a rundown industrial neighborhood of Dallas in 2004.

The acronym NTR stood for "North Texas Refinery." (The company would later be renamed Elemetal though the Miami branch that employed the three amigos remained NTR Metals.)

The Loftus brothers have said they recognized "enormous potential in gold" even then, at a time when prices were low.

"Our founders saw a nascent blossoming industry ripe with potential," a glossy in-house magazine for employees and clients reported in 2016. "They knew it was only a matter of time before the market corrected. And as we all know the market did more than correct—it skyrocketed."[1]

The brothers were right: their fledgling gold firm boomed after the financial crisis wrecked the global economy at the end of 2007. Stocks were tanking. Banks collapsed. Everyone wanted gold. The metal seemed like the market's only sure thing. Like funeral homes and pawnshops, gold is recession-proof.

On March 16, 2008, the day Wall Street bank Bear Stearns went under, an ounce of gold sold for roughly $1,000.[2] Over the next three years, gold would nearly double in value, hitting an all-time high above $1,900.[3] That growth far outstripped the Dow Jones Industrial Average, which grew by just 6 percent over a similar period.[4]

"The founders often joke that their biggest struggle was expanding fast enough to meet the booming market," the company magazine states.[5]

The Loftus brothers were two sides of the same coin. John was a quiet, intelligent, and analytical former commodities trader. Steve was the entrepreneur, a relationship man always asking questions. It had been Steve who recognized the opportunity in gold—and he saw more opportunities everywhere. Steve came up with ideas for expansion; John applied the brakes. Together, they were the company's brain trust.

John would become CEO, but Steve ran the show. Employees used to joke that on the company's organizational chart, Steve represented the white space. He controlled everything.

Elemetal's office Christmas parties grew legendary. One year, the company flew in its entire national staff for a holiday extravaganza in the ballroom of the Omni Dallas Hotel. As a cover band played classic-rock hits, employees competed in casino night games. The prizes included flat-screen televisions, new computers, and Louis Vuitton handbags. The whole shebang must have cost upward of $1 million, staff whispered.[6]

Conservative celebrities with a doomsday flair cut commercials endorsing gold companies. In 2010, Fox News host Glenn Beck pitched a company called Goldline on his syndicated talk-radio show.[7] As his hook, he used the collapsing US economy and, for good measure, even mentioned Germany's undoing before the rise of Hitler.

"I want you to read the headlines today," Beck told his nine million weekly listeners. "I want you to read about the stock market. I want you to read about housing sales. I want you to read in the last thirty months we've added $4.4 trillion to our debt. I want you to read up on the Weimar Republic."[8]

The solution, according to Beck? Gold.

"It is always the flight of last resort, it is always the hedge against inflation," the talk-show host explained. "I don't know what's going to happen. I really don't. But I would ask that you consider your options. And call Goldline." (Goldline's executives were later accused of fraud, although criminal charges were dropped after the company agreed to refund millions of dollars.)[9]

That kind of panicky demand—coupled with the needs of manufacturers, jewelers, and Silicon Valley firms—fueled Elemetal's sales. Many industries depend on gold. Because it is a good conductor and does not corrode, gold is increasingly used in electronics. Circuit boards in laptops, cell phones, cameras, even cars contain small amounts of gold. Phones contain an average of 0.034 grams of gold, worth about $1.70, according to the US Geological Survey.[10] But tech companies generally account for just 10 percent of gold demand.[11] Half of annual gold demand still comes from the jewelry industry. Investors seeking gold bullion (coins, ingots, and bars) make up a quarter of demand, while central banks account for the remaining 15 percent.

At the same time gold demand was spiking during the financial crisis, the economic turmoil also drove up Elemetal's supply. As Americans pawned their jewelry and antiques for cash, the supply of scrap gold soared by a third.[12] In other words, the financial crisis helped Elemetal coming and going, by creating both robust supply and ravenous demand. The more gold Elemetal could buy, the more it could sell to Fortune 500 companies. It was an ideal time to be in precious metals. There were new faces in Elemetal's office almost every day. The company had a start-up energy, former employees said, even though its location—an industrial suburb full of warehouses, strip clubs, and a hose-supply store—was far from glamorous. The only thing holding them back was finding enough gold.

By the year of Beck's rant in 2010, the Dallas company had nearly thirty scrap-buying branches around the country, including NTR Metals' warehouse office in the Miami suburb of Doral, where the three amigos would soon work. Elemetal even expanded to the United Kingdom, and later to Germany, Spain, and Hong Kong.

Still, there was more room to grow. Elemetal was essentially a glorified middleman. It operated as a gold dealer buying and selling metal. Any gold that came into Elemetal branches was resold to the American arm of a competitor, the Swiss conglomerate Metalor, which had its own refinery. Elemetal needed its own plant to refine gold, which was a far more profitable business.

The Loftus brothers could make so much more money—if only they owned a refinery.

◇◇◇◇◇◇◇◇

The small town of Jackson, Ohio, sits nestled in the Appalachian hills of the state's southeastern corner, near the West Virginia border. It was founded in 1816 and populated by a "Great Welsh Tide" of pioneers from Wales. Decades ago it boasted fine hotels and mansions, thanks to its status as a capital of America's booming iron trade. But like many Midwestern towns where manufacturing jobs were evaporating, Jackson, with a population of about sixty-three hundred, descended into a generational economic depression.[13] For a glittering moment in the twenty-first century, it seemed gold might be Jackson's way back to prosperity.[14]

As the recession loomed, Jackson had one solitary success story, an unexpected player in a growth industry: Ohio Precious Metals.

The refinery had started melting gold on a tiny site in 1974.[15] It was far from the centers of the precious-metals trade in New York, Los Angeles, and Miami, as well as the mines of the western United States. But it survived by buying and refining small amounts of scrap gold.

In 2004, the same year the Loftus brothers founded NTR Metals in Dallas, a wealthy local businessman named Alan Stockmeister bought Ohio Precious Metals.[16] He believed in gold's promise as strongly as they did.

Stockmeister was the closest thing modern-day Jackson had to a tycoon. Aside from Ohio Precious Metals, Stockmeister Enterprises had interests in construction, real estate, banks, movie theaters, a plumbing business, and hotels. He also owned the local newspaper.

Stockmeister pumped money into the facility, moving it into a former Campbell's Soup factory on the outskirts of town. All of a sudden, Jackson boasted one of the five biggest gold refineries in the United States, along with Republic in Miami; Metalor in North Attleboro, Massachusetts; Johnson Matthey in Salt Lake City; and Kennecott Copper in Magna, Utah.

When the recession sparked a scrap-gold boom, Ohio Precious Metals couldn't keep up, even with the aid of a $9.47 million loan from President Barack Obama's 2009 stimulus bill.[17] There was no way the plant, which employed fewer than a hundred people, could refine all the gold coming in. Stockmeister didn't have the cash to invest in new equipment and technologies.

But Elemetal and the Loftus brothers did.

In April 2012, the companies announced what they called a merger but was in practice an acquisition led by Elemetal. The Dallas company got its refinery. OPM acquired a new supply of gold—and the resources to process it. A lucrative partnership had been born. Even the *Wall Street Journal* noticed.[18]

"It's pretty much hand in glove," Stockmeister told the paper of his deal with Elemetal.

The week after it sealed the takeover of Ohio Precious Metals, Elemetal paid $7 million for a modern office building in Dallas, a real corporate headquarters.[19] The Dallas company began shipping equipment and workers to Jackson, many of them refugees from Laos who had originally worked in Elemetal's small assaying operation in Texas. They tended to stick out in rural Ohio. Other newly hired workers came from the surrounding area. By the fall, the refinery's workforce had nearly doubled in size to 180 employees. State and local leaders rallied round.

When Elemetal announced in 2013 that it would open a new metals recycling plant in a nearby town that would create five hundred jobs over five years, Ohio governor John Kasich spoke at a news conference alongside Elemetal executives. "The one thing we can't do is slow down," Kasich said. "I'm your friend and I am committed to you."[20]

State legislators amended the tax code to ensure the facility would stay in Ohio rather than move to Texas. "There are only a few other companies in America that can refine precious metals . . . with the quality and volume that they do," State Representative Terry Johnson wrote in a local newspaper. "Virtually all the jewelry at Tiffany's came through their factory in one form or another."[21]

Elemetal cared about its image, securing a "conflict-free" certification from an industry-backed group certifying that its gold did not come from war zones in and around the Democratic Republic of the Congo. "We are proud to be the first compliant gold refinery in the United States," the refinery's president, Bill LeRoy, said in 2012. "OPM has shown continuous commitment to the responsible sourcing of precious metals and . . . high quality, socially responsible gold products."[22]

But as NTR's imports soared the next year, Elemetal executives developed a severe case of what former employees and refinery workers describe as "gold fever." The bosses didn't ask many questions—the gold was pouring in and that was all that mattered. While the higher-ups stayed silent, one former worker at the refinery said he and his colleagues grew suspicious about the source of all that metal. Through Google searches, they found disturbing photos of Peruvian children diving in mercury-tainted pools of water with hoses to suck up tiny particles of gold. One of the workers showed the pictures to an Elemetal supervisor. "So what?" the manager replied. "They're making fourteen cents a day."

At the end of the day, no one was looking very closely at the foreign gold the company was bringing in. Not Elemetal's compliance program or corporate management. Not customs officials in South America or the United States. Not the precious-metals industry's regulator, the US Treasury Department's Financial Crimes Enforcement Network, which is tasked with enforcing anti–money laundering laws such as the Bank Secrecy Act. And certainly not the private gold exchanges and industry groups that vouched for Elemetal's gold.

These entities—based in Chicago, London, and Hong Kong—certify refineries as "good delivery" after testing the purity of their metal. Of those three, the London Bullion Market Association, the most prestigious industry group, also touted rules requiring refineries to demonstrate effective compliance and sourcing policies to ensure their gold came from responsible mining operations. Making a good delivery list is the pathway into global markets and Fortune 500 companies.

Ohio Precious Metals made the Chicago Mercantile Exchange's good delivery list a few months after the 2012 merger with Elemetal.[23] Then, in April 2013, it was added to the Hong Kong exchange. A press release touted OPM as the only US-owned refinery to make the cut.

Later that year, the London Bullion Market Association added OPM, too.[24] It was a major coup for Jackson.

The London good delivery list had been founded in 1750 as a way for England's Royal Mint to guarantee it was dealing in quality gold. On its website, the association boasted it was the "de facto standard trusted around the world." Any company on the list had passed compliance tests meant to ensure a supply "free from metal that has financed conflict or been used for money laundering or terrorist financing."[25] For Elemetal, it was outstanding marketing. Only two other US refineries were on the list at that time.[26]

Elemetal's client list now resembled a who's who of America's biggest companies.[27] By 2015, nearly seventy of the Fortune 500 were buying its gold. Jackson's refinery was feeding dirty gold—mined illegally in vast stretches of Perú's scarred rain forest—to almost every major US industry.

Among its clients were major tech companies: Apple, Google, HP, and IBM.

Autos: General Motors and Ford.

Chemicals and pharmaceuticals: Johnson & Johnson, Dow Jones, Merck.

Defense: Lockheed Martin.

Retailers: Macy's, Staples, Gap, Ralph Lauren, and JCPenney.

Verizon and JetBlue Airways were on the list, too. Even Starbucks and the Walt Disney Company were buying Elemetal gold.

The company's metal suffused the entire US economy. And that meant nearly every American consumer was complicit in the catastrophic environmental destruction overwhelming Perú's La Pampa.

CHAPTER 11

The Crackdown

NTR'S GOLD SUPPLIER, PEDRO DAVID PÉREZ MIRANDA, AKA PETER FERRARI, wasn't completely aware of it, but his world was shifting beneath his feet.

President Ollanta Humala, who took office in 2011, was under pressure to do something about the sprawling illegal gold mines in southeastern Perú that were drawing international scrutiny.

Not only were the environmentalists and conservationists on his case, but legitimate miners—a politically powerful and influential group—were pushing him to do something about the activities in La Pampa that were giving the entire industry a bad name.

In February of 2012, the government made illegal mining a criminal offense punishable by up to eight years in prison.[1] Two months later, congress also took aim at those who were financing the activity, passing a mouthful of a legislative decree: "The Efficient Fight Against Money Laundering and Other Crimes Related to Illegal Mining and Organized Crime."

The preamble to the law captured just how alarmed the government was: "We are witnessing a worrying increase in crime related to illegal mining activities, which, in addition to seriously damaging the ecosystem, life and health of the people, also represents a serious destabilization of the socio-economic order."

Under the new rules, those caught laundering money generated by illicit mining, drug trafficking, kidnapping, extortion, or terrorism could face up to twenty-five years in prison.

Illegal mining had taken its place in the pantheon of national threats.

The new rules created new headaches for gold buyers like Ferrari. The provisions required them to register their companies with the Ministry of Mines and keep detailed records on who sold them gold and where it came from. In many ways the rules seemed impossible to comply with. At Ferrari's gold-buying shop, people often came in with jewelry or coins to sell—whether they were family heirlooms passed down for generations or stolen, it was impossible to tell.

In theory, sellers were supposed to show receipts to prove they were the rightful owners, but most often they would simply sign a statement swearing the items were theirs.

For gold miners, that process was even trickier. Although the miners had to present their mining titles and other documents, there was no way for them to *prove* the gold actually came from those mines. And most of the gold buyers in Lima really didn't want to know.

The less scrupulous found easy ways around these new regulations. A number of mines produced little but legal justification, charging illegal miners a fee to say that gold was being extracted from their legitimate operations. And gold merchants often bought or swapped lists of tax ID numbers and names—lists that allowed them to fill out purchase orders even if the actual seller wasn't strictly legal. Also, dodgy lawyers would create companies and books of invoices that could be used by gold dealers.

Despite the workarounds, the new laws had an almost instant impact.[2] From 2012 to 2013, the volume of Perú's once-rising gold exports dropped 3 percent, in part as a result of the new requirements.

Yet despite the crackdown, Ferrari and NTR Metals defied the national trend. During that same period, three companies that were suspected fronts for Ferrari's operations (Mano de Dios, Minerales Gold MPP, and Comercializadora de Minerales Rivero) exported $238.5 million worth of gold and precious metals—up sharply from just $61 million the previous year.[3]

And Ferrari himself seemed unfazed, keeping up a routine that many casual associates found at odds with his hard-partying reputation. Though he seemed to live in a world surrounded by vices—and often acted and dressed like a narco kingpin—he was also something of a health nut.

José Estuardo Morales, one of Ferrari's longtime associates, said he was hired as a driver and often that meant following the gold magnate in a car as he jogged down the beach in Lima in the pre-dawn hours.

Morales said his boss's public persona and actual personal life were almost comically divorced. His one true vice was women. All his other vices were subordinate. He exercised regularly to look good when he went out clubbing. And he kept his clubbing under control so he could work out.

"He was a health freak," Morales said. "He never did a gram of coke in his life."[4]

Ferrari also credited his healthy lifestyle (not the often-rumored plastic surgery) for his youthful looks. "I don't smoke, I'm an athlete, I have no vices at all," he told reporters in 2018. "I'm more than 50 years old but I don't look like it. I've never been sick."[5]

Another secret to Ferrari's youthful appearance might be that he rarely got his hands dirty—literally—in the gold trade. Although he had been in the industry for decades, he claimed he'd never owned a gold mine or even visited a mining camp.

But that didn't matter. Perú's goldfields, particularly the ones in La Pampa, were teeming with tens of thousands of desperate miners, people literally working around the clock digging up gold. To the government and environmentalists, those miners and the army of gangs that protected and extorted them were one of the primary threats to the very stability of the nation.

But to gold buyers like Ferrari they represented an efficient legion of freelancers who beat a path from Madre de Dios to shops in Lima to sell their metal. And that arrangement allowed Ferrari to keep his distance. In his telling, he was simply a city-bound merchant. "Of course I've never been to Madre de Dios," he often repeated. "I'm not a miner."[6]

But he wasn't telling the whole truth; he had been to Madre de Dios. A number of people, including friends, fellow gold buyers, and taxi drivers, remember the flamboyant "Peter Ferrari" meeting with gold merchants in the region's capital, Puerto Maldonado, hitting the clubs, and picking up women impressed by the muscular city slicker.[7]

CHAPTER 12

The Raid

ON DECEMBER 4, 2013, AGENTS FROM PERÚ'S NATIONAL CUSTOMS AND Tax Authority, SUNAT, raided a shipping warehouse in Lima's airport district of Callao.

Inside, authorities found 508 kilos of gold worth $18 million destined for the United States and Italy.[1] According to press reports, the gold belonged to six companies that had been targeted because they fit the profile of money laundering fronts—all recently created and doing booming business.

But one company in particular caught authorities' attention. Comercializadora de Minerales Rivero SAC was exporting the lion's share of the gold, 304 kilos worth $11.2 million, most of it bound for NTR Metals in Miami.[2] In fact, NTR's parent company, Elemetal, had already paid for the shipment.

Minerales Rivero had been registered that same year and had begun exporting gold in June. By November, just five months later, the upstart company had exported a staggering 4,665 kilos of gold worth $188 million.

Even more intriguing for regulators, the company was registered to Peter Ferrari's nephew, Miguel Ángel Rivero Pérez, and it was registered to the same address the gold merchant used for his gold-buying operation, on La Paz Avenue.[3] (It was just one obvious red flag that Steve Crogan, Elemetal's compliance officer in charge of approving NTR's client list, never caught.)

When police questioned Ferrari's nephew, he told them the gold he was exporting came from a legitimate mining operation called

Estrellitas de la Loma, registered in Piura, in northeastern Perú. But the owners of that company said they had never done business with him or any of his companies.

"Therefore, we presume the metal comes from an illegal source," the police said in a report, noting the seized metal was 92.56 percent pure gold, "a composition that is similar to the gold that is exploited in Madre de Dios."

Police believed the nephew was a front man for Ferrari. One of Ferrari's multiple lawyers—he burned through them with alarming speed—described Ferrari's protégé as a clueless dupe.

"He had no idea what he was getting into," the lawyer said. "He was just a car washer and cut Peter's grass."[4]

For Ferrari, the accusation that Minerales Rivero was a front company was absurd. What kind of criminal mastermind tries to hide behind a company registered under his nephew's name, and using his own company's address?

"If I was really trying to hide something, if I really needed a front company, I would set it up under someone who had nothing to do with me," he said. "We weren't hiding anything."[5]

It's unclear what triggered the raid by Peruvian authorities, perhaps a failure to pay customs fees and taxes. Whatever the reason, some in the police force had a theory: Ferrari and his crew had gotten greedy. "I think they quit bribing customs officials and so customs actually did its job," said one police investigator who worked on the case.[6]

The airport raid rattled Perú's gold merchants and the international import companies that relied on them.[7] In addition to Elemetal, among those that had gold seized were Kaloti Metals, a Miami-based dealer that sold gold to a refinery in Dubai, Swiss conglomerate Metalor, and the Italian firm Italpreziosi—though none of those companies would incur the scrutiny of US authorities like Elemetal.

"The seizure announced the arrival of a new era in policing the multi-billion dollar illegal gold trade in Perú, sending a message to the Peruvian companies that were moving illicit gold into the legal markets that they would never again have it so easy," wrote the nonprofit news site InSight Crime.[8]

The seizure sent Ferrari's crew into a panic.

Ferrari's customs broker, Andrés Tejeda, quickly called his friend and business partner Juan Pablo Granda.

"We have a big problem," Tejeda said.

Granda let out a long sigh of frustration.

He was far from Lima, standing on a hill near the Incan citadel of Sacsayhuamán. It is a Quechua name pronounced roughly as "sexy woman," to the delight of tour guides leading English-speaking groups, and the place where fifty mounted Spanish conquistadors had defeated a much larger force of Incan warriors during the siege of Cusco in 1536. Granda knew the seizure of Ferrari's gold could lead to Elemetal discovering how much gold NTR's three amigos had bought from the notorious precious-metals broker, blowing up their network of lies.

The airport bust also terrified many people in Ferrari's network of alleged cutouts and straw men. Joseph Leyva Miyashiro, the young man who'd once been the gold magnate's driver, suddenly realized the implication of having casually signed documents for his one-time boss. When the police informed him that he was a registered shareholder of Mano de Dios—a company that had exported more than $100 million worth of gold to Miami—Leyva was living with his grandparents and making $500 a month working at a business that filled fire extinguishers.

Luis Rolando Madueño Chocano, the retiree who was paid to sign mountains of documents, discovered he was the unwitting owner of a bank account that was being run by one of Ferrari's alleged front companies. Although Madueño could barely make ends meet, investigators informed him that his bank account—the one he'd opened with $50 and on the instruction of Ferrari's crew—had received seventeen wire transfers from the United States totaling more than $10.6 million. Madueño never saw any of it.[9]

Meanwhile, Ferrari was trying to figure out what went wrong and how he could avert disaster. It didn't take long to find a solution. A month after the seizure, as police and investigators were trying to determine the origin of the gold and how it traced back to Ferrari, a team of lawyers showed up at the government warehouse where the metal was impounded.

The attorneys carried an order from a judge in Campo Verde, a far-flung town of sixteen thousand people about 450 miles northeast of Lima, to release the gold to Ferrari. The customs officials had no choice but to hand back the bullion. (The judge would later admit that he was paid by the gold merchant's associates to write up the order, and he was jailed on corruption allegations in a separate case.)[10]

Five days later, on January 8, 2014, a company called Sumaj Orkro SAC deposited approximately 127 kilos of gold destined for South Florida's Kaloti Metals with a transport carrier named Hermes, police said.[11]

Authorities suspected this was some of the same gold pried out of the government warehouse with the court order just days earlier. As they moved in to block the export, they discovered that Sumaj Orkro's legal representative was Alberto David Miranda Pando, one of Ferrari's cousins.

Ferrari had stolen his gold back—Granda was certain.

When the news broke, the American was back in Lima grilling chicken wings, fish, and sausages on the rooftop pool terrace of his apartment building for a weekend party. He saw a television report about authorities seizing the gold. A stack of bars flashed across the screen—and Granda saw his own handwriting. He had numbered each bar with a black marker and then recorded its weight in his spreadsheets. His numbers were still on the bars, along with a new notation from authorities showing their weight. He ran to his computer. Those weights matched the numbers in his ledger. They were the same bars. Ferrari had stolen them from Elemetal and resold them to Kaloti.

The gold seizure, recovery, and apparent double dealing might have been just another footnote in Ferrari's byzantine business operations, but together they would come back to haunt him.

In an insurance claim, Elemetal asserted that it had already paid for the gold that was initially seized from Minerales Rivero in Lima's airport district, although the US precious-metals importer never acknowledged the three amigos were dealing with Ferrari or any of his presumed shell companies. (As for Kaloti, the company denied buying any gold from Ferrari that he allegedly stole from Elemetal.)

Granda never trusted Ferrari, who was technically the client of his NTR colleague, Renato Rodriguez. Granda viewed the gold dealer as a prima donna, always nickel-and-diming NTR and threatening to take his business to Kaloti, where he still had accounts. All the other Peruvian gold dealers hated him too; he was flamboyant and never paid his taxes, they said, drawing unwanted attention from authorities and the media. In meetings, he mumbled so much Granda could barely understand him.

Now Ferrari was about to make the three amigos' careers at NTR a living hell.

CHAPTER 13

La Base

THE PERUVIAN POLICE INVESTIGATION OF THE AIRPORT GOLD SEIZURE brought Peter Ferrari's run of good fortune to an abrupt halt. No longer could he allegedly gin up new companies under the names of underlings and associates to stay ahead of the law. But authorities thought he was already cooking up a solution to keep moving gold: smuggling it out of Perú.

On an exclusive block of Lima's Batallón Libres de Trujillo street, Ferrari had what he called *La Base*, The Base, a sprawling home tucked behind a large brick wall that gave him the room and privacy to go about his business. It was a spot where workaday vans and BMW sports cars would pull in day and night, and burly security men prowled the premises.

Some of Ferrari's employees had been told the house belonged to Gabriela Pérez del Solar, a congresswoman who had shot to fame as a member of the country's female volleyball team that won the silver medal at the Seoul Olympics in 1988.[1] Though there were no indications she knew what Ferrari and his men were up to, the fact that they were operating (or at least claimed to be) from the home of a well-known politician and celebrity only seemed to underscore his credentials as a legitimate businessman.

It was at *La Base* that the crew accumulated the gold they bought at their small storefront on La Paz Avenue and melted it down into chunky ingots.

As Perú's crackdown intensified, wily gold traders saw a solution in the nation's porous borders: they could smuggle illegal gold to neighboring countries and forge papers to make it look like it had been mined there. For anyone wanting to buy Peruvian gold, the places to go quickly became Ecuador and Bolivia. The borders were little-policed stretches of jungle and mountains. Metal could flow across easily. Ferrari denied ever smuggling gold across international borders, but a former employee said he witnessed his boss and his men stacking the gold bricks into wooden crates and putting them on trucks headed to Ecuador and Bolivia.[2]

And regional export statistics suggest *something* strange was happening.

In 2013, before the airport bust, Perú exported nearly 60 metric tons of gold to the United States.[3] The next year, with Peruvian customs officials more carefully scrutinizing precious-metals outflows, that figure plummeted to just 18 tons.

At the same time, exports from Ecuador and Bolivia skyrocketed. Bolivia's gold shipments to the United States tripled from 9.5 tons in 2013 to almost 32.9 tons the following year. Ecuadorian exports shot up from 9.8 tons to 23.3 tons. Those spikes in Ecuador and Bolivia accounted for nearly all of the "shortfall" in Peruvian gold exports. Of course, no major new mines had opened in Ecuador and Bolivia to produce these streams of raw gold. Mining statistics from the US Geological Survey show that Ecuador steadily produced between 3 and 5 tons per year and Bolivia extracted around 7.[4] That hadn't changed.

Sensing the seismic shift in South America's gold trade, NTR's three amigos—with Renato Rodriguez as the point man—set up shop on the other side of Perú's borders, snapping up the smuggled gold and shipping it to the United States.

In the year following the airport raid in Lima, NTR's imports from Ecuador tripled to $337 million and its deals in Bolivia jumped tenfold to $270 million.[5] Meanwhile, its purchases from Perú plummeted 92 percent, from $980 million in 2013 to a piddling $79 million in 2014.

The sudden shift should have been a red alert to compliance officers at NTR's parent company, Elemetal, as well as its competitors and the banks that financed the entire industry. Elemetal did seem to know what was going on. In one contemporaneous internal email, a company executive acknowledged that "exports of precious metals from Lima ha[ve] all but stopped. . . . Our customers have advised that precious metal is transiting the border to Bolivia and Ecuador."[6]

Even though Elemetal compliance officer Steve Crogan established several Latin American countries as "no-fly" zones where the company could not purchase gold because of know-your-customer and security risks, the Elemetal bosses didn't stop their star salesmen from buying "Ecuadorian" and "Bolivian" metal that was clearly being smuggled from Perú.[7] (The "no-fly" countries were Mexico, Venezuela, Guyana, French Guiana, Suriname, Brazil, Paraguay, and Uruguay. With the exceptions of Mexico and Brazil, the other nations produced relatively little gold.)

With the Peruvian gold market shut down, Granda's friend, the customs broker Andrés Tejeda, proved instrumental in helping the three amigos get back on their feet. Because the Bolivian city of La Paz had no direct flight to Miami, all the smuggled Peruvian gold that ended up in La Paz had to be flown back to Lima—with false papers stating it was mined in Bolivia—and then shipped to South Florida. Tejeda pulled the shipping logs to find out which companies were sending gold from La Paz to Lima. That's how NTR identified who in Bolivia had gold to sell. Then Rodriguez would fly there to woo the Bolivian dealers and buy their supplies of smuggled Peruvian gold.

It was good business, but Rodriguez hated Bolivia. The food was mediocre, there weren't any good hotels, and the women were hardly to his taste. It felt like the 1970s. He didn't want to be there and he half-jokingly blamed one person: Granda, NTR's director of Peruvian operations, who was in charge when the Peruvian police seized Ferrari's gold at the Lima airport.

"Finally landed in La Paz," Rodriguez texted his two colleagues late in 2014 via the encrypted messaging system WhatsApp. (During their travels, the three amigos freely exchanged text messages on WhatsApp, imagining no one outside their tight-knit trio would ever read them.)[8]

"Never been so happy," Barrage replied in mockery.

"This is all Juan's fuck up," Rodriguez said.

"Had he not fucked up Peru you wouldn't be chasing ounces in modern day 1972," Barrage agreed.

"He a lying fuck up," Rodriguez said.

Granda jabbed back: "At least I am not in Bolivia."

"Fuck off," Rodriguez said. "Bolivia is keeping us afloat. Bolivia is where it's at."

Granda reminded Rodriguez that all the gold ending up in Bolivia was coming from Granda's territory in Perú. But because the gold was being shipped to the United States as if it had originated in Bolivia rather than in Perú, all the commissions went to Rodriguez. Granda was getting stiffed.

"Yea, tell all of my Peru gold good night," Granda said. "I think [Barrage] is smuggling the gold out of Peru so you won't pay me lol [laughing out loud]."

"You Peruvians fucked it up," Rodriguez rejoined.

Barrage then transmitted a picture of small Black children with the message: "That's the thanks I get for feeding a village of niglets."

Granda's response: "Lmao."

Laughing my ass off.

PART II

CHAPTER 14

The Perfect Patsy

NTR'S THREE AMIGOS WERE ALWAYS JUST ONE STEP AHEAD OF THE LAW.

As authorities in one South American country caught on, the gold dealers would open up operations in another. When exporting gold from Perú became increasingly risky, they slipped off to Bolivia, Ecuador, and Chile.

In Ecuador, Samer Barrage and Renato Rodriguez landed a spectacular client: a deep-pocketed Miami Beach–based investor named Jeffrey Himmel, who was exploring investment opportunities in his wife's native country. Himmel, who was introduced to NTR's dealers by an Ecuadorian businessman, decided on importing gold from the mountains in Ecuador to sell to refineries in the United States. For a decent return on his investment, Himmel thought he had found the perfect buyer in NTR Metals in Miami. But NTR's dealers—still reeling from the seizure of their gold shipment at the Lima airport in late 2013—would soon see Himmel as the perfect patsy for their smuggling racket.

It somehow seemed improbable that the sophisticated sixty-year-old Himmel—a former investment banker known for his marketing genius in resurrecting consumer products such as Ovaltine and Gold Bond Medicated Powder—would ever cross paths with the gold traders from NTR, let alone do business with them.

After graduating from the prestigious Wharton School at the University of Pennsylvania in 1975, Himmel became a certified public accountant and worked at what was then one of the Big Eight accounting firms. But he had always wanted to work with his father, arguably one of the twentieth century's great market-ing geniuses. So, in 1983, when Martin Himmel took his consumer products company public, Jeffrey Himmel signed on with his pops. Himmel Senior's business model was simple: buy a fading consumer pharmaceutical product and revive it with a wave of catchy adver-tising. His wizardry at branding earned a tidy fortune for the old man, a high school graduate: $43 million when the Himmel family cashed in on a stock offering.[1] "What I need to know, they don't teach in college," a young Martin Himmel had told his mother when she urged him to leave his job as a soda jerk and enroll in college. He was right.

When Himmel's dad went to visit the fancy executives in charge of the ailing products he wanted to buy, he never asked to see the financials, at least not at first. What he wanted were the letters cus-tomers sent the company. Martin Himmel needed to know people cared about the product; if they did, the product could be revived. It didn't matter what it was. Using that philosophy, Martin Him-mel helped turn cast-off brands like Doan's Pills for Backache Pain and Lavoris Mouthwash back into household names in the 1980s. Another smart investment, a trademark called Topol he acquired for $200,000 in 1973, would generate $23 million per year in sales at its peak in the early 1980s, according to the *New York Times*. In refashioning the brand, Martin Himmel recalled an old print ad from the 1930s: if you blew smoke into a handkerchief, it turned gray. And what emerged was Topol Smoker's Toothpolish for a disease he dubbed "yellow ugly tobacco stained teeth." *Fortune Magazine* labeled the Himmel business model "scavenger" entrepreneurship.[2]

Himmel Senior had one method for reviving products: get on television as often as possible to repeat the same core message. Jef-frey Himmel often said he'd rather do thirty thousand television and radio spots over the course of a year than pay through the nose for one Super Bowl ad. Competitors called this strategy "the Him-mel Hammer." When the family sold their firm in 1986, they made another $47 million. But that was the end for the father–son duo. The new bosses fired them the day after the deal closed.

Out of a job, Jeffrey Himmel had no shortage of options. Be-tween 1987 and 1990, he worked on Wall Street as Wilbur Ross's right-hand man at Rothschild, Inc., during the corporate restructuring boom. (Ross became secretary of the Commerce Department under President Donald Trump.) During Himmel's years in investment banking, he had so little time to spend with his children that he would schedule standing appointments in order to see them: a weekly dinner on Thursday and breakfast Saturday morning. He didn't take a vacation the entire time.

In 1991, he yearned to return to his roots in consumer products, hoping to fulfill a promise he had made to his dying father. Himmel told his father, on his deathbed, that he had finally bought the rights to the nutritious chocolate powder known as Ovaltine, a lifelong dream for the two of them. The deal wouldn't close for another nine months, but the fib put a smile on his father's face.

It was Jeffrey Himmel who came up with having child actors deliver the advertising line that would make the drink famous: "More Ovaltine." But it was a single mother who wrote in to the company, admonishing Himmel that the children ought to be polite and say, "More Ovaltine, please." With that finishing touch, Himmel immediately tweaked the ad and "More Ovaltine, please" would turn into an iconic advertising catchphrase of the 1990s. (In 2007, Himmel sold Ovaltine to Nestlé for $30 million.)[3]

Himmel—who wore shoulder-length gray hair alongside perfectly round glasses that lent him an owlish countenance—owned homes in Manhattan and Southampton, New York. He loved tennis and built not one but two tennis courts—one hard, one clay—at his Long Island home where tennis stars sometimes trained before the US Open. His life took a radical turn in 2005 when he agreed to be the godfather of a friend's baby girl at a baptism in Miami. At the celebration, Himmel, by then divorced, met Patricia, the aunt of the baby being baptized. She was beautiful. During the country club after-party, Himmel trembled from the other side of a window watching her talk to other guests. He gave her a business card and they talked by phone. On July 4, they had their first date. Five months later, on her birthday, he proposed. They wed the following March at the Mandarin Oriental Hotel on Brickell Key, a man-made island off of downtown Miami.

South Florida is halfway between New York, where Himmel lived, and Guayaquil, Ecuador, where his wife's family lived. They agreed to settle in the Miami area. In 2008, the couple bought a $6 million waterfront home on Miami Beach's Palm Island.[4] The palatial Mediterranean revival estate was archly named Casa di Sole e Mare, Italian for "House of Sun and Sea." Three years later, his wife opened Violetas, a home-decor store on Miracle Mile, an upscale shopping district in the affluent Miami suburb of Coral Gables.[5]

For the New York transplant, everything seemed perfect in Miami. But the perennial entrepreneur was still itching to launch another business—something to cap his career. He was looking for new opportunities and hoping to spend more time in his new wife's native Ecuador. But Himmel made a mistake that would doom his Ecuadorian venture.

He trusted a man named Paul Borja.

∞∞∞∞∞∞∞

Paul Borja was a gregarious and squat *Guayaquileño* with a sharp sense of humor, a crude tongue, and a habit of hugging women a beat too long. He had grown up in the wealthiest circles of Ecuadorian high society.

Now he lived in Miami, where he had started a real estate appraisal service and a general-contracting firm. Borja, who had met Himmel in Guayuaquil's social scene, constantly pestered him with different investment opportunities, from buying South Florida real estate to investing in a utility-metering company back in Ecuador. None of the projects interested Himmel. Not until Borja mentioned gold in early 2012. The pitch sounded alluring.

Ecuadorian gold, Borja claimed, was some of the highest purity metal in the world. In most countries, a ton of rock veined with gold—known as ore—yielded less than two grams of gold before processing, which then further reduced the haul. But Ecuadorian quartz ore—*cuarzo*—contained an incredible seven or eight grams of gold, Borja said.

Even better: There was little competition. Foreign mining companies wanted little to do with Ecuador. The risk of doing business there was viewed as high because of Ecuador's then president Rafael Correa, a socialist often mentioned in the same breath as Hugo Chávez of Venezuela and Fidel Castro of Cuba. The country did not look kindly on foreign, multinational mining companies that could bring environmental devastation to Ecuador.

As he listened to Borja, Himmel leaned back in his chair. They had arranged to meet at his wife's store. Surrounded by tastefully gilded furniture and accessories, Himmel began thinking that gold had the ring of success. He had already considered so many investment opportunities in Ecuador, mainly businesses that would take local products and market them far more lucratively in the United States. None passed his careful scrutiny.

One venture he pondered involved Ecuadorian fishermen. They raised some of the highest-quality shrimp in the world. But when it came to the delectable crustacean, American shoppers cared only about low prices, not quality. In a similar vein, Ecuadorian cacao was renowned for its delicate flavor, but the US gourmet chocolate market was too crowded to make an investment worthwhile. Buying a television station in Ecuador didn't make sense either because of tight government oversight of the media. Those were only a few of the nonstarters.

As Himmel sat with Borja, the Ecuadorian made his pitch: He had forged relationships with the small, locally owned mining companies and artisanal miners who dominated Ecuador's gold industry. By buying gold at a discount from the small miners and selling it to American refineries, Borja claimed, they could make a 10 percent profit in just seven days, the amount of time it took to haul gold from the Ecuadorian mountains, fly it to Miami, and get paid. Borja already had accounts open with an eager local buyer: NTR Metals. He offered to serve as Himmel's man on the ground in Ecuador, finding gold to buy, making sure the payments arrived on time, and arranging the shipments to NTR.

All he needed was cash. Himmel's cash.

Himmel was intrigued. But first the former Wall Street banker wanted to do his due diligence and ensure that there was a logical supply chain from the mountains in Ecuador to the refineries in the United States. On October 16, 2012, he and Borja drove to the modest industrial offices of NTR outside Miami. Rodriguez and Barrage—two of NTR's three amigos—were waiting for him.

In customary fashion, Himmel sold himself—all his accomplishments on Wall Street, as well as his philanthropic efforts with the American Diabetes Association. He told Barrage that the gold trader and Himmel's wife had something in common: they were both of Lebanese descent. When Barrage mentioned that his wife, Iska, was expecting, Himmel was only too happy to recommend his family pediatrician. He was practically purring. But for all his business savvy, he had no idea that the more he talked, the more he looked like a tasty meal to the sharks sitting across the table.

Later that day, Himmel wrote his new friends and partners an email.

"Samer, we wish you and Iska blessings with the upcoming birth of your daughter. Samer, we have a lot in common, Lebanese family and my birthday, Christmas!" Himmel enthused. "The Lebanese community is so small here in Miami, and in Ecuador, I am sure we know a lot of people in common. . . . Paul and I look forward to building a successful business together."[6]

Rodriguez replied twenty minutes later.

"Jeffrey, you beat me to the punch," the gregarious salesman wrote. "I always like to send a follow-up email thanking our clients for the meeting. It was great to meet you as well and I look forward to working with a fellow New Yorker!!"

The next morning, Barrage chimed in. As it turned out, he and Himmel did have friends in common, thanks to their Lebanese ties.

"Small world indeed," he said.

Their meeting was a smash, but, careful as always, Himmel studied the gold trade for a few more months to see whether it really made business sense. The true profit, he discovered, was closer to 1 percent, not the 10 percent margin Borja had promised. But even 1 percent in seven days was enticing. He was in, with a logical buyer for his gold imports, NTR.

For NTR, "the Bank of Himmel" was a turning point.

On March 1, 2013, Himmel registered a Florida company called MVP Imports, using his wife's store in Coral Gables as the mailing address on the corporation papers.[7]

The acronym MVP didn't stand for "most valuable player."

It was personal.

MVP paid tribute to his wife, Patricia.
Mi vida Patricia. Patricia is my life.
MVP.

∞∞∞∞∞∞∞

In the fall of 2013, Himmel's new company, MVP Imports, began to buy gold mined in the mountains of Ecuador and then ship it to Miami. The gold went straight from Miami International Airport to NTR's office in Doral.

For NTR, the arrangement would prove ideal. Himmel had large sums of money on hand to cut quick gold deals ahead of competitors in Ecuador. And his role provided a bonus: Himmel was the importer of record on customs papers, not NTR, which would come in handy after the airport gold seizure in Perú, because NTR's dealers were looking to avoid scrutiny. Little did Himmel know.

In terms of gold production, Ecuador was a blip on the global stage, producing 2 percent of the supply that Perú did.[8] But because the two nations shared the Andes mountain range—and veins— Ecuador was understood to be the last untapped gold market in South America. The profits were strong and steady, and Himmel had a vision that drove his passion for an industry he admittedly knew little about. In Ecuador, where he hoped to retire with his wife, Himmel had a long-term goal that went beyond importing gold. He dreamed of bringing technology to Ecuador to create a more environmentally responsible method of mining gold.

"I'm looking to build something new," Himmel told his friends, saying he wanted both to make money and help the people of a poor country. He wanted to transform how Ecuadorian miners extracted gold. To prevent mining waste from being dumped into waterways, Himmel planned to build an 11.5-mile pipeline stretching from the mountain mining sites to a waste treatment plant.

By this point, even President Correa was eager for change and foreign investment. "Our mining laws have been a total disaster," Correa said in 2014. "It has been a failure on the part of the government."[9]

Not only would Himmel's treatment plant clean up the environment and save lives, it would also—because the miners' mercury-based practices were so inefficient—boost the amount of gold recovered. The whole enterprise, priced at $65 million, would pay for itself in just a few years, according to his projections.[10] And to encourage the participation of the mining community, all of the processing plants that joined in the pipeline would receive half of the profits from the venture.

Himmel was no passive investor. He and his wife moved to Guayaquil, Ecuador's commercial capital. He traveled to rural shantytowns to visit the artisanal mines perched on the sides of mountains in southwestern Ecuador's aptly named Provincia de El Oro, the Province of Gold. But Himmel suffered from claustrophobia and could barely make it past the low entrances of the narrow mining shafts.

Though the mines were intimidating, Himmel delved deep into the logistics of his supply chains. Trucks ferried his gold from mountain towns to a secure vault in Machala, the nearest big city, and then on to light aircraft—*avionetas*—bound for the international airport in Guayaquil. From there, couriers checked crates laden with gold into the cargo holds of American Airlines passenger flights to Miami. Unlike most gold dealers, Himmel wasn't a speculator. He financed his import business with lines of credit and his own capital. From NTR's perspective, his cash spared the company the risk of having its paid-for gold seized by customs, as had happened with Peter Ferrari's shipment, leaving the company short $10 million.

By the end of their relationship, MVP Imports would buy $337 million worth of gold in Ecuador and turn around and sell it to NTR Metals. Other Miami refineries approached Himmel about taking his business. But he stayed loyal to Rodriguez and Barrage.

◇◇◇◇◇◇◇◇

Two of Ecuador's biggest gold exporters in 2014 were linked to a trio of brothers named Alberto, Javier, and Jordi March Game.[11] One of the companies, a longstanding chemical business called Spartan del Ecuador, had diversified into precious metals in 2013 as the Latin American gold rush boomed.[12] The other company, Clearprocess, had been formed in 2012 and found quick success. It declared $189 million in revenue in 2014 after making no money the previous year, according to court records.[13] (Alberto March said

Clearprocess couldn't do business until 2014 because that's when the company acquired its export license.)[14]

Spartan was one of the suppliers that Borja found for Himmel's company, MVP Imports. Although their business relationship was short-lived—MVP Imports bought gold from the company only between November 2013 and spring 2014—Himmel's association with the March brothers would provide a mountain of gold.[15] In 2014, Spartan del Ecuador sold $128 million worth of gold to MVP, which was then resold to NTR in Miami.[16]

Himmel had every reason to believe that all of the gold was coming from the Ecuadorian mountains. That's what the customs documents and mining records showed. That's what the bank transactions showed.

But Ecuadorian prosecutors—who would later accuse the three March brothers of participating in a money laundering scheme—believed the gold had actually been smuggled into Ecuador from Perú after that country's crackdown on illegal mining.[17] (The March brothers have maintained that Spartan and Clearprocess dealt only in legal gold with all the required paperwork and that they had no contact with NTR.)[18]

∞∞∞∞∞∞

For the time being, Himmel was happy with the flow of gold from Ecuador—he was buying the metal at a 4 to 6 percent discount, pocketing about a 1 percent profit as he had predicted. When Himmel was in town, he would meet with Rodriguez and Barrage for lunch at Hillstone, an upscale restaurant in Coral Gables, where they would talk business over the appetizers and family over the steaks.

Still, the accountant in Himmel wanted to do more double-checking. He asked Rodriguez and Barrage if he could see their books. Gold was a business built on trust. Himmel had to be sure that NTR would pay him when the gold arrived in Miami. He knew all too well that if NTR started having cash flow problems, he would become an unsecured creditor, unlike the banks that would be first in line to collect on their notes. Himmel told Rodriguez and Barrage that if they expected to keep his business they would have to introduce him to the boss of NTR's parent company, Elemetal, in Dallas.

Himmel wanted to meet Elemetal's cofounder, Steve Loftus, face-to-face.

In early May 2014, Himmel flew to Dallas. He toured Elemetal's old processing plant on the city's seedier side. It was filled with scrap gold and old radios that contained microchips with trace amounts of precious metals that the company melted down.

Loftus took Himmel to his colonial-style home outside Dallas, where Himmel met his wife. Their neighbor was billionaire Mark Cuban, who owned the Dallas Mavericks and starred on the reality TV show *Shark Tank*.

Loftus and Himmel had good chemistry. They were both irrepressibly creative business minds. Himmel had ideas and started pitching Loftus. Elemetal should start a commemorative coin business, he said. Himmel, with his marketing nose, could help attract customers. Loftus seemed receptive. Himmel was still excited when he got back to Miami. He wrote an email to Loftus and the other Elemetal executives he had met in Dallas.

"Your straight-shooting and passion for your business are outdone by only the red bean and rice soup in the [Elemetal] cafeteria," Himmel gushed in a May 2, 2014, message.[19]

"We highly value our relationship with NTR Metals, and look forward to growing together," Himmel said. "I am going to give some thought to the commemorative coin business. Whether it is selling a commemorative World Cup coin, Pope Francis coin in Argentina, or better yet in the Vatican, or other branded product, I will give this further thought."

Nothing would come of it. NTR was already shifting its focus from Ecuador to yet another South American country where Rodriguez and Barrage had found a new way to buy smuggled gold, thanks to a young entrepreneur who was obsessed with the precious metal.

CHAPTER 15

The College Student

THE GOLD DEALER THAT NTR'S THREE AMIGOS FOUND IN CHILE COULD not have been more unlike Jeffrey Himmel.

A twenty-one-year-old college student from a family of jewelers and devout Evangelical Christians, Harold Vilches Pizarro had none of Himmel's business acumen or riches.[1] But what he lacked in experience, he made up for in burning ambition.

Vilches formed his first company, Inversiones Aurum Metals, in 2012.[2] A year later, the company managed to export $16 million worth of gold, more than 40 percent of Chile's scrap-gold exports.

By the time Vilches was carrying gold on flights to Miami for NTR Metals in late 2014, the chubby, dark-haired young man had already churned through several precious-metals buyers, including double-crossing a major player in the United Arab Emirates.

For Vilches, who had been around gold his whole life and who dreamed of building his own refinery in the United States, the high-stakes world of precious-metals dealers seemed like a natural fit.[3]

Vilches's uncle, Enrique Vilches Millar, was the founder of a successful chain of jewelry stores in Chile. As far back as Vilches could remember, his father, Mario, a retired Air Force mechanic, had worked with Enrique. Then, when Vilches was in middle school, Mario split with his brother to start his own company. He opened a jewelry store and a scrap-gold business where he bought used trinkets and gold produced by small-scale miners, melted it down, and resold it to jewelers.[4]

During summer vacations, Vilches helped out in the family business. He took inventory at the jewelry store, which his mother ran, and delivered ornaments to the scrap-gold shop. He would put the jewelry in an envelope, tuck it into his pocket, and jump on the metro. Twenty minutes later, Vilches would emerge in Santiago's bustling city center, where the stately façades of colonial-era churches broke up blocks of apartment buildings and office towers. At a scrap-gold shop tucked inside a faded yellow mall, Vilches would watch, transfixed, as his father tested the jewelry with acids to make sure it was gold and melted it with a blowtorch. After Mario sold the gold, he'd give Vilches stacks of cash to take back to his mother at the jewelry store.[5]

Other than his occasional duties at the family business, Vilches led the relatively carefree existence of an adolescent raised in an upper-middle-class home in one of the wealthiest countries in Latin America. He attended private school, played tennis in his free time, and frequented an Evangelical church with his family.

As Vilches was preparing to enter college, however, his life took an unexpected turn. Early one morning, his father had a stroke while working at the scrap-gold shop and fell into a coma. He was found lying on the floor with the shop's security gate halfway open.[6] Vilches's mother abandoned the jewelry store to stay by her husband's side at the hospital. It fell to Vilches and his siblings to take charge of the family business. Overnight, Vilches went from worrying about his college entrance exams to providing for his family. Although he didn't know it at the time, his father would never go back to running the family business.[7]

In 2012, Vilches opened his first company: Inversiones Aurum Metals. The scrap-gold shop was registered to his dad, which made it hard for Vilches to carry out bank transactions and anything else that required a signature. In order to keep selling gold, he needed a company in his own name.

It wasn't just an administrative change. Vilches thought he could find a more efficient way to conduct business and hopefully expand the company.[8]

The way his father had set it up, the family business was labor intensive and the profit margin thin. They had to keep a large inventory at the jewelry store so buyers had options, but that meant a lot of money was tied up in earrings and necklaces. Sales were only good around the holidays, so the store had to sustain itself all year off the profits from Mother's Day and Christmas.

Vilches's sister had dropped out of college to run the jewelry store, and Vilches was struggling to coordinate all of the small transactions at the scrap-gold shop while studying business at a local university. If he could close the jewelry store and invest that money in the scrap-gold shop, he thought, he could buy and sell larger quantities, maybe even to exporters instead of jewelers. The business plan was risky, but if it worked, his family could make a lot of money. It was a plan that would eventually lead him to NTR Metals.

At first, Vilches claimed, he did everything by the book.[9] To obtain larger quantities of gold, he worked in the scrap-gold shop for half the day, then spent the afternoon going from one competitor to the next with cash in hand to buy their inventory. He amassed as much jewelry as he could, melted it down, and sent two exports, worth about $20,000 each, to Miami-based Republic Metals Corp., NTR's rival, which operated one of the biggest precious-metals refineries in North America. (The Rubin family, which owned Republic Metals at the time, said it had no knowledge of any dealings with Vilches.)

Jewelry was subject to a 19 percent sales tax in Chile, which was slapped onto the used gold ornaments Vilches bought. But if the jewelry was for export, the government was supposed to return the money after the gold had been sent abroad.[10]

The government's process for verifying the information on the tax refund form was time-consuming, however, and Vilches made countless trips to the tax agency's office to plead with the official in charge of his case. In the end, it took a whole year to get a lousy $7,600 back.

Clearly, he realized, he was never going to make any money following the rules.

So Vilches found a loophole. Gold jewelry purchases were taxed at a high rate, but gold coins were considered currency, making them tax exempt.[11] If he bought gold coins and melted them, he wouldn't have to pay sales tax.

Vilches opened an account with a coin broker and rented an office in an upscale neighborhood. He imported three bright-blue furnaces from China to melt gold. He wasn't sure how to use the machines, since his dad had always used a blowtorch, but he found instructional videos on YouTube.[12]

Then, after a disagreement with Republic about its payment system, Vilches started searching for a new buyer.

CHAPTER 16

Moving Up

IN THE SUMMER OF 2013, A GOLD BROKER CAME TO GONZALO FARIAS'S office in Santiago to tell him about a new supplier.

Farias, a pale, soft-spoken businessman who ran a gold export company called Grupo EFAD, was always meeting with potential suppliers and looking for ways to expand his business.

He had started years ago in the jewelry trade and currently bought gold from small-scale miners and exported it to the United States, South Korea, and Europe. That summer, he was on the cusp of landing a major deal with an Emirati precious-metals company called Fujairah Gold.

Farias thanked the broker for coming and told him he had certain rules about who he was willing to work with. In particular, there were three families Farias wanted nothing to do with. He wrote the three last names on a piece of paper and handed it to the broker.

One of them was Vilches.

Farias had known the Vilches family for years and had once owned a jewelry store in the shopping mall where Vilches's father, Mario, worked. They'd greeted each other every morning for more than a decade, but Farias had kept the Vilches family at arm's length. Chilean police had detained Mario's brother, Enrique Vilches Millar, in the late 1990s on suspicion that he had financed an international gold-smuggling operation, although he was later absolved of criminal charges. Enrique had also been jailed in 2002 for tax evasion.[1] He would later be sentenced to five years' probation for tax crimes. The fact that Enrique was an Evangelical pastor did little to assuage Farias's concerns.

The broker was convincing, however, and before long he'd per-suaded Farias at least to meet with the new gold supplier, a young man named Harold Vilches.

When Vilches arrived at Farias's office a few weeks later dressed in a suit, the gold exporter was struck by how young he was.

The twenty-year-old college student was polite and respectful. He seemed reserved, but he clearly understood how to make a business deal. He assured Farias that all he wanted was an op-portunity to work hard and build his own business. And Farias, who had a son the same age, decided to give Vilches a chance—as long as he passed a background check and promised to do every-thing by the book.

It was an act of goodwill Farias would soon come to regret.

At first, there was nothing unusual about Vilches's gold deliv-eries, but as time wore on he started sending Grupo EFAD more and more gold. By early 2014, he was selling the company 30 kilos a week. There were days when Vilches had 10 kilos to sell—more than $400,000 worth of gold.[2]

Farias didn't ask a lot of questions. Asking someone in the Chil-ean gold trade to reveal their suppliers just wasn't done. Gold com-panies jealously guarded their networks to keep them from being poached by competitors. Farias, who had recently signed a contract with an Emirati company, Fujairah, to provide 100 to 120 kilos of gold a month, was happy to have the extra material. He assumed Vilches must have a Rolodex of suppliers because of his family's connections. (Farias has not been accused of any wrongdoing.)

And at first, that had been the case. Vilches had gotten the gold he sold to Grupo EFAD from Chilean sources, including gold coins.[3] But coins and used jewelry weren't dependable sources of gold. Chile had stopped minting 100-peso gold coins in the 1970s, and Vilches could only buy large quantities when someone with a stock-pile decided to sell.[4]

He began to look for gold in Argentina, which was only a few hours away on the other side of the Andes Mountains.[5]

Through a contact at a scrap-gold shop, he got the phone num-ber for a supplier in Argentina. Vilches gave the supplier a call, and a few days later two men showed up outside his office building with 5 kilos of gold. They were in business.

Vilches was careful not to buy too much from the Argentines at once, just 5 to 10 kilos at a time. They were smuggling the gold over the border without paying taxes, and Vilches declared it as having come from melted coins. If he bought too much, he was afraid the cover story would seem suspicious.

Unbeknownst to Farias, Vilches was also secretly lobbying Fujairah to cut out the middleman and do business directly with him.[6] He'd spotted the company's name on some export paperwork for the gold he sent Grupo EFAD and realized that he was losing money by not selling directly to Fujairah.[7]

In May 2014, Vilches sent emails to a Fujairah executive and a Uruguayan broker who worked with Fujairah in Latin America.[8] Vilches claimed he was having problems with Grupo EFAD and said he wanted to sell his gold directly to Fujairah.

"I'm a real gold seller, I sell 100 kilos a month to Efad," Vilches wrote. He said his family had been in the gold business for thirty-five years and that he could sell Fujairah 100 kilos of gold a day. But, he added, he would need "something like a bank letter of credit" as a method of payment.

The email to the broker, though in Spanish, was poorly written and riddled with grammatical errors. But that didn't deter Fujairah. At the company's request, the broker traveled to Chile to meet with Vilches.[9] After Fujairah had reviewed his paperwork and its lawyers had conducted a background check, Vilches signed a lucrative deal with the company.[10] In the contract, he promised to deliver a total of 2,930 kilos of gold over the coming months, all of it from legal Chilean sources.[11] And just like that, Farias lost his deal with Fujairah to a now twenty-one-year-old upstart.

Fujairah gave Vilches access to a standby letter of credit—a guarantee in case the company didn't pay for a shipment within seventy-two hours.[12] The letter of credit—which was initially capped at $1.6 million and eventually increased to $5.2 million—essentially promised that Fujairah would be responsible for any unpaid loans Vilches's company accrued at its bank, Banco Santander. Vilches needed the letter of credit to guarantee the loans he would take out to buy gold.

Providing a guarantee is common in export deals, but the letter of credit Fujairah gave Vilches's company was unconditional.[13] The bank wouldn't need to check with Fujairah before applying it.

Before he could get loans to buy gold, Vilches had to present his business plan to Banco Santander. His only experience making formal business presentations up until that point had been the mock presentations he gave in his college classes.[14]

When Vilches presented his PowerPoint to the bank executives, he got the impression that they didn't believe he was actually the boss of his company. Even so, they approved the loans with the standby letter of credit as a guarantee. (Neither Fujairah nor Banco Santander has been accused of any wrongdoing.)

The deal with Fujairah was a big win. If everything went according to plan, Vilches could make between $2 and $6 million. But the deal was also risky. Chile didn't have enough scrap metal to produce the amount of gold he'd promised to deliver.[15]

Farther north in Perú, however, the Amazon rain forest had plenty of gold.

∞∞∞∞∞∞

Shortly after Vilches met with Fujairah's Latin America broker for the first time, he traveled to Lima to meet with a Peruvian businessman named Rodolfo Soria Cipriano.[16] Soria was a gold supplier for both NTR and Peter Ferrari.[17]

Vilches had found Soria's name online by searching for a list of Peruvian gold exporters and had simply sent him an email. During their first meeting, they talked about tennis and soccer and gambled at a casino before getting down to business.[18]

Vilches enjoyed chatting with Soria, but he found that buying gold in Perú was very different than it was in Chile. Soria traveled with armed bodyguards and picked Vilches up at the airport in an armored car.

At first, Vilches and Soria discussed exporting the gold legally, according to Vilches. They hoped to avoid taxes by sending shipments through a special customs zone in Arica, a sleepy port city in northern Chile near the border with Perú. After doing some research, however, they realized that they would still have to pay taxes. For gold entering Chile, taxes were steep—above 40 percent.[19]

As Vilches understood it, Soria had access to large quantities of gold—some of which had been mined informally, though, Soria assured him, not in the troubled Madre de Dios region.[20] Soria sold to

NTR Metals, but ever since the 2013 seizure of Ferrari's shipment in Lima, Peruvian officials had been scrutinizing exports and it had gotten a lot harder to do business.[21]

According to Vilches, they decided that in order to dodge taxes and government scrutiny, Soria would bring the gold to Tacna, a Peruvian town just thirty minutes from the border. From there, Vilches would smuggle it into Chile.[22] (Soria has not been charged with gold smuggling.)

To pull this off, Vilches bought a cheap gray Mazda Demio sedan with local license plates and rented an apartment in Arica.[23] He flew from Santiago to Arica with $1 to $2 million in cash in his carry-on luggage. Vilches was often accompanied by his girlfriend's fifty-three-year-old father, a taxi driver named Carlos Rivas Araya, and his sister's twenty-seven-year-old boyfriend, Javier Concha Montes. Neither of them had much business experience, but Vilches preferred to hire people he could trust. Vilches's girlfriend, whom he'd met on the first day of college, worked as a secretary in his Santiago office.

Once in Arica, Vilches and his employees pried off the door panels of the Mazda sedan, wrapped the cash in plastic, and hid it inside.

Vilches's apartment had an open-air parking area, but his strategy was to act as if he wasn't doing anything wrong. If a neighbor walked by, he'd wave and call out, "Hey, neighbor, how's it going?" He figured the neighbor would assume he was repairing the car.

Once the car door panels were secured, according to Vilches, he and his employees drove across the Chilean border to Perú and picked up the gold from Soria's safehouse in Tacna.[24] Vilches used his handheld spectrometer to analyze the precious metal while Soria ran the stacks of cash through a counter machine.[25] Then Vilches cushioned each 2- to 3-kilo gold bar in a sponge so that if a police officer banged on the car doors at a border checkpoint he wouldn't hear the sound of metal clanging against metal. Vilches typically hid around 50 kilos of gold in the car at a time.

But no one ever banged on the car doors. Border guards were on the lookout for cocaine and human trafficking, not gold. On one trip, Vilches crossed back into Chile at three a.m. only to find the border guard fast asleep. He had to rap on the glass to wake up the guard so he could get his passport stamped.

Once the gold was in Chile, Vilches hired a secure transport company to take it to Santiago and send it to Fujairah on a cargo plane. He told the company his gold came from legal sources. Hiring a secure transport company made his operation appear more legitimate. Like removing the car door panels in broad daylight, it signaled to the world that he had nothing to hide. It was a strategy best summed up in Chilean Spanish as *ser patudo*—which roughly translates to being shameless—and it suited Vilches well.

The scheme worked for a while. Over the summer of 2014, Vilches's crew made seven trips from Chile to Perú and back, moving some 300 kilos of gold worth more than $10 million.[26]

It was a profitable business. Vilches bought gold at below-market prices and because he wasn't declaring it to customs officials, he didn't have to pay taxes.[27] Then he falsified paperwork to make the gold appear to have come from legitimate sources.[28] Vilches also continued to get regular shipments from Argentina, although smaller quantities than he brought back from Perú.[29]

His sudden wealth started to attract attention at the university, where his classmates spread rumors about why he'd gone from driving a Kia to sitting behind the wheel of an Audi.[30]

Then, in mid-August, on the eighth trip Vilches's crew made to Perú, they ran into trouble.[31] A secure transport truck had just been the target of a spectacular armed robbery at the Santiago airport, which press reports referred to as "the theft of the century."[32] Vilches, who was on his way back from a business trip, got an email from the operations manager at the secure transport company he used explaining that the company couldn't move anything of value at the moment.[33]

The problem was that two of Vilches's crew members, Rivas and Concha, had just crossed the border into Chile with 48 kilos of gold hidden in the car doors. It was a holiday weekend, and they didn't want to stash roughly $2 million worth of gold in the Arica apartment for three days until businesses reopened and they could find another transport company.[34]

Rivas and Concha called Vilches to ask if they could take the gold on their flight back to Santiago. Vilches wasn't sure how big of a customs presence there was at the Arica airport, so he told his employees to go without the gold first to scope out the situation.[35]

But Rivas and Concha, itching to get home and spend the long weekend with their families, ignored their boss's advice and walked up to a customs official at the Chacalluta Airport with a black duffel bag containing fifteen ingots. They said they were planning to transport the gold bars on Sky flight 124.[36]

Unfortunately for the duo, Perú's national customs agency had recently alerted its counterpart in Chile that smugglers might be moving illegal gold into neighboring countries. Chilean customs officials in Arica had begun to closely scrutinize gold shipments.[37]

The customs official at the Chacalluta Airport asked Vilches's employees where their gold was from. Concha, flustered, said they'd purchased it from artisanal miners in the area. But 48 kilos was an unbelievably large quantity for small-scale miners and Arica wasn't known for artisanal gold mining.[38]

Did they have a receipt? the customs official wanted to know. Rivas and Concha lied and said they did, then hurriedly called Vilches, who had just arrived in Santiago.[39]

"Why did you say that?" Vilches groaned at Concha after he'd explained his bluff about the local miners.

Vilches raced to the office and wrote a receipt listing one of his companies as the seller and another as the buyer, then hastily shot off an email.

At the airport, Concha and Rivas explained the receipt by telling the customs official that their company had to write its own receipt because the artisanal miners didn't have one. The receipt didn't prove the origin of the gold, however, and the customs official seized the shipment.[40]

Concha and Rivas called their boss with the bad news. They nervously talked over each other as they tried to explain what had happened, which only added to Vilches's irritation.[41]

Meanwhile, customs officials pulled Rivas's and Concha's travel records. They learned that the pair had recently traveled to Tacna, in Perú, so they sent photos of the seized gold to their Peruvian counterparts in customs.[42] The Peruvians said it appeared to have come from their country. A subsequent lab analysis showed that the gold was 98.9 percent pure, which Chile's national mining agency told customs officials was a higher quality than small-scale Chilean miners in the region were capable of producing.[43]

The Chilean customs agency issued a complaint against Rivas and Concha, and prosecutors in Arica opened an investigation.[44]

That was the beginning of Vilches's problems with Fujairah, which had been promised the 48 kilos.[45] Vilches told the company that he'd had some administrative issues with customs that had delayed his shipment.

Then, in mid-November, things got much worse. Vilches's lender, Banco Santander, notified Vilches that it planned to close all of the accounts associated with his company as a result of violations of the bank's policies.[46] Vilches assumed it was because the bank had learned about the seizure in Arica, which had been in the news.[47]

The problem was that Vilches owed Banco Santander money from the loans he'd taken out to buy gold. When the bank closed Vilches's accounts, it used the letter of credit from Fujairah to pay itself back.[48] Because the letter was unconditional, the bank didn't have to check with Fujairah first.

A Fujairah executive frantically emailed Vilches to ask why his bank had executed a letter of credit, collecting $1.6 million, when Fujairah had already paid for all of the gold shipments.[49]

One of Vilches's lawyers responded and explained that customs officials had seized some of Vilches's gold. Not long afterward, Vilches's bank collected another $1.6 million from Fujairah using the same letter of credit. The Fujairah executive fired off four more emails demanding an explanation. The bank eventually collected an additional $2 million, bringing Fujairah's total losses to $5.2 million. The company was livid.[50]

The Arica seizure marked the end of Vilches's exploits in Perú. It was now too risky to smuggle gold across Chile's northern border, so Vilches turned his full attention to Argentina.[51] Unbeknownst to Fujairah, he'd already found a new buyer.

Several months before his business relationship with Fujairah fell apart, Vilches had asked Soria if he knew anyone who was looking for a new gold supplier.[52]

Soria said he knew just the guy, according to Vilches.[53]

"I'm going to send you the contact for a man named Renato Rodriguez at NTR," Soria told him. "He'll help you with everything."

CHAPTER 17

A Suitcase Full of Gold

IN MID-NOVEMBER 2014, HAROLD VILCHES LANDED IN MIAMI WITH A suitcase full of gold.[1] It was the first time he'd ever set foot in the United States.[2]

He checked into a Hyatt hotel in downtown Coral Gables.[3] He had come to Miami to meet Renato Rodriguez and Samer Barrage.

Starting a business relationship with NTR Metals had been easy.[4] Once Vilches had gotten Rodriguez's number from Rodolfo Soria, the Peruvian gold supplier, he'd called the NTR dealer on WhatsApp. Rodriguez asked for some standard paperwork, and, according to Vilches, the company's compliance department approved his application in just a few weeks.[5]

While Vilches's last name might have raised suspicions in some circles inside Chile, outside the country his family's connection to a successful chain of jewelry stores proved useful. It was only natural for him to be exporting gold.

In fact, when Vilches's gold-smuggling scheme imploded a few years later, Elemetal's general counsel Trey Gum would cite Vilches's family business as justification for the company's decision to buy gold from the twenty-one-year-old college student. "The information NTR Miami received was that Mr. Vilches came from a family of established jewelers with close ties to the evangelical community in Chile," Gum told *Bloomberg*. He said NTR did not establish a relationship with Vilches until after its representatives visited his companies in Chile.[6] (Gum has not been accused of any wrongdoing.)

For the NTR dealers, the call from Vilches in the fall of 2014 couldn't have come at a better time. Gold shipments directly from Perú had dried up after the seizure at the Lima airport. While NTR's three amigos were importing hundreds of millions of dollars' worth of gold shipped from Ecuador and Bolivia, they still hadn't managed to fill the void created by the crackdown in Perú.[7]

On Vilches's first day in town, Rodriguez and Barrage picked him up from the Hyatt around lunchtime and took him to Houston's, an upscale restaurant known for steaks and burgers.[8]

Vilches immediately liked the two Miami businessmen. Rodriguez was friendly and easygoing, and Barrage shared Vilches's passion for reading about international markets. He seemed to have a deep understanding of the global gold trade and a knack for business strategy.[9]

Partway into the lunch, Vilches decided to test the waters.

"I could bring gold from Argentina," he ventured.[10]

"Would it be hard to import it into Chile?" the NTR dealers asked. "Argentina has various restrictions."

Vilches wasn't sure they'd understood what he meant, so he changed the subject and asked about their business dealings in Perú. He wanted to feel them out before he shared more about his Argentine smuggling scheme.

(Rodriguez would later deny Vilches's accounts of their conversations, saying the Chilean led him and Barrage to believe that his gold came from melted-down coins—never mentioning it was smuggled from Argentina or Perú into Chile.[11] The conversations between Rodriguez and Barrage and Vilches in this book are largely based on Vilches's recollections, which US investigators found credible and later used to build their criminal case against NTR's three amigos.[12])

Rodriguez and Barrage told Vilches that Soria was a good friend whom they had met in Lima on several occasions. In fact, Rodriguez said, Soria had told them about Vilches's smuggling operations in Perú.[13]

The NTR dealers complained that it had become increasingly difficult to import directly from the Andean nation. Large quantities of Peruvian gold were being smuggled to Bolivia and Ecuador for export to the United States, they added, and they imported from both countries. Vilches interpreted this as a hint that they were also smuggling gold.[14]

Now sure it was safe to confide in the Miami businessmen, Vilches tried again.

"I can bring gold from Argentina without paying taxes," he said.[15]

Rodriguez and Barrage asked how risky that would be.[16]

It would depend on his ability to justify to customs officials the amount of gold he was exporting, the young Chilean explained.[17] But Vilches already had a way to substantiate the precious metals exports. He would say they came from gold coins he melted into bars.

The NTR dealers said Vilches should give his plan a try. Once the shipments got to the United States, they said, they were home free. NTR was a prestigious company accredited by the London Bullion Market Association, the international trade association representing precious-metals companies, and by COMEX, a major metals exchange. No one would question the gold.[18]

After lunch, Rodriguez and Barrage gave Vilches a tour of NTR's office and laboratory.[19]

They showed him the cinder-block warehouse where workers poured molten gold into brick-shaped molds and the metal shelves that stored gold bars the size of bread loaves.[20] When they stopped in Barrage's office, Vilches noticed a whiteboard on the wall behind his desk. On it, Barrage had written the names of gold suppliers in two columns: on the left, the ones whose applications were still under review by the company's compliance department, and on the right, the ones who had already been approved.[21] Barrage was highly focused on this aspect of the business, Vilches learned, and celebrated every approval as a major win.[22]

Before Vilches left Miami, Rodriguez took him to set up a US company and open a US bank account. Vilches had told Rodriguez he was having trouble keeping his Chilean bank accounts open because of anti–money laundering controls, and Rodriguez had offered to introduce him to an accountant friend who could help him open a US corporate account.[23] Vilches's US company, Aurum Metals LLC, was up and running in no time.

Between meetings on the three-day trip, Vilches managed to squeeze in some shopping at a luxury mall in Coral Gables and lounge in the hotel pool. One evening, Rodriguez and Barrage took him to a club. Miami, he thought, was beautiful, laid-back, and very expensive.[24]

By December, Vilches's new operation was in full swing.[25] He bought gold from his supplier in Argentina, who smuggled it over the border into Chile, and then exported it to NTR in Miami. On the customs paperwork, Vilches wrote that the gold was Chilean.[26]

The operation required a great deal of coordination and Vilches gave everyone in his crew a different role. His wife, Scarlett, whom he had recently married, took care of administrative tasks, paying bills, coordinating the arrival of the Argentine smugglers, and organizing the withdrawal of cash when NTR paid Vilches for the gold exports.[27]

His wife's father, Carlos Rivas, served as his right-hand man. Rivas accompanied Vilches on trips and—though he had no formal training—was put in charge of company security. Rivas and another employee, Javier Concha, shuttled shipments of gold to Miami in their carry-on luggage.[28]

It was unclear where the gold originated. Vilches's contact in Argentina told him most of it had been purchased from refineries in Buenos Aires. All Vilches knew for sure was that he paid 4 to 6 percent below market price, which meant that the gold wasn't exactly coming from the national bank.[29]

The shipments were sent to Chile via couriers at least once or twice a month. They hid the gold in a gray Ford Fiesta and drove it along a winding pass of hairpin turns through the Andes Mountains. In the winter, when the pass was blanketed in snow, the road could be treacherous.[30]

Once they arrived in Santiago, the smugglers delivered the gold to Vilches's office. He paid them in dollars, which they wrapped in plastic and hid inside the car doors before returning to Argentina.[31]

Vilches and his father-in-law watched YouTube videos to teach themselves how to cast gold into ingots and stamp the bars with the gold's weight and purity. They imprinted each ingot with an elaborate crown—the seal of Aurum Metals—in order to make the gold seem more legitimate.[32] Then Vilches arranged the export paperwork, which included a sworn declaration claiming the gold came from melted coins.[33]

He also needed to provide customs officials with receipts for the gold coins, and for this he enlisted the help of a coin broker named Dagoberto Muñoz Paredes.[34]

Muñoz was a well-known character in Chile's scrap-gold industry. A short, dark-haired man with a round face and a mischievous grin, he preferred to conduct business in what Chileans call a *café con piernas*—a "coffee shop with legs"—where pretty waitresses in miniskirts tottered around on high heels delivering cappuccinos.

Muñoz ran a no-frills coin website. When he first started doing business with Vilches in 2013, the college student had been like any other customer. He told Muñoz how many coins he wanted and Muñoz bought them from other clients, charging a small commission.[35]

Once the gold began flowing in from Argentina, however, Vilches got Muñoz to issue fake receipts showing Vilches's companies had purchased thousands of gold coins from a company registered in Muñoz's name. Vilches also got Muñoz to sign sworn declarations that he'd witnessed Vilches melt the coins.[36] (Muñoz claims Vilches tricked him into signing the sworn declarations and approving the receipts.)[37]

Last, Vilches obtained a certificate of analysis from a laboratory certifying the gold's composition.[38] To avoid arousing suspicion, he bought copper and mixed it with the smuggled metal before sending a sample to the lab.[39] That way, the composition matched typical Chilean gold coins.

Once all of the paperwork was in order, either Rivas or Concha would take the gold to Miami in their carry-on luggage.[40] At first, Vilches had tried to send the gold using a secure transport company, but he quickly realized that it wasn't practical given the amount of uncertainty in his smuggling operation.[41] If the Argentine smugglers were delayed crossing the border, for example, it was cheaper to change a plane ticket than to reschedule a secure transport.

Vilches occasionally took the gold to Miami himself when he had meetings, but he mainly left the hassle of the eight-hour flights to his father-in-law and Concha. Rivas and Concha transported only a few bars at a time, but even three bars, weighing 4.5 kilos each, were worth roughly half a million dollars total.[42]

In Miami, they declared the gold to customs officials, who reviewed the export documents and weighed the bars but never subjected them to much scrutiny. Then the couriers handed the suitcase to a secure transport company guard who met them at the airport.[43] The guard drove the gold to NTR's office in an armored truck.[44]

Vilches exported $5.5 million worth of gold to NTR in December, crowning a successful year in the illegal gold trade.[45] He and his crew had carried out sixty exports in 2014—many containing gold smuggled into the country from Perú and Argentina. In total, they'd handled over $50 million in gold.[46]

The young Chilean celebrated his success by buying a $1 million mansion north of Santiago.[47] He moved his entire family, including his wife, his parents, and his sister, into the house.[48] The five-bedroom, eight-thousand-square-foot home bordered an artificial lake surrounded by lush vegetation. The grounds included two swimming pools and a jacuzzi where Vilches could soak while watching swans glide serenely on the lake.[49]

CHAPTER 18

El Patrón del Mal

WHILE VILCHES ENJOYED HIS SUCCESS, NTR METAL'S THREE AMIGOS WERE hustling to find more South American gold for the US market. Juan Pablo Granda had held the title of NTR's director of Peruvian operations for just three months when the seizure of Peter Ferrari's gold at the Lima airport in late 2013 wiped out his company's billion-dollar gold business. The next year, Granda would have to start all over again. He needed to rebuild NTR's Perú business from the bottom up.

There would be no more deals with Ferrari; he was too hot. Even the country's other major gold dealers—including several who hadn't been involved in the airport bust—were feeling pressure from the Peruvian government.

Gold was so scarce that for the first time Granda traveled to Puerto Maldonado, the city near the epicenter of Perú's illegal mining industry, La Pampa. Before that, he'd stuck to the big cities of Lima and Cusco, where the big gold dealers were. The trip was an adventure.

"Just landed in Puerto 93 degrees," Granda wrote from the sweltering jungle city on October 1, 2014.[1]

"Stay safe," Rodriguez replied.

"I'm like Pablo coming to Ecuador to get the coke," Granda said.

"Pablo" was the infamous Colombian drug lord Pablo Escobar, who fascinated Granda. Late at night, the American gold dealer binge-watched a Colombian telenovela called *El Patrón del Mal* (*The Boss of Evil*), which glorified Escobar's gory battles with the Colombian government, the DEA, and rival cartels. The series, broadcast on Netflix, featured a scene in which Escobar went to Ecuador to buy his first kilo of cocaine.

Now Granda, who also enjoyed comparing himself to the conquistador Francisco Pizarro and the Inca king Atahualpa, was in Puerto looking for his first load of jungle gold. Rodriguez texted him and Barrage asking for more details about the seller and the export company handling NTR's transaction.

"It's all under the table no docs," Granda said.

"So who is legalizing it?" Rodriguez replied.

Granda explained that the supplier was selling the gold to a couple of exporters known as *los curas*—"the priests" in Spanish. The men had once studied in seminary together. God hadn't worked out, but gold had. One of the priests' companies would handle the deal and falsify paperwork to ensure the gold appeared legally mined.

"[They] provide the papers," Granda texted Rodriguez.

Then Granda seemed to reconsider the wisdom of putting so much smuggling talk in writing.

"What r u trying to [do], set me up," he asked Rodriguez.

Granda and his NTR partners sometimes worried authorities were monitoring their conversations. Yet crossing the line into South America's underworld of narcos, gold collectors, and money launderers fueled their machismo. They had bragging rights their straitlaced friends in Miami could never claim.

Granda, in particular, seemed reckless in his WhatsApp correspondence while trying to impress his best friends back home—a dentist, a physician, a university employee, and a pair of engineers. "As far as security, I already have to worry about intelligence officials monitoring my calls with exporters anyways," Granda wrote in a WhatsApp message to one friend. "Peru is #1 in drug exports and illegal mining exports."[2]

A few weeks later, in another message exchange, he ratcheted up the braggadocio. "Peru exports the most illegal drugs in the world, and the only thing that they export more than that is informal gold," Granda wrote in a November 12, 2014, message to his friends, using the euphemistic term "informal" to describe metal that wasn't quite legal.

Granda also told his friends about the time he went to Bolivia with Rodriguez to meet a potential customer in a bar. The man, a

German national, thought the dark-skinned Granda was a local—and bragged he could get him a kilo of cocaine for $700, a significant discount from the market price of at least $1,000.[3] Granda turned down the offer but later helped the client relocate from Bolivia to Cusco and bring $1 million with him.

There was only one slight hitch with the German.

"On Friday," Granda told his friends, "my customer from Cusco put out a hit on him for some bad business."

◇◇◇◇◇◇◇◇◇

Just as Rodriguez hated going to Bolivia, Granda loathed Perú's jungle boomtown of Puerto Maldonado.

The roads were dirt. There was only one nice hotel and not a single decent nightclub. He didn't think the girls were pretty either. But soon Granda found a solution to this problem—a way to find gold without traveling back and forth to Puerto. With Ferrari and other top Lima gold dealers now allegedly smuggling their metal to Bolivia and Ecuador instead of exporting it directly to the United States, there was little work for customs brokers in the capital. That meant Granda's fast friend, customs broker Andrés Tejeda, would be looking for an opportunity just when Granda needed him.

There was still a trickle of gold coming out of La Pampa and into Lima. But Perú's field of competition was changing quickly. Buyers from India and Dubai—who couldn't have cared less about breaking the mining, corruption, and money laundering laws that worried Granda—started to dominate the market.

Every week, Tejeda pulled the export rolls at the customs office. The paperwork revealed which Peruvian companies still had access to gold and were willing to export it from Lima, despite the government crackdown.

It fell to Granda to poach the suppliers from his Indian and Middle Eastern competitors.[4] Once they had the gold in hand, Granda and Tejeda would falsify mining documents to make it seem like the metal had come from legal mines. They set up dozens of front companies to ship the gold. Then they arranged for Elemetal to wire the payments not to those shell companies but to exporters already approved by its compliance office. That way no one in Dallas would ask questions about where the gold was coming from because Elemetal believed it had already done its due diligence. And no one thought to check the shipping labels on the packages of gold arriving in Miami. If they had, they might have questioned why Elemetal was buying gold from dozens of shell companies but only paying a single, preapproved account.

On the Peruvian side, Tejeda would doctor customs paperwork and greenpalm the right officials to ensure NTR's gold shipments made it safely out of Lima. The customs broker even set up his own front companies to sell gold, then kicked back cash from the commissions to Granda after the deals were done. To keep track of their off-the-books customers, Granda kept secret Excel spreadsheets filled with company names, invoices, payment records, and pictures of the gold bars they were shipping. Tejeda was good at finding customers but bad at closing deals. In one meeting with a client, the hard-partying customs broker fell asleep. The bemused gold collector snapped a photo of himself holding Tejeda's hand so that it looked like the sleeping man was picking his nose.

Granda and Tejeda had learned from one mistake made by Ferrari's alleged black market operation: His companies exported too much gold. That made them stand out. So Granda and Tejeda tried to avoid drawing attention: Instead of selling a lot of gold through a few large front companies, they sold a little gold through a lot of small companies. It was far easier for the companies to go undetected.

There were still a few whales out there. Granda's biggest customer, a firm from Cusco called Veta de Oro del Perú—Golden Vein of Perú—wound up selling him nearly one ton of gold a month. The company told Granda it was all clean. He never went to visit Veta de Oro's mines—that would just slow down the deals. And no one from the country's mining agency was checking to see whether the mines listed on its papers were producing gold or even existed. (Several years later, Peruvian officials would accuse Veta de Oro of buying suspicious gold. The company remains under investigation but has not been charged.)[5]

By the end of 2014, NTR's Peruvian office was back in business, buying $79 million worth of gold—most of it from Madre de Dios, the fabled land of outlaw miners.[6]

CHAPTER 19

Land of the Jaguar

FOR THE FIRST WAVE OF CONQUISTADORS WHO PARTICIPATED IN THE subjugation of the Aztecs and the Incas, the rewards had been almost unimaginable. Gold, silver, and precious stones had been there for the stealing, allowing them to amass fortunes that would last generations.

And yet rumors swirled that there was still fabulous wealth hidden somewhere in the jungles of the Amazon or tucked away in the mountains the Incas called the Antis, now known as the Andes. One of the roots of these stories has been traced back to the Muisca people of the Colombian highlands. In an elaborate ceremony, their leader, the *zipa*, would cover his body in gold dust—literally becoming *El Dorado*, or the Golden One—and then wash it off in Lake Guatavita as gold objects were tossed into the water as offerings.

But over the years that story metastasized into tales of an entire city, region, or civilization—just as grand, or even grander, than the Aztecs and Incas—steeped in gold. The culture was sometimes referred to as Meta, Omagua, or Paitití, but all versions shared similarities with the El Dorado myth: a land rich in precious metals, jewels, amber, and pearls waiting for the taking.[1]

One of the most persistent tales put that civilization—in this case called Paitití—in the vicinity of Perú's Madre de Dios region, where NTR Metals sourced its gold.

Madre de Dios lies about three hundred miles east of the Incan capital of Cusco, where the Andes give way to the Amazon. But even for that empire of conquerors, which had subdued hundreds of tribes, Madre de Dios was untamable.

The Incas saw their world divided into four sectors, known as the Tahuantinsuyo. Madre de Dios was in Antisuyo, the Land of the Jaguar. It was a region they raided looking for coca leaves, bird feathers, honey, and gold—and that was fiercely defended by jungle tribes.

The Incas made several attempts to conquer the Land of the Jaguar but all failed. In one instance, in the fifteenth century, Incan ruler Inca Yupanqui floated downriver with ten thousand warriors to subdue the region. Only a thousand men survived the trip; the rest were killed by riverbank tribes.

Even if the story—recounted by Garcilaso de la Vega in his *Comentarios Reales de los Incas*, published in 1609—was not entirely accurate, it captures the general sentiment of the Incas: that Madre de Dios, the Land of the Jaguar, was fierce and dangerous, capable of eating entire armies.[2]

When the Spanish arrived, the region's fearsome reputation only amplified rumors of a wealthy kingdom hidden in the eastern lowlands; if the tribes were so vicious, the thinking went, they must be safeguarding *something*.[3] While decades of Spanish expeditions failed to find the fabled Paititi, news of its existence rang louder than ever. In 1623, Spanish explorer Juan Recio de León provided a secondhand, but detailed, description of the kingdom, which he placed southeast of Cusco. Recounting tales told to him by local tribes, he described a massive lake with "many populated islands with an infinite number of people and the master of all of them is the Great Paititi."

He wrote, "The Indians of those islands are so rich that they carry on their necks many pieces of amber . . . seashells and clumps of pearls."[4] The description was likely a reference to the area around Lake Titicaca, which straddles current-day Perú and Bolivia and is considered one of the ancestral birthplaces of the Inca.

The first detailed expedition into the Madre de Dios region came in 1861 when Peruvian Colonel Faustino Maldonado and a group of adventurers rafted down the entirety of the Madre de Dios River until it flowed into the Madeira River in Brazil. In March 1861, their boat capsized, killing Maldonado and three of his colleagues. But he became the namesake of the province's capital: Puerto Maldonado.

By the end of the 1800s, the quest for gold and riches in Madre de Dios had shifted to something less mythical but equally lucrative: rubber. With the advent of the automobile industry and the industrial revolution, demand for latex from Amazonian rubber trees sparked an international rush into some of South America's most pristine jungles in search of the valuable sap. And that rush gave birth to one of the region's most controversial and colorful characters: Isaias Fermin Fitzcarrald.

During his short and brutal life (he died at thirty-five), Fitzcarrald would massacre hundreds of natives and enslave hundreds more in hopes of building a railroad over a seven-mile-long, fifteen-hundred-foot-high mountain pass that would connect two watersheds and would give rubber companies unfettered access to Madre de Dios.

His discovery of that mountain pass, now known as the Isthmus of Fitzcarrald, was called by Peruvian historians "the most important geographic discovery of the nineteenth century."[5]

But he's better known for his cruelty.[6] In 1895, he used hundreds of indentured servants to haul the steamship *Contamana* over the isthmus. The feat was immortalized by German filmmaker Werner Herzog in his 1982 film *Fitzcarraldo*, with Klaus Kinski playing the title role.

Less than two decades later, the rubber boom was over. By 1912, the English had planted rubber trees in their colonies in Malaysia, Sri Lanka, and Africa, ending South America's monopoly on rubber.[7] Puerto Maldonado and other towns along the rubber trail languished.

Until the gold rush.

CHAPTER 20

"Major Unwanted Heat"

IN ECUADOR, NTR WAS PLEASED WITH THE STEADY FLOW OF GOLD IT was acquiring from Jeffrey Himmel's import company, MVP. But Himmel's right-hand man, Paul Borja, wasn't.

Although Borja was making hundreds of thousands of dollars, he knew an untapped market existed that no US company would enter: Africa.

The continent has vast reserves of gold. But some of the mines, especially in war-torn Central Africa, are controlled by violent rebel groups and worked by children. African gold is radioactive. No clear-headed American compliance officer would run the risk of doing deals in Africa, although there are widespread reports of European and Middle Eastern companies sourcing billions of dollars' worth of gold there every year.[1] The US government hadn't paid much attention to South American gold, but the 2010 Dodd-Frank Act did require companies to disclose purchases of minerals and precious metals from conflict zones in and around the Democratic Republic of the Congo.[2]

In October 2014, Borja asked Himmel if he would be interested in meeting with a group of businessmen from the Central African Republic, which shares its southern border with Congo. The men had gold to sell—at a steep discount.

The meeting was set for the early fall of 2014 in Guayaquil. Their offer was alluring. They could sell at as much as a 12 percent discount. That was double to triple the discount Himmel was getting in Ecuador. But a price that low immediately raised red flags.

Criminals desperate for cash will often unload tainted goods at well below market price, knowing that whatever funds they receive are better than nothing. The proposed discount was a classic warning sign of money laundering.

Since 2012, the landlocked, resource-rich Central African Republic has been divided by a brutal civil war between government forces and feuding Muslim and Christian militias. Thousands have been killed, and many more displaced. A thriving illicit trade in commodities like gold, diamonds, coffee, and timber fuels the conflict, according to United Nations reports.[3] Just months before the businessmen approached Borja and Himmel, President Barack Obama had authorized US sanctions against governmental and rebel leaders.[4]

After the meeting in Ecuador, Himmel emailed NTR's Renato Rodriguez in Miami to tell him about Borja's idea of importing gold from Africa.

"Renato, isn't it a violation of US law to be doing business with this country?" Himmel asked.[5]

Rodriguez could read Himmel's mood. There was no way the Miami multimillionaire wanted to get mixed up with African "blood gold." And there was no point in NTR putting a prized cash cow at risk.

"Any metal out of Africa could be conflict metal with child labor and terrorist funding," Rodriguez replied. "I cannot say for certain that it is against US law, however, [it] would bring some major unwanted heat on anyone importing metal from Africa."

In other words, Rodriguez advised, steer clear. And Himmel's bank, Wells Fargo, agreed.

Himmel told the Central African Republic businessmen no, as politely as he could.

"We will have to pass on this opportunity," Himmel wrote in a follow-up email. "Our refinery in Miami and our bank are both concerned with doing business with countries viewed as having human rights violations. And according to Amnesty International, the Central African Republic is currently experiencing a human rights crisis of epic proportions."[6]

One of the gold dealers wrote back.

"Dear Jeffrey," the man replied via email. "I regret your refinery's decision. . . . I hoped that our transaction could help rebuild this beautiful country that has suffered for many years from the international lust of the great powers because of its mineral wealth."

Whatever the protestation, the deal with the Africans was not going to happen. Himmel wanted no part of something illegal. But he didn't know that Borja and Rodriguez—men he trusted—were already using him as a pawn to import vast amounts of suspicious gold.

Not from Africa—but, prosecutors would later allege, from Perú. Himmel was none the wiser.

After all, he trusted that all the paperwork Borja gave him about their Ecuadorian gold and its origins was accurate. That was a problem. A big one. No one was checking to see whether Borja was honest except Himmel himself—and Rodriguez. The episode with the businessmen from the Central African Republic illustrated Himmel's blind spot. When he was trying to check their bona fides, who did he call? Rodriguez.

There was no one else to tell him he was putting himself in grave danger.

CHAPTER 21

Things Fall Apart

AS 2014 DREW TO A CLOSE, NTR'S THREE AMIGOS WERE GETTING nervous again.

Juan Pablo Granda, in particular, was spooked after reading a news article about smuggled Peruvian gold ending up in Bolivia.[1] "Did you read it?" Granda asked Samer Barrage via WhatsApp on December 7.[2]

"There is even one that came out on Reuters," Barrage responded. "Looks like a hot topic all of a sudden."[3]

"Shit," Renato Rodriguez chimed in.

"It doesn't mention us though," Barrage said.

But it still gave Rodriguez pause.

"Should I postpone [the] Bolivia trip?"

Despite the scare, less than two weeks later Granda and Barrage were bragging to each other about their respective "mules," a metaphor commonly used in the drug trade. They even swapped pictures of the young men from Perú and Colombia carrying gold in backpacks. Barrage had taken over Colombia as his personal territory for Elemetal.

"Just another day in Colombia," Barrage texted, attaching additional photos of gold bars with and without black shrink-wrapping. "150kg."

The haul was worth as much as $6 million.

"Nice," Granda replied.

"The mules had to shit the packets," Barrage joked.

"Lol," Granda said. "Let me know when he moves 300 [kilos] in one day."

⬦⬦⬦⬦⬦⬦⬦⬦

In mid-January 2015, Rodriguez and Barrage traveled to Santiago to visit their new Chilean gold supplier.[4]

In a meeting at Harold Vilches's office in Las Condes, an upscale neighborhood with stunning views of the Andes Mountains, the three men celebrated the success of the smuggling operation. Although they hadn't discussed Vilches's scheme on the phone, the NTR dealers told the Chilean that they knew he'd begun to send smuggled gold to Miami, according to Vilches, because the amount he was exporting suddenly increased.[5]

Vilches had another idea to export even more gold. Over lunch at an elegant steak restaurant called Santabrasa, he told the NTR dealers that he had a contact who was offering him gold in Africa. Would NTR be willing to buy it?[6]

Despite what Rodriguez had told Himmel about the dangers of buying African gold, the NTR executives warmed up to the proposition, according to Vilches.[7] But they couldn't buy the gold if the customs documents said it had originated in Africa.[8] If Vilches moved the gold through Europe before exporting it to Miami, however, the indirect route would disguise its origins. Then he could sell it directly to NTR.[9]

Rodriguez and Barrage said they could even advise him on how to transport the gold, according to Vilches. NTR had offices in Europe, including in England and Spain, and the company was familiar with European customs laws.[10] (Rodriguez and Barrage have denied Vilches's account of this conversation and said they never discussed buying gold in Africa.)[11]

The next night, Vilches took Rodriguez and Barrage to Palomino, a strip club where he'd recently gone for his bachelor party. The Miami salesmen plied Vilches with drinks.[12]

While they were in Santiago, Rodriguez and Barrage also met with Gonzalo Farias of Grupo EFAD, who had been one of Vilches's first customers. Rodriguez had emailed Farias before the trip to ask for a meeting, and Farias, who was always looking to expand his network, was happy to oblige. But he had no idea the dealers were working with Vilches, with whom he'd had a falling out.

At a hotel in Las Condes, Rodriguez and Barrage gave Farias an aggressive sales pitch. They wanted to poach him from Republic

Metals; Farias had sold gold to the Miami-based refinery for years. Republic was offering a better price, however, and Farias didn't have enough gold to feed the demand of two US buyers. They left the door open to the possibility of working together at some point in the future. (The Rubin family, which owned Republic Metals at the time, said it has no knowledge of any dealings with Farias.)

Before the NTR dealers left the meeting, Farias asked who else they planned to meet with in Santiago. At some point, he told them, they'd likely cross paths with a young gold exporter named Harold Vilches.

"If you meet with Harold Vilches, you're going to end up with nothing but problems," Farias warned. "Be careful with Vilches because he's a criminal."

The NTR dealers lied, saying they had no plans to meet with Vilches. They assured Farias they didn't want any trouble.

◇◇◇◇◇◇◇◇◇

Unbeknownst to Rodriguez and Barrage, trouble was already brewing in Chile.

After customs officials had seized Vilches's gold near the Chile–Perú border the year before, they'd taken a look at national export data and noticed a huge spike in the amount of scrap gold leaving the country.

In fact, scrap-gold exports had nearly tripled in Chile between 2013 and 2014, shooting up from $37 million to $100 million.[13] There was no way Chile was suddenly producing that much scrap gold. The country didn't have enough pawnshops to explain the increase. Customs investigators realized with alarm that they didn't have sufficient controls in place to regulate gold exports.[14]

Officials at the Santiago airport started to pay closer attention to the gold bars leaving the country, sometimes taking photos of shipments. But no matter how suspicious a shipment seemed, they had few legal justifications to seize it. They also had little information with which to evaluate the accuracy of the export paperwork, including the laboratory certificates documenting the gold's composition.

In January 2015, the national customs office in Valparaíso imposed new regulations. Exporters were now required to obtain a certificate of analysis from an accredited laboratory and include more detailed information about the gold's origins in their sworn declarations.[15]

The following month, in an unrelated effort to tighten anti–money laundering laws, Chilean lawmakers added smuggling to the list of illegal activities that constituted a base crime for the offense.[16] That meant any effort to disguise the origin of money derived from gold smuggling was now legally considered money laundering.[17]

For police and prosecutors, that would come to mean a great deal. In a money laundering investigation, they could employ all sorts of techniques that were off-limits in a simple smuggling case, including phone taps.[18]

∞∞∞∞∞∞∞

The tightening restrictions in Chile weren't the only problem NTR's three amigos faced.

In early 2015, Vilches happened to be in Miami to meet with his accountants and stopped by the NTR office. Rodriguez and Barrage were in the midst of processing a shipment from Bolivia, but they took a quick break to take Vilches out to lunch.[19]

On the drive to the restaurant, Vilches overheard the NTR dealers discussing a problem with their insurance company. From what he understood, it sounded like the insurer was refusing to cover a gold seizure in Perú. The dealers had to talk to their bosses and they seemed worried. They were blaming their misfortune on that rogue Peruvian gold dealer Peter Ferrari, who had double-crossed them. Vilches knew of him by reputation but had never met him.[20]

∞∞∞∞∞∞∞

While Vilches and Chile were still supplying ample gold, at least for the time being, the monthly numbers from the three amigos' other territories were weak.

By early February 2015, it was obvious the NTR dealers were not getting their hands on enough gold, as a result of stricter enforcement in Perú. They needed to buy more smuggled metal in Bolivia and Ecuador—fast.

"MTD is an ugly picture," Barrage texted Granda on February 2, referring to NTR's month-to-month gold buys.[21]

"We need more Peruvian gold from Bolivia and Ecuador," he wrote on WhatsApp. "Can u make it happen?"

"Anything for [Rodriguez]," Granda replied.

But they had more urgent business.

A day earlier, Elemetal executives had summoned them to Dallas. The bosses wanted the three amigos to meet with attorneys from Jones Day, the white-shoe law firm. Elemetal had asked the firm to investigate the Peruvian government's seizure of NTR's gold shipment at the Lima airport in late 2013 and its subsequent theft and resale by Peter Ferrari. The company had filed a $10 million insurance claim on the lost gold. But the insurer was fighting it—suspecting the three amigos knowingly bought illegal gold from Ferrari—and had opened its own investigation. Now, to get reimbursed, Elemetal's corporate attorneys at Jones Day needed to prove NTR's three amigos had been duped into buying dirty gold and had not been involved in Ferrari's gold heist. And they needed to do it before the insurance company put the trio through recorded depositions. But they couldn't keep delaying.

When the three amigos arrived in Dallas, Barrage made sure to remind his subordinates of an important point: The insurance investigator wanted to look at their cell phones. They couldn't let that happen.

"Do not bring your cells to the depos," Barrage texted via WhatsApp.[22]

Four days later, the three amigos met with the insurance company investigator. Barrage had coached Granda and Rodriguez through their cover stories: They had no clue the seized gold was being shipped by Ferrari. They had nothing to do with his theft.

Under oath, the men insisted they had been suckered by his shell companies. The investigator kept pressing. Yes, they were aware of who Ferrari was, but they barely knew him. Certainly, they had never knowingly done business with him. They wouldn't budge, alternating between evasiveness and confrontation.

When the investigator asked to see their phones, the three amigos told him that they'd forgotten and left them behind.

"I didn't want to be interrupted [if the phone went off]," Rodriguez told the insurance man.

"I didn't bring mine," Granda said.

"Poor guy," Barrage texted the other two during a break in the deposition. "Have him frustrated."

The investigator had been stymied.

∞∞∞∞∞∞

Whereas all three amigos gave depositions, one key Elemetal employee refused: compliance chief Steve Crogan, who had done a sloppy job of vetting the Ferrari front companies submitted by Barrage and Rodriguez.

Rather than give a statement under oath to the insurance investigator, Crogan resigned from Elemetal in April 2015 and refused to cooperate with the inquiry. Days before he turned in his notice, Crogan was asked by an Elemetal auditor if he was aware of any "non-compliance or violation of laws and regulations in regards to [anti–money laundering] procedures and the Patriot Act," according to an April 3 email.

"I am not aware of any violations of procedure and relevant laws," Crogan wrote back two hours later.[23] (The audit would find no "material flaws" in Elemetal's compliance, revealing yet another failure of oversight at the company.) Of course, by this point Crogan should have realized how badly his compliance program had failed. He was likely worried that discussing it on the record might hurt his career. After Crogan left, he set himself up as a consultant in Massachusetts, advising businesses on complying with money laundering laws. Elemetal executives described his departure as "acrimonious." In the end, no one at the company would ever know what Crogan knew about NTR's dealings with Ferrari and when he knew it. He has never spoken to the news media or publicly about his role at Elemetal.

But in the months before he left Elemetal, Crogan did share some information with an old colleague from his days as a US Customs agent.

Digging through Peruvian customs records late in 2014, the three amigos had found what they thought was evidence of Ferrari trying to fence the gold he stole from NTR. Rodriguez had told Crogan that some of the gold was heading to an NTR competitor,

Miami-based World Precious Metals Refining. It was an insult added to injury. Not only had NTR paid Ferrari for the gold he later allegedly stole, but WPM was paying him too. Ferrari was getting paid *twice* for the same metal.

Crogan had written back asking for a few more details.

"My next call is to HSI," said Crogan, using the acronym for Homeland Security Investigations. "Can you give me a few quick [bullet points] on this fact pattern so I express it correctly before talking to the 'G'?"

∞∞∞∞∞∞

The "G-man" Crogan spoke with was a quick-tempered Cuban-born Miamian named Colberd Almeida.

Almeida, thirty-eight, was a career federal agent who went by "Cole." He had joined what was then known as the US Customs Service in May 2001 after a stint as a federal air marshal, and then investigated Chicago's drug trade before coming back home to Miami in 2004. The Midwest was too cold for his South Florida family.

In 2011, a supervisor ordered Almeida to start looking into gold imports. HSI's data analysts had noticed the huge volumes pouring into Miami. The bosses wanted to open a case. But Almeida knew nothing about precious metals. He needed help. One of the first people he turned to was Steve Crogan. As a retired Customs agent now working in the gold industry, Crogan became a valued source. He would occasionally contact Almeida with tips.

In an email on September 5, 2014, Crogan reached out to the agent with a new lead.[24]

Ferrari was selling gold allegedly stolen after the 2013 airport raid to a Peruvian company called Empresa Minera Gold Fish, controlled by his nephew, Crogan told Almeida. Gold Fish was turning around and selling the gold to World Precious Metals. Another Ferrari company called Premium Gold was doing the same thing.

"Peter Ferrari is well documented in the annals of [Customs] for drug money laundering between Peru and the United States," Crogan wrote, adding that Ferrari had been the target of a 2001 Customs investigation into Metalor.

They spoke on the phone.

"I'll look into it," Almeida promised, although he got dozens of such tips and had never heard of Peter Ferrari.

Crogan may have thought he was helping out a buddy in US law enforcement by feeding him information on a suspected criminal. Perhaps he also hoped Homeland Security could help recover Elemetal's missing gold, the seizure of which had reflected poorly on him as a compliance officer.

But Crogan didn't seem to realize that Ferrari presented a huge liability to himself and the company. The three amigos had lied to Crogan about their own dealings with the Peruvian gold dealer and still hadn't come clean.

In emails back and forth with Crogan, the three amigos joked with the compliance officer like a friend.

"I hope that you are doing better than Tom Brady," Granda wrote Crogan, teasing him about an upcoming National Football League match-up between the New England Patriots and Miami Dolphins.

That Sunday, in a season-opening upset, the Dolphins beat Crogan's Pats 33 to 20.[25]

CHAPTER 22

Mama Customs

WHEREAS JEFFREY HIMMEL REFUSED TO BUY GOLD FROM AFRICA BECAUSE he considered it suspect, Harold Vilches was willing to take the risk to expand his Chilean gold empire.

In mid-February 2015, Vilches and his father-in-law, Carlos Rivas, landed in Dar es Salaam, Tanzania, a port city on the Indian Ocean.[1] Groggy from four flights and nearly two days of travel, they walked off the plane into a wall of oppressive heat.[2]

Vilches's local contact, a Spanish gold broker, met them at the airport and they shared a taxi to the hotel. Looking out the car window, Vilches could see rows of unpainted shacks and barefoot children kicking up dust as they plodded along dirt roads. The taxi blew past motorcycles and men riding bikes.

"What a shithole," thought Vilches. Unlike some of its neighbors in South America, Chile was a stable country with a prosperous economy. Its capital, Santiago, was more akin to Madrid than La Paz, with a metro that put some public transit systems in the United States to shame. The poverty in Tanzania was a shock for the young man.

For weeks, Vilches had been on the fence about making the trip. Other people who had done business in the region cautioned that he might get scammed or even robbed. But the allure of an untapped gold market was too great. In the end, Vilches asked his lawyer to run a background check on the Spanish broker, crossed his fingers, and hoped for the best.[3]

The hotel the Spaniard had chosen was a spectacular five-star resort on the beach. Another of Vilches's employees, Javier Concha, who had gone to Miami to make a gold delivery, joined them the next day.

The Spaniard introduced the Chileans to a local gold broker who went by the name Tanga and claimed to be in the Tanzanian military. Tanga was portly and dripping in gold: he wore a gold watch on his wrist and a thick gold chain around his neck. He didn't speak Spanish, but he spoke to the Spaniard in French and the Spaniard translated for Vilches's crew.[4]

Tanga said he could easily sell the Chileans 1,000 kilos a month—a metric ton of gold. He didn't say where the precious metal was from, but Tanzania was full of gold mines. The country was Africa's fourth-largest gold producer and small-scale miners alone unearthed 20 metric tons a year.[5] Vilches knew the conditions in the mines could be terrible and that they sometimes employed children, but he tried not to think too much about that.[6] After all, the gold was being offered at a 30 percent discount.[7]

A few days into the trip, Tanga took Vilches to the office of a company that he said could take care of the export paperwork.[8]

As Vilches and his employees waited inside the office, a secure transport truck pulled up outside and guards jumped out carrying a half dozen safes. Each strongbox was packed full of gleaming gold bars and nuggets. It was the largest amount of gold Vilches had ever seen in one place.[9]

He asked if he could test a sample.

A woman wearing a customs uniform, whom the office employees called "Mama Customs," consulted with the staff in Swahili. Then she indicated that Vilches could touch the gold.

He picked up a piece and held it in his palm. Based on the color, it appeared to be high quality. Then he used his handheld spectrometer to analyze it. The metal was remarkably pure: 90 percent gold. When Vilches tested samples from the other safes, some of the readings came back as high as 96 percent. His eyes practically bulged.[10]

Vilches's doubts about traveling to Tanzania immediately evaporated. "Wow," he thought. "This is where the business is at."

He returned the gold to the safes. Then Mama Customs grabbed his hands and turned his palms so they were facing up. She ran her fingers over them to make sure he hadn't hidden any gold. Vilches had never seen anyone do this before. It seemed theatrical.

Vilches agreed to buy 50 kilos as a test shipment. The total for taxes, insurance, and secure transport came to $109,000.[11] He would pay for the gold itself once it arrived in Miami and he could get it analyzed in a lab. The Tanzanian company asked for some documents and said they would take care of the receipt and the rest of the paperwork. The company showed Vilches a certificate stating that the gold had been unearthed by licensed miners. It looked like everything was in order.[12]

As Vilches waited for the export paperwork, he kept in touch with Rodriguez and Barrage, updating them on his progress. They encouraged him to finalize the documents so the gold could be exported. They were all going to make a lot of money, the NTR dealers said, according to Vilches.[13] (Rodriguez and Barrage have said they never discussed buying gold in Africa with Vilches.)[14]

Then one day, Vilches and his crew were sitting in the hotel lobby with the Spaniard when Tanga arrived in a state of agitation. He spoke to the Spaniard in rapid-fire French as he nervously glanced over his shoulder. Tanga thought someone, probably a police officer, was following him, the Spaniard explained. "He said it must be because of you guys, because they know there's a buyer from America here," he said.[15]

It was unusual for a foreign gold buyer to show up in Tanzania with hundreds of thousands of dollars and Vilches, Tanga said, was attracting unwanted attention. Foreigners—at least those with US companies—tended to avoid buying gold in the region.

But Vilches didn't think he was to blame. He wasn't doing anything illegal in Tanzania; in fact, the gold appeared to have all the required paperwork. If someone was following Tanga, he thought, it must be because the Tanzanian was involved in something shady.

After a brief exchange with the Spaniard, Tanga abruptly walked out of the lobby and jumped into a taxi. "Let's follow him!" the Spaniard yelled, running out the door and diving into Tanga's taxi just before it took off.

Vilches and his crew hurried out of the hotel and jumped into another taxi. They told the driver to follow Tanga.[16]

The driver did his best to keep up as Tanga's taxi sped away. They managed to stay on his tail for a few blocks, but lost sight of him outside the tourist district.[17] Within a few minutes, Tanga was long gone.

As they were trying to figure out what to do next, the driver delivered some unsettling news. "Someone is following us," he said in English, glancing in the rearview mirror. Vilches turned to look out the back window and saw a black Toyota SUV with tinted windows following closely behind.[18]

His mind started to race. What if someone was trying to rob them? What if they were being kidnapped? Vilches began searching on his cell phone for the nearest Chilean embassy. Nothing came up in Dar es Salaam. "Shit!" he thought. Then he searched frantically for another nearby embassy, any embassy, where they could ask for help.

Suddenly, as they were approaching an intersection, two more black Toyota SUVs crossed in front of the taxi and slammed on their brakes. Five men carrying machine guns jumped out of the cars and pointed their weapons. A woman followed behind them and opened the taxi door, flashing what appeared to be a police badge. She demanded to see the Chileans' passports. Rivas, his hands shaking, handed over the travel documents.

The woman instructed the Chileans to follow the SUVs to the nearest police station. Then she and the armed men climbed back into their vehicles. A few minutes later, they arrived at a plot of land that looked more like a farm than a police station. There were chickens pecking the dirt in one corner and people eating lunch at wooden tables.

The men led Vilches and his employees to a table where an officer who appeared to be in charge demanded to know who they were and what they were doing in Tanzania. Vilches tried to respond in English, but the officer didn't seem to understand. Then Vilches tried speaking in what he remembered of high school French. That didn't work either. Exasperated, the official motioned to a man who, from what Vilches gathered, had spent some time in Ecuador.

"He speaks Spanish! He speaks Spanish!" the official said. But when Vilches spoke to the man in Spanish, he didn't seem to comprehend a word.

After an hour of utter confusion, all Vilches understood was a warning that Tanga might be dangerous. "How on earth did I get here?" he wondered.

Just as he was starting to lose hope, two men walked into the police station. Vilches recognized them as two gold dealers whose office he'd visited earlier on the trip as he was scoping out suppliers. The dealers spoke with the police and after a few minutes Vilches and his crew were allowed to leave.[19]

The new gold dealers took Vilches, Rivas, and Concha to another luxury hotel, this one even more expensive than the last.

That night, Vilches and his crew crowded into the same hotel room and slept in their clothes. They wedged a chair under the door handle and left their bags packed so they could leave at a moment's notice.

The Chileans were afraid to go outside, so over the next few days the new gold dealers brought diamonds to the hotel and showed the Chileans pictures of gold bars. The dealers were aggressive. "Take it, take it," they insisted. "You can pay me later." Vilches suspected that they had somehow arranged for the Chileans to be detained so they could rescue them in an effort to win their business. He wasn't even sure if the people who had detained them were actually police.

By this point, Tanga and the Spaniard had reappeared. Vilches, who had already invested more than $100,000 in Tanga's gold, decided not to take his chances on a new supplier. Tanga had offered no explanation for his earlier disappearance and although Vilches regarded him with growing suspicion, he'd sunk a lot of money into the deal. In addition to the $109,000 to cover taxes and insurance, Tanga always seemed to need money for something. Vilches was paying for his hotel room and giving him $200 a day for expenses, which the Chilean suspected went toward prostitutes. Every time Vilches saw Tanga he was accompanied by a different woman. The trip was turning into a disaster.[20]

Finally, near the end of February, Tanga announced that the gold was ready for export. He told Vilches it would be waiting for him at the airport customs office. Vilches planned to transport the shipment in his carry-on luggage.

When the Chileans arrived at the airport, however, neither Tanga nor the gold was there. Vilches frantically called the Tanzanian, who said he was waiting in another area. But after searching for a few minutes, it became apparent that Tanga was lying.[21]

"I'm going to stay here and resolve this," Vilches told his crew. "I'm not going to lose my money." But Concha and Rivas, still shaken from the encounter with the armed men, convinced Vilches that it was too dangerous. It was time to go home.

As they boarded the flight, Vilches's mind was racing. Had everyone been in on the scam? he wondered. Even Mama Customs? Had the gold even belonged to Tanga in the first place? Maybe Vilches had just been the latest in a string of foreigners the Tanzanian had duped using the same six safes full of gold. (Neither Tanga nor "Mama Customs" have been accused of any wrongdoing.)

Vilches felt sick to his stomach. He'd been in Tanzania for weeks. Between the money he'd paid to export the gold and the five-star hotel rooms, airfare, and other travel expenses, he'd lost $300,000.[22]

When they landed in Amsterdam for their connecting flight, Vilches ran to the bathroom and threw up.

CHAPTER 23

"Jeffrey, We Just Had a Problem"

THANKS TO THE FERTILE FIELDS THAT SURROUND IT, MACHALA IS KNOWN as "the banana capital of the world." In more recent years, Ecuador's fourth-largest city has also become a gold-trading hub. The port city sits on Ecuador's southwest coast just two hours from the mining towns of Portovelo, Zaruma, Piñas, and Atahualpa in the Vizcaya mountain range, a branch of the Andes, where gold has been mined for centuries.[1]

Today, roughly six thousand miners work hundreds of small mines, using simple and destructive methods. Their gold is sold in rough bars to dealers known as collectors, who travel back and forth between the Ecuadorian mining towns and Machala.[2]

When Jeffrey Himmel decided to import gold from Ecuador into the United States, it turned out the Ecuadorian traders weren't just obtaining the precious metal from Ecuador's mines. In the border towns of Ecuador, smugglers sold tons of illegally mined Peruvian gold to local collectors. Much of it ended up in Machala.[3]

As Himmel launched his gold-buying business in Ecuador, like all American precious-metals dealers, he was required under US law to set up an anti–money laundering compliance program. The Bank Secrecy Act mandates that dealers who trade more than $50,000 worth of precious metals, stones, or jewelry per year "know their customers."[4] In Ecuador, because of the influx of illegally mined gold from Perú, it wasn't so easy to know the actual source of the precious metal.

As part of his due diligence, Himmel met with his Miami bankers at Wells Fargo and consulted with Elemetal's compliance officer, Steve Crogan, and its CEO, Bill LeRoy, along with his Ecuadorian lawyers, bankers, and transport and logistics couriers.

Himmel told them all that he was determined to avoid dealing with illegitimate gold exporters. "The support of Wells Fargo is essential to the success we have enjoyed and hope yet to cultivate in the future," Himmel wrote his bankers in an email. "In summary, I want to be in this business for the long-term, and do not want to take any risks of non-compliance with [the Treasury Department], US Homeland Security Investigations, and any other relevant rules and regulations."[5]

Everything was moving forward with his plans in Ecuador, from buying gold to introducing technology that would increase metal yields and establish sound public health initiatives. They included an ambitious, environmentally friendly pipeline to help clean up waste in the mines. Ecuador's president Rafael Correa had even agreed to provide land for Himmel's pipeline and processing plant project. In a meeting with local miners in Zaruma-Portovelo, Himmel told them, "What we're going to do here in Ecuador is not for you, it's for your children and your children's children." It was an easy sell.

∞∞∞∞∞∞∞∞

In the early evening of March 5, 2015, the bedside phone at Jeffrey Himmel's Guayaquil home jolted him from a nap. On the other end of the line was the number two man at Tevcol, the courier company that routinely carried his gold from Ecuador's mountain mining towns to the regional airport in Machala, where it would be flown to Guayaquil and then to Miami in the late evening.

The Tevcol executive had a startling message to deliver, one that made little sense to Himmel.

"Jeffrey, we just had a problem. Your gold shipment was seized by the Ecuadorian authorities," the executive said. "We're looking into what happened."

"Where?" asked Himmel, tired and confused.

"At a border town near Perú."

"Why the hell are we doing business there?"

Himmel's mind was exploding. There was no logical reason for his gold to be anywhere near the border, two hours away from the Ecuadorian mountains where he thought his supply of gold was mined. His company, MVP Imports, had never done a gold transaction at the border with Perú, at least as far as he knew.

But instead of buying gold from the mountain mines of Ecuador, somebody had betrayed Himmel—by setting up a deal with smugglers from Perú. And the only people who logically could have been responsible for betraying Himmel were Paul Borja and NTR Metals. But it wouldn't end there. Someone or something in the Ecuadorian border town had tipped off the local cops, who pulled over the Tevcol truck carrying MVP's load of gold and seized it. Now Himmel was out $2 million for the eighty-three bars.

Because the gold was picked up near the Ecuador–Perú border, rather than the agreed-upon venue of Machala, Himmel feared his insurance wouldn't cover the lost metal. He was never going to see his money or gold again—and worse, he could be in serious trouble with the law because his shipment had been smuggled into Ecuador. His reputation, carefully crafted over several successful decades in business, might never recover.

Himmel called Renato Rodriguez to tell the NTR trader he'd been double-crossed. Now, he had no choice but to shut down his whole business. MVP Imports appeared to be involved in criminal fraud. If Himmel kept the company going—knowing what he now knew—he could end up in prison.

Not only was MVP dead, but so was Himmel's dream of a gold-mining ecotopia in Ecuador.

Rodriguez was sympathetic and promised to help Himmel recover his gold.

⬦⬦⬦⬦⬦⬦⬦

Although the three amigos had no qualms about breaking the law on the gold trail leading from Perú to South Florida, at home they tended to play by the rules.

One April day in 2015, Samer Barrage found himself doing something strange for an international gold smuggler: putting in a call to the FBI. A suspicious bar of gold had been brought to NTR Metals' office in Doral, Florida.

It all started when a trio of Miami robbers held up a TransValue armored truck loaded with gold in a made-for-Hollywood heist on March 1, 2015. The truck was hauling a total of 275 pounds of gold worth about $5 million, heading to a shipping destination south of Boston. But that evening, the TransValue couriers stopped unexpectedly along a dark stretch of Interstate 95 about fifty miles east of Raleigh, North Carolina, coughing and crying uncontrollably. Somehow, before the trip even began, the robbers had snuck into the truck, placed pepper spray in the cab, and remotely activated it so the two drivers would get sick and have to pull over. The robbers were able to tail the couriers because they had also placed a GPS device under the truck. Immediately after it pulled over, they pulled up in a white minivan and confronted the TransValue couriers at gunpoint.

"*Policía!*" they yelled. The two guards exited the tractor-trailer without their guns. The robbers gave instructions in Spanish, tied the guards' hands behind their backs, and led them into nearby woods. Then the thieves cut the padlock on the truck's trailer and offloaded five-gallon buckets that contained ten gold bars, along with forty silver coins. They put the loot in their van and fled.[6]

The next month, a Miami pawnbroker who had been a regular NTR customer appeared at the warehouse holding a twenty-six-pound gold bar worth a half million dollars. Guillermo Morales said he had obtained the slab of yellow metal in an international transaction and asked if NTR's refinery would be interested in buying it.

"I can't make that decision," an NTR employee told Morales. "Let me check with someone here who can."

He called for his boss, Barrage, who ran the warehouse facility in Doral when he wasn't in Colombia overseeing the company's gold deals in Latin America. Barrage knew Morales. And he knew NTR could make an easy profit of thousands of dollars by buying and selling the gold bar. But, instinctively, he also knew something wasn't right.

"It's kind of a big bar," Barrage told the pawnbroker, as he improvised a plan to dig deeper into the source of the beautifully refined precious metal.

He asked an NTR employee to weigh the gold using a scale equipped with a camera capable of capturing its distinctive markings. Barrage immediately recognized the familiar RMC logo and stamp of one of NTR's chief competitors, Republic Metals Corp., which operated a massive refinery just a few miles away. The seal was unmistakable, Barrage thought. He told Morales NTR could not purchase the gold bar without the correct paperwork, including a certification of the gold's origin.[7]

"Okay," Morales replied, exiting NTR's facility with the gold bar—but no deal.

Barrage quickly consulted with an off-duty Doral police officer working at the refinery. They both suspected the same thing: the bar that Morales was trying to sell was part of the gold shipment stolen the previous month from the courier truck.

"We should call the FBI," Barrage told the cop.

Within minutes, FBI agents hustled over to NTR's refinery.

Thanks to Barrage, the FBI agents had the lead they needed to break the case, and soon arrested the three armed robbers as well as players on the periphery of the gold caper, including Morales.[8]

"Both remarkable and vexing. . . . Mr. Barrage called the FBI and turned in the suspected stolen gold in 2015—while he was in the middle of his own conspiracy to launder money by purchasing gold," an attorney for Barrage would later remark.

In the end, nine of the stolen gold bars were never recovered. A Miami jeweler admitted to melting down most of the loot and selling it to other local jewelers. In the process, he made more than $1 million for the robbery ring and proved why gold is so coveted by criminals: once it is melted and transformed, it becomes impossible to trace.

CHAPTER 24

The Golden Chicken

MVP IMPORTS' GOLD SHIPMENT IN ECUADOR WASN'T THE ONLY BUSINESS deal NTR Metals was about to lose.

Before returning to Chile after his ill-fated Africa trip in 2015, Harold Vilches stopped in Miami. Over lunch at an Argentine restaurant, he told Renato Rodriguez about the mishaps in Tanzania. Rodriguez was sympathetic—after all, Vilches hadn't lost any of NTR's money—and encouraged the young Chilean to move forward, according to Vilches. He also warned Vilches about developments back home in Chile: customs officials had recently seized gold from another company and they appeared to be taking a close look at the country's gold exports.[1]

When Vilches returned to Santiago, he researched the seizure to figure out what the other company had done wrong. He also hired a high-powered lawyer named Marko Magdic, who was the former head of the Interior Ministry's Department of Organized Crime, to help him understand the ins and outs of export regulations. (Magdic has not been accused of any wrongdoing.) Armed with this information, Vilches compiled a folder with nineteen documents to substantiate his exports. He gave one copy to customs officials at the airport and another to his employees to bring to Miami. Vilches wasn't going to take any chances.[2]

But his string of bad luck continued.

On April 29, the eve of Vilches's twenty-second birthday, he took a suitcase containing five gold bars to the Santiago airport. Vilches was accompanied by his lawyer, his father-in-law, and another employee, Javier Concha, who was going to travel to Miami with $700,000 worth of gold.[3]

Vilches knew from obsessively checking customs rules online that the Chilean government was changing the requirements for analyzing gold exports. The government planned to mandate that certificates of analysis come from a lab with a specific accreditation. What Vilches hadn't realized was that the new rules had already gone into effect.

A customs official inspecting Vilches's shipment thought his claim that the gold had come from coins sounded dubious. The official scrutinized Vilches's paperwork and noticed that the laboratory where he'd sent the gold didn't have the required accreditation.[4]

The paperwork contained other inconsistencies as well. A receipt for one of the bars indicated that it was 84 percent pure gold, but the laboratory certificate said 90 percent.[5]

The official called a customs lawyer, who directed him to seize the gold.[6]

"I have to take this," the official told Vilches.

"Why are you going to take it?" Magdic asked, pressing the official to explain what was wrong with the export documents. "You just need to tell us what paperwork is missing and we'll come back tomorrow with whatever you need."[7]

The official wouldn't budge.

Vilches was livid. "Again?" he thought. "Right before my birthday?"

When it was clear that they weren't getting the gold back, Vilches called Rodriguez at NTR in Miami to share the bad news. The dealer told him to be more careful going forward, according to Vilches.[8] (Rodriguez denies this.)[9]

But what neither of them knew was that Vilches already had a target on his back. In fact, in that same airport, not far from where the gold was seized, an elite federal police brigade had been investigating Vilches for over a month.[10]

∞∞∞∞∞∞∞

There is a fable in Chile about an ambitious farmer who has a chicken that lays golden eggs. For a while, the man is content with the golden eggs, but one day he decides that the chicken must also be made of gold. As with the golden goose of Aesop's fables, the farmer kills the chicken only to discover that she's flesh and blood.

No more chicken. No more golden eggs.

It was a story Chilean prosecutor Emiliano Arias Madariaga would think about often over the next year as he investigated Harold Vilches. A less ambitious gold smuggler might have kept a low profile and it could have taken years for law enforcement to catch up with him. But this young guy seemed to be in a hurry. Overnight, he'd gone from a nobody to Chile's largest scrap-gold exporter, leaving a trail of lawsuits and customs complaints in his wake.[11]

In mid-March, the national customs agency had sent the prosecutor a summary of its findings about Chile's exponential increase in scrap-gold exports. The report included a list of companies whose exports appeared to have skyrocketed over the past two years. The strange thing was that the companies hadn't declared any imports that might explain how they'd been able to export far more scrap gold than Chile produced.[12]

The report intrigued Arias, an animated prosecutor with thick black hair who was constantly sipping strong yerba mate tea. As the head of the office that prosecuted cases originating at Santiago's international airport, he thought he had seen all types of trafficking and smuggling. But gold was something new.[13]

Arias ordered the anti-drug-trafficking brigade at the Santiago airport to launch an investigation. He didn't have evidence that the gold smuggling was tied to drug trafficking—although he hadn't yet ruled out that possibility—but it looked like the case might involve money laundering, and the brigade certainly had a lot of experience with that. They were part of the PDI—the federal investigative police force—Chile's equivalent of the FBI.[14]

The case landed on the desk of Juan Pablo Sandoval Valencia, a serious, straitlaced agent with a round face and a beard. Sandoval came from a small town in southern Chile known for producing honey and had studied marine biology in college. Before finishing his degree, however, he'd felt called to police work and had applied to join the PDI. He'd spent years on the front lines of Chile's drug war—the country's geography made it a natural transshipment point for cocaine produced in Bolivia and Perú—and developed a cynical view of the world.[15]

Sandoval didn't consider his years studying marine biology wasted time. On the contrary, the investigative methodology was similar. Spending hours in a car staking out drug dealers and hours on a boat watching whales weren't as different as they might seem. Both took a lot of patience and a lot of attention to detail.

The order to investigate came with a stack of customs reports on scrap-gold exports and companies that had violated customs regulations. The 2014 seizure of gold from Vilches's company in northern Chile was described in detail. It didn't take long for Sandoval to zero in on Vilches.[16]

One of Vilches's companies, Comercializadora e Inversiones Alfa y Omega, seemed particularly suspect. In 2013, the company hadn't exported any gold, but in 2014, it had exported 920 kilos, worth almost $37 million, making it Chile's top scrap-gold exporter. The second largest exporter was Aurum Metals, which also belonged to Vilches and had exported $12 million worth of gold in 2014. Between these two companies and a third one Vilches owned, the young Chilean had managed to export more than half of the scrap gold shipped out of the country that year.[17]

Chile's Financial Analysis Unit, which monitors bank transactions, had also flagged Vilches's companies. A report from the agency said that Aurum Metals appeared to be part of a complex network of people and companies bringing suspicious amounts of money into Chile. Aurum Metals had opened an account at Banco Santander in July 2014, for example, and between August and September the company had received $7 million, which it withdrew in hundred-dollar bills.[18]

That was one of the things that struck investigators as they started to unravel Vilches's web of companies and financial transactions: for a college student, the guy sure was moving a lot of money. And he was also moving a lot of gold, sending hundreds of kilos of the precious metal to the United States and the United Arab Emirates.[19]

"This kid is either the son of a millionaire, just won the lottery, or he's involved in something illegal," thought Arias, the prosecutor, as he read Sandoval's first report.

Investigators suspected that Vilches was working for someone else, perhaps a larger criminal organization or a family member. There was no way someone with his lack of experience could pull this off alone.[20]

The best way to figure out what Vilches was up to, they decided, was to intercept his phone calls.

CHAPTER 25

The Wire

IN THE SUMMER OF 2015, HAROLD VILCHES THREW HIMSELF INTO A NEW
project. He'd outgrown his office, where he could only fit small machines capable of melting up to one kilo of gold at a time. He needed
somewhere he could house larger pieces of equipment.[1]

Vilches found a warehouse in a gritty part of Santiago that he
could rent with an option to buy. It had a thousand square feet
of open floor space surrounded by twelve-foot walls bristling with
barbed wire.

Vilches studied as much as he could about security. The important thing, he learned, was to slow down an intruder long enough to
call the police.

He spent more than $100,000 fortifying the warehouse with ar-
mored doors, security cameras, and an Israeli motion sensor system
that triggered a pepper spray dispenser. He also imported machines
from the United States that could melt five kilos of gold at a time.
Inside the warehouse, Vilches built an office, a laboratory, and a
vault that only he could enter.[2]

But for all the security measures he took, it never occurred to
Vilches that Chilean authorities would record his phone conversations—a vulnerability investigators exploited by obtaining a judge's
permission to tap his phone.[3] When the young gold exporter made
or received a call, it was recorded on a federal police computer at
the Santiago airport. Police officers took turns sitting in front of
the computer and listening around the clock. The case agent, Juan

Pablo Sandoval, could also get the calls on his cell phone from wherever he happened to be.[4]

Every few weeks, Emiliano Arias, the prosecutor, would ask the police for a copy of the recordings and pass the CD off to his assistant, a lawyer named Nicolás Rodríguez Videla.

Rodríguez Videla spent weeks doing nothing but listening to Vilches's phone calls from seven in the morning to five in the afternoon, hunched over a desk in a cubicle with pea-green walls and dim fluorescent lighting.[5] Rodríguez Videla, a lanky young man with a shy smile and protrusive eyes, documented the calls in an Excel spreadsheet, color coding the entries based on whether they were relevant to the investigation.

Unlike most people his age, who preferred to send text messages or communicate via WhatsApp, Vilches talked on the phone a lot. He frequently called his mom, his dad, and his wife.

The calls between Vilches and his wife were the hardest ones for Rodríguez Videla to document. The couple would talk for fifteen minutes about their classes at the university—which professors they liked, which classes they hated—and about their families. Then Vilches would briefly mention a gold shipment before they went back to discussing the mundane details of their daily lives. Rodríguez Videla had to listen to the entire conversation to make sure he didn't miss those relevant tidbits.[6]

Because neither the prosecutors nor the federal police had previously investigated gold smuggling, they approached the case as if the target were a drug trafficking operation. They documented smuggling routes and schedules, identified Vilches's network of collaborators, and looked at the financial maneuvers the group used to move millions of dollars into Chile.[7]

The more investigators learned, in fact, the more it seemed like a drug trafficking operation, minus the drugs. From the phone calls, they discovered that Vilches periodically received large quantities of smuggled gold from Argentina, which he paid for in cash, before sending the merchandise to Miami. They also learned that Vilches was setting up a secure bunker with a laboratory.[8]

The phone calls quickly dispelled their suspicions that Vilches was working for someone else. It was clear that the college student was the one giving the orders.[9]

Soon, investigators expanded the phone taps and began intercepting calls from Vilches's wife, his father-in-law, and his employee Javier Concha. They also recorded Vilches's communications with the NTR dealers in Miami, with whom he seemed to have a friendly relationship.[10]

Meanwhile, Chilean customs lawyers pored over Vilches's export paperwork. They also sent samples of the gold they'd seized at the Santiago airport to a laboratory for testing. The results didn't match the information Vilches had included in his export paperwork.[11] Whereas Vilches claimed his shipments came from melting coins, which contain gold and copper, a laboratory analysis showed that Vilches's gold had high levels of silver, platinum, palladium, and lead.[12] Investigators suspected it had originally been mined in Perú.[13]

As the information poured in, prosecutors, federal police, and customs lawyers updated each other through a WhatsApp chat group.[14]

The team went into high gear when Sandoval, the case agent, picked up calls that the Argentine smugglers were crossing the border into Chile. He had two hours to drop whatever he was doing and drive to Vilches's bunker, where he would park and wait for the smugglers to arrive.[15] Sandoval snapped photos of them getting out of their gray Ford Fiesta, entering the compound with a black duffel bag, driving to a supermarket to buy booze, and covering stacks of dollar bills in plastic wrap in the parking lot of a fast-food restaurant before heading back to Argentina.[16] When the smugglers were in Chile, Sandoval and his colleagues worked around the clock. Sometimes they didn't go home for two days straight.[17]

It was also clear from Vilches's intercepted phone calls that his crew hadn't witnessed him melt thousands of coins, like his export paperwork claimed—they were faking a legal activity to hide the illicit origins of the gold from Argentina and the money they made from selling it.[18] And to investigators, that meant Vilches was laundering money when his businesses bought smuggled gold and exported it to NTR Metals in Miami.[19]

It was the crucial piece of evidence Chilean law enforcement needed.

But to prove this in court, they would have to show that Vilches wasn't actually buying as many gold coins as he claimed.[20]

Over two months in 2015, for example, receipts showed that Vilches's company Alfa y Omega had purchased 11,796 one-hundred-peso gold coins for a total of $7.8 million.[21]

When investigators asked Chile's central bank—which mints the country's currency—about gold coin production, however, the bank said it hadn't minted 100-peso gold coins since 1976. That year, it had minted just 3,000. Investigators also asked Santiago's official exchange how many gold coins brokers traded every month and learned that the number was around 120.[22]

As the evidence piled up, the police could have easily captured the Argentines when they crossed the border or nabbed them as they entered Vilches's bunker. But investigators wanted to take down the entire organization, and building a money laundering case took time.[23]

For more than a year, investigators allowed Vilches to smuggle gold into Chile and export it to NTR in Miami as they secretly watched and documented his every move.[24]

To give the money laundering investigation time to prosper, Arias assigned the customs complaint from the Santiago airport seizure to another prosecutor named Pablo Alonso Godoy. The complaint accused Vilches of making false customs declarations, which was a far less serious crime than money laundering.[25]

Arias didn't combine the cases because the customs case couldn't be legally kept secret. Keeping the cases separate reduced the chances that Vilches would learn he was also being investigated for money laundering.

When Vilches came to Alonso's office in downtown Santiago to give a statement in the customs case, he pestered the prosecutor about wrapping up the investigation.

"How long are you going to hold on to my gold?" Vilches demanded. "I have clients in the United States who are waiting for it."[26]

⬦⬦⬦⬦⬦⬦⬦

NTR's three amigos were running out of options in their quest for more gold.

They had already scurried from Perú to Ecuador, then to Bolivia and Chile, staying one step ahead of investigators. But they still had South America's fourth-biggest gold-producing nation: Colombia.

Though Colombia didn't have as much gold as Perú or Brazil, it still had plenty of precious metal buried deep in remote jungles. But some of the players in Colombia's illegal gold trade—guerrilla groups battling the Colombian government and major drug trafficking organizations—made Perú's illegal gold traders look like the minor league.[27] As in Perú, illegal gold mining had become a bigger source of profits for the country's fearsome criminal groups than cocaine.[28]

Elemetal had opened a subsidiary in Colombia in 2013, NTR Metals Zona Franca, and Samer Barrage was part owner. The Miami businessman had family in Colombia and traveled there frequently, often spending weeks at a time.[29]

According to business records, one of NTR Metals Zona Franca's suppliers in Colombia was a company called Enmanuel Gold SAS.[30] The company, whose legal representatives were later arrested in 2017, was allegedly part of a criminal organization run by a woman known in the underworld as "the queen of gold," according to prosecutors.[31] The queen's group was accused of buying illegal gold, passing it off as a legal product purchased from artisanal miners, and sending a staggering three tons of the metal to companies in Cali, Colombia, and Miami. The illicit mining operations that allegedly provided precious metal to Enmanuel Gold produced so much silt and debris they stopped a river in its tracks, authorities say.[32]

By the end of 2015, as its other South American gold sources dwindled, the majority of NTR's imports would come from Colombia.[33] That year, the company imported $722 million in gold from the country, accounting for more than half of all Colombian gold exports to the United States.

PART III

CHAPTER 26

"A Conflict Diamond Is a Conflict Diamond"

AS NTR'S THREE AMIGOS CONTINUED TO HUSTLE FOR GOLD IN PERÚ, Bolivia, and Colombia—where the illegal precious-metals business was a snake's nest of drug traffickers, international smugglers, and money launderers—a Miami-based federal investigation into dirty gold was in danger of stalling out.

A year had passed since Elemetal compliance officer Steve Crogan tipped off Homeland Security Investigations special agent Cole Almeida about Peter Ferrari in September 2014. In order to move forward, Almeida needed to convince a prosecutor to take on his case. Agents investigate. But prosecutors make cases in court. If an agent can't get a prosecutor to buy in, the investigation withers on the vine. Almeida needed a prosecutor who believed the US government should take down dirty gold.

He had first taken his investigation to the narcotics unit of the US Attorney's Office in late 2011. The prosecutor assigned to the case left the anti-drug squad soon after. The next prosecutor didn't seem to know what to make of the evidence.

To Almeida, the heart of the case seemed clear: The bounty of gold being shipped to Miami came in large part from countries dominated by the drug trade. In that part of the world, Almeida believed, it was safe to assume that large spurts of new investment had only one source: cocaine sales to Americans. Equally suspicious: The South American nations were shipping a seemingly impossible amount of gold to the United States. Almeida could see the discrepancy simply by comparing customs records to foreign mining statistics. Every year, Perú, Bolivia, Ecuador, and Colombia exported far more gold than their mining agencies reported was being dug out of the ground. Where was all that excess metal coming from? The difference between what was formally mined and what was exported to the United States could only be explained by illegal gold—gold that would never have been reported to the mining agencies in the first place.

But the prosecutors Almeida talked to scratched their heads. What was the crime? they asked. How could they prove the money to buy the gold was coming from drugs? The tainted cash was being converted to precious metal far away in South America, not in the United States. And it's not like the gold coming into the United States was being secretly smuggled in hidden cargo holds. The import companies like NTR were declaring their metal loads at US Customs.

Almeida was left slapping his forehead. "A conflict diamond is a conflict diamond. I don't care if you declare it at the border as being okay. It's still a conflict diamond," he would tell the prosecutors, noting by way of comparison the US ban on buying African-mined diamonds that fuel warfare. "It's the same with gold."

After years of gathering evidence with little result, it was clear to Almeida that the narcotics prosecutors weren't taking him seriously. So he went to the narcotics section chief, veteran prosecutor Lynn Kirkpatrick, and told her he wanted to take the case to a rival unit within the Miami US Attorney's Office, the economic crimes section, which investigated financial malfeasance and fraud.

Kirkpatrick urged him to reconsider. She thought the case had potential. And she saw a solution to Almeida's problem: a young prosecutor named Frank Maderal who had just joined her team.

"I've got a new guy," Kirkpatrick said. "He's brilliant. He wants to do money cases. Talk to him."

∞∞∞∞∞∞

In an ideal world, a junior federal prosecutor like Francisco "Frank" Maderal wouldn't have been at the top of Almeida's list to handle the gold case.

Maderal, thirty-three, was green. He'd been an assistant US attorney for less than three years—and he had already angered more than a few supervisors and colleagues with his independent streak and distaste for bureaucracy. He'd been transferred into narcotics, on the US Attorney's Office's seventh floor, a few months back. It was far from his dream job. The narcotics unit seemed to be coasting on a fading reputation. In the 1980s and 1990s, the office had won national acclaim for prosecuting Colombia's infamous Medellín and Cali cartels, not to mention Manuel Noriega, the Panamanian strongman and narco ally who was captured in a US invasion in 1989. After bringing charges against members of the Medellín cartel, Miami's then US attorney, Leon B. Kellner, was placed under heavy guard when intelligence officials discovered that the cartel planned to have him killed.[1]

"A special weapons and tactics team from the Miami Police Department took up positions around the courthouse," the *New York Times* reported.[2]

In the 1990s, however, drug-smuggling routes began shifting away from the heavily policed corridor between Colombia, the Caribbean, and South Florida. Mexico was the new pipeline, and so the biggest cases were now on the United States' southwestern border. By the end of the decade, 80 percent of the US cocaine supply entered through Mexico.[3] After the September 11, 2001, terrorist attacks, the FBI pulled back from its intense focus on drug investigations. The bureau eliminated its drug squads in Miami, crippling the narcotics unit's investigative power.

The US Attorney's economic crimes section, three floors down from narcotics, was where Maderal really wanted to work. That's where the big cases were these days. In economic crimes, prosecutors followed the illicit money trail, which took them everywhere in an international hub like Miami. They targeted Ponzi schemers, healthcare fraudsters, and tax cheats and went after banks and financial institutions that accepted their dirty money. Occasionally, they could force sweeping systemic changes in the way the US financial system worked. The economic crimes prosecutors often compared the narcotics folks to the aging 1972 Dolphins: always talking about their undefeated season. But what had they done lately? Nowadays, narcotics cases were mainly takedowns of "pill mills," cash-only storefronts where unscrupulous doctors sold pain-killers to addicts. Prosecutors in economic crimes liked to think they could change people's lives and have an impact on society. That's what Maderal—tall, confident, and sporting black hair a touch longer than most prosecutors would wear—wanted to do.

But precisely because the narcotics section wasn't doing big, complex cases with multiple defendants, the seventh floor held more potential for a maverick like Maderal. "You can do more on seven than you can on four," legendary narcotics prosecutor Dick Gregorie told Maderal, referring to the units—as all the prosecutors did—by their floor number. "Try to do the most complicated thing you can."

CHAPTER 27

Operation Arch Stanton

ON SEPTEMBER 11, 2015, COLE ALMEIDA DROVE FROM HOMELAND SECURITY'S building in western Miami-Dade County, practically a stone's throw from the Everglades, to meet Frank Maderal at the US Attorney's Office on the northern fringes of downtown Miami.[1]

The stone-and-glass James Lawrence King Federal Justice Building sits blocks away from the waterfront and the American Airlines Arena where LeBron James, Dwyane Wade, and Chris Bosh won NBA championships for the Miami Heat. But it feels a world apart from the prestigious addresses where corporate lawyers file fat hourly bills. Just a few blocks west of the federal building lie the Florida East Coast Railway train tracks and Interstate 95, the highway that urban planners in the 1960s decided to stick like a knife through the heart of Overtown, Miami's historic African American community.[2]

When Almeida arrived at the prosecutor's office, Maderal greeted him wearing a bow tie. Red with blue polka dots. The HSI agent couldn't help staring. Maderal looked like a schoolboy, not an assistant US attorney.

"This guy is the genius?" Almeida thought to himself.

But he was out of options.

If the gold case was going to get done, Maderal and Almeida were its best hope. Maybe the last one. In a conference room, Almeida laid out his case with the benefit of a few PowerPoint slides. He suspected US precious-metals companies were lying about their sources of gold in Latin America. There were dozens of gold dealers

157

in Miami, several of which became targets during the investigation. But there was only one big refinery: Republic Metals. And Republic's records showed what seemed to be irregular transactions totaling hundreds of millions of dollars. The company declared it was buying gold from one country but was then sending the payments to a third party in a different country. That raised all kinds of red flags. Why wouldn't you pay the person you bought the gold from directly? And how many other companies were doing the same thing? There could be billions of dollars of dirty deals out there.

Maderal, who at the time was investigating a drug-tainted money laundering case in Perú, learned from a confidential informant that gold had become the most effective way for hiding narcotics proceeds because it was so difficult to trace. For South American cocaine syndicates, he was told, the gold trade opened up lucrative opportunities to boost profits exponentially from their drug sales in the United States. Could there be a connection to Miami's explosively growing gold imports?

The prosecutor thought precious-metals dealers were regulated in the same way as banks, but he wasn't sure. Because gold, diamonds, and other gems are so susceptible to abuse by money launderers, the federal government considers precious-metals dealers to be "financial institutions." That means the United States' anti–money laundering compliance and disclosure rules apply to them, as well as to other industries where dirty cash could be laundered. Casinos, for instance, have to follow the rules laid out in the Bank Secrecy Act. So do stockbrokers, car dealers, and pawnshops. Even travel agencies are covered. Like banks, none of those businesses can allow themselves to be used by narco-traffickers and other criminals. They are required by law to "know their customers." Maderal said he'd look into how the law applied to the gold trade. It could be an angle to pursue. Right now, maybe they had a case worth looking at. But it was far too early to tell whether they had a crime they could prove in court.

A few days later, Maderal called Almeida back.

He had dug into the tiny type of the Code of Federal Regulations, the 180,000-page bible for prosecutors. Under Title 31, Subtitle IV, Chapter 53, Subchapter II, Section 5312 of the 1970 Bank Secrecy Act, gold dealers were subject to the same regulations as banks.[3]

"I think we're on to something here," Maderal told Almeida.

"No shit," Almeida said.

∞∞∞∞∞∞∞∞

Prosecutors and agents delight in choosing code names for their investigations.

They sometimes drip with machismo.

The FBI's probe into the Trump campaign's potential ties to Russia was codenamed "Operation Crossfire Hurricane." The infamous Bureau of Alcohol, Tobacco, Firearms and Explosives investigation that allowed suspected gun smugglers to purchase weapons and sell them to Mexican drug trafficking outfits was "Operation Fast and Furious." An attempt to crack down on banks working with payday lenders, escort services, and other shady businesses was "Operation Choke Point." Maderal was far more subtle in his approach to naming the gold case. Maybe too subtle.

When the prosecutor suggested "Operation Arch Stanton," Almeida drew a blank. Maderal chuckled. The name came from a 1966 Clint Eastwood spaghetti western called *The Good, the Bad and the Ugly*.[4] The plot centers on a stolen cache of Confederate gold, which is supposedly buried in an old grave. The name on the tombstone? Arch Stanton.

(Spoiler alert: The gold was actually hidden in a neighboring plot marked "unknown" next to Stanton's.)

Maderal had watched the movie as a child and seen it a dozen times since. It was a popular flick then and now, but even cinephiles would struggle to make the connection. The reference was beyond obscure.

"What a nerd," thought Almeida, who suggested "Operation Barred Gold" instead.

Although agents normally got the privilege of naming cases, not prosecutors, Maderal stuck to his guns. His case, his rules. Operation Arch Stanton it was.

At least if the name leaked out, Almeida said, only die-hard Clint Eastwood fans would have any idea that Operation Arch Stanton was about gold.

"Man, you're a grumpy cat, Cole," the prosecutor replied.

CHAPTER 28

The Prosecutor

COLE ALMEIDA HAD EVIDENCE: STACKS AND STACKS OF RECORDS GATH-ered from US Customs and Border Protection and Miami import-export brokers in the gold trade.

He kept the files in binders. It was good information, but Almeida's organizational methods didn't strike the younger, digitally savvy prosecutor, Frank Maderal, as very sophisticated, even for the shoe-leather digging on which federal agents prided themselves.

"Do they have this stuff electronically?" he asked.

The prosecutor wanted to know more. Which US companies were buying the most gold? Where were they getting it from? If looking at this one aspect of the gold trade produced hundreds of millions of dollars in shady deals, surely there must be other areas for investigators to plumb. Maybe there were billions of dollars' worth of suspect trades. They just had to look in the right place.

Maderal didn't know what he was getting himself into.

He had never done a case as complex and far-reaching as gold, which spanned two continents and involved secretive refineries, elusive shell companies, and unsavory businessmen operating deep in far-off jungles. By the time the NTR case wrapped up, it would involve not only several prosecutors from the US Attorney's Office but more than twenty-five agents and analysts from three federal law enforcement agencies—with offices both domestic and foreign—and the assistance of sovereign governments in at least three South American nations.

It would even prevent Maderal from fulfilling a promise he had made to his wife, Andrea, a dermatologist, that he would return to private practice the following year, in 2016.

Like almost all federal prosecutors, Maderal had gotten his start in the major-crimes unit, where newbies are sent to bone up on simpler cases. Maderal's early cases had garnered a few press releases from the Department of Justice. But at the end of the day, they were routine stuff, nothing groundbreaking. Tax-refund thefts, cyber-crimes, and the shooting of a police officer outside Miami.[1] Nothing that even earned a mention of his name in the *Miami Herald*.[2]

Maderal wasn't just inexperienced; he was rebellious, from the way he handled cases to the quirky outfits he wore. Most days, he came into the office wearing khaki slacks and boat shoes without socks. Suits were for court. Worse, he didn't always do what his bosses wanted. In fact, in the very first trial he had been given—with marching orders to finish off a case brought by another prosecutor against a young hospital worker accused of stealing patients' Social Security numbers—Maderal asked a judge to dismiss the indictment because he felt the evidence collected by the previous prosecutor wasn't strong enough to merit the charges. Getting the indictment thrown out damaged his standing in the office. Team players didn't do that. He had questioned the judgment of a colleague. Who did the new guy think he was?

But Maderal, the son of a successful Cuban immigrant gastro-enterologist and a bubbly Louisiana mother who worked as a registered nurse, was ambitious and smart. He had wanted to be a prosecutor ever since he did a summer internship with a federal judge in South Florida while he was studying at Georgetown University Law Center. It didn't happen right away. After graduating in 2007, the first job offer he got was working as a corporate lawyer in downtown Miami. Dull, tedious stuff. The money was good, but the work made him a task rabbit for clients who knew exactly what they wanted and how they wanted it done. There was no freedom.

Within a year, he got out, snagging a coveted clerkship with the same judge back in South Florida district court. One day, he ran into Miami's US attorney, Wifredo Ferrer, and asked him out for coffee. In hindsight, a lowly clerk ambushing the top prosecutor in one of the nation's biggest districts was a mortifying overreach. But Ferrer, who had served as deputy chief of staff and counsel to US Attorney General Janet Reno during the administration of President Bill Clinton, graciously agreed. The overture got Maderal on his radar, although there were no openings at the time; the federal budget had been slashed in the recession, leading to a hiring freeze. In 2011, Maderal moved on to a fancy law firm in the affluent suburb of Coral Gables. Finally, the next year, a spot at the US Attorney's Office opened up and he was offered a position.

In his first years as an assistant United States attorney, Maderal discovered something about himself. It was an odd trait for someone who chose a career in law enforcement: after a successful prosecution, Maderal could barely stand to watch when defendants were led away from the courtroom to prison. Even when he put away a man for downloading child pornography—a crime that enabled the abuse of minors—Maderal had to avert his eyes when the US Marshals handcuffed him. The defendant's mother was sitting a few rows back in the Key West federal courthouse. She had sobbed her way through the entire trial. Now, she was practically wailing.

In 2015, Maderal got out of major crimes and into the narcotics unit. This was his chance. From the time he joined the US Attorney's Office, the other prosecutors pegged him as a "short-timer," someone who wanted to say he'd done his time in public service before jumping back into the higher-paying world of private practice.

He was going to prove them wrong.

CHAPTER 29

"Dude, This Is Insanity"

AFTER TALKING THE GOLD CASE THROUGH WITH COLE ALMEIDA, FRANK Maderal saw the only way forward: US Customs numbers.

He asked the Department of Homeland Security to send raw electronic data on gold trades to his office on the seventh floor. The spreadsheets made the trades so much clearer. Instead of having to sift through stacks of paper—where each gold transaction took up several pages of dreary customs forms—the spreadsheets represented each transaction as a single line of data.

Each line told him which companies were exporting gold from Latin America to the United States. Not just that: the numbers also revealed when the companies sold it, how big the shipments were, how much they were getting paid, and who was buying all that metal. He trawled through the vast spreadsheets, each with hundreds of thousands of line entries, looking for trends.[1]

One nation stood out: Perú, which at the time produced 11 percent of the raw gold being imported into the United States.[2] As much as a spreadsheet can shock a federal prosecutor, the customs data for Perú bowled him over. The vast majority of Peruvian companies exporting gold to the United States, the data revealed, had no history in the gold business. Most had never even existed before now. Gold wasn't a business you got into one day and out of the next. It took time to develop suppliers and expertise. But the Peruvian gold was coming from companies that appeared out of thin air. After shipping the gold—sometimes tens of millions of dollars' worth—the companies would vanish. Poof. Then another exporter would pop up in the old one's place. When Maderal broke down his spreadsheet into three-month quarters, he saw the companies weren't even sticking around for an entire year. They'd be gone and replaced after a single quarter. It all added up to billions of dollars of gold being shipped by what were essentially ghost companies. Here today, gone tomorrow. All heading into Miami, the closest US port to South America. All heading into Maderal's jurisdiction.

Operation Arch Stanton was gaining momentum.

Together, the small team of federal investigators was figuring out who the biggest Peruvian exporters were. But who was buying their gold? The hub of the case had to be the big US refineries that imported South American gold. They were the ones who could be prosecuted. And only a handful of them were scattered across the country, in Massachusetts (Metalor), Ohio (Elemetal), Utah (Asahi), and Florida (Republic). The potential suspects were in plain sight.

But one jumped out: Elemetal.

The company's huge gold business, routed through its South Florida subsidiary NTR Metals, seemed to come out of nowhere.[3] The raw numbers alone looked suspicious. In 2011, NTR bought virtually no gold from Perú. Then, in 2012, the company imported $73 million. The next year: $980 million worth. How had that happened? A billion dollars' worth of gold out of practically nothing? Even more puzzling, after 2013, NTR's imports from Perú fell off a cliff.[4] Instead, in 2014, it started importing huge amounts of gold from neighboring countries where it had never before done much business: Ecuador and Bolivia. In 2015, the pattern switched again. Now, the gold was coming from Colombia and Chile.

Making simple line graphs of NTR's imports by year and country opened Maderal's eyes to how obvious the pattern was. When Perú died, Ecuador and Bolivia picked up the slack.

After those markets failed, NTR turned to Colombia and Chile.

"Dude, this is insanity," the prosecutor told Almeida.

It seemed improbable a business could grow like that. Not unless NTR was breaking the law somehow. How else could the Miami importer source so much gold so quickly from countries like Ecuador and Bolivia with scant histories of exporting large amounts of precious metals? The company couldn't be buying that much gold and at the same time ensuring its suppliers weren't criminals. In

Maderal's mind, a case was beginning to take shape: it was a crime under the Bank Secrecy Act to buy gold without running thorough due diligence on suppliers, as he and Almeida had discussed at their first meeting. Not the most serious crime. But somewhere to start.

And maybe, just maybe, NTR was doing more than turning a blind eye, Maderal thought. Maybe NTR's traders were engaging in something far worse: dealing with foreign criminals who hid behind shell companies to move dirty gold from the Peruvian jungle to Miami. That was money laundering. The traders, who worked on commission, had an incentive to break the law. So did NTR's parent company, Elemetal. The more gold its traders bought in Latin America, the more gold Elemetal could sell to Fortune 500 companies. It was a volume business, run on incredibly tight margins.

Compared to money laundering, a Bank Secrecy Act violation for not having a bona fide compliance program was a parking ticket. It carried a maximum prison sentence of five years but was usually resolved with a fine. Money laundering could get you twenty years. Money laundering was the better case—if Maderal and Almeida could prove it.

As they researched the companies NTR was buying gold from, one name kept popping up: Pedro David Pérez Miranda, aka Peter Ferrari. Simple Google searches showed Ferrari was not someone an American gold company should be doing business with. The Peruvian press had been reporting for years on his alleged connections to drug traffickers and illegal mining. Searching through Spanish-language news stories also led the federal investigators to what seemed like a major breakthrough: Just before NTR seemed to abandon Perú's precious-metals market at the end of 2013, local authorities had seized a shipment of Ferrari's gold at the Lima airport. NTR's imports from Perú fell by 91 percent in the year after the airport seizure. It seemed more than a coincidence.

Even more suspicious, the export companies in Ecuador and Bolivia that started selling gold to NTR had never before traded precious metals. That left a nagging question the customs data couldn't answer: Where was all the gold really being mined? It sure looked to Maderal and Almeida like the answer was Perú—that its ample supply of gold was simply being smuggled into neighboring countries. They suspected NTR's traders were hopscotching from country to country, buying up Peruvian gold but doctoring paperwork to make it look like it was mined in a legitimate place. Whenever local authorities cracked down, NTR's traders likely moved their operations to another spot on the South American map.

Maderal knew he had to be careful, however. The data had become his bible, his gospel for building a case. That didn't mean it was infallible. It had been compiled, after all, by US Customs officials sitting in cubicles in Maryland. The bureaucrats could have made a mistake that Maderal and Almeida wouldn't see until it was too late. Maybe Customs had accidentally coded some lead imports as gold trades and sent flawed spreadsheets. Maybe the fluctuations in gold volumes Maderal was seeing had to do with some kind of new regulations in Latin America that he didn't know about. Maybe the changes were simply the result of market forces as the ounce price of gold moved up and down. Or maybe the exporters had simply found new buyers in Switzerland or China and were no longer selling their gold to importers in the United States. A defense attorney could use the things Maderal didn't know to pick apart his case and exonerate NTR.

On his own time, Maderal studied data analysis and visualization. It wasn't normal practice for a prosecutor. But Maderal, a former physics major who ended up pursuing a classical studies degree at the University of Florida, had a knack for numbers. He kept thinking about Dr. John Snow, the nineteenth-century English physician who discovered that cholera was a water-borne disease, not a miasmic plague spread in the air. By mapping the homes of people who fell ill in an 1854 cholera outbreak, Snow saw a cluster of sickness around the Broad Street well pump in London's Soho district. His work created the field of epidemiology. Snow's decision to map was crucial. Had he compiled a bar chart of deaths per day, say, rather than a map, he might have missed the source of the cholera. Data doesn't teach you anything by itself; you have to know how to look at it.

At night, Maderal dreamed of what he wasn't seeing in his data, sometimes waking up in a cold sweat. All his wife knew was that he was working a big case. Sworn to secrecy under a federal grand jury, he couldn't tell her anything more.

∞∞∞∞∞∞

While Maderal tossed and turned, the bosses at Elemetal were delighted with their star salesmen, the three amigos. Juan Granda, in particular, was singled out for perks for rebuilding the Perú business after the seizure of NTR's gold at the Lima airport.

On November 8, 2015, the company invited Granda to its skybox at AT&T Stadium in Texas to watch the Dallas Cowboys take on their biggest rivals, the Philadelphia Eagles. (Granda was a Cowboys fan because growing up his single mother couldn't afford to take him to see the Miami Dolphins, and the games were blacked out on local television.)

It was all-you-could-eat food and unlimited drinks with what felt like fifty people packed into Elemetal's thirty-person on-field box. Elemetal's cofounder, Steve Loftus, and his wife were there.

The Eagles beat the Cowboys in a thrilling 33–27 overtime win.

CHAPTER 30

Turf War

DESPITE HIS HESITATIONS, FRANK MADERAL WAS MAKING PROGRESS.

The prosecutor had a target: NTR Metals and its parent company, Elemetal. He had a Bank Secrecy Act case, at a minimum, with the potential of adding on far more serious money laundering charges. But now he had a problem. And it was something beyond his control.

On January 12, 2016, through the grapevine of the US Attorney's Office, Maderal caught wind that the FBI was working a gold case, too. The FBI investigation also involved NTR Metals. But it was coming from a different angle. It had something to do with buying gold from Chile.

When Maderal called up the FBI team working the case, the agents gave him unsettling news. A colleague in his office named Michael Sherwin was already building an investigation into illicit gold trading between Chile and South Florida.

"You need to talk to AUSA Sherwin about it," an FBI agent told Maderal. "You need to talk to him."

"Oh no," Maderal thought.

Another federal prosecutor—especially a senior one like Sherwin—could derail the biggest case of his budding career.

∞∞∞∞∞∞

Assistant United States Attorney Michael Rafi Sherwin, forty-seven, was an intensely focused Midwesterner who graduated from the University of Notre Dame Law School in 1998.[1] The son of a

Vietnam War fighter pilot, Sherwin studied Arabic while taking law courses and developed a keen interest in the Middle East. Rather than practicing law after graduation, he joined the US Navy as an intelligence officer. Just a few years later, he would be stationed in Turkey when Al-Qaeda terrorists attacked the World Trade Center towers and the Pentagon on September 11, 2001. Thanks to his expertise on the Arab world, Sherwin found himself advising some of the most powerful men in the George W. Bush administration, including General Tommy Franks, who was in charge of the US Central Command and oversaw the wars in Afghanistan and Iraq.

Because of his military intelligence background, Sherwin worked big cases after joining the US Attorney's Office in Miami in 2007. He was recruited by a senior prosecutor to assist in a major case involving the so-called Cuban Five, a ring of Miami-based Cuban spies whom the Obama administration later quietly exchanged for an American intelligence officer imprisoned by the Castro regime, as well as the American aid worker Alan P. Gross.[2] Sherwin was even enlisted by the Department of Defense for a one-year stint to assist in the Afghan government's prosecution of hundreds of accused terrorists being held in Bagram, the US detention center that came to be seen as equivalent to Guantanamo Bay.[3] Now Sherwin worked in the economic crimes section, where Maderal himself hoped to end up.

Maderal may have been a rising star—but next to Sherwin, he was a featherweight.

∞∞∞∞∞∞∞

Federal prosecutors work for the same boss: the people of the United States. But that doesn't mean they're always playing on the same team. Collaboration between prosecutors is not a fixture in the Department of Justice. When two prosecutors find themselves investigating separate but related cases, there's not only a collision of egos; in many instances, the competition triggers a race to an indictment. The first prosecutor to bring charges gets the upper hand, even though such speed may make it impossible to bring a comprehensive case.

Now, there were two rival gold investigations in the very same US Attorney's Office in Miami—and they were about to collide.

As the senior prosecutor, Sherwin could try to take the whole case for himself. Maderal was determined not to let that happen. It was his only major case. He'd spent months working on it, provoking mockery from some of his colleagues who wondered what he was up to. They were constantly in court; he spent his days sequestered in his office poring over spreadsheets. If Maderal ended with nothing to show for it, his career as a prosecutor might never recover. Maybe he would be a "short-timer" after all.

First things first, Maderal had to figure something out: How much did Sherwin know about NTR Metals? Was Sherwin building a grand takedown of the gold industry in Miami—like the case taking shape in Maderal's mind—or did he just want to arrest a couple of smugglers, charge them, and move on? On January 14, 2016, he sent Sherwin an email.

"Hey Mike, when you have some time today, I'd love to get the scope on what that [FBI] group is seeing goldwise . . . and if you're interested I can tell you what we're seeing," he said.[4]

A few days later, Maderal rode the elevator three floors down to Sherwin's office in the economic crimes section. Sherwin was in the middle of resolving a major affordable-housing fraud case. "I don't have a lot of time for this right now, Frank," Sherwin said.

More than a month passed, and Maderal still wasn't getting the information he wanted.

Maderal's frustration began to boil into fury. He couldn't tell what exactly Sherwin was investigating or whether the other prosecutor was broadening his probe to encroach into what Maderal felt was his territory: the whole damn gold-smuggling trade between South America and Miami. He thought Sherwin was holding back on his gold case, refusing to show his cards. To get answers, Maderal would have to raise the stakes.

CHAPTER 31

La Vuelta Larga

BY EARLY 2016, HAROLD VILCHES, THE PRECOCIOUS CHILEAN GOLD DEALER, was spending so much time in Miami that he decided to rent an apartment.[1] The hotel stays had started to add up.

Vilches found a flat in Brickell, the city's gleaming financial district, in a high-rise that boasted two infinity pools and a hot tub set in a tropical garden. But he had little time to enjoy it. His life might have seemed glamorous from the outside, but running a gold-smuggling operation was hard work.

Vilches would travel to Miami for a week at a time to meet with his accountants, the NTR dealers, and potential clients. He often had so many meetings lined up that he didn't have time for lunch. He'd return to the apartment in the evening exhausted and buy a 7-Eleven hot dog before collapsing into bed. At one point, Vilches was traveling so often he'd seen all of the movies offered on LAN's Santiago–Miami flight.[2]

Getting money back to Chile had also become a headache.

At first, NTR had paid Vilches's Chilean companies for gold shipments. Then, after banks in Chile closed Vilches's accounts, NTR switched to paying his American company through his US bank account. But Vilches couldn't wire the money back to Chile because his accounts there had been closed.[3]

So Vilches enlisted the help of a stockbroker named Luis Patricio Mella Pino.[4]

Mella ran a brokerage firm in downtown Santiago and offered money exchange services. In January 2016, he traveled to South

Florida and opened a US company for the sole purpose of receiving money from Vilches's gold exports.[5]

To get Vilches's money back to Chile, Mella developed an elaborate scheme, which he called "*la vuelta larga*"—the long trip. It entailed converting Vilches's payments from NTR to Chilean pesos and then back to dollars in Chile using a series of companies. Vilches needed dollars to pay the Argentine smugglers.[6]

But Vilches didn't seem to understand that Mella's scheme took time. In a call recorded by Chilean investigators, he pressured the broker to move the money more quickly.

"Those jerks from customs confiscated 60 kilos from me," Vilches complained, explaining his urgency to get paid.[7]

Vilches also laundered his money through Chilean real estate. He bought a property near the coast using part of a $732,000 payment from NTR, visited it once, and then immediately put it up for sale.[8] Vilches claimed it was a wedding gift for his wife that he'd sold when money got tight after the Santiago airport seizure, but prosecutors were convinced it was a money laundering scheme.[9]

∞∞∞∞∞∞

While Vilches was hustling gold deals with NTR in Miami, Chilean prosecutor Emiliano Arias was making his own inroads through his American contacts.

As the head prosecutor for cases originating at Santiago's international airport, Arias often worked with the FBI and the DEA. The more he learned about the illegal gold market, the more he became convinced that it made sense to work with US investigators in this case as well. After all, he thought, the demand for Vilches's dirty gold was driven by US consumers, whose voracious appetite for the precious metal came at the expense of South American rain forests.[10]

Arias contacted the FBI through an agent stationed in Chile with whom he had worked on previous cases. He shared the outlines of the investigation with the agent and with the FBI's assistant legal attaché at the US Embassy, a woman named Lourdes McLoughlin.[11]

Working with the FBI had its advantages. US agents shared information about Vilches's American operations as well as the identities of the NTR dealers Vilches was talking to on the phone.[12]

But the collaboration also slowed down the Chilean investigation. By that point, customs officials and police had gathered reams of documents, transcribed hours of phone calls, and photographed the Argentine smugglers on their trips to Santiago. Chilean law enforcement wanted to arrest Vilches and the smugglers while they were in the middle of a gold sale, but the FBI needed more time for its investigation.[13]

The problem was that under US law, the gold Vilches imported into Miami didn't appear to be illegal. It had all of the proper documentation from Chilean customs authorities. The FBI needed time to prove NTR knew it was importing illegal gold. And Chilean authorities feared that if they arrested Vilches before the FBI was ready to move in Miami, the NTR dealers would find out and flee the United States.[14]

Arias thought it was important to strike only after the investigation had progressed far enough in the United States.[15] If the feds didn't take down NTR's operation in South Florida, the company would just find another Harold Vilches.

CHAPTER 32

The Go-By's

ASSISTANT US ATTORNEY FRANK MADERAL HAD FEW "GO-BY'S"—PREVIOUS blueprints of successful prosecutions—to model his gold case on.

Federal prosecutors often pulled old indictments of similar cases to learn how their colleagues had taken down criminal operations. Sometimes in building a new indictment they simply swapped out the names and changed important details.

While US prosecutors had intermittently targeted the gold industry over previous decades, they tended to focus on the domestic scrap trade, not on imports from abroad. For instance, Chicago prosecutors had shown how members of Mexican drug lord Joaquin "El Chapo" Guzmán's feared Sinaloa cartel used $100 million earned from selling cocaine in the American Midwest to buy scrap gold from pawnshops, jewelers, and antique stores. The drug dealers then resold the gold to a corrupt couple in South Florida, the proprietors of a "we buy gold" store called Golden Opportunities, who wired millions in payments back to a Sinaloa front company in Mexico. (Golden Opportunities resold much of the scrap gold to Republic Metals, which was not implicated in wrongdoing.)

It was a simple, effective money laundering operation. There was almost a beauty to El Chapo's criminal alchemy: cocaine turned into dirty cash, then into gold, then finally into clean cash. At that point, the cartel could reinvest the money into the production and smuggling of drugs or use it to buy real estate and luxury goods or simply put it in the bank. The Golden Opportunities case showed how international organized crime groups manipulate America's hush-hush gold industry to launder money and keep their businesses running.[1] Even minor industry players like Jed and Natalie Ladin—the hard-working, well-liked couple who owned Golden Opportunities—can wind up playing supporting roles in vast criminal operations.

But the El Chapo case didn't involve illegal mining or require any work overseas. It didn't give Maderal the road map he needed. Maderal did have another dirty gold investigation in mind, however. Except it wasn't a model to emulate but a disaster to avoid.

In 2012, prosecutors in the Southern District of New York—the famed Manhattan office that attracts the best, most ambitious public-service-minded lawyers in the nation—tried to bring a civil case that would expose the nexus between Latin America's gold trade, foreign drug traffickers, and US precious-metals refineries. The case opened auspiciously enough, with prosecutors moving to seize $31 million held in US bank accounts connected to a Peruvian family, the Sánchez Paredes clan, suspected of trafficking cocaine. The civil complaint said the clan was selling gold to refineries to launder drug money and was moving the cash through bank accounts held by the Italian refinery Italpreziosi and Miami-based Republic Metals, the major competitor to Elemetal.[2]

Going after Republic was a mistake. The company's high-powered lawyers were soon able to demonstrate that Republic had tipped off the DEA in Miami about the Sánchez Paredes organization. Within a month, the New York prosecutors dismissed the civil complaint against Republic, saying in a press release that the American refinery was "an innocent owner, and a bona fide purchaser."[3] The next year, in 2013, the remaining case against Italpreziosi was dismissed when US prosecutors said the Peruvian government refused to hand over critical evidence.[4] (Italpreziosi has denied any wrongdoing, saying it bought the gold in good faith after proper vetting.)[5]

Maderal would have to find his own way to bring down NTR. There was nothing to model his case on.

No federal prosecutor had ever done what he wanted to do—and won.

◇◇◇◇◇◇◇◇◇

With the circumstantial evidence against NTR Metals building, Maderal had to make a tactical decision: When to tell parent company Elemetal that it was the target of a criminal probe.

No one at the US Attorney's Office thought it was a good idea to let Elemetal know it was on his radar. Tipped off, the company might start covering its tracks. But Maderal ignored those warnings. It seemed like a win-win. Either Elemetal would try to destroy evidence—and expose itself to obstruction charges—or it would comply with his grand jury subpoena, delivering documents that could potentially show top executives were aware of the smuggling.

On April 16, 2016, Maderal sent a "target" letter to Elemetal's headquarters in Dallas, along with the grand jury subpoena demanding thousands of pages of emails, as well as customs, corporate, and financial records.[6]

It was a shock-and-awe approach.

A few days later, when a partner from the major law firm Jones Day called Maderal, the prosecutor breathed a sigh of relief. The law firm was a monster, the largest in the United States and one of the most prestigious in the world, with forty-three offices in eighteen countries. It employed twenty-five hundred attorneys, many of them graduates of Ivy League schools. Some were former federal prosecutors.[7]

Maderal knew Jones Day wouldn't try to destroy records. He was going to get Elemetal's files if the company hoped to survive. And the prosecutor would soon find out how much those files had to say about NTR's three amigos, Juan Pablo Granda, Samer Barrage, and Renato Rodriguez—and their gold dealings with Peter Ferrari.

∞∞∞∞∞∞∞

Maderal still had a Michael Sherwin problem.

All he knew was that the rival prosecutor's case centered on Chile. But in April 2016 an attorney at Jones Day reached out to Maderal to let him know that Elemetal's compliance officer had been contacted by an FBI agent about Peter Ferrari and Perú. The problem was this: the agent wasn't working with Maderal.

Maderal wanted to own the gold investigation. If any federal agent was working an angle on gold, he wanted to know. In the vast bureaucracy of the federal government, it was the only way to maintain control of his case. "We want everyone to be in our tent pissing out, not outside the tent pissing in," he told Cole Almeida. "If someone from the Postal Inspector Service calls us and says they have a gold case, we welcome them into our team. We don't want anyone else out there doing a gold case without us."

Could this new FBI agent, Maderal worried, possibly be working for Sherwin? Was Sherwin making a move to steal his gold case? For months, the other prosecutor had been treating him like a mushroom, Maderal thought. Keeping him in the dark and feeding him shit. Increasingly anxious, the younger prosecutor fired off an email on April 21, 2016, to FBI special agent Eric McGuire. Maderal also copied his own unit chiefs, Lynn Kirkpatrick and Richard Getchell, in what looked like a power play.

The prosecutor urged the FBI agent to stop communicating directly with Elemetal because the company had hired legal representation. He couldn't have random agents contacting his target out of the blue. Then Maderal zeroed in. "Is there an AUSA who you have spoken with about the Peter Ferrari/Peru NTR Metals issue?" he asked.

McGuire didn't respond well.

"Thanks for copying Lynn and Dick instead of just calling me to discuss this first," he curtly wrote to Maderal, after taking the prosecutor's bosses off the chain.[8]

Later that day, McGuire provided a more comprehensive response, copying in Sherwin on the follow-up email. McGuire said he was not involved in the FBI's probe of NTR, which was being run by Sherwin and an FBI special agent named Refina Willis. McGuire's interest stemmed simply from a confidential informant who had contacted him with intel on NTR and Ferrari.

Now Maderal needed to play nice. He tried to bring everyone together. "I think it would be a good idea for us all to sit down and compare notes," Maderal wrote back. "We're taking a big picture, top-down approach. . . . We're already working with [prosecutors in] Ecuador and Peru, and I'm going to try with Bolivia, but I'd very much like to get the details of your case. . . . We already have an OCDETF [Organized Crime Drug Enforcement Task Force] open, and several agencies including FBI . . . but we have room for more."

Maderal was dangling his cooperation and information in exchange for Sherwin's assistance. The OCDETF, a Justice Department initiative that provided money and other resources to major drug investigations, was another incentive. The FBI agent leading Sherwin's probe, Refina Willis, responded that maybe they could get together on Wednesday.

"Meeting Wednesday would be great," Maderal wrote back. "We'd like to show you what we're seeing in terms of NTR's big-picture activity and hear some more about what you're seeing out of Chile. I assume it's gold, probably purchased with narcotics proceeds, probably smuggled out of Peru, and then exported out of Chile through a front company . . . to the US."

Maderal wanted the FBI on his team. Not only did the bureau have the Chile end of his case, but it was also the behemoth of federal law enforcement. No other agency had the manpower, technical resources, money, and sheer ability to "flood the zone" on a major case. And Willis, who like Sherwin had served in military intelligence, would be a valuable addition. It was her first big case. She was hungry. And she was a team player. Although Willis was willing to engage with Maderal, Sherwin was still giving his colleague the silent treatment. The next day, Maderal launched an email salvo directly at his colleague.

"I'm sure you're swamped, but what's the plan here?" Maderal wrote Sherwin at 1:24 p.m. on April 26, 2016, leaving his bosses and the other agents off the message. "I've been keeping you up to date on our refinery investigation for months . . . and I've been hoping to coordinate and assist each other's investigation, but I've been getting the cold shoulder."

Sherwin was sitting in a plea negotiation when Maderal's message came through on his smartphone. Reading through it, Sherwin grew so agitated he could barely register what the defense attorney sitting across the table from him was saying. Eight minutes after receiving the message, Sherwin fired an email back to Maderal.

"There is no cold shoulder—I do not operate like that—it achieves nothing," he responded. "I am only here to indict cases that have proper evidence and claw back as much stolen money as I can for the victims—I could care less about section parochialism and statistics—never have and never will."

Maderal barked back.

"Frankly, you have been operating like that: For months I have been attempting to ensure we have the targets divvied up so there is no overlap and wasted effort and so we can share evidence," he wrote forty minutes later. "You've wanted none of it. . . . I've updated you on our case from the beginning and not one word from you. . . . All I am asking is to avoid competing toward the same target and share evidence."

Finally, Maderal delivered an ultimatum to the senior prosecutor.

"If you can't agree to that because you're hoping that you'll be able to swoop in and make something of your own against NTR, then at least just come out and say that, and we'll take it from there."

It was like the glory days in narcotics. Back then, case discussions often grew so heated that federal prosecutors nearly came to blows, at least according to the old-timers. Maderal was a man possessed. This was his only case. Sherwin knew how much the case meant to Maderal, but he wouldn't allow a junior prosecutor to talk to him this way. He had served overseas and the military sense of chain of command still mattered to him.

Right then and there, Sherwin decided he was going to take up this dispute with his former supervisor in the narcotics section, Dick Getchell, who was now Maderal's boss.

It took Getchell to make peace. When Sherwin told Getchell about Maderal's hotheaded email, the narcotics unit deputy chief immediately apologized. Prosecutors didn't act like that anymore. Especially when one clearly held rank. "Mike, I know you," Getchell told Sherwin. "I know you wouldn't steal a case from someone else. I know you're busy as shit. We want you to help Frank with the case. He said he looks up to you."

Maderal could certainly use Sherwin's expertise. He had never done a corporate case, unlike Sherwin, who was working on an investigation that would soon bring down a prominent South Florida affordable-housing developer on fraud charges.[9] But first, Getchell said, the junior prosecutor had to apologize. "Look, Frank," the supervisor said. "Mike is pretty tough. He lived in tents in Afghanistan. You don't want to settle this with a fist fight."

When they had cooled off, Sherwin went three flights up to Maderal's office. For Sherwin, the gold case was just one of several large cases on his plate and he was already working fourteen-hour days. He liked the gold case but had come to realize what a career-maker it could be for his colleague.

"I don't need any extra cases," he told Maderal.

The senior prosecutor began to look around his colleague's office. It resembled a conspiracy theorist's closet. Charts and maps and photos were taped on the walls. And yet there was something compelling about the crush of information. He had seen his fair share of these makeshift war rooms during his service in Afghanistan and Iraq. "I'm impressed, Frank," Sherwin said. Maderal was clearly deep into the gold case. They started comparing notes. Maderal said he was working a "know-your-customer" angle against NTR Metals. Sherwin didn't think much of that approach. The criminal exposure for NTR on a Bank Secrecy Act case was weak, he said. The executives could just fob it off on an incompetent compliance officer, something out of their control, he warned. Surely there was something stronger. The investigation needed targets: individuals who could be held responsible for felony crimes.

The gold case now belonged to Maderal. Sherwin arranged to have all his evidence sent upstairs to narcotics. The case agent, Refina Willis of the FBI, said she'd be happy to work with the new prosecutor. Sherwin briefed Maderal on the work he'd done so far.

It all started with Harold Vilches.

◇◇◇◇◇◇◇◇

Two months earlier, on February 1, 2016, Sherwin and Willis had flown to Santiago to meet Emiliano Arias, the Chilean prosecutor investigating Vilches.

During a three-hour meeting, the Chileans walked Sherwin and Willis through Vilches's smuggling routes. They took the Americans to Santiago's airport to show them customs records and play wiretap recordings. Looking at photographs of the smuggler, Sherwin couldn't get over how young Vilches was, just twenty-two years old. "This guy's a punk-ass kid," the prosecutor thought. Finally, the Chileans took them on a rare visit to Chile's Casa de Monedas, or House of Coins, which mints money. Also inside the mint's vaults: millions of dollars' worth of gold that had been seized from

Vilches. Sherwin and Willis were the first non-Chileans allowed into the vault.

When Sherwin got back to Miami, he empaneled a grand jury to begin subpoenaing Vilches's financial records. The Chileans formally requested US assistance with their investigation in an April 18, 2016, letter, two days after Maderal sent his subpoena to NTR's parent company, Elemetal.

Vilches was exporting more scrap gold than Chile produced, Arias wrote to Sherwin.

This output was impressive—so impressive it defied belief.

Sherwin may have been leaving the case, but he was giving Maderal a gift—a viable target—and a compelling way to strengthen his investigation against NTR.

Young Harold Vilches was about to become a star witness.

CHAPTER 33

"I'm Finished"

HAROLD VILCHES'S WHIRLWIND GOLD-SMUGGLING CAREER FINALLY started to catch up with him in February 2016. That month, Chilean prosecutors charged him with smuggling in the case of the gold bars customs officials had seized at the Santiago airport the previous year.[1]

Vilches had also begun to suspect his phones were tapped. When he made calls, he could hear static in the background that was sometimes so loud he could barely understand the other person on the line.[2] By March, Vilches had stopped discussing his smuggling activities on the phone. He even refused gold offered by the stockbroker Luis Patricio Mella, who had helped him move his NTR payments to Chile.

"What would you pay me for a little kilo of gold from Argentina?" Mella asked in a call recorded by Chilean investigators in early March.

"Nothing, Pato, I'm not buying that," Vilches responded, using the broker's nickname.[3]

Vilches assumed the phone taps were related to the Santiago airport case; he didn't know about the money laundering investigation. He tried to keep a low profile and continue his operations under the radar.[4]

On May 1, Vilches sent another gold shipment to the United States.[5]

Vilches's father-in-law, Carlos Rivas, carried the gold in his suitcase like normal. But as he was passing through US Customs at the Miami airport, officials ushered him into a small room. A group of people he assumed were customs agents took a sample of the gold and analyzed it. Then they handed him a copy of the report. Rivas didn't think much about the interaction, which he assumed was a routine customs inspection. But Vilches, back home in Santiago, thought it sounded unusual. He asked Rivas to send him a photo of the report.[6]

Vilches opened the WhatsApp message on his phone and scanned the document for the name of the agency that had taken the sample. It was the FBI.[7]

"Fuck," Vilches thought. "I'm finished."

◇◇◇◇◇◇◇◇

In April, Chilean federal police agent Juan Pablo Sandoval and his boss Juan Figueroa traveled to Miami to meet with the FBI team assigned to the case.[8]

They also visited Miami International Airport so they could get a better understanding of how Vilches's gold entered the country. The investigators knew from working on drug trafficking cases that US officials carefully screened luggage for cocaine and marijuana. But gold shipments, they were surprised to learn, passed through airport controls without much scrutiny. Officials looked at customs declarations and weighed the gold bars. That was about it.[9]

Back in Chile, a corruption scandal was rocking the country. The attorney general had moved prosecutor Emiliano Arias from his post to a special team investigating political corruption. Arias had asked to take three prized cases with him: two human trafficking probes and the Vilches investigation.[10]

The gold case fascinated him. It stretched from Perú and Argentina to the United States and the United Arab Emirates. It was also a crime Chilean prosecutors hadn't seen before. Vilches appeared to have found a niche that no other criminal group in the country had discovered. The amount of gold he had moved in a short period of time was mind-boggling. And, Arias had to admit, the case was entertaining. The key player was a twenty-two-year-old college student who sent his father-in-law on grueling eight-hour trips to Miami with suitcases full of gold. One of his associates held business meetings in *cafés con piernas*, the Chilean equivalent of Hooters. You couldn't make this stuff up.[11]

◇◇◇◇◇◇◇◇

At the end of May, Vilches got more bad news: he was being charged with fraud in a case involving Fujairah Gold, the Emirati importer that had accused him of swindling millions.[12]

In the indictment, prosecutors alleged that Vilches had fooled Fujairah into believing he could provide the company with large quantities of legal gold. Then, they argued, once he'd struck a deal, Vilches started taking out loans he had no intention of paying back using Fujairah's standby letter of credit as a guarantee. That led Vilches's lender, Banco Santander, to collect $5.2 million from the company. And that wasn't all. Prosecutors said Vilches had promised to transfer $500,000 to Fujairah to start paying the company back but had purposely changed two digits in the company's bank account number to ensure the transfer wouldn't go through. Vilches then told the company he'd successfully transferred the money, investigators said.[13] (Vilches claims the wrong digits were an innocent mistake.)[14]

The Fujairah case made the news in Chile, prompting Elemetal to order NTR to suspend all operations in the country.[15]

Chilean investigators decided they couldn't continue waiting for the FBI. Now that Vilches had been charged with fraud, it was only a matter of time before the Argentine smugglers stopped bringing him gold. Authorities had to act quickly.[16]

They hatched an elaborate plan. A police officer stationed at the border would quietly notify customs agents that the Argentines had entered the country. Then the customs agents would pull over the Argentines and several other cars to make it look like a routine inspection. They would search the cars and confirm that the Argentines were carrying gold without letting the smugglers know they'd spotted it. Then, when the Argentines delivered the gold in Santiago, the federal police would pounce.[17]

On the appointed day, customs officials and federal police had everyone in place. But at the last minute they got a call that the mountain pass between Chile and Argentina was closing. It was wintertime in South America and there was too much snow. They would have to wait.

Then Arias, the prosecutor, was transferred again, this time to head an office in a city an hour and a half south of Santiago. He had to pass the Vilches case off to his replacement, an affable prosecutor named Tufit Bufadel Godoy.[18]

Unlike everyone else who had worked on the case, Bufadel had some experience with metals exports.[19] He'd previously prosecuted a case involving stolen copper cables exported to China as scrap metal. He'd even gone to China for several weeks during the investigation.

By the time the Vilches case landed on Bufadel's desk, however, it appeared to have stalled. Vilches and his crew had stopped bringing gold into the country, and they'd stopped talking about anything of interest on the phone.[20] Vilches had been put on nighttime house arrest a week after he was charged in the Fujairah case and was prohibited from leaving the country.[21] Every night, he was awoken by the local police ringing the doorbell and had to get out of bed and sign a piece of paper to confirm he was home.[22]

It quickly became clear to Bufadel that he would need to build a case from the evidence investigators had already collected.[23] They were unlikely to get anything new at this point.

Bufadel went to his boss to explain the situation.

"You have to find a way," he told Bufadel.

At that point, Vilches was the target of three public probes: a case stemming from the 2014 seizure in the city of Arica in northern Chile, the Fujairah fraud case, and the 2015 Santiago airport case. That was in addition to the secret money laundering investigation. To strengthen the money laundering case, Bufadel decided to combine it with the Santiago airport seizure.[24]

Once he started writing the indictment, Bufadel realized he had plenty to work with. Over the past year, investigators had documented millions in gold shipments in meticulous detail, down to the exact weight of each gold bar. They had phone tap recordings, photographs, customs records, and bank account information.[25]

It was enough for a judge to issue an arrest warrant.[26]

Next, police had to carefully plan the arrests so that everyone in Vilches's crew was captured at the same time.

∞∞∞∞∞∞∞∞

As federal prosecutor Frank Maderal took control of the gold case in Miami, Perú's epicenter for illegal mining, Madre de Dios, was spinning out of control.

Despite Peruvian president Ollanta Humala's efforts over the last three years to crack down on dirty gold, a crush of wildcat miners hungering for metal continued to invade indigenous reserves and national parks.

Every year, the miners dumped forty tons of mercury into Amazonian rivers, according to Perú's environment ministry. The fish that local people depended on—especially in rural and indigenous communities—were loaded with toxins. The people needed the fish to survive, but each bite was poison. Scientists who took hair samples from residents found levels of mercury up to sixteen times greater than was considered safe. They estimated fifty thousand people had ingested unsafe levels of mercury, and those numbers would grow as mining spread.[27]

On May 23, 2016, Humala declared a sixty-day state of emergency in the region that would later be extended for another two months.

"Forty-one percent of the population of Madre de Dios is exposed to mercury pollution," Perú's environment minister said at a news conference announcing the declaration.[28]

Things were so grave that the government banned the catching and sale of *mota punteada* (*Calophysus macropterus*), a common species of local catfish that fed at the bottom of rivers and absorbed tremendous amounts of mercury. Instead, local officials would provide uncontaminated fish and clean drinking water. The government also committed to sending three hospital ships downriver to provide medical aid, as well as setting up scientific stations to monitor mercury levels in the water. News media outlets from around the world covered the declaration.

All the attention was bad for business. The gold miners weren't just outlaws cutting down trees anymore; now they were being portrayed as killers.

Four days after Perú declared a state of emergency, NTR's three amigos reached out to each other. Juan Pablo Granda texted Samer Barrage and Renato Rodriguez to complain that their bottom line was already taking a hit. They had only brought in 86 kilos of gold that month. A good month netted at least 94.

"You should have pulled your weight," Rodriguez said.[29]

"I have failed," Granda replied. "Spot price and state of emergency in Madre de Dios got us."

He wasn't the only NTR trader whose numbers were slipping. The totals from Bolivia and Guyana—where Rodriguez was buying smuggled Peruvian gold—were falling, too.

Granda thought there was no excuse for the slowdown.

"Those countries are looser than Barrage's ass after riding a horse," he complained.

CHAPTER 34

The Fellowship of the Ring

NOW THAT FEDERAL PROSECUTOR FRANK MADERAL HAD CONVINCED HIS colleague Michael Sherwin to let him have the whole gold case, he needed a bigger team. And he wanted to play quarterback.

Normally, federal investigations work like this: An agent collects evidence of criminal activity and presents it to a prosecutor. The prosecutor reviews the material and determines whether there is enough evidence to bring charges and try the case.

Maderal hated that approach. He didn't think it would work for something as complex as gold. He needed to connect dots that extended across two continents, acting more as an investigative supervisor than a prosecutor. He had the FBI and Homeland Security Investigations working parallel investigations in Chile and Miami. There were thousands of pages of documents to review. He would have to oversee all the work, keep the agents on track, and stop their bosses from pulling them back into other cases. No matter what, if he wanted to nail down the case in Perú, where NTR had bought so much gold from Pedro David Pérez Miranda, aka Peter Ferrari, he needed more help.

That was a problem: neither the FBI nor HSI had a presence in Perú, aside from a couple legal attachés. The Drug Enforcement Administration, on the other hand, had one of its biggest global offices in Lima, with more than twenty special agents, and a long history of intelligence gathering and source building in the Peruvian cocaine trade. After Bolivia's left-wing president Evo Morales kicked the agency out in 2008, Lima replaced La Paz as a key office for the DEA in South America—responsible for managing operations across the "southern cone," a region that covered Perú, Bolivia, Brazil, Argentina, Uruguay, and Chile.¹ Only the office in Bogotá, Colombia, where the DEA had made major cocaine cases for nearly a generation, was more important regionally.

So Perú was the DEA's turf.

"You can't go into their backyard without bringing them into the case," Maderal's supervisor told him.

It had been difficult enough getting the FBI and HSI to work together. But Maderal had an ally in DEA supervisor Carl Beckett, who was in charge of the Lima office's anti–money laundering unit. When Beckett came to Miami on an unrelated case, Maderal decided to show him a list of the Peruvian front companies he was investigating. Beckett knew all about them. DEA special agent Tim Schoonmaker and his colleagues had been sniffing around them for months while looking into dirty gold. Many were Peter Ferrari's companies. Beckett said the Peruvian police had their own investigations into the companies, too. Maybe the Peruvians would help Maderal, like the Chileans had helped Sherwin. Beckett didn't need to be sold on the importance of gold. He saw the nexus between illegal mining, gold smuggling, and drug trafficking. He knew it was all one massive pot of money. Hitting Perú's illegal gold industry would hurt the narcos' pocketbooks. He had been listening to Schoonmaker's lectures.

Maderal began planning a trip to Perú. It would be the first time the dirty gold team met together—in person—in one place. Getting the FBI, HSI, and DEA to sit down at the same table as equals was itself a milestone.

He called their union "The Fellowship of the Ring."

Just as in Tolkien's fable world, where the elves and dwarves and humans struggled mightily to band together in the face of the dark lord Sauron, federal law enforcement agencies are loath to collaborate. It's not that the agencies necessarily distrust each other—although some do. It's more the impediment of a vast, territorial bureaucracy where agents from the DEA may have no clue what their colleagues at the FBI are doing—and don't want them stepping on their turf. Everyone wants to be first with a big case. It matters who gets to kick down the door.

But for Maderal to make his case he knew he needed them all to work together. Fighting dirty gold would require the cooperation of three gigantic federal law enforcement agencies as equal partners on a scale rarely seen in America's criminal justice system. No one was going to hoard the informants or the territory or the glory. They had to collaborate or the case would fall apart. It was too vast and too complex for one agency to handle alone. The case needed a field general. And it was going to be the prosecutor.

In addition to wanting to secure the DEA's cooperation, Maderal had another reason for going to Perú. He had spent weeks searching through the money laundering statute in the prosecutor's handbook, convinced that what NTR's gold dealers were doing must be against the law. He needed to find the crime that the company and its dealers were committing. Sitting in his office late one night, surrounded by reams of paper and legal books, Maderal made a breakthrough: The US money laundering statute allowed prosecutors to charge anyone suspected of "promoting" illegal activity in a foreign country. If NTR's dealers were buying illegally mined gold from Ferrari, that was enough to trigger a money laundering conspiracy charge.[2]

Usually, the government uses the money laundering statute to charge drug traffickers for "concealing" proceeds from the narcotics trade in investments like luxury real estate, foreign cars, and seemingly legitimate businesses.[3] But concealment didn't seem to apply to Maderal's case.

By law, a "promotion" money laundering charge could only be based on a so-called specified unlawful activity enumerated in the statute. Drug trafficking? That was there. Kidnapping? That too. Extortion? Also listed. But illegal mining? It wasn't an option. So, Maderal had to get creative if he wanted to make a criminal case.

Deep in the throes of his research, he discovered another way forward: the money laundering statute *did* consider crimes against a foreign nation that would require extradition under a bilateral treaty to be "specified unlawful activities." Perú and the United States have had an extradition treaty since 2001, and it included illegal gold mining. As a result, Maderal could use illegal mining to underpin his money laundering conspiracy case against NTR.[4]

It was a brilliant bit of lawyering—and the first time any federal prosecutor would use that approach to make such a case in the United States, the US Attorney's Office resident money laundering expert, prosecutor Tony Gonzalez, would later tell Maderal. (While it seemed like a breakthrough to the prosecutors, the federal agents working the case had already come to the same conclusion on their own.)

Still, Maderal would have to prove beyond a reasonable doubt that illegal gold mining was taking place in Perú. He would also have to prove that NTR and its dealers were participating in a money laundering conspiracy when they bought dirty gold from Ferrari and his crew. For NTR, turning a blind eye to Ferrari's apparently illicit network would be no excuse. Under the statute, ignoring obvious signs of criminal activity wasn't a valid defense.

Now the gold investigative team needed to go to Perú to prove that NTR had promoted "specified unlawful activities"—specifically illegal mining—when it bought Ferrari's gold.

On June 6, 2016, Maderal met FBI special agent Refina Willis and HSI special agent Cole Almeida at Miami International Airport. They were joined by Willis's partner at the FBI and a last-minute arrival: a young agent from the DEA's Miami office.

No one at DEA Miami wanted in on the gold case—until they found out DEA Lima was getting involved. Then, they felt like they couldn't be left out. Just before the trip, a Miami supervisor walked into the young DEA agent's office. He had been on the job a couple of months. He didn't know anything about gold.

"You're going to Perú," the boss said. The agent barely had time to ask why. The flight was in a couple hours.

At the airport, the newcomer approached Maderal, who was wearing a Patagonia baseball cap and holding a small duffel bag. They'd never met.

"Are you Frank?" he asked.

"Yeah," Maderal said. "How'd you know?

"You look like an AUSA," the agent replied.

∞∞∞∞∞∞∞∞

When the team of federal investigators arrived at the Lima airport later that night, they were met by a black armored van from the US Embassy. The van delivered them to the JW Marriott in Lima's most exclusive neighborhood, Miraflores, a seaside district that had been sacked and burned by the Chilean army in the late nineteenth century. Now, Miraflores was packed with restaurants, nightclubs, and department stores catering to foreign tourists and Lima's jet set.

Maderal and the agents looked around the hotel. Practically every guest checking in was holding the special brown passport issued to US government employees. Peruvian counterintelligence had probably bugged the whole place. There might even be cameras in the rooms. Nothing sensitive about the case could be discussed inside the hotel.

The next morning, DEA special agent Tim Schoonmaker and his partner Steve Fischer—a grinder newly arrived in Perú who talked like a Jersey beat cop and was still working on his Spanish—picked them up in the van and drove to the US Embassy across town. It was only a six-mile drive, but in the hellish traffic of Lima—ranked as the world's third-most congested city—the trip took nearly an hour.[5]

When it was inaugurated in 1995, during the height of Perú's violence, the massive US Embassy in Lima was the largest outpost of American diplomacy in the Western Hemisphere. The Peruvian architect who designed it said it was supposed to evoke Incan architecture. A local critic, however, called it a "great dumb box."[6]

Waiting at the embassy were the legal attachés from the FBI and HSI, as well as Carl Beckett, the DEA supervisor, and some staffers from the US State Department. The DEA didn't have a conference room in its corner of the embassy big enough to squeeze them all in. They had to borrow one from the State Department, with fake leather chairs and whiteboards mounted on the wall.

The room may have been standard for government offices. The meeting taking place within it was not. The three biggest US law enforcement agencies were sitting around one table talking about the same case.

Beckett opened with an exhortation.

"I don't see agency," he told them. "We're all one team. Team USA."

It had to be said. That's how unusual it was for the FBI, HSI, and DEA to be at the same table eager to cooperate. Then Maderal, the quarterbacking prosecutor, took over. A torrent of gold was coming out of Perú, destroying the rain forest and enriching drug dealers, he said. The federal agents had to prove that NTR Metals and their trio of dealers knew they were buying suspect metal in order to back up a money laundering charge. First off, Maderal needed the Peruvian government to hand over all its customs records and the results of its investigations into Pedro David Pérez Miranda, aka Peter Ferrari. Maybe the Peruvians had a witness that the United States didn't know about or a crucial piece of evidence buried in some file. Maderal's probe was still in the so-called vacuum cleaner phase: he needed to suck up every piece of information he could find.

Schoonmaker said the DEA would get the records Maderal wanted. Then the HSI attaché said, no, he would get them. The competition to play a major part in the case was already heating up. Everyone wanted a piece of it. Maderal told the team he wanted indictments out by September. That was only three months away. They had to get to work. It was rah-rah stuff. But he could see the agents' eyes lighting up around the table. They had a massive, one-of-a-kind case and they all knew it. Now they just needed to make it.

First they broke for lunch. There was a chicken restaurant the DEA agents liked in an open-air shopping center not far from the embassy. Maderal walked up the steps to the mall. A curly-haired man, wearing gold chains, was trailed by several bodyguards as he walked down. Maderal and the man almost collided, but the prosecutor veered right and the man went left. As the man's posse proceeded down the street, Schoonmaker leaned toward Maderal.

"Dude," he whispered. "That was Pedro Pérez Miranda."

"Who?" Maderal asked.

"Peter Ferrari," he said.

∞∞∞∞∞∞

The next day, the DEA wanted some time with Maderal. Schoonmaker wanted him to meet the Peruvian prosecutor investigating Ferrari. But it quickly became clear that Maderal's Peruvian counterpart, a pale, wide-eyed man named Lizardo Pantoja, wasn't much interested in cross-border collaboration.

Pantoja seemed nervous. Jumpy. Lizardo, the Americans couldn't help thinking, was an apt first name. At any moment, the prosecutor might leap onto the wall and scurry away through an open window.

But Pantoja may have had good reason to be afraid. Peruvian prosecutors are generally career officials. They don't snag cushy jobs at corporate law firms like their US counterparts. For that reason, some fear attacking power. Maderal could indict a sitting US senator, and unless he royally botched the case his career wouldn't suffer. In fact, taking down a senator might help him make a name for himself. But if Pantoja indicted the wrong guy—say, a politically connected businessman with alleged narco ties like Peter Ferrari—his career could be finished. Or worse, his life. Peruvian prosecutors, judges, and witnesses often face intimidation and threats in the course of their work. Law enforcement officials in the country have even been murdered under suspicious circumstances.

Prosecuting someone like Ferrari seemed to terrify Pantoja, the Americans thought. Still, Maderal made his pitch. He wanted to stop the destructive illegal gold trade and planned to use all the resources of the United States government. Would Pantoja help him? Would he give him access to his Ferrari files?

"Okay," Pantoja limply said. "*Sí*."

It was clear he was just saying that to get the Americans out of his office. There was no glimmer of inspiration in Pantoja's eyes. Only fear and dread.

The Peruvians would be no help.

ᗅᗅᗅᗅᗅᗅ

On their final day in Perú that June, Maderal's team planned to do a flyover of La Pampa—the sprawling stretch of rain forest that had been felled by illegal miners—but the DEA plane's engine was on the fritz. Maderal wouldn't get to see the devastation firsthand.

Still, he got some other news that boosted his confidence in the case. The Peruvian customs agency had shared its gold statistics. The export records matched up perfectly with US import records, company for company, kilo for kilo, dollar for dollar. There was no indication of a sudden shift of Peruvian gold away from the United States to a third country like China or Switzerland. Maderal's data bible was accurate. No more sleepless nights. At least not about the numbers.

But now he had another concern: Working with agents abroad, especially the DEA, always made him wary. The agency depended on its relationships with foreign cops and prosecutors. It needed them for tips and investigative legwork. Sometimes the DEA agents and the locals became friends and allies. Thanks to their in-country knowledge, the agents stationed abroad saw the bigger picture: they needed to help their counterparts build local cases and strengthen their own institutions in order to stop transnational crime. To Maderal, however, it seemed like some agents forgot their ultimate goal was to bring charges in the United States. Sometimes they would go native. He called it "T. E. Lawrence syndrome," after the famed British soldier who helped the Arabs fight for their freedom during World War I and in the process became "Lawrence of Arabia," a hero as much Arab as British. Maderal feared that at some point during the gold case, Schoonmaker would go full T. E. Lawrence.[7] The DEA agent had only a few months left on the job. It was clear to the prosecutor that Schoonmaker was hell-bent on making the best possible case—and didn't care who he pissed off.

The only question in Maderal's mind was how long it would be before he found himself dealing with "Schoonmaker of Perú."

CHAPTER 35

His Last Case

TIM SCHOONMAKER DIDN'T LOOK AT DRUG CASES THE SAME WAY MOST OF his colleagues did. In part that was because of his background. No DEA agent has a "typical" path into the agency. But his journey was more peripatetic than most.

Born in New York State in 1960, Schoonmaker grew up a faculty brat in Ohio, where his father was a professor of chemistry at Oberlin College. His mother worked as a rare books librarian. As a young man, he excelled both in the classroom and as an athlete, and his grades were strong enough to enroll at Carleton College, a top liberal arts school in Minnesota, where he became a geology major and played right wing on the varsity soccer team. He worked on a ranch in Montana over summer breaks. After graduation, he hitchhiked through the American West before traveling up to Alaska and then all the way back down to Mexico.

Now what? Schoonmaker couldn't face any more time in the classroom. He didn't want to sit in an office. His roommate from Carleton had dropped out and joined the US Air Force Pararescue squad. It sounded like a daredevil's dream. Pararescue troopers were trained to save downed airmen from hostile territory and harsh terrain in active combat.[1] In peacetime, they plucked mariners off shipwrecks in swirling seas, rescued stranded mountaineers, and stood by at Cape Canaveral for space shuttle launches in case of disaster.[2] The unit's mantra: "These things we do, that others may live."

Ninety men were invited to the pararescue school's selection course in 1983. Just five trainees graduated a year later. Schoonmaker was one of them. Although he was a reservist, it was a dangerous full-time job. In his spare time, he lived in Corvallis, Oregon, enrolled in a veterinary program at Oregon State University, and rode broncos on the school's rodeo team. He was a lousy cowboy. The broncos bucked him off. He liked caring for animals, but he knew he wouldn't last another four years in the classroom, let alone a lifetime in a sterile vet's office. He missed the outdoors. He missed the action. For a while, he worked on professional ski patrols at Oregon's Mount Hood and Crystal Mountain in Washington.

Pushing thirty, he worried about finding a career. He had a serious girlfriend, who would soon become his wife. A roommate said federal law enforcement agencies were eager to hire military veterans. Schoonmaker researched his options. The FBI seemed hidebound and uptight. The agents had backgrounds as lawyers or accountants. But the Drug Enforcement Administration, now that was something else.

Richard Nixon established the DEA in 1973, in response to what he termed an epidemic of narcotics plaguing America's streets.[3] "This administration has declared an all-out global war on the drug menace," he told Congress. The war on drugs—which stemmed from America's long adherence to largely ineffective prohibition-style policies—had begun.[4]

The DEA's early agents tended to be men who had served as local police officers or in the Vietnam War. They specialized in undercover work, dressing up as hippies and members of the counterculture. In the 1980s, the cocaine boom turned their focus to the root source: Latin America.

Schoonmaker joined the DEA in 1992, passing through basic training at Quantico, Virginia, and was assigned to the agency's Portland office. Still filled with wanderlust, he hungered to serve overseas. In 2000, he got his wish, moving his young family from Oregon to Santa Cruz, Bolivia. Living there taught him Spanish—street Spanish, not the kind he had studied in a six-month DEA language program in Washington, DC—as well as the importance of working with local cops. Cases couldn't get done without them. Finding ones he could trust was the hard part.

When he rotated back to Salt Lake City after six years abroad, he became a DEA supervisor. It was the worst mistake of his career. Schoonmaker wasn't cut out for desk work. Overseeing agents—instead of building his own cases—left him feeling powerless and uninspired. He couldn't even get a $200 purchase order without a counter-signature from his boss. And his brusque manner and supreme confidence in his own abilities and judgment did not help him manage up the chain of command. He was not a political animal.

In late 2009, Schoonmaker put in for a downgrade back to agent. Three years later, he asked for a transfer to Perú.

It was time to get back to doing what he loved.

∞∞∞∞∞∞∞∞∞

The DEA had changed since Tim Schoonmaker joined the agency. Some would say it had grown up. Others, that it had lost its edge.

In Bolivia, Schoonmaker had gone on jungle raids with the national police, guns drawn. Perú wasn't like that. In Perú, the DEA agents waited until after the local cops had busted the drug labs and stacked up the cash, coke, and guns. The DEA only showed up when the cameras did. That didn't mean the work wasn't dangerous. Schoonmaker never took the same route home from the US Embassy two nights in a row. He drove a bullet-proof SUV and carried a gun. He worried about his teenage children and the petty crime that sometimes turned deadly on Lima's streets. Peruvian nightlife started much later than it did in the United States. His daughter complained that her midnight curfew in Lima meant she could only see her high school friends for an hour before having to head home.

Schoonmaker may have missed live operations, but he discovered a passion for building money laundering cases. Most DEA agents hated them. That was just because they didn't understand how simple money laundering really is, Schoonmaker thought. Drug trafficking organizations excel at smuggling drugs, not laundering money. The narcos can dissolve cocaine into the fabric of jeans, camouflage it in pet food, and mix it into plastic. They can dig tunnels under the United States–Mexico border. They can even hide drugs inside women's breast implants.[5]

Their operations generated huge amounts of money, but hiding all that cash was tricky, especially for the relatively unsophisticated

Peruvian drug gangs. While the Colombian and Mexican cartels hired lawyers and accountants who knew how to manipulate international real estate markets and the global banking system to hide illicit funds, Perú had no international drug cartels. The Peruvian drug gangs were smaller, regionally based outfits, a neighborhood corner store compared to the corporate-like empires run by the Colombians and Mexicans. They were often familial in nature, so the DEA called them "clans."

Seizing the clans' drugs was a temporary solution. After all, they could always grow more coca. Money was their real Achilles' heel. Targeting their cash and investments was a backdoor way to cripple their operations. Without financing, they couldn't maintain their elaborate cultivation and smuggling networks or buy protection and corrupt local officials.

After arriving in Perú, Schoonmaker crafted a thirty-one-page presentation on Peruvian narcotics money laundering that he would show to bosses and colleagues.[6] To figure out where the narcos were, Schoonmaker argued, all you had to do was walk into a jungle or mountain town and ask who owned that brand-new hotel or mansion.

"Unlike cocaine, which is easy to hide and move, Peruvian clans' assets are easy to locate and identify," Schoonmaker wrote, "and hard to hide. In almost every community, narcotics-derived assets can be easily detected simply by identifying the new impressive office buildings, hotels and markets that stand out from the surrounding community. The titleholders of these assets rarely can justify their ownership and usually they can be easily linked to clan heads, resulting in the seizure of the assets, the arrests of clan heads, and the dismantlement of these clans."

Though the DEA brass acknowledged the importance of money laundering, many field agents wrongly assumed that cracking a money case required the help of a forensic accountant. Schoonmaker knew it wasn't that different from a narcotics investigation: all it took was an agent willing to go through bank statements, corporate documents, and tax records—and finding a confidential source with the insider knowledge to explain it all.

Cracking heads and incinerating kilos of cocaine weren't going to solve the drug problem. There was a better way.

∞∞∞∞∞∞∞

After Frank Maderal returned to Miami on June 10, 2016, Tim Schoonmaker was cautiously optimistic.

Finally, an American prosecutor wanted to make a gold case. The DEA agent liked that Maderal seemed aggressive. He'd ignored a fellow agent in Quito who warned him to stay away from the Miami prosecutor and instead take his case to the Southern District of New York.

"He's an arrogant jerk," the other agent said. "I won't work with him. He's completely disrespectful."

"I can handle him," Schoonmaker replied.

So Schoonmaker set out on his main mission: figuring out what laws Peter Ferrari was breaking in Perú in his dealings with NTR's three amigos.

From Elemetal's files, which the company had begun delivering to Maderal in response to his subpoena, Schoonmaker could tell the NTR Metals traders were likely falsifying customs paperwork. Making that into a case was possible—but Maderal felt criminal charges just for that offense would be marginal. It would be like going after Elemetal over a parking ticket. On the other hand, if Schoonmaker could find evidence of Ferrari committing criminal activities in Perú, then Maderal would be able to say NTR's gold dealers had "promoted" those crimes by buying his gold. That would be a serious money laundering charge that could stick in a federal court.

Schoonmaker knew there was one law the Miami prosecutor could use to nail Ferrari and NTR's traders: in 2012, as the gold boom devastated larger and larger swaths of rain forest, Perú's government had made illegal mining a crime. The DEA agent had a solid grasp of Peruvian law in general. But the nation's mining statutes were spread out across different parts of the legal code. Figuring them all out would be a nightmare. Luckily, Schoonmaker had "Pequeño."

Pequeño, "little guy," was a Peruvian national police sergeant Schoonmaker had handpicked for an assignment on his special intelligence team, an eight-man squad of DEA-paid Peruvian cops who helped the feds make drug cases. Pequeño was Schoonmaker's number two guy on the so-called vetted unit, named because the DEA had to put each member through rigorous background checks.

His real name was Ramón Barboza Montes. He had been on the force thirty years and knew everybody, from the criminals to the cops to the prosecutors. He also had street cred and always dressed in plain clothes. (The one time Schoonmaker saw him in uniform, the American burst out laughing. Pequeño looked ridiculous with his billed cap and braided tassels.)

"I want to know everything you need to do to be able to pull gold out of the ground legally," Schoonmaker told his sergeant. "Everything from that point until you export it, what you need to do to do it legally. I need every single thing."

The unit's office quickly filled up with legal codes and documents. Gold exporters needed to compile dozens of records—from mining permits to tax declarations to metallurgical analyses to copies of the identity cards of their gold suppliers. The team boiled all the material down into digests, and Schoonmaker translated them for Maderal in Miami, sending him photos of each document to show how they should be filled out.

Although Ferrari had filled out all the right paperwork, the Americans believed his documents were riddled with lies. To confirm that suspicion, Schoonmaker would have to persuade Lizardo Pantoja, the Peruvian prosecutor, to turn over his trove of evidence.

For Maderal, the Peruvian export forms were a breakthrough. The prosecutor now had a potential Peruvian crime, illegal mining, to buttress his US money laundering indictment. In their deals with Ferrari, he could argue, NTR's traders were promoting illegal mining by buying gold from a known dealer of illicit precious metal.

But for Schoonmaker it wasn't nearly enough. As much as he cared about making the US case against NTR and its three dealers, a worry was worming into his mind. Charging them in the United States would only be a job half done. Illegal mining was a Peruvian problem hurting Peruvian people and Peruvian rain forests. If Perú wanted to truly eradicate dirty gold, Schoonmaker believed, the Peruvian government would have to make its own criminal case, too. Local criminal charges would send a signal to the wildcat gold miners and their criminal financiers that the nation would no longer tolerate illegal mining. Schoonmaker believed that Pedro David Pérez Miranda was a poster boy for the entire dirty industry; Peter

Ferrari had to be the target. The local press would eat up his demise with wall-to-wall coverage. Schoonmaker had seen Peruvian prosecutors let dozens and dozens of other money laundering cases languish. They wouldn't be able to do that with a defendant as high-profile as Ferrari.

To Schoonmaker, failing to stop illegal mining now could also seriously destabilize Perú. As wildcat miners sought fresh territory to exploit, their dredges and bulldozers were creeping closer and closer to the mountainous area controlled by the rebel group known as the Shining Path. The Peruvian government had reduced the Shining Path's influence to the rural highlands on the eastern-facing slopes of the Andes Mountains, a remote region known for its bountiful production of coca—and for the gold that flowed down its waterways into the Amazon.[7] If the rebels got a foothold in the lucrative gold business, Schoonmaker feared, the new cash flow might revive a brutal guerrilla war.[8]

The first step to making sure that didn't happen in Perú? Seeing Ferrari arrested and brought to trial—in his native country. If such a notorious gold trader could slither away, then it meant open season on the rain forest—and it would also render meaningless everything the Americans hoped to accomplish with their own criminal cases back in Miami. None of it would matter if the Peruvians didn't take down Ferrari. And Schoonmaker had only a few months to make that happen. Federal law enforcement officers have a mandatory retirement age of fifty-seven. Schoonmaker's retirement was set for February 2017. On March 1, he liked to joke, he would turn into a pumpkin.

This would be his last case.

∞∞∞∞∞∞∞

NTR's three amigos, Juan Pablo Granda, Samer Barrage, and Renato Rodriguez, had little clue they were popping up on the radar of federal investigators looking into dirty gold.

Granda was busy collaborating with Andrés Tejeda, the Peruvian customs broker, to rebuild NTR's gold trade in Perú. Barrage spent much of his time in Cali, Colombia, cultivating new suppliers in the gold market. Meanwhile, Rodriguez, who had seen business dry up in Bolivia and Ecuador, lost eighty pounds with daily trips to the gym and a low-carb diet of chicken, fish, and veggies. He still baked for his twin girls but wouldn't touch the cookies himself. Now, with a goatee and a trendy long-on-the-top, short-on-the-sides haircut, he looked a bit like a European soccer player. Rodriguez still kept in touch with his old customer Jeffrey Himmel, who had been out of the gold trade for more than a year since the fiasco in the Ecuadorian border town. (The tennis-loving Himmel had gifted Rodriguez two rackets to keep him fit.)

Himmel still had no idea that Rodriguez or Barrage or anyone else at NTR was responsible for the mess in Ecuador. In the summer of 2016, when Himmel used his contacts at the American Diabetes Association to help Rodriguez's ailing mother, the NTR trader ended an email to Himmel with an affectionate exhortation: "Be well, my friend!"

∞∞∞∞∞∞

All was not well for Elemetal, NTR, and its trio of top gold dealers.

In early June, after Harold Vilches had been charged with fraud in the Fujairah case, Elemetal had dumped the young Chilean exporter as a client.

Elemetal's attorney, Trey Gum, said in later press coverage that the company "reported the matter to appropriate governmental authorities" and suspended its business in Chile.[9]

Then, in mid-June, Ecuadorian authorities arrested seven businessmen, including the three brothers linked to Spartan del Ecuador, a major supplier for Himmel's MVP Imports, and accused them of money laundering.[10] (The March brothers insisted they were innocent victims of political persecution.)[11]

On June 26, 2016, Barrage texted Granda and Rodriguez a link to an article about the March brothers' case.[12] The story claimed another company linked to them, Clearprocess, was buying Peruvian gold and that Clearprocess and Spartan were doing business with two specific South Florida precious-metals companies. NTR was not mentioned in the article. Maybe the three amigos had some breathing room, but they couldn't take any chances. The article stated that Ecuadorian authorities were tapping phones.

"Don't like the fact that calls were intercepted," Granda wrote back to Barrage.

"Keep telling you guys about the calls," Barrage said. "Hopefully this helps."

"Yea, you are right," Granda replied. "But the calls with the customers, I might just have to do everything face to face. U don't speak with customers so u don't have those situations. We need to find a way to avoid this."

"Should be nothing to avoid," said Barrage, who had often warned the other two against speaking on the phone with customers. "That's the whole point, you #simplebitch."

What the three amigos didn't know was even worse.

For months now, in response to prosecutor Frank Maderal's April subpoena, Elemetal had been turning over reams of internal records to the feds: more than ten thousand pages of payment records and compliance files on NTR customers from Perú, Bolivia, Chile, and Ecuador, as well as 179 gigabytes of emails revealing all employees' correspondence.

But despite the array of internal information, the files weren't turning up evidence of money laundering, both the feds and Elemetal's attorneys could see. In June, however, Maderal got a critical tip that NTR's three amigos were using WhatsApp to communicate on their cell phones. He told Elemetal's lawyers at Jones Day to see if they could obtain them. The chats could provide a mountain of potentially incriminating evidence.

Elemetal executives and their lawyers knew they had to get a hold of the texts: the more information and cooperation Elemetal provided to Maderal, they reasoned, the less likely it was that the executives or the company would be charged. The executives may have turned a blind eye to suspicious movements of gold across Latin America—and set up a Swiss cheese compliance program—but they didn't believe they bore any responsibility for gold smuggling.

In their minds, the blame should fall squarely on the three amigos.

CHAPTER 36

─────────

The Secret Weapon

THE SAME DAY NTR'S THREE AMIGOS EXCHANGED FRANTIC TEXT MESSAGES about the arrests in Ecuador, the DEA's Tim Schoonmaker drove to the office of *comandante* Jorge Domínguez Grandez, a Peruvian National Police supervisor.

Domínguez commanded a fraud section of the Peruvian police's newly formed anti–money laundering directorate. His team had been brought in to investigate the big Lima airport raid in late 2013, when Peruvian customs officials seized $18 million worth of gold mostly belonging to Pedro David Pérez Miranda, aka Peter Ferrari. Schoonmaker was convinced that Domínguez held the keys to bringing down the gold smuggler.

The commander's unit had compiled a 120-page investigative report on Ferrari's gold business laying out all the ways he had broken Perú's mining and customs laws. The legal mines where Ferrari said his gold originally came from? Empty and nonfunctional. The gold suppliers who had submitted copies of their national identity cards? They were straw owners, little old ladies and people Ferrari's crew met at neighborhood social clubs.

The Peruvian police couldn't prove exactly where Ferrari's gold was coming from. But they knew it wasn't coming from where he claimed on his companies' paperwork. That made it illegal gold. And that was a crime. Schoonmaker knew the report could not only support the United States' case against NTR and its three gold dealers; it could also provide a basis for the Peruvians to charge Ferrari in Lima. Yet the local authorities were just sitting on the report.

In their meeting, the *comandante* seemed to have little inter-est in helping his American colleagues. Unfortunately, Domín-guez explained, it wasn't in his power to give the DEA the report. Schoonmaker would have to go back to the Peruvian prosecutor, Lizardo Pantoja, who was handling the case. Pantoja was the one who had the report and the thousands of pages of mining permits, corporate records, and customs documents that served as under-lying materials. The prosecutor would have to sign off.

Eager to search through the documents, Schoonmaker called Pantoja and asked if he could send a special US unit armed with high-tech hand scanners—known as the Document and Media Exploitation Section—to copy the Peruvian police records.

"I can scan this whole thing for you," Schoonmaker told the prosecutor, explaining how the Americans could digitize every single page and turn them into a searchable database, helping investigators from both countries. Pantoja agreed but wouldn't give him a specific time when the squad could come to his office. Schoonmaker called again. And again.

Pantoja wouldn't return his messages.

∞∞∞∞∞∞∞∞∞

For a prosecutor, Frank Maderal was savvy with data. But the spreadsheets he was getting were growing more complicated. Fig-uring out what it all meant was an intractable problem for the US Attorney's Office—but not for Homeland Security Investigations (HSI), which routinely undertook complex studies of customs data.

The investigative agency grew out of the merger between the US Customs Service and the Immigration and Naturalization Service that formed US Immigration and Customs Enforcement (ICE). They were all part of the alphabet soup of agencies under the massive De-partment of Homeland Security, created by Congress in 2002 in the aftermath of the 9/11 terrorist attacks.

It was an uneasy alliance. ICE's Homeland Security Investiga-tions probed money laundering, human trafficking, drug smuggling, and transnational crime. The immigration enforcement side of ICE targeted undocumented immigrants. It rounded up those who com-mitted crimes and others who had overstayed their visas. And it was yet another agency—US Border Patrol—that made headlines for boarding buses and asking people for their immigration papers.[1] But in the public mind, it was all ICE.

HSI's capabilities went far beyond other units of the Department of Homeland Security. HSI kept forensic accountants on contract to help agents and prosecutors. Maderal asked for a data whiz. He got one: Danielle DiLeo, a forensic accountant who worked at Deloitte, one of the world's biggest accounting firms, and was on special assignment to HSI's Trade Transparency Unit. (She had gone with Maderal and the federal agents to Perú, spending the entire plane ride and much of her time in Lima plugging away on her computer.)

DiLeo would become Operation Arch Stanton's secret weapon.

Her biggest challenge was taking two separate and critical spreadsheets and marrying them together, a technical problem that baffled Maderal and Cole Almeida. One spreadsheet from Customs listed NTR's gold imports. The other spreadsheet, submitted by Elemetal in response to the subpoena, showed which exporters the company paid for gold. It was thousands and thousands of lines of data. But the payment records didn't necessarily match the import records. Customs had one format for recording data; Elemetal had another. The work was painstaking, a logic puzzle. DiLeo would identify an import and then search for a payment record to that supplier for roughly the same amount of gold. NTR was doing so many deals with so many different companies that it was sometimes nearly impossible to sift through. And it got more complicated: The Customs records often told one story, but the payments told another. On many occasions, DiLeo found, NTR would buy gold from one company but then wire a payment to a seemingly unrelated firm. Sometimes NTR would accept fifty shipments of gold from a company, but not pay it a cent. DiLeo would have to calculate the value of all those shipments and then look for a company that had been paid a similar amount in aggregate to find a match. It took months.

But at the end of the process, the investigators had a far more complete picture of who NTR was doing business with—and how the three amigos were skating by Elemetal's compliance program.

The married spreadsheets became a map for Operation Arch Stanton.

∞∞∞∞∞∞

In Miami, Elemetal's lawyers at Jones Day thought the company might not have much to worry about from the federal investigation.

The thousands of emails between the three amigos that the company turned over to the government showed no signs of criminal activity. But in June 2016, someone slipped the feds several of Granda's WhatsApp messages, which suggested he was communicating with money launderers in his gold deals. Prosecutor Frank Maderal shared them with Jones Day. Early the next month, the Elemetal bosses told Barrage that both his subordinates, Granda and Rodriguez, needed to turn over their cell phones to Jones Day. The firm's lawyers wanted to do an internal review of their WhatsApp messages to see if they contained evidence of money laundering. (Elemetal didn't ask for Barrage's phone because Maderal had not suggested that the firm's vice president of Latin American operations was engaged in similar communications.)

When Barrage delivered the news, his two colleagues weren't happy.

"That's easy for you to say, Sam," Granda objected. "They don't want your phone."

The three amigos drove in Rodriguez's Lexus from NTR's suburban office to downtown Miami. In a Jones Day conference room, Granda and Rodriguez met with the firm's attorneys Chris Pace, a former federal prosecutor in Miami, and Cristina Soto, an Ivy League–trained lawyer. The Jones Day lawyers told both NTR employees that investigators suspected they were communicating with money launderers about gold deals in their WhatsApp messages. Both denied it.

But they didn't have much of a choice: turn over the phones or lose their jobs.

Granda and Rodriguez's dilemma illustrates a common problem in the corporate world. In criminal investigations, corporations and employees don't always have the same interests. Sometimes they can be directly opposed. To deal with this issue, US courts have established what is known as an "Upjohn warning." Under Upjohn, company lawyers generally have an obligation to tell employees that they represent the company, not the employees. If interests potentially conflict, the lawyers should also advise the employees that they may want to hire their own attorneys. Elemetal's lawyers say they warned Granda and Rodriguez several times that the company's interests and theirs were diverging, but the two gold traders maintain they were never given such a warning.

After the US Attorney's Office delivered its subpoena to Elemetal in April, NTR's three amigos learned that federal authorities were investigating Miami's entire gold industry for money laundering. That's why their emails were being collected, or so they thought at first. But as months went by, it became increasingly obvious Elemetal's top gold traders at NTR were targets of the investigation. Now, the parent company's lawyers were telling Rodriguez and Granda that the prosecutor suspected they were doing gold deals with money launderers in South America and that investigators wanted to see the WhatsApp messages on their cell phones. It should have been time to start worrying that Elemetal's executives did not have their backs. But the three amigos—who were propelling Elemetal's business—believed the company was on their side. After all, Jones Day and Maderal, the prosecutor, hadn't found anything in their thousands of emails. They looked sparkling clean.

And besides, maybe giving Elemetal's lawyers access to their WhatsApp messages wasn't such a big deal, they thought. Most of the messages involving dirty deals were in a rough code. As for the more explicit ones—Pablo Escobar and mules and smuggled gold—everyone in the South American gold industry talked like that. The Elemetal bosses, they figured, weren't going to sell out their star employees. That would mean giving up the company's entire Latin American operation—and exposing the executives' own cushy corporate lifestyles to possible legal liability. Even after the fiasco with Ferrari, when NTR's valuable shipment was seized by authorities at the Lima airport, Elemetal executives had seemingly ignored the improbable new supply of gold coming out of Ecuador and Bolivia—gold that they had been told in internal emails was largely mined in Perú and smuggled across the border.

Why would Elemetal's executives do anything else but keep turning a blind eye?

But the three amigos could not have been more naive about how their employer had turned on them.

In the Jones Day conference room that July, Rodriguez seemed more worried that federal agents might see his personal information, including photos of and chats with his family members. The three amigos often exchanged photos of the escorts they frequented, too.

"We are not handing this over to the government," Rodriguez told Pace. "We will do a query with key words and only hand over what is pertinent to the investigation."

Pace, Elemetal's lead lawyer at Jones Day, pacified him.

"It's grand jury secrecy," he said. "They can't post it on the internet."

In the end, Granda and Rodriguez decided to give up their cell phones to a technician who made copies of their WhatsApp messages. They went downstairs to eat pizza at a lobby café and waited to retrieve their phones.

"I feel like I just got raped," Rodriguez complained, thinking that Elemetal's lawyers had lied to them.

If the three amigos had been wiser and better informed, they would have quit their jobs, driven onto the MacArthur Causeway connecting downtown Miami to South Beach, and thrown their phones into Biscayne Bay instead of turning them over to Elemetal's lawyers.

∞∞∞∞∞∞

The DEA's Tim Schoonmaker still couldn't get the Peruvians to cooperate with him, but his case was gaining momentum in other ways.

He, Maderal, and the rest of the feds were growing increasingly focused on Granda, Barrage, and Rodriguez. As NTR's on-the-ground traders, they had direct involvement in its seemingly illegal gold deals with Peter Ferrari. The question was just how far up Elemetal's hierarchy the criminality extended.

Thanks to his contacts in the police force, Schoonmaker's right-hand man, Pequeño, had made a major discovery: an American insurance investigator looking into NTR's $10 million claim from the seizure of Ferrari's gold shipment at the Lima airport had left his card with one of the Peruvian cops on the case.

If anyone had evidence that the three amigos knew they were buying illegal gold, it was the insurance investigator, a New York lawyer named Peter Rossi. He'd gone through Elemetal's compliance files and deposed NTR's three gold traders. Now Schoonmaker had his number.

On August 5, Schoonmaker called Rossi at his New York office.

"Were these guys duped?" Schoonmaker asked. "In your judgment, did they know what they were doing?"

"Tim, there is no doubt in my mind. They knew exactly what they were doing," Rossi replied.

During the depositions, Rossi said, it grew clear that Granda, Rodriguez, and Barrage didn't want to help his investigation. They were confrontational, evasive, and defensive. They admitted knowing Ferrari but said he was just another guy in the gold business. They insisted they had no special relationship with him.

Rossi didn't believe them.

CHAPTER 37

"*Investigaciones!*"

THE SUN HAD YET TO RISE ON SANTIAGO'S UPSCALE LAS CONDES neighborhood on the morning of August 12, 2016, when Chilean federal agents Juan Pablo Sandoval and Juan Figueroa pulled up outside Harold Vilches's apartment building. They were accompanied by a team of colleagues from the PDI, Chile's FBI equivalent.[1]

At the gate to the handsome beige brick building, they pressed the intercom buzzer and told the concierge they had an arrest warrant. Once inside the lobby, they instructed him not to let anyone leave the building.

Sandoval knew from the phone taps that Vilches owned a gun, but he was almost certain it was safely hidden in the bunker.

"*Investigaciones!*" the police shouted as they knocked on the door to apartment 404.[2]

Vilches had already gotten up at three that morning when the local police came to check on him to enforce his nighttime house arrest. His first thought when he heard someone at the door was that the police had returned, forgetting that they'd already stopped by. He rolled out of bed in his pajamas and went to the front door.

Through the peephole, Vilches could see four police officers. But they weren't the local guys who came to check on him every night. These officers had federal police jackets emblazoned with the letters *PDI*. Vilches was confused. Maybe they were burglars, he thought. He'd heard of cases in which thieves dressed up as police in order to get inside the victim's apartment.[3]

Sandoval told Vilches he had a warrant for his arrest and Vilches, now convinced he was dealing with real police, opened the door.[4]

Inside the apartment, Sandoval tried to explain why they were there.

"No, no, I've already resolved that," Vilches said dismissively, believing the police had come because of the Santiago airport case. "You can talk to my lawyer."[5]

"I'm talking about another case," Sandoval replied. "I know you have a case in Arica and another one here. This is something else."

The federal agents fanned out across the apartment, seizing computers and cell phones. Vilches went to wake up his wife before the police could get to her.[6]

To Vilches, the show of force seemed excessive. His only crime, as he saw it, was not paying taxes. It wasn't as if he'd killed someone.

The police told Vilches and his wife to sit on the couch. Dazed, still wearing their pajamas, the couple tried to respond to a barrage of questions. Did they have any weapons in the apartment? Any money? Any gold? Any drugs?[7]

"No, no, I don't have anything like that," Vilches insisted.

At first, his wife also seemed to be under the impression that the police were there because of the airport seizure case, which Vilches had assured her he had under control. When the agents told Vilches's wife they also had a warrant for her arrest, she had a panic attack. Tears streamed down her face as she attempted to answer their questions.[8]

Then prosecutor Tufit Bufadel and his boss, José Luis Pérez Calaf, entered the apartment. Vilches was still half asleep, but he understood one thing: if Pérez Calaf, the top regional prosecutor, was there, that meant Chilean authorities considered this an important case. And that was bad news.[9]

As police escorted Vilches and his wife out of the building in handcuffs, they were ambushed by a TV news crew, which had been tipped off about the arrests.

"What do you think about being accused of gold smuggling?" a reporter asked, jamming a microphone through the open car door as Sandoval guided Vilches into a police vehicle.

"It wouldn't be the first time," Vilches retorted.[10]

Simultaneously, other federal agents were arresting Vilches's associates.

As the police knocked on their doors, the members of Vilches's crew tried to warn each other. Their calls were picked up by the wiretaps—the first interesting conversations police had recorded in months. "The police are entering!" one member of the crew shouted to another. "Here too!" the person at the other end of the line shouted back.[11] The police seized laptops, cell phones, and checkbooks.[12]

They had gotten the keys to Vilches's bunker while searching his apartment and asked him for the codes to his safes. Vilches had keys as a backup in case the power went out and his high-tech security system failed.[13]

But even with the keys, getting inside the bunker was like entering a bank vault. Once they got past the wall topped with barbed wire and the armored doors, the police needed an intricate combination of keys to open the interior doors. Inside the vault they found 116 million Chilean pesos in cash, equivalent to more than $150,000. The gun Sandoval had heard about on the wiretaps turned out to be a fake. It had just been for show.[14]

After the members of Vilches's crew had been booked at the police station, they were taken to the courthouse. They spent the day waiting in jail cells.

The hearing started at six thirty that evening and continued past midnight.[15] Bufadel, his eyes bloodshot, struggled to stay awake.[16] He had been up and working since before dawn.[17]

Nicolás Rodríguez Videla, the junior lawyer who had spent weeks listening to Vilches's phone calls, had also been up since early that morning making copies of key wiretap recordings and a PowerPoint presentation to explain the case.

Because investigators had never been able to seize gold from the Argentine smugglers, the prosecutors had to show the judge that the border crossings matched up perfectly with the dates Vilches sent gold shipments to Miami.[18]

Bufadel played phone tap recordings and showed the judge surveillance photos and export records.[19] He was determined to convince the judge that Vilches and his coconspirators should stay behind bars while awaiting trial. He knew the only way to get the crew to cooperate was to keep them in jail long enough that they got a taste of what it would be like to spend years in prison.[20]

All six defendants faced money laundering charges; all but one were also accused of smuggling gold, forming part of a criminal organization, and presenting false customs declarations.[21]

But to Vilches, it seemed as if prosecutors were exaggerating his crimes. They tried to pass off what he insisted had been figures of speech—like "la vuelta larga" (the long trip) to explain the scheme to transfer his NTR payments to Chile—as code language and portrayed his export business as an organized criminal enterprise. The young Chilean was livid. He started muttering under his breath during the hearing, refuting what the prosecutors were saying.[22]

Vilches's lawyer, Marko Magdic, had been unable to attend the hearing, so another lawyer from his firm stepped in. The lawyer, Matías Schmidt, gave the best court performance Vilches had ever seen.

Schmidt claimed the gold Vilches had exported was from coins and said the stacks of receipts proved its legal origins. Although prosecutors insisted there weren't enough gold coins in Chile to explain that amount of gold, Vilches's lawyer argued that a lot of coin sales weren't registered by the official Chilean exchange. He said the number of gold coins on the market fluctuated wildly from day to day depending on whether someone with a stockpile decided to sell.[23]

(Although Vilches now admits that roughly 90 percent of the more than $20 million in gold he sent to NTR was from Argentina, he maintains that some of it actually had come from other sources including gold coins.[24] In addition to the coins traded on Santiago's formal exchange, many more circulate on the informal market. Some are rumored to have been stolen from state coffers by General Augusto Pinochet and his cronies during Chile's brutal military dictatorship.)[25]

Vilches's lawyer kept talking until the judge finally interrupted him. "Are we going to keep listening to your monologue or should we continue with the hearing?" he asked.[26]

After both sides had made their arguments, the judge decided there was room for doubt. Because investigators had never detained the Argentine couriers at the border crossing, they didn't have direct evidence that the gold had been smuggled. The judge ordered the release of Vilches and four other defendants on house arrest. The sixth defendant was instructed to report to the police station every month.[27]

Bufadel, the lead prosecutor, was crestfallen.[28] His marathon twenty-hour day had been for nothing. Instead of going home to rest, he had to go home knowing he needed to start preparing an appeal.

Vilches, thinking he'd at least won this fight, left the courthouse with a huge smirk on his face.[29]

But prosecutors immediately appealed the judge's decision, and a week later an appellate court ordered that the crew be held behind bars until their case was resolved.[30] To avoid the media spectacle of getting hauled back to jail, Vilches and his wife turned themselves in.

CHAPTER 38

"DEA Sucks"

STILL BEING STALLED BY HIS "PARTNERS" IN PERUVIAN LAW ENFORCEMENT, DEA agent Tim Schoonmaker realized he had no choice but to run an end around on the prosecutor Lizardo Pantoja and the police *comandante* Jorge Domínguez.

Domínguez's boss, the general in charge of the anti–money laundering directorate, was unusual: He liked the DEA, unlike some of his colleagues in Peruvian law enforcement. The general often asked American investigators for help on his own cases and, perhaps seeking to build trust, readily agreed to give Schoonmaker the report.

It was packed with information—but incredibly dry. Schoonmaker distilled it for the Operation Arch Stanton team the old-fashioned way: not in PowerPoint but on a giant thick-stock paper graphic. The four-by-four, double-sided diagram told the story visually. It mapped out Peter Ferrari's shell companies, the chronology of how and when they formed, and all their gold and financial dealings. It was so bulky he had to fold it up eight times to fit it into his briefcase. His colleagues thought he was crazy. They laughed when he fished it out of his briefcase and carefully unfolded it. But even they had to admit it told the story well.

Getting the Peruvian report that underlay the graphic may have been a victory—but it destroyed any relationship the DEA had with Domínguez and Pantoja. Domínguez grew openly hostile in meetings. When the *comandante* came to the US Embassy for a meeting, he kept asking one question: "Why am I here?"

Schoonmaker tried to persuade him to move against Ferrari. The Peruvians, he argued, had stacks and stacks of evidence proving the mines where Ferrari claimed to be buying gold were fallow and that his shell companies were bogus. The Peruvians had to make an example of him, Schoonmaker said.

"Why aren't you guys moving on the case?" Schoonmaker asked Domínguez. "I've read the thing. You have everything you need."

The *comandante* got up and left.

Pantoja seemed even worse.

When Schoonmaker walked into the prosecutor's office soon after he had gotten the report, he saw something that shocked even a DEA veteran used to working in foreign countries. On Pantoja's whiteboard scrawled in Spanish was a message loud and clear: "DEA Sucks."

Pequeño, Schoonmaker's ally in the Peruvian police, thought he knew what was going on.

Under Peruvian law, the police and prosecutors only had a certain amount of time to charge Ferrari. The clock had started ticking at the beginning of 2014, shortly after the Lima airport raid. If Pantoja didn't charge Ferrari by early 2017, the outlaw dealer who was allegedly laundering millions through gold trades would walk free.

"So that's their game plan," Schoonmaker told Pequeño. "They're trying to run out the damn clock."

From his decade working with foreign authorities in Latin America, Schoonmaker had come up with a theory about why local law enforcement failed to get things done. It was a checklist that he would work through to figure out what was really going on.

First was incompetence. Second, bureaucracy. Third, fear. Fourth, ignorance. And, finally, the worst of all, corruption. Schoonmaker could work with incompetence by training local cops. With his strong Spanish, he could navigate bureaucracy. In subordinates, his confidence whisked away fear. And ignorance? Well, he was a natural teacher. But corruption was tough. It often went all the way to the top. Proving corruption against foreign officials required the DEA to walk a political tightrope. They were guests abroad and could be expelled.

In his gut, he was approaching an inescapable conclusion: Pantoja and Domínguez simply did not want to charge Ferrari. They even seemed reluctant to run surveillance on the alleged gold launderer, the target of a major criminal probe. Something sinister appeared to be going on. (Pantoja and Domínguez were never accused of wrongdoing.)

∞∞∞∞∞∞∞

Elemetal's five-year run in South America was heading for a crash landing.

On September 15, 2016, *La Republica*, a major daily newspaper in Lima, reported that authorities were charging a ring of gold dealers in relation to an October 2015 seizure of 18 kilos of gold worth $600,000.

At the center of that ring was a notary named Joule Vila Vila who worked for Peter Ferrari, among other gold traders. Vila Vila was already on the government's radar, accused of ginning up a fake company and using more than fifty straw men to defraud the municipality of Lima. (In 2019 he would be arrested on charges stemming from that case.) But in 2016 he was free and, according to investigators, using those same skills for dirty gold deals. The article implicated Juan Granda and his company, NTR Metals, by name as being the importer of the shipment.[1]

It didn't take Granda long to figure out that his Peruvian business partner, Andrés Tejeda, might be involved.

Before the story broke, the customs broker had called Granda and told him that in order to avoid any problems with Peruvian authorities, Granda would have to pay a bribe of $40,000 to a senior police official. Granda refused, thinking Tejeda intended to pocket most of the money for himself. After the attempted shakedown, Granda's name appeared in the story, but Tejeda's did not.

Granda immediately got a panicky call from his NTR colleague Samer Barrage, who had read the story.

"You have to get out of Lima," he told Granda. "You have to leave now."

Granda dropped everything and flew to Miami, only returning later to Perú to clear out his apartment and recover his belongings. He had been in the country three years. In that time, he had helped Elemetal acquire more than $1 billion in Peruvian gold, almost all of it illegally mined.

His plan was to join Barrage at Elemetal's affiliate in Colombia. He applied for a Colombian work visa and laid low in Miami at his mom's house until it was approved in December.

Elemetal's executives knew they had a problem. Granda had essentially been forced to flee Perú. NTR's biggest customer in Chile, Harold Vilches, had been arrested. Another supplier in Ecuador had been criminally charged. The bad publicity was killing Elemetal's reputation in the precious-metals industry. And on top of that they had prosecutor Frank Maderal breathing down their necks. Even over the summer, they had discussed suspending more of their Latin American business. Now, it seemed they had no choice.

On September 16, 2016, Elemetal formally stopped doing business in Perú, Ecuador, Bolivia, and Chile—its most profitable markets—but not Colombia.[2]

At the end of September, the company turned over the three amigos' WhatsApp messages to Maderal. The prosecutor had subpoenaed the chats after Elemetal told the government it had collected them from Granda's and Rodriguez's cell phones in July. But it had taken more than two months for the Jones Day lawyers to make heads or tails of the messages. First off, they were written in Spanish and Jones Day only employed a limited number of Spanish-speaking lawyers. Second, the messages had downloaded into an indecipherable jumble of conversations where it was difficult to tell who had sent a message and who had received it. Finally, many of the benign-sounding messages only became significant when the lawyers compared them to NTR's gold purchases and compliance files.

Maderal had no idea what a mother lode he was getting.

Senior Elemetal executives could now see clearly that their star gold traders were engaged in criminal behavior. Cooperating with Maderal and proving they had no idea what the three amigos were up to was the only way they could avoid criminal charges themselves.

CHAPTER 39

Inside the War Room

THOUSANDS AND THOUSANDS OF DOCUMENTS WERE BEING DELIVERED to Frank Maderal's war room on the seventh floor of the US Attorney's Office in Miami. Internal emails between NTR's three amigos and Elemetal's compliance office. WhatsApp messages, including additional chats from Samer Barrage's cell phone, which had been collected in October. Travel records. Customs forms. It was a treasure trove. Exactly what the feds needed to make their international gold case.

But the records were gathering dust in Maderal's conference room. As far as Tim Schoonmaker could tell, no one was going through them. Homeland Security's Cole Almeida had the Miami end of the case. It was Almeida's job to examine those records. As the agent who opened the case, he was considered the lead investigator, "first among equals." And he'd found some promising nuggets. But there were still thousands and thousands of pages to read.

Schoonmaker was thinking the worst. His own retirement was scheduled for February, just a few months away. Maderal seemed to be working other cases. Schoonmaker worried his own bosses at the DEA would lose interest. He had promised them indictments. Gold smuggling wasn't in the DEA's lane. Without results, what was the point of months of investigation? He couldn't let his last big case wither and die.

Someone needed to call out Almeida and Maderal for not reading through the records yet. Who cared if he pissed them off? He was on his way out the door anyway. Fuck it.

Schoonmaker called Almeida in the fall.

"It's all there," Schoonmaker told him. "There's no reason we shouldn't put it together and we need to put it together now. Why isn't it getting done?"

Schoonmaker said he would even fly up to Miami to help.

"We're working on it, Tim," Almeida snapped back. "What more do you want us to do? I'm the one that brought you this case. I don't need you busting my balls."

∞∞∞∞∞∞

In the US justice system, federal prosecutors charge companies but rarely go after executives at the top. Why? The head honchos at major corporations often insulate themselves by saying they were relying on the company's compliance officer, auditor, or general counsel. Often layers and layers of deniability lie between them and the crime.

After the financial crisis in 2008, dozens of bankers were prosecuted. But none came from the prominent New York investment banks such as Bear Stearns and Lehman Brothers that were once considered "too big to fail." Certainly no major CEOs went down for their role in tanking the US economy.[1]

Brandon L. Garret, an expert in corporate prosecution at the University of Virginia law school and author of the book *Too Big to Jail*, told the *New York Times* that he has talked to prosecutors off the record about why more individuals are not charged at major companies.

"Some say they don't have the resources," Garret said. "It's one thing to settle with a big company and another thing to do serious investigations of dozens of people. Others say these aren't really intentional crimes, or it's difficult to establish intent in individual cases. Others just repeat the party line, which is, 'We target individuals whenever we have the evidence.'"[2]

Like many federal agents, Schoonmaker distrusted the coziness he saw between federal prosecutors and the high-priced criminal defense attorneys who represent big companies and wealthy executives. There was too much overlap between the two. They had all gone to the same schools, clerked for the same judges, and worked at the same firms. Successful prosecutors often jump ship to corporate law firms midway through their careers.

Schoonmaker hoped to gather evidence against the Elemetal executives he believed responsible for NTR's massive purchases of illegally mined gold, but he wondered if fancy Frank Maderal was willing to take them on. "This never stops if we don't put executives in jail, Frank," Schoonmaker said. The agent was still upset Maderal had told Elemetal that the feds were building a case against it.

But Maderal understood just how difficult it was under existing law to hold executives responsible for the actions of their underlings. It was wrong, he thought, to charge people with weak evidence and bring a case destined to result in dismissal or acquittal. That could ruin someone's life.

CHAPTER 40

The Flip

AFTER HIS ARREST FOR MONEY LAUNDERING, HAROLD VILCHES BECAME a national celebrity in Chile.

A well-known TV program, *Contacto*, aired a twenty-five-minute special on the case entitled "The King of Gold." Reporters for the program traveled to Perú's Madre de Dios region to show the rain forest destruction wrought by the illegal gold trade. As the camera panned over miles of deforested patches where the ground and the water had turned orange from contamination, the narrator described the scene as "apocalyptic." "It looks as if a bomb has made everything disappear," he said.[1]

Contacto also unearthed old videos of a young Vilches strumming his guitar and interviewed his uncle Enrique, the founder of a successful chain of jewelry stores, who said he had nothing to do with his nephew's business ventures. The TV reporters even tracked down the mother of one of the Argentine smugglers and interviewed her through a crack in her front door.

Federal police had hoped to arrest the Argentine smugglers the next time they crossed the border, but after the *Contacto* report aired, they did not return to Chile.[2]

Following Vilches's arrest, the FBI got back in touch with Chilean prosecutors. The collaboration had stalled when prosecutor Emiliano Arias left the case and Vilches stopped exporting gold.[3] Vilches's arrest made the case against NTR and its three gold dealers a lot stronger, and the FBI wanted to turn the young exporter into a confidential informant.

Tufit Bufadel, the prosecutor who took over the case, had been disturbed by the images of environmental destruction in the *Contacto* report. He understood that using Vilches to take down NTR and its traders was the only way to stop the pipeline of illegal gold flowing through Chile to Miami. If Chilean prosecutors threw Vilches into jail without helping the FBI build their case, he thought, NTR would quickly replace Vilches with another exporter. Bufadel thought of it like an illness. If prosecutors attacked the fever and not the virus, the fever would return. NTR was the virus. He agreed to help US investigators.[4]

Meanwhile, Vilches was miserably adapting to jail. He'd spent the first few nights crammed into a filthy cell with six other people. His cellmates included a Russian who said he had been arrested for trafficking women. Vilches tried his best to stay away from the man, but the cell was so small that he woke up in the middle of the night to find his foot touching the Russian's head. The young Chilean slept fitfully, his stomach in knots and growling with hunger. The food, delivered on trays without any utensils, was practically inedible.[5]

During the day, the prisoners were allowed to walk around the jail yard. The most common question they asked one another was why they had landed in jail. Vilches lied and said he had been arrested for check fraud. He didn't want to draw attention to himself by saying he traded gold. But the Russian appeared to have no qualms about revealing why he was there, seemingly oblivious to the fact that the other prisoners didn't look kindly on those who had harmed women or children.

One day, a group of inmates attacked the Russian. They cornered him in the jail yard and punched him until he fell to the ground. Then they began kicking his head. Vilches, who was nearby, could hear the loud, liquid thuds of the blows to the Russian's skull.

The guards ran over and yelled at the prisoners to back away. As they helped the Russian to his feet, he covered his face in his hands. Blood poured between his fingers and splattered onto the ground. He could barely walk.

"Nothing happened here," a jail official told the inmates. "The Russian tripped and fell and he's going to the infirmary."

After seeing what had happened to the Russian, Vilches decided he needed to integrate himself by any means possible. There was a Ping-Pong table in the yard and Vilches started challenging his fellow inmates to matches so they would view him as a friendly guy. After a few days, he was transferred to a special wing where most of the other inmates were accused of financial crimes or involved in cases that had attracted media attention. It was safer than being among the general jail population.

Vilches's cell contained a cement bunk bed covered by thin foam mattresses and dirty blankets crawling with bedbugs. He took the top bunk and his father-in-law took the bottom. The toilet was in the open, and the showerhead, which was nearly on top of the toilet, ejected a torrent of freezing cold water.

The gold smugglers were struggling. Every morning, Vilches had to psych himself into getting out of bed. His father-in-law walked in endless circles around the jail yard and refused to eat. He was furious at Vilches for dragging his daughter into the gold-smuggling scheme.

Vilches worried constantly about his wife, who was awaiting trial in a women's jail. He could only communicate with her through letters his lawyer delivered. Vilches wrote to his wife to reassure her that they would start their lives over as soon as they were freed. Their marriage didn't have to end because of this unfortunate episode. His wife's letters in response were affectionate, but she confided that she felt anxious and alone.

To pass the time, Vilches purchased a small TV from another inmate and watched Chilean national soccer games and boxing matches. He also got his hands on a contraband cell phone and looked at the media coverage of his case.[6]

Initially, Vilches planned to fight the charges. But one of the minor players in his ring decided to talk to prosecutors and was quickly released from jail.[7] After that, prosecutors made Vilches and the rest of his crew wait three weeks before taking their declarations. Those three weeks were the longest of Vilches's life. The wait had exactly the effect prosecutors intended. "I can't stay in here my whole life waiting," Vilches thought. "I can't even stay in here six months, let alone a year." His wife was suffering, his father-in-law was suffering, his crew was suffering. It was too much.[8]

It didn't take long for prosecutors to convince Vilches to cooperate. He faced five years in prison for money laundering and smuggling.[9] He was out the 116 million pesos police had found while searching his bunker plus more than $2 million in gold that customs officials had previously seized. Vilches told his lawyer that if he could negotiate a good deal they would all be willing to talk.[10]

He soon learned that Chilean prosecutors weren't the only ones interested in his cooperation. One day, when Vilches's lawyer came to visit, he shared some unsettling news. In a small room used for attorney–client meetings, Ignacio Pinto Basaure told Vilches that the FBI had contacted him.

"What?" Vilches said. "I don't understand."

Pinto explained that the FBI was investigating NTR and its gold traders in Miami and that it wanted Vilches to share information about his dealings with them. "In reality, they don't want you for anything," Pinto said. "They just want you to talk about your clients." The lawyer warned Vilches that if he didn't cooperate, he might face serious charges and federal prison time in the United States.

"This couldn't get any worse," Vilches thought.[11]

∞∞∞∞∞∞

One morning in October, more than a dozen agents and prosecutors packed into a freezing cold meeting room at the Santiago prison complex where Vilches was being held.[12]

Vilches's wife, father-in-law, and former employee Javier Concha had already spoken with investigators and been released from jail. Vilches had insisted on going last because he wanted to ensure that prosecutors kept their end of the deal.[13] By the time it was Vilches's turn, he had spent two months in pretrial detention.

He was escorted to the meeting room in a yellow vest that said "prisoner." His lawyer was waiting outside. Knowing that Vilches likely hadn't had anything to eat all morning, Pinto gave him a piece of chocolate. Vilches was handcuffed, so Pinto practically had to feed it to him.

"Harold, don't freak out, but there are a lot of people in there," Pinto warned.[14]

Inside the room, Vilches saw four Chilean prosecutors, two customs officials, two federal police agents, two officials from the country's tax agency, and three FBI agents. He sat down at a small table across from one of the prosecutors, who had a laptop open to take notes.

"Harold, tell them everything," Pinto told his client.[15]

It didn't take much prompting to get the young gold exporter talking.

For five hours, Vilches recounted his adventures, starting with the trips to Perú and continuing with his smuggling operations in Argentina, the disastrous foray into the Tanzanian gold market, and the business relationship he'd built with the NTR gold dealers in Miami.[16]

Vilches was an entertaining storyteller; Bufadel, the lead Chilean prosecutor, thought he seemed to relish the attention.[17] As one investigator later told *Bloomberg*, "All you lacked was the popcorn."[18]

But Bufadel was also struck by how much the young exporter, now twenty-three, had changed in the span of a few weeks.[19] Vilches looked like he'd lost twenty pounds and the arrogance that had been on display at the first hearing seemed to have faded. The weight of the legal troubles he faced had finally sunk in.

The three FBI agents, including Refina Willis, couldn't interrogate Vilches because they didn't have jurisdiction in Chile. They occasionally interrupted to consult with their Chilean counterparts, who asked Vilches questions on their behalf. More than anything, they wanted details about Vilches's interactions with NTR and its dealers. (Frank Maderal had planned to fly down, but his flight was delayed.)[20]

Much of what Vilches said confirmed what Chilean investigators had learned from the surveillance and phone taps. But some information, including Vilches's trip to Africa, was news to them.[21]

There was one question Vilches seemed unable to answer. He didn't know with certainty where the gold he bought from the Argentine smugglers had originated. Bufadel was convinced it was Peruvian, but he was never able to prove it.[22]

The next day, Vilches was released from jail. He was confined to his apartment on house arrest, which made him feel claustrophobic, but it was better than being behind bars. At least his apartment building had a swimming pool.[23]

CHAPTER 41

Jumping All the Way

WHATEVER WAS HAPPENING WITH THE PERUVIAN INVESTIGATORS, Tim Schoonmaker knew it would have to wait.

The United States' case against NTR was strong, he realized. It could be stronger still. One more element would put a real bow on the case: A cooperator in Perú. Someone who could put NTR's three amigos, Juan Pablo Granda, Samer Barrage, and Renato Rodriguez, in league with Perú's most infamous alleged gold smuggler and money launderer, Peter Ferrari.

Documents and text messages and emails were good in court. But they were complex and boring. Juries could get lost in them. Defense attorneys could argue they were being cherry-picked. A credible cooperating witness could bring those dull documents to life by giving testimony that wove them into a narrative of unmistakable corruption and malfeasance. That was the gold standard. The FBI had already gotten themselves a prize in Harold Vilches; now it was the DEA's turn.

Schoonmaker and his partner Steve Fischer drew up a list of targets they could flip inside Ferrari's operation. Schoonmaker had been doing this for years. He knew what buttons to press. He learned everything about potential cooperators before contacting them, meticulously planning out how the approach would be made. You didn't want to scare the person off. But you also wanted to make it very clear that if they didn't flip, they would feel the full weight of the United States government.

The DEA agents were confident they could flip the first name on their list: Andrés Tejeda, the customs broker who had collaborated with NTR's three dealers and Ferrari both before and after Peruvian authorities seized his shipment of gold at the Lima airport in late 2013. They had overwhelming evidence to hold over Tejeda's head. The Peruvian police report that had been so hard to obtain revealed exactly how Tejeda set up front companies to disguise Ferrari's role in selling illegal gold to NTR.

Tejeda was the perfect target for recruitment as a cooperator. He was in the middle of Ferrari's entire alleged criminal enterprise. He had the whole picture, with Ferrari at the center of the wheel and all the spokes extending outward. In fact, Tejeda was so central to Ferrari that he had become one of the main targets of the Peruvian investigation. And the Lima-based customs broker was vulnerable: he had a wife and a teenage child. The couple was expecting a baby. Doing prison time would destroy his family. That gave the agents even more leverage.

First, the agents needed to get Tejeda alone in a way that wouldn't make the customs broker suspicious or, worse yet, tip off Ferrari. So they concocted a ruse.

Tejeda traveled frequently for business. He had a visa to the United States. Why not tell him he had a problem with his visa? That way Tejeda would have to come to the US Embassy in Lima, where the DEA's Schoonmaker and Fischer would be waiting. Schoonmaker asked his embassy colleagues to contact Tejeda and tell him that there was an issue with his visa that required him to come to the embassy. That wasn't too out of the ordinary. People had issues with their visas all the time.

When Tejeda showed up for his appointment in November, Peruvian police at the outside gate checked his documents and put him through a metal detector. They took his phone. They patted him down. They asked him why he was there. A visa problem, he said, before being ushered into the compound.

Tejeda approached the embassy down a long, flag-lined walkway. The building was the size of two city blocks—a massive white fortress with tiny windows and surrounded by a ten-foot wall. He walked up to the heavy double doors and pulled them open.

Another metal detector was inside. It was an intimidating gauntlet but nothing out of the ordinary—yet.[1]

Once inside, Tejeda was led to a windowless interview room off the main lobby. This wasn't how visa issues were normally handled.

Schoonmaker and Fischer were waiting inside.

When Tejeda entered, they stood up.

"Tim Schoonmaker, DEA," the agent introduced himself.

"Steve Fischer, DEA."

"*Mierda*," Tejeda thought. Shit.

Schoonmaker was wearing a dark suit, a change from his normal slacks and button-down. Looking casual wasn't an option. "You are here for a visa issue," Schoonmaker said. "But there is a larger issue here, *señor*."

Schoonmaker and Fischer laid out everything they knew about Tejeda's role in Ferrari's alleged racket, rattling off all the fake companies he had set up and all the customs papers he had forged. They had the customs broker cold. He was looking at a minimum sentence of ten years in federal prison. But there was still a way out: cooperating with the DEA.

"This is how you can help yourself and help your family," Schoonmaker told him. "This is how you can help your young child."

The agents acknowledged that they couldn't make any promises to Tejeda about sparing him prison time in exchange for cooperation. That would be up to the prosecutor and federal judge in the United States. But if Tejeda helped, Schoonmaker would put in a good word. A lot of good words.

"In my opinion, you're going to be better off helping us and cooperating with us than you are trying to fight us," Schoonmaker said. "But it's your decision. If you want to walk out right now, that's fine. I'm fine with that. This is your decision."

As much as Schoonmaker might have wanted Tejeda to cooperate, the DEA agent knew what it would mean for the customs broker—and for his family—if he agreed. His life would never be the same.

The door was right there. But Tejeda didn't bolt.

They had him.

Everything Schoonmaker knew about the case led him to believe that NTR's dealers, Granda, Rodriguez, and Barrage, were

criminals. He just needed Tejeda to confirm it all: the false paperwork, the bribes to customs officials, the phony export companies
set up to evade Elemetal's compliance office, the illegally mined
gold. Schoonmaker told the customs broker to tell the truth. "It's
like diving off a cliff," he said. "You just gotta do it. You can't dive
halfway off a cliff. You'll hit the rocks. Don't cooperate halfway.
Don't try to think you can snow us. Don't do it. Walk out instead.
It's all or nothing."

Tejeda jumped. All the way.

Over this and subsequent meetings, he would tell Schoonmaker
and Fischer how he started out in 2013 helping Ferrari export illegally mined gold through a series of phony companies to NTR's
Miami office.[2] When Peruvian customs officials started asking questions about these out-of-nowhere spikes in gold shipments from
companies no one had ever heard of, Tejeda would bribe them or
shut down the suspect firm and create a new company. He met
NTR's three amigos for the first time at Ferrari's birthday party at a
Lima restaurant early in 2013. They hit it off. Over more meetings,
including one at Ferrari's house, they devised the plan that saw hundreds of millions of dollars' worth of illegally mined gold smuggled
from Perú to the United States. When authorities finally cracked
down, Tejeda helped Granda come up with a new scheme: rather
than moving lots of gold through a few companies, they would
spread the shipments among many companies to avoid raising suspicion. Of all the gold shipments Tejeda helped arrange, he said,
maybe $50,000 was legal.

In other words, Tejeda could testify that Granda, Barrage, and
Rodriguez knew they were buying Ferrari's dirty gold, which would
solidify the US money laundering case.

Two or three hours passed as Schoonmaker and Fischer questioned their new confidential informant at the embassy. Now, they
had to turn to the most important subject of all: Tejeda's safety. If
anyone found out the customs broker was cooperating, his life could
be in danger. Schoonmaker gave him a piece of advice: Don't tell
anybody. "Not your family, not your wife, nobody," Schoonmaker
said. "The last thing you want is for the word to get out. It just takes
one slip of the tongue."

The DEA agents gave Tejeda their cell phone numbers.

"If anyone threatens you," Fischer said, "you call us. You don't wait. You call us."

The DEA could move the customs broker and his family away from Lima if it came to that. They could even move him to the United States.

Schoonmaker told Tejeda they would meet again. There was so much more to go over. Now that Tejeda had started cooperating, he belonged to the United States.

CHAPTER 42

Clash of the Titans

OPERATION ARCH STANTON WAS BEING NAILED DOWN.

The American investigators already had a major cooperator in Chilean gold trader Harold Vilches. Now, they had the Peruvian customs broker, Andrés Tejeda, too. The two men—who didn't know each other—told similar stories about their dealings with NTR's three amigos. Even better, some of their claims were backed up in customs data and parent company Elemetal's files, none of which Vilches or Tejeda had seen.

Tejeda's cooperation, however, would lead to an internal conflict among the American investigators that undercut the spirit of their collaboration.

Prosecutor Frank Maderal insisted the new informant be flown to Miami right away. He wasn't necessarily concerned that Peter Ferrari would harm Tejeda. The Peruvian's crew weren't killers. Rather, the prosecutor just wanted the assurance of knowing where Tejeda was. If the customs broker took an unplanned vacation at a time when he was needed to testify—or even worse, decided to stop cooperating and vanish—it could threaten the gold case.

"I need to know he's available," Maderal told the DEA's Tim Schoonmaker on the phone.

Schoonmaker disagreed. It was easier to continue debriefing Tejeda in Perú where he was comfortable. Bringing him and his family to the United States—where they didn't speak the language or know anybody—could seriously unsettle him. It could also inadvertently tip off Ferrari that something was wrong. Why would one of his top lieutenants suddenly move his family to the United States? Moreover, someone would have to babysit Tejeda and help his family as they adjusted to their new home, a time-consuming and expensive responsibility that would eat into the agents' ability to work the case.

"Frank, have you ever done one of these before? You better talk to Refina and Cole about this," Schoonmaker said, referring to the other federal agents on the gold team. "It's not as easy as you think. Moving him needs to be a last resort."

Then it got more heated.

Schoonmaker insisted he had to inform the Peruvians of Tejeda's cooperation. They still had a criminal case open on the customs broker in Perú. Sooner or later, they would find out he was talking to the feds. Keeping them out of the loop could break the trust the DEA was building in Perú. His bosses agreed. But the prosecutor wouldn't budge.

"I'm making a criminal case for the United States government," Maderal said. "Not Perú."

"That's not fair, Frank," Schoonmaker replied. "The DEA, we operate here. We're not here for one case. This isn't about your parochial bullshit. I am looking out for the long-term interests of the DEA and the US government in Perú. If we don't tell them and they find out, all hell is going to break loose."

They were practically screaming.

"If you tell the Peruvians, it's going to leak out," Maderal said. "It's going to leak out and get back to Ferrari and screw the whole case up. You can't switch hats and say, 'Now I'm a diplomat.' You don't have the right to throw a wrench in our case like this."

"You're not my boss, Frank," Schoonmaker yelled back. "You can't tell me what to do."

But at the end of the day it was Maderal's case. Schoonmaker backed down. And Maderal, in turn, agreed to let Tejeda stay in Perú. Still, the argument with Schoonmaker left the prosecutor shaken. Something he had predicted about the DEA agent was, in his eyes at least, coming true.

"Tim's going T. E. Lawrence on me," Maderal thought. "I knew this would happen."

CHAPTER 43

"Does Your Wife Know You Went There?"

IN MID-DECEMBER, HAROLD VILCHES, THE CHILEAN GOLD-SMUGGLER-turned-informant, traveled to Miami—this time without gold bars in his carry-on luggage. He was there to testify before a US grand jury.[1]

In the US legal system, grand juries decide whether a prosecutor has enough evidence to charge someone with a crime. The jury, made up of as many as twenty-three people, listens to testimony and reviews records. It is run exclusively by the prosecutor—no defense attorney is present.

Assistant US Attorney Frank Maderal had summoned Vilches to Miami to testify against NTR's three amigos. If Vilches was convincing, the grand jury would be more likely to indict.

Getting him there had taken some negotiating. The young Chilean was still under house arrest in Santiago and prohibited from leaving the country. Chilean prosecutors had to ask the court to lift Vilches's travel ban. After some back-and-forth, it was decided that Vilches could go to Miami if the Chilean prosecutor Tufit Bufadel and federal police agents went with him.[2]

Vilches had far more experience traveling to the United States than his government-appointed chaperones. He glided through US customs, quickly filling out the entry forms at the self-check-in machines. Once he was in the baggage claim area, Vilches realized that he'd left his lawyer, the prosecutor, and the federal police agents far behind. "Some security," Vilches thought as he sat down on his suitcase to wait.[3]

Lourdes McLoughlin, the FBI legal attaché, picked up the Chileans from the airport and took them to a hotel near the bureau's regional headquarters in Miramar, a city north of Miami.

The Chilean federal agents struck Vilches as very serious. They kept their uniforms on at all times, even inside the hotel. Bufadel, the prosecutor, was different. On the first morning in Florida, Vilches went downstairs to the breakfast buffet and saw the prosecutor sitting at a table by himself. Vilches sat down next to him.[4] They started chatting and developed a friendly rapport.[5]

In the days leading up to the grand jury, Vilches met with Maderal every day to go over his testimony. The Chilean officials also had meetings with US investigators, but they mostly waited around for Vilches to testify.

To pass the time, some of the Chileans went to malls. It was right before Christmas and they wanted to buy gifts for their families. Vilches offered to request their rides; he knew how to get around Miami and already had the Uber app downloaded on his phone. In the evenings, they went out to eat before returning to the hotel. Vilches watched Netflix until he fell asleep.[6]

Bufadel interpreted Vilches's eagerness to share rides as concern that he could be locked up in Miami if he wasn't in the company of a Chilean official—although Bufadel wouldn't have been able to help since he had no authority on US soil.[7]

When Vilches wanted to go out to eat or leave the hotel for any reason, he would send the prosecutor a message asking if he'd come. "I'll get the Uber," Vilches would offer. And when Bufadel left the hotel without him, the young Chilean seemed to wait anxiously for his return. Bufadel, amused, thought the mastermind behind a massive gold-smuggling operation now seemed more like a lost puppy glued to the hotel window until his master came home.[8]

Vilches had a harder time getting along with the FBI agents. McLoughlin and Refina Willis seemed to alternate between treating him brusquely and kindly. At one point, when Vilches recounted his visit to a Santiago strip club with the NTR dealers, Willis seemed offended. "Does your wife know you went there?" she asked.[9]

On the last day of the trip, Vilches finally got down to the business at hand. The newly minted government informant testified under oath before a grand jury at the federal courthouse in downtown Miami. He gave a condensed version of the story he'd recounted numerous times to investigators. As he spoke, the women in the grand jury seemed to look at him sympathetically, as if he could have been a son or a nephew who had gotten in over his head.[10]

The Chilean investigators weren't allowed to watch the grand jury proceedings, so after checking out of the hotel they went to Fort Lauderdale with McLoughlin, the FBI legal attaché, to get something to eat. McLoughlin parked the car in a lot near the beach.[11]

When they returned after lunch, one of the car windows had been smashed open. All of Bufadel's belongings, including the gifts he'd bought for his family, were gone. Bufadel returned to Chile with only the clothes on his back.[12]

The trip was also a strange experience for Juan Pablo Sandoval, the Chilean federal agent who had spent a year listening to Vilches's phone calls, but little time with him face-to-face. Vilches didn't seem to understand the extent of the Chilean police involvement in the case and treated the agents with scorn. He appeared to be under the impression that the investigation had originated in the United States.[13]

Sandoval finally got a chance to set the record straight on the plane ride home. After takeoff, he walked over to Vilches and sat down next to him.

"Harold, if you hadn't done so many exports in one month, you would have gone unnoticed," Sandoval told him. "What caught my attention was that your company from one moment to the next started doing seven or eight exports a month."

"I know," Vilches conceded. "I screwed up."[14]

As they spoke, the young man started to soften. He confessed that he felt guilty for having involved his wife and father-in-law in the scheme. They were both devout Christians and had been deeply shaken by the arrests.[15]

The Chileans arrived in Santiago the next morning after an overnight flight. As Vilches stepped off the plane, he felt exhausted but at peace.[16] The last few months had been harrowing, but he was only twenty-three. He had his whole life ahead of him.

CHAPTER 44

Schoonmaker's Last Gambit

THE PERUVIAN AUTHORITIES STILL WEREN'T MOVING AGAINST PETER Ferrari, the man they thought was the country's Pied Piper of gold smugglers.

Tim Schoonmaker couldn't believe it. Ferrari was out on the town, visiting restaurants and nightclubs. His gated compound was just a few miles from the US Embassy. Occasionally, Schoonmaker would see Ferrari at the gym down the street from the embassy, where the bronzed Peruvian tended to avoid lifting weights in favor of tanning beds and the sauna.

In late December, Schoonmaker scheduled a meeting with Peruvian prosecutor Lizardo Pantoja and Pantoja's supervisor. It was the DEA agent's last chance at a power play, only days before the deadline for charging Ferrari would expire. Schoonmaker told the Peruvians that the United States was now preparing its own indictments in the gold case. They would be handed down soon. "How is it going to look if we indict all these Peruvians for illegal gold mining and money laundering in Perú, and you guys don't do anything?" Schoonmaker asked. "Our cases should run concurrently. You guys will look like superstars." If Peruvian authorities failed to charge Ferrari, he added, it wouldn't just look like they lacked the stomach to take him down; worse, it might appear that Ferrari had paid them off.

The DEA had received reliable information, Schoonmaker claimed, that there was corruption among the Peruvian investigators. If Perú's case against Ferrari was allowed to expire, the United States could only conclude it had been stymied by corruption. Schoonmaker told the prosecutors he was telling them all this because he trusted them and knew they would help. What he was really doing was silently pointing the finger at Pantoja. No more games. "When the US indicts, everyone is going to look at your case and see all the evidence you had and they're going to start asking why you didn't do anything," he said. "I'm telling you the [Peruvian] attorney general is interested. The money-laundering directorate is interested. The media is interested. It's going to be high profile."

Pantoja turned white.

CHAPTER 45

La Venganza

PEDRO DAVID PÉREZ MIRANDA, AKA PETER FERRARI, RANG IN THE NEW YEAR of 2017 breathing easy.

He knew that the airport raid on his gold shipment in late 2013 had sparked a police investigation and that his employees and associates had been hauled in for questioning, but that was three years ago and nothing had come of it. Ferrari had always maintained his innocence, so he figured the authorities must have come to the same conclusion and let the matter drop.[1]

Even so, he was taking precautions. All the companies that the police said had been set up in the names of family members and associates as cover were no longer in business. Ferrari claimed he'd quit selling gold altogether, too spooked by the raid. Police believed he was playing possum. He may have quit exporting gold directly from Perú but instead was smuggling it overland to Bolivia and Ecuador and exporting it from there, they claimed.

It was just after two a.m. on January 3, 2017, days after Tim Schoonmaker played his ace on Lizardo Pantoja, the prosecutor, when police finally swung into action against Ferrari's sprawling gold empire, swooping in on eleven different properties simultaneously—offices, warehouses, apartments, homes. Among the targets was Ferrari's residence in the exclusive La Planicie section of Las Molinas in Perú's capital. A wealthy enclave built around a golf course, it was a neighborhood of walled-off residences that were equal part bunker and home—the type of place where those with status and wealth could isolate themselves from the grinding poverty and crime of the capital.

As news cameras rolled, more than thirty police officers, investigators, and detectives surrounded the compound, laden with flak jackets and brandishing automatic weapons. Pouring over the wall on a ladder, the police were prepared to find Ferrari—the dangerous don with ties to drug cartels and a small army of security.

What they encountered instead was Pérez Miranda, the family man. After they barged past a life-sized Santa Claus mannequin stationed by the front door, authorities would report they found the playboy and his girlfriend lounging in the kidney-shaped swimming pool. Also at the house were several of Ferrari's grown children and a score of his grandchildren.[2] His daughter, Jacqueline, was so startled by the raid—believing her family was the victim of a home invasion—that she jumped from a second floor balcony into a courtyard and sprained her ankle. Local television would say she, or Ferrari's girlfriend, was trying to escape from authorities by crawling across the roof to another house.[3]

Lizardo Pantoja didn't let Schoonmaker know the bust was coming. But the DEA agent had been tipped off. The Peruvian police needed manpower for all the raids and someone in the prosecutor's office asked Schoonmaker's special intelligence unit for extra bodies.

After the cops went in, Schoonmaker called one of his unit's junior members who had been sent to Ferrari's house. Would Pantoja let Schoonmaker come observe? When the question was passed to the prosecutor, who was standing nearby, Schoonmaker could hear his answer.

"That asshole?" Pantoja said bitterly in Spanish. "No."

The raid on Ferrari's house was bizarre. For one, Pantoja allowed Ferrari to keep his cell phone. As police searched the property, Ferrari stalked the premises wearing a tight black T-shirt and making frantic phone calls. According to observers, the Peruvian cops also failed to search one of Ferrari's cars—even though they searched others parked next to it—and left one upstairs bedroom untouched while rummaging through the rest of the house.[4] That was basic policing 101, Schoonmaker thought when he was briefed later. A major failure.

Among the items seized from Ferrari's compound were cars (but no Ferraris), rifles, and flak jackets. To the TV crews, the small arsenal meant the gold dealer was ready to go to war. But the shotguns and protective gear were simply the tools of the trade, Ferrari argued, the sort of items anyone would have who handles millions in gold and cash. The raid of the compound and questioning of the guests lasted more than sixteen hours, well into the next evening. When it was over, Ferrari was escorted by five police cruisers to the central station in downtown Lima as if they had a high-profile escape risk on their hands.

Of all the evidence collected during the raid, there was one item that fired the imagination of the press. In one of the rooms, Ferrari had a framed poster of *Scarface*, the 1983 Brian de Palma movie about a Cuban immigrant in South Florida who becomes a ruthless drug lord.

Carlos Neira, a longtime investigative reporter with *El Comercio*, had followed the gold magnate's case for years. He, like others, was convinced that Ferrari was up to no good, but he was also uncomfortable with how the police seemed to be trying to smear the controversial businessman in the press before the case went to court. Police reports played up the gold merchant's enviable lifestyle and over-the-top personality to paint a picture. The guns, the women, the pool, the wealth, the cars. It all looked bad, but none of it was incontrovertible proof that he was a criminal. "So he had a Tony Montana poster on the wall," Neira said. "The police and the media made a big deal about that. But that doesn't make him guilty of anything."[5]

Neira suspected there might be people in the police department who were still bitter that Ferrari had escaped drug charges two decades earlier. Charges, they must have felt, that should have led to his conviction.

"Was this revenge for Ferrari's crimes in the 1990s?" the reporter wondered.

∞∞∞∞∞∞∞∞

Fourteen days later, on January 17, Ferrari, his nephew, Miguel Ángel Rivero Pérez, and his business partner and bodyguard, Alfredo

Néstor Egocheaga Rosas, also known as "Cookie," sat shoulder to shoulder during an excruciating day in court.[6]

Peruvian prosecutors were asking the judge to put them behind bars for eighteen months to let the investigation proceed. If Ferrari and his crew were trying to project the image of workaday businessmen, they missed the mark. The gold magnate was wearing a gray blazer over a white shirt with a pocket square. His hair was slicked back. Miguel Ángel Rivero was wearing a white tuxedo jacket with a black shirt. They looked like extras from *Scarface*, or like they were ready to go clubbing.

And during the first few hours of the hearing, they very likely thought the day would end over celebratory drinks.

Lizardo Pantoja, the prosecutor who had drawn so much scorn from Schoonmaker, appeared to make a mess of his presentation. Despite having led a three-year investigation into the trio of men, it often seemed like he was dealing with the case for the first time. During a disjointed and rambling two-and-a-half-hour exposition, he mumbled and stuttered his way through a pile of documents. He spent much of his time in silence, frantically rifling through the papers. And he wasted more valuable time reading through a ridiculously long list of bank checks that Ferrari's companies had received from NTR Metals, Republic, and other US gold buyers—payments that no one was disputing. Judge Richard Concepción Carhuancho repeatedly interrupted him to try to get him back on track and had to caution the defense team from laughing at him.

At one point, Pantoja accused Ferrari of having a slew of prior convictions—including fraud and failure to pay child support—that simply weren't true. Whether he had misread a document or intentionally tried to slip something into the record never became clear. (Pantoja and his team refused multiple interview and information requests over the course of two years.)

The three men were being accused of organized crime, money laundering, and illegal mining—allegations they all denied. But the entire case rested on the illegal mining charges. If there was no dirty gold, there was no dirty money, and therefore no money laundering. And without illegal mining, the crime ring that police were describing, with Ferrari as the capo, was simply a sprawling family business.

But making the illegal mining connection wasn't easy. After all, Ferrari wasn't actually operating illegal mines, and he claimed that he rarely traveled to mining regions.

What Pantoja did have was damning documentary evidence. To prosecutors, it was clear that Ferrari and his nephew had lied about their gold suppliers, ginning up fake companies and fake receipts to create a paper trail. And the one paper trail that seemed legitimate was also problematic. Ferrari had cut eleven checks worth more than $3.7 million to Rodolfo Soria, a man the government was investigating for allegedly laundering money from illegal mining. (Soria was the Peruvian exporter from whom both NTR and Chilean Harold Vilches had once bought gold.) Finally, Pantoja said lab reports of the seized gold indicated it was similar in purity and composition to the metal coming out of the illegal mines in Madre de Dios.

For Ferrari's defense team, the government's evidence was flimsy. Despite the yearslong investigation, Pantoja didn't have a single witness or informant who claimed they had seen Ferrari or his crew knowingly buy illegal gold. In addition, prosecutors had neglected to set up a sting—send in an undercover cop to offer him illicit metal.

"Why would you ask for pretrial detention if during three years you never did an investigation?" Ferrari's lawyer asked. The nephew's lawyer was even more blunt: "You're asking to put them behind bars to justify the fact that you didn't do your job over the course of three years."[7]

It was also clear, however, that Ferrari and his crew had extremely bad timing. Perú had only made illegal mining a criminal offense in February 2012. If the case had started several months earlier, they might all be facing a slap on the wrist. Now—with the illegal mining and aggravated money laundering charges—they were looking at twenty-year sentences.

Given a chance to speak, the gold magnate described himself as a victim of changing social norms. "Ever since I was fifteen, for more than forty years, I've been buying and selling gold," he told the judge. "I've perfected my knowledge of the business, the way we all do it, which is informally. Perú is full of informal mining."

"I don't buy gold outside of my establishment [in Lima], the clients I have I've made over time. They come to me with their gold and I buy it," he continued. "I always assumed it was legal gold, maybe it was informal, but always legal."

While the government talked of the hundreds of millions of dollars that passed through his bank accounts, Ferrari argued the money wasn't truly his. Rather, it belonged to the gold buyers and the gold vendors. He was just a middleman who took a small commission "like everyone does."

Carhuancho, the judge, wasn't moved. After reviewing the evidence against Ferrari in his office, he returned at 8:51 p.m. to deliver his ruling. But rather than a short statement, he launched into an elucidation of the evidence that lasted almost four more hours. He made the case much more convincingly than Pantoja. As one courtroom observer said, "The only real prosecutor in the courtroom was the judge."[8]

Carhuancho said it was painfully clear to him that Ferrari and his crew had repeatedly lied to investigators about the origins of their gold and tried to hide its true source behind dummy companies. And his association with Soria, the alleged money launderer, also raised serious questions. The only logical conclusion, he said, was that the gold was being illegally mined. Ferrari knew it, and he was trying to cover his tracks. "This is the very definition of money laundering—trying to hide the presumed illicit source—which in this case is illegal mining," the judge said.

Authorities focused on four of Ferrari's companies to make their case. All of them followed the same pattern: they appeared out of nowhere, exported hundreds of millions of dollars' worth of gold, and then disappeared.[9]

Business Investments, the only company in which Ferrari was officially listed as the general manager, operated from April to October of 2012, exporting 3,412 kilos of gold worth $174 million—almost all of it to Republic Metals in Miami. Business Investment's active life span was just seven months, but it appeared to be the longest-lived company in Ferrari's stable of businesses.

Less than two weeks after Business Investments ceased activities, La Mano de Dios (Hand of God)—the company that originally won the contract with NTR Metals—sprang to life, exporting

2,153 kilos of gold worth $108 million. It operated for less than three months.

Eight days after it was shelved, Minerales Gold began operations, exporting $135 million worth of gold before it was sidelined. "We have been able to prove that all [these businesses] were created under the names of cutouts and or straw men," police investigators explained in a report, "but all of them were under the direction and guidance of their leader Pedro David Pérez Miranda [aka Peter Ferrari]."[10]

Shortly before one a.m., Carhuancho, the judge, ordered Ferrari and his two associates to spend the next year and a half in jail pending investigation. Then the weary judge rang a bell ending the proceeding.

Ferrari and his associates sat stone-faced—stunned by the turn of events and worn down by the marathon hearing. As they were escorted out of the courtroom, their families sobbed.

CHAPTER 46

Kings of the World

DESPITE THEIR TESTY RELATIONSHIP, FEDERAL PROSECUTOR FRANK MADERAL and DEA agent Tim Schoonmaker still had to work together. But not for much longer.

Schoonmaker was set to retire on February 30, 2017.

But he had no desire to end his career just yet. There was much more to do on the gold-smuggling case, including going through the complete stack of Elemetal files and WhatsApp messages the company had handed over to the investigators.

His mandatory retirement date could not be more inconvenient. As soon as his tenure at the DEA ended, he and his wife would lose their government housing in Lima and their government-issued cars. He would lose his diplomatic visa and have to apply for a new one. His son wasn't set to graduate high school in Lima until June 30, 2017. They didn't want to make their boy move in the middle of his senior year. Schoonmaker had already tried to get an "age waiver" a few months back that would allow him to stay until the end of June. Maderal had even written a letter saying how important the gold case was and how crucial Schoonmaker was to finishing it off. It didn't matter. The DEA denied his request to stay on.

The other agents stopped him in the halls of the US Embassy.

"That's bullcrap, Tim," they'd say.

As Schoonmaker tried to make arrangements for a new apartment and visa, the twenty-six-year veteran lost it. He wasn't coasting to retirement. Far from it. He was working a major case until his last day on the job. The top DEA commanders were always talking

248

about how the agency was a family. Now it was clear to him that they were not family. Not when it mattered. Knowing he had no bridges left to burn, Schoonmaker fired off an email to the agency's chief of operations in Washington, DC. In it he said the DEA had a duty to look after its long-term employees. All he had asked for was four more months. Four more months to get his son through high school. And they said no.

"It's too late to do anything for me," Schoonmaker told his bosses. "So this isn't something I'm asking for myself. The decision has been made, I've already made arrangements for my family. I have less than six weeks until I'm out of here. So I'm not asking for myself. What I'm asking for is for people who come after me. How about doing better for them than you did for me? How about showing them more respect and consideration than you did for me? And more than for me, for my wife. Because it's been my wife for 26 years who's borne the burden of my job. And she's done it faithfully. She's been a faithful support to me through thick and thin. She's been the one who's had to endure threats to her husband and her family, of her kids getting blown up, and long nights waiting for her husband to come home. If not for me, how about doing it for her, or for the next wife?"

The next day the DEA's regional director in Lima called Schoonmaker into his office.

"Oh fuck," he thought.

"Tim, put in for an extension," the director said. "Don't say anything about your family. Talk about the gold case. But put in for an extension."

The DEA finally did the right thing and granted him a four-month extension. His retirement date was being pushed back to June 30. That gave his son time to graduate from high school. And it gave Schoonmaker time to help nail NTR's three amigos.

He would be there when they got indicted, he swore.

∞∞∞∞∞∞

Though Peter Ferrari had been arrested in Perú, no one was getting indicted in the United States until the American investigators went through each and every page of the subpoenaed Elemetal materials. There were tens of thousands of pages.

Maderal had done some digging and found a few goodies, including Juan Pablo Granda's reference to himself as Pablo Escobar. They all knew that would be catnip for a jury and the media. There was still more to be done. The information was scattered. Someone had to go through and organize it, pull out the most damning material that could be used against the three amigos, who it was clear could now be charged criminally.

It was hard work. Homeland Security special agent Cole Almeida was stretched thin. Maderal seemed busy on other cases, working not just complex investigations into Venezuelan kleptocrats raiding the national oil company but also targeting drugs being sold on the dark web by a Frenchman nicknamed Oxymonster who competed in international beard-growing competitions.[1]

Even when Schoonmaker threatened to take his end of the case to another prosecutor in New York, no one seemed willing to dive into the records. Schoonmaker didn't care anymore about the pecking order or which agent was "first among equals." Someone had to take the time to read the documents. (Steve Fischer, his partner at the DEA in Lima, had dropped the case, worn out by his colleague's all-consuming intensity.)

This was Schoonmaker's last shot. Early in 2017, Schoonmaker flew up to Miami. When he got to the US Attorney's Office, he asked the assistants two questions: Who came in first? And who left last? He would enter the office with the early birds and leave with the night owls. If Schoonmaker wanted to go through everything, he would need as much time as possible. The DEA agent wanted to build the material into a timeline of malfeasance for Maderal. "This case is going to be so self-evident that you're going to have to charge," he told the prosecutor.

For the next six days, he shut himself in Maderal's windowless war room on the seventh floor. The documents, obtained through a grand jury, were confidential. So he had to sit there, day after day, reading them on a secure computer. He read and read and read. When he found a nugget, he would copy and paste it into a Word document. The records—especially the WhatsApp messages between the three amigos—were loaded with incriminating evidence. Thinking their communications were encrypted and secure, and would never be turned over to the feds by their bosses, the NTR traders had talked openly about smuggling gold.

"We need more Peruvian gold from Bolivia and Ecuador," Samer Barrage wrote in one exchange. "Can u make it happen?"[2]

They talked about hiding gold and forging paperwork to make it look legitimate.

"It's all under the table, no docs," Granda texted.

Back and forth, they swapped pictures of couriers and shrink-wrapped packages of gold bars.

The three amigos were so cocky, Schoonmaker thought—they acted like kings of the world. With each discovery, he stuck his head out into the hall. Maderal's office was just on the other side.

"Frank, you won't believe this, get in here!" Schoonmaker shouted.

Maderal came scurrying across.

"Holy shit, this is great."

By sheer force of how much time they were spending together working the same case, Maderal and the agents began to bond. The rough-and-tumble agents made fun of Maderal when they ordered pizza and the lean prosecutor peeled the cheese off his slices and left the crust. They laughed when a parade of Amazon delivery people traipsed into Maderal's office carrying mountaineering gear for his upcoming ascent of Mount Rainier.

By the time Schoonmaker was finished working on the timeline, he had combined the WhatsApp messages with the bounty of information the dirty gold team had gathered from NTR's due diligence files, the customs records, and internal emails. It showed exactly which gold deals the three amigos were talking about when they exchanged their messages: Who they were buying from, how much, and at what price, along with all the devious ways in which they had disguised the metal's real source. The document was a clear and detailed rendering of a criminal conspiracy. To the DEA agent, it was clear as day: NTR's three gold dealers knew what they were doing was illegal. Their own words clearly showed they were plotting to buy smuggled and illegally mined gold around South America and ship it to the United States. It was more than enough to charge them with a money laundering conspiracy that supported Peter Ferrari's illegal mining.

"Dude, this is so slam dunk," the DEA agent said. "We've got them. It's really a slam dunk."

∞∞∞∞∞∞

The gold case was working up the chain of NTR Metals.

FBI special agent Refina Willis, assisted by the Chilean authorities, had flipped Vilches. Schoonmaker, despite resistance from a hostile Peruvian prosecutor, had flipped Tejeda. Now, they had to corral the three amigos.

Renato Rodriguez was lowest on the NTR totem pole. He had been hired before Granda, but Granda, the young financial whiz, had outshone him with the incredible volume of gold he procured from Perú. And unlike Granda, Rodriguez had a family. The feds could use that as leverage to flip him against his boss, Barrage. Maybe even against the Elemetal executives.

Schoonmaker had put out an alert on Rodriguez's travel. The next time the NTR trader flew out of Miami for a business trip, the DEA in Lima would be notified. Schoonmaker wanted to meet him at the Miami airport when he returned.

In January, his email dinged. Rodriguez was flying back to Miami. Schoonmaker got himself a flight and called Maderal. Time to flip Rodriguez. Just like he had with Tejeda, Schoonmaker carefully planned out the approach. Rodriguez would get off the plane and head for US Customs. Then he would be selected for enhanced screening and taken to a back room, where Schoonmaker would be waiting.

He would tell Rodriguez about the trove of evidence that US authorities had collected on his illegal activity. He would ask him to cooperate and wear a wire. It was either that or prison. Even if Rodriguez said no and walked, the pressure of knowing he was under investigation would be tremendous. Schoonmaker had seen other targets drive themselves crazy after declining an approach to cooperate. They would convince themselves they were being tapped and surveilled, even if no one was watching them. They were always waiting for the door to fly open and the handcuffs to go on. Sometimes, they couldn't take it anymore and came back begging to be wired up.

But then Almeida, the Homeland Security agent, called. He wanted to do the flip. It was his turn.

Schoonmaker groaned.

"I know I can flip him, Cole," Schoonmaker said. "I know I can do it. Can you do it? If you think you can, go ahead. But if you don't, it's on you."

"I got this, Tim," Almeida replied. "This one's mine."

Instead of going to the Lima airport, Schoonmaker went home.

∞∞∞∞∞∞

Around eight p.m. on a warm South Florida evening in early February, Cole Almeida and Refina Willis knocked on Renato Rodriguez's door at his home in Miami-Dade's far western reaches, just shy of the line that prohibits urban development into the Everglades. The agents didn't have a warrant. It was a "knock and talk." Rodriguez's wife and twin daughters were home.

The gold dealer knew NTR was under investigation. But having two federal agents on his doorstep with his family at home spooked him. By design, Almeida and Willis didn't push him too hard. They didn't want to scare him off. They asked a few general questions about his work trading gold for NTR, as well as his interactions with the Chilean dealer Harold Vilches. Rodriguez was cautious, but he didn't ask for a lawyer. Almeida and Willis left within an hour.

Maybe the agents had created an opening.

Rodriguez immediately called Elemetal's lawyer Chris Pace at Jones Day. The trader could not seem to grasp that Pace was not his attorney—and he did not realize the company now considered him a criminal suspect whom it would be only too happy to throw to the government.

"Renato, I am not your lawyer and I cannot advise you," Pace said. "I am representing the company."

"But what would you do if you were my lawyer, hypothetically?" Rodriguez asked plaintively.

"I can't give you advice as the company's lawyer," Pace replied, "because I might give you advice that is in the company's best interest, not yours."

The visit also alarmed Rodriguez's colleagues, who discussed it over lunch soon after in Cali, Colombia.

"Renato needs to get a lawyer," Granda told Barrage. "You have to tell him to get a lawyer."

Two weeks later, Almeida called Rodriguez again. He needed to come to the US Attorney's Office in downtown Miami. Time to go for the flip. Willis was there too. Almeida painted a bleak picture. Rodriguez's life was about to be destroyed by a federal prosecution—unless he agreed to cooperate against Barrage and Granda.

"You're on the *Titanic* and I'm throwing you a life vest," Almeida told Rodriguez.

It was a line he had practiced before the interview.

"Don't be an idiot. I'm warning you. This is your opportunity."

But Rodriguez was loyal. He was godfather to Barrage's daughter. There was no way he would betray him.

"I didn't do anything wrong," he kept saying.

Then Maderal walked into the room. But Rodriguez wouldn't budge.

"I just want to let you know the next time I see you will be in court after you're arrested," Maderal said.

Rodriguez went home.

∞∞∞∞∞∞

Operation Arch Stanton was approaching go-day.

After months of painstakingly building his landmark gold case, Maderal now faced a formidable challenge: taking the seemingly endless threads of evidence his team had collected since September 2015 and weaving them into a case strong enough to charge NTR's three amigos in federal court.

Prosecutors can file criminal charges through two kinds of legal instruments: indictments and complaints. Most prosecutors don't want to show defendants their hand before a trial. So they choose to charge through bare-bones indictments written in legalese. But Maderal was convinced the smarter approach in this case was to draft a criminal complaint. Complaints require supporting documents called affidavits that explain the evidence underlying the charges. Maderal planned to attach a richly detailed narrative-style affidavit to his complaint. He wanted to lay out a vivid portrait of illegal mining, gold smuggling, and money laundering across two continents, one that captured the widespread environmental damage to the Amazon rain forest and the powerful role of drug traffickers in the illicit multi-billion-dollar industry. His goal was to show a judge that the impact of the three amigos' money laundering activities went far beyond dirty gold and dirty cash. And he thought the tale might interest the American news media, which had done precious little big-picture reporting on Miami's robust gold trade.

The crafting of the complaint and affidavit with case agents took several weeks, mainly because of the prosecutor's insistence on sending a powerful message. "Why does it matter?" Maderal would say to Almeida and Willis. "We need to show why it matters." What they came up with in the war room read something like a thirty-page term paper, but it made Maderal's point.[3]

"Illegal mining is responsible for the devastation of large swaths of rainforest," the affidavit stated. "In Peru, illegal mining is supported by human trafficking, forced adult and child labor, and prostitution in and around mining camps. Areas in which illegal miners burn down the rainforest and strip away the surface of the earth remain barren because of contamination from chemicals such as mercury."

○○○○○○○○○

In Jackson, Ohio, few people outside the executive ranks of Elemetal's refinery seemed to have any idea about the federal investigation in Miami. But all was not well.

Elemetal's decision to shut down its Latin American gold business in late 2016 was a colossal blow to the refinery's business. With so much less gold coming in, its workforce was slashed from more than two hundred to as few as fifty. Things may have been going downhill anyway. As the economy began to recover in 2012 and investor panic subsided, gold prices sank precipitously and the domestic market dried up, too. The decline started almost at the exact moment Elemetal acquired Ohio Precious Metals as part of its grand expansion. From April 2012, when the merger went through, to early 2017, gold's value declined roughly 20 percent.

On February 3, 2017, with seemingly little idea of the gathering storm around Elemetal, Ohio governor John Kasich made a telephone call to Alan Stockmeister, the former owner of the Jackson refinery. He was now chairman of Dallas-based Elemetal, as well as a top donor to both the Ohio GOP and Kasich's failed presidential bid for the 2016 Republican presidential primary.[4]

Kasich told Stockmeister he was being appointed to the board of the Ohio State University, the largest in the state.

"I feel privileged, humbled and thrilled," Stockmeister remarked to the *Jackson County Times-Journal*.[5]

∞∞∞∞∞∞∞

With its multi-billion-dollar business in Latin America shut down, Elemetal was desperate to salvage whatever it could from NTR Metals in Miami.

In the early spring, Samer Barrage and Elemetal CEO Bill LeRoy went to the downtown Miami offices of their rival Kaloti Metals & Logistics, the company that exported South American gold to Dubai and that NTR had suspected of trying to buy a portion of its metal shipment that had been stolen by Peter Ferrari.

Their offer: Selling Elemetal's and Barrage's joint Colombian gold operation "as is" to Kaloti, which would be allowed to vet each account.

The incentive for the sale's pitch: Privately, LeRoy suspected his three gold dealers at NTR—including Barrage—would soon be indicted for their corrupt dealings in South America. Kaloti's owner politely turned them down. He wanted no part of what even to outsiders was clearly a crisis about to explode.

"You Have Nothing to Worry About"

ON MARCH 9, 2017, DAYS BEFORE FEDERAL AGENTS WERE SET TO ARREST Juan Pablo Granda, Renato Rodriguez, and Samer Barrage, the news outlet *Bloomberg* published a big scoop.[1]

The lengthy magazine-style narrative was a yarn about a young Chilean gold smuggler named Harold Vilches who crisscrossed South America hunting for dirty gold to export to NTR Metals and others. But he'd gotten caught and now Vilches was cooperating not only with Chilean authorities but also with the FBI, *Bloomberg* reported.

At one point, more than a dozen law enforcement officials had crowded into a room to hear him being interviewed. Vilches loved the audience. "[He] fed off the attention," *Bloomberg* reported, citing anonymous officials. "He laughed and seemed to shrug off the seriousness of his situation. His confessions took on the air of a performance."

Vilches knew everything about NTR's three amigos and their gold-smuggling scheme. According to the story, he had testified before a federal grand jury in Miami in December. The piece mentioned Rodriguez and Barrage by name, detailing their first meeting with Vilches in Coral Gables. It quoted them denying everything Vilches had said.

The story was delivered into Frank Maderal's email inbox the day it was published. "Did you see this?" the perturbed prosecutor asked Homeland Security agent Cole Almeida.

Tufit Bufadel, the Chilean prosecutor, their colleague and collaborator, was quoted by name. Had he and his colleagues really leaked to *Bloomberg*—one of the largest business news media outlets in the world—not caring that it might endanger the US case? Maderal was worried sick, not about Barrage and Rodriguez, who had families tying them to the United States, but about Granda. He was young and single. He had relatives in Ecuador, and a passport from that country. Was he going to flee Miami before the feds could arrest him?

Maderal and the agents had to hustle out a criminal complaint with an arrest affidavit so it could be signed by a magistrate judge before Granda could run off to Ecuador. The young prosecutor didn't even show the paperwork to his narcotics supervisor, Dick Getchell, for final approval before presenting it to a judge. If the case fell apart, it was all on him.

⚬⚬⚬⚬⚬⚬⚬⚬⚬

Granda and his family say he never intended to flee the country.

But there is no doubt the three amigos knew they were up against it now.

"In exchange for his release from jail, Vilches provided extensive testimony that has allowed Chilean prosecutors and the US Department of Justice to try to build a huge, multinational gold smuggling case," the March 9 *Bloomberg* story said.

After *Bloomberg* published, Elemetal CEO Bill LeRoy told the NTR trio to meet him in Miami.

First, the three amigos had to get their stories straight. They met at Blue Martini, a tacky nightclub at a shopping mall in southwest Miami. Over drinks, Granda told his colleagues that he was ready to leave the company and get another job in Colombia. Barrage said the same thing. Both were willing to go so that perhaps Rodriguez could stay on and run the remaining business out of Colombia.

The next day, March 15, 2017, the three amigos were supposed to meet LeRoy at NTR's warehouse office in Doral. But Barrage said there had been a change of plans. Instead, Elemetal's CEO wanted the three to come to his hotel near Miami International Airport.

LeRoy got down to business immediately, telling them Elemetal's Latin America business would never reopen and that they were losing their jobs immediately with no severance. NTR's three amigos asked if the parent company was going to hire lawyers for them. LeRoy said Elemetal would deal with that issue later on. "You have nothing to worry about," he told them. "You guys have been good to us, we'll be good to you." He said nothing about how Elemetal had been turning over evidence about the three NTR dealers to the US Attorney's Office and the federal grand jury for months.

LeRoy himself had testified against the three men before the grand jury—and had asked Maderal months before if Elemetal should fire them. No, the prosecutor said, he didn't want to tip them off.

After their grim meeting with LeRoy at the hotel, the three amigos gathered again at a nearby Starbucks. They were out in the cold, again, just like in the 2008 financial crisis. But Barrage encouraged them to stay positive.

"We'll figure something out," he told them. "We'll find something to do."

Granda decided to get his mind off things and go shopping for clothes at the Dadeland Mall in Kendall. Bags in hand, Granda got a call from his mother.

"The FBI is here," she said.

At her home in Cutler Bay.

Waiting for her son.

A new voice came on the line. It was FBI special agent Refina Willis. "You need to come home," she said. Granda replied that he was on his way. It seemed the FBI just wanted to ask him some questions, as they had earlier with Rodriguez. His mother was thinking about brewing the agents coffee, although her left arm was in a sling because of a recent fall.

Granda still didn't have his own lawyer. On the drive down, he called Elemetal's general counsel, Trey Gum. LeRoy had said Elemetal would be good to him, but Gum didn't seem to have gotten the message.

"I'm Elemetal's lawyer, Juan," Gum told him. "Not yours. We can't help you."

Twenty minutes later, around one thirty in the afternoon, Granda walked through his mother's front door. Willis and two other FBI agents were sitting in her living room with expressionless faces, backs ramrod straight. Granda tried to greet them. But Homeland

Security special agent Cole Almeida and his partner had followed Granda through the door, two dark shadows at his back.

They weren't there to question him.

They were there to arrest him.

The charge? Conspiracy to commit money laundering.

Almeida told him he had five minutes to get ready. He should leave behind anything valuable that he didn't want to store in a jail locker. Off came Granda's gold Rolex. His gold bracelet. His gold necklace. The pair of shoes he was wearing. They had laces, which would be taken away from him at lockup. (Shoelaces were forbidden because of the risk inmates might try to hang themselves.)

The last thing he said to his mother as the agents took him out the door was to call Barrage. He would get him a lawyer. Elemetal might have abandoned him, but Barrage wouldn't.

"Sam will take care of me," he said.

His mother sobbed in shock.

Willis asked her if she needed anything or wanted to make a phone call.

"Leave me alone," Granda's mother told her. "Please leave me alone. I need to breathe."

On the drive Granda and the agents made small talk about the Miami Marlins, who were in spring training and headed for another dismal season. No one said anything about the case. Half an hour due north on the Ronald Reagan Turnpike, and the agents pulled up to Homeland Security's office in Doral. The building, a modern four-story concrete-and-glass structure, was a short drive from NTR's warehouse.

The federal agents escorted Granda inside for processing and questioning.

They put him in a yellow-walled, first-floor concrete block interview room. The six-by-six space was cold and brightly lit. There were no windows. Granda was seated across a small table from Almeida and Willis. Wearing a black Ralph Lauren polo shirt with an oversized electric-blue horseman on the chest, Granda was about to feel the full force of the federal law enforcement system.

No more small talk.

Almeida pulled out a copy of the thirty-page criminal complaint and affidavit.

Granda—a dark beard on his lower jaw and neck, his hair worn in the popular hipster style, buzzed short on the sides, longer on top, and slicked back—began to read.

"Beginning around January 2013, Juan P. Granda and others conspired to commit money laundering by sending billions of dollars from the United States to Latin America with the intent to promote the carrying on of organized criminal activity, including illegal mining, gold smuggling and the entry of goods into the US by false means and statements, and narcotics trafficking," the document stated. "Granda undertook this conspiracy in connection with his employment as the Director of Operations for NTR Metals, a precious-metals refinery. Other NTR employees joined Granda in this conspiracy."[2]

There was no mention of Barrage or Rodriguez, except by the aliases of "Salesperson 1" and "Salesperson 2." No one else had been arrested. As he got to a lengthy section that dealt with the cooperation of a customs broker identified as "Confidential Source 1," Granda's eyes nearly popped out of his head. The source's testimony laid out how he had helped Peter Ferrari and the three amigos export a bounty of illegal gold from Perú. There was only one person "CS1" could be, Granda thought: Andrés Tejeda, the customs broker who had helped him and his colleagues build NTR into a dominant gold buyer in Perú.

"Lying motherfucker pinned the whole thing on me," Granda thought to himself. "I knew he was a rat."

After Granda finished reading, Almeida advised him of his Miranda rights.

Granda knew he was trapped. His survival instincts kicked in. All he wanted to do was figure out what the agents needed from him—and then give them as little as was necessary to escape this sterile room.

But his boiler-room sales techniques were never going to work on a pair of federal agents who had already buttoned up their entire case.

Granda told Almeida he was willing to help the agents with their investigation but he needed to discuss some things with a defense attorney first. And he had a question: Were the feds going after a bigger fish than just Elemetal? He was already angling.

"We're not making any promises here but we will talk to the [prosecutor] on your behalf," Almeida said.

"I want to be as cooperative as possible, but I don't want to get mixed up in something I don't understand," Granda replied.

It could be a promising start to the interview. Granda was already talking about cooperating and trying to figure out how he could get released and sleep in his own bed at his mother's home rather than in a federal lockup. Almeida asked if he knew Rodolfo Soria—one of NTR's former gold suppliers in Perú.

"I might have met him a couple of times but to me he was just an individual in the gold business," Granda answered.

"You might have met him or you met him?" Willis asked.

Granda was hedging. When the agents asked about Ferrari, Granda claimed he could barely remember the man's full real name. He looked cool, but as he answered questions he took long pauses, sucked his teeth, and stared down at the table.

"We really want you to be honest. We really want you to cooperate," Almeida said. "Are you lying to us at this point?"

"With respect, I'm not lying."

Then Granda countered: he said he could help the feds track down NTR's seized gold that Ferrari had stolen in Perú and resold to other American companies. But Almeida and Willis didn't bite. They wanted to talk about the WhatsApp chats, which figured prominently in the affidavit. Why did a successful American gold dealer compare himself to a modern-day Pablo Escobar?

"At that point in time, I had been watching the Pablo telenovela," Granda said sheepishly.

Then Almeida pointed to a text Granda sent on his 2014 trip to Puerto Maldonado, the center of Perú's illegal gold mining: "It's all under the table no docs."

"So you guys fabricate paperwork, in essence," Almeida said.

"No, we don't," Granda replied, trying to explain that the miners couldn't ship the gold out of the country, so they needed to sell it to companies with valid export licenses. All he meant in the messages, he claimed, was that the gold needed papers. It needed to be "formalized." Nothing fishy.

Almeida cut him off. "You know as well as we know that's not what happened," he said. "Those documents were fabricated. The officials were paid off in order to get shipments out of the country. . . . Peter Ferrari's companies couldn't come up with documents. So they had to bribe officials."

"Yeah I remember that, that's true."

"You knew about it," Almeida insisted. "You actively participated in it."

"No, I'm being honest with you. I would not have risked myself to participate in that. I was telling Sam [Barrage] and Bill [LeRoy] this today: We weren't this organized crime [family] that everyone thinks or is being presented. . . . With the amount of money I made in salary and commission, there's no way I would risk putting myself in this situation. . . . It wasn't illegal gold. There was informal material but it was in the process of formalization."

"We're going down the wrong path here and I'm going to cut this short," Almeida interrupted. "We don't need to dwell on the process of formalizing gold."

Then the agent brought up the photos of gold "mules" that Granda and Barrage had exchanged. Granda was getting flustered.

"That's one of the things I want to clear up," he said. "If you want the truth, it might not be what you're looking for. These are jokes that go back and forth in this business. . . . I know on this page what it looks like, but that's not the case and I don't know how I can prove that."

Willis, who had said little so far, jumped in. There was chatter in the messages about buying "Peruvian gold" from Bolivia and Ecuador. But Granda denied that he and his partners ever moved any gold across the Peruvian border, even as he acknowledged smuggling was commonplace. "You can't control where the individuals [in Ecuador and Bolivia] get their gold," he explained.

"What you can control," Willis scolded, "is purchasing it from them and we know that's what you guys were doing."

It was all a running joke, Granda said. They didn't smuggle gold.

"We know your running jokes," she replied. "We've read everything. This is not even the tip of what we've read."

"Those are jokes," Granda said again.

"Yeah, obviously those are jokes," Almeida interjected, "but the jokes have a lot of truth behind them as well."

Granda was a hustler. But it was quickly becoming apparent that he couldn't wiggle his way out of this corner. He was trapped, and it started to sink in that the agents would likely take him into federal custody.

"I can tell you I've never smuggled gold. I'm being one hundred percent honest," Granda said, wearily rubbing his left hand over the right side of his face, his elbow resting on the table. "It all sounds so incriminating. That's why I want to help you guys because I know the texts you're going to find are super incriminating. There might be a text in there saying I killed somebody, but I don't want you to think that I literally killed somebody."

"Juan, you're facing twenty years in prison," Almeida responded. "I just want you to understand that."

"That's why I want to be honest with you," Granda said, grasping for a lifeline from the federal agents, who suggested they could help him if he came clean. "Can I ask both of you guys a question? You guys are investigating us and everything you see makes us look super guilty, right, but you guys are looking for a bigger fish, something bigger than Elemetal. . . . Let me know what you are looking for and I can see how I can help you get there."

"We're looking for the truth," Almeida replied, his voice rising. "It's simple. It's not complicated. Tell us the truth, starting with Peter Ferrari. How you guys were able to pay off the customs officials. . . . How you switched companies on purpose to try to evade law enforcement. . . . That's what we want to know. When you start doing that, we can continue."

Granda didn't fold. He said NTR's three amigos had no idea they were buying Peter Ferrari's gold until the seizure at the Lima airport in late 2013.

"If you can't admit to that, then we're done here because I don't want to be spinning my wheels all night," Almeida said.

"I can't admit to something I didn't partake in," Granda said.

"Have you ever done any gold smuggling?" Almeida asked. "That's a simple question."

"My job is to coordinate exports."

"Have you ever committed any gold smuggling? Yes or no?"

"No."

"Do you know anybody at NTR that was directly involved in smuggling gold?"

"No."

That was that. An hour had passed—and the flip had flopped.

Almeida and Willis had given Granda every opportunity to talk. He didn't seem to understand how much trouble he was in. He still thought he could talk his way out of the interview room. But he was headed straight to a federal lockup.

CHAPTER 48

The Depth of Their Betrayal

SHORTLY AFTER JUAN PABLO GRANDA'S ARREST, ONE-TIME GOLD IMPORTER Jeffrey Himmel's email pinged with a message from his lawyer. Attached was a thirty-page criminal complaint and affidavit against Granda. The document laid out a sprawling money laundering conspiracy carried out by Granda and two other NTR traders named only as "Salesperson 1" and "Salesperson 2."

Reading through the complaint, Himmel choked when he got to paragraph number 11. Granda, it stated, and the two anonymous salespeople were "NTR's Miami-based sales team responsible for finding and buying gold in Latin America and the Caribbean."

In that horrifying moment, Himmel knew the prosecutors were talking about Samer Barrage and Renato Rodriguez. It was almost two years to the day since Ecuadorian authorities had seized his $2 million shipment of gold and he had shut down his company, MVP Imports. In that time, he had stayed close with Rodriguez, whose mother he had helped with her diabetes. He now realized it was not just Paul Borja, Himmel's right-hand man in his Ecuadorian gold venture, who had double-crossed him; Rodriguez and Barrage had deceived him too.

The depth of their betrayal was spelled out in a section titled "Illegal gold smuggled through Ecuador and Bolivia in 2014." Much of the $337 million worth of gold that MVP had imported from Ecuador was not Ecuadorian gold, the affidavit said, as he had been led to believe by Borja and the Ecuadorian miners. In fact, the affidavit alleged, it had been smuggled over the border from Perú.[1]

"This was their plan right from the get-go," Himmel realized.

Then it got worse. The affidavit named MVP Imports as NTR's intermediary for buying gold, saying his company had been used to "mask" NTR's illicit role. The prosecutors even noted that MVP's principal address was the small boutique home store, Violetas, owned by his wife. The only saving grace was that neither his name nor his wife's was mentioned in the affidavit. But it wouldn't take long for someone to figure out the connection.

When a *Bloomberg* reporter got in touch, Himmel declined to comment. But to contain the potential scandal, he sacrificed one of his proudest achievements: his recent election as the upcoming chair of the American Diabetes Association. By the time *Bloomberg* published a story three weeks later, he had resigned from the ADA to protect the organization. From the media coverage alone, his carefully honed reputation as an ethical businessman and philanthropist might never recover.[2]

His nightmare was only just beginning. Three of the complaint's forty-five paragraphs—and a single chart—dealt with MVP Imports and Ecuador. Within a few days, the FBI called him on his cell phone. It totally spooked him. He was at South Miami Hospital visiting a friend dying of cancer. "I can't talk to you," Himmel told the agent. "I'm going to put you in touch with my lawyer." Then his wife called.

There were federal agents at their waterfront estate in Miami Beach.

"Do not talk to them," he told her.

The stakes were higher than Himmel ever could have imagined. He now had to convince prosecutors that he was a dupe, not a criminal coconspirator working with NTR's three amigos in their gold-smuggling racket.

∞∞∞∞∞∞∞

Samer Barrage knew he would be next to get arrested.

The criminal complaint against Granda listed Barrage as "Salesperson 1."

He was already consulting a criminal defense attorney. The exposure was huge. Not only were NTR's Chilean gold exporter

Harold Vilches and Peruvian customs broker Andrés Tejeda cooperating with the feds, but also they'd arrested Granda. Who knew if
he would flip too?

Four days after his former colleague was busted at his mom's
home, Barrage pulled up an internet browser on his computer.

It was around ten p.m. on a Sunday, March 19, 2017.

He looked at flights to Colombia. There was one leaving from
Miami to Cali in five hours, at three Monday morning. Barrage
had made more than forty trips to Colombia before. But they were
always planned in advance. He had never left under these circumstances, buying a ticket and leaving hours later. Only twice had
he even ever flown before nine a.m. With the net closing around
him, he couldn't stay in Miami. All of his industry contacts were in
Colombia. If he wanted to salvage any of his business, he needed to
go back. Barrage booked the flight, packed, and told his wife he was
off to Colombia. Then he drove to the airport, leaving his Volks-
wagen GTI in short-term parking.

Prosecutor Frank Maderal had placed a travel alert on Barrage
and Rodriguez just in case something like this happened. The feds
were planning to arrest the two men in due course, but not until
they'd had a chance to grill Granda. When Barrage bought the
ticket, alarm bells went off at Homeland Security. But no one was
awake to hear them. Cole Almeida wouldn't find out about Barrage's middle-of-the-night departure until the Homeland Security
agent woke up the next morning.[3]

"He's taking off," Almeida told Maderal. "He's trying to flee."

They had to chase him to Cali.

∞∞∞∞∞∞

Maderal was frantic. He hadn't slept for days, stressed out about
the next big move in his gold case. He hadn't even put the final
touches on the criminal complaint for Barrage's and Rodriguez's
arrests.

They hadn't expected Barrage to run. Would Rodriguez be
next?

Tim Schoonmaker, the DEA agent, flew up from Perú. He and
Maderal were holed up in the war room, hastily adapting the

language in the affidavit of Granda's criminal complaint for another complaint charging Barrage and Rodriguez.

The prosecutor, however, could not risk waiting around for a federal magistrate judge to sign off on the complaint. He told Almeida and the FBI's Refina Willis to pick up Rodriguez and bring him to Homeland Security's office for processing.

Rodriguez had known this moment was coming. Almeida had already made two passes at persuading him to flip. After they arrested him at his Miami home, the two agents brought Rodriguez to Homeland Security's office for questioning. But in the stark gray interview room, little progress was made. Almeida, despite his maverick personality, was a stickler for paperwork. He took such a long time filling out forms that Rodriguez's defense attorney, Sabrina Puglisi, was able to email Maderal and tell him and his agents to back off. No one was going to talk to her client.

Schoonmaker couldn't believe it. He had driven out to Homeland Security Investigation's office in Doral to take a crack at Rodriguez. Almeida had already tried and failed to flip the NTR dealer weeks earlier. Now it was the DEA's turn. But Rodriguez's lawyer's email made it impossible. Once a lawyer invokes a client's right to silence, federal agents have to respect that.

The DEA agent called Maderal. He was apoplectic.

"Cole wasted four fucking hours doing paperwork," Schoonmaker shouted.

But Maderal knew it was too late.

"Tim, stop," the prosecutor said. "The interview is over; that's the law."

Schoonmaker was a few months away from retirement. He didn't want to break the rules. But he didn't mind getting creative.

So he volunteered to drive Rodriguez to the Federal Detention Center in downtown Miami for booking. He knew he couldn't speak to the defendant. But no one said he couldn't talk to the FBI agent, Willis, who was riding in the passenger seat.

Schoonmaker turned to the agent.

"Man, I would be freaking out if I was in this guy's place," Schoonmaker said, gesturing with his eyes in the rearview mirror to Rodriguez. "All the evidence we have, he's looking at ten years.

He's got one chance to maybe get to see his wife again, and his only chance is to cooperate. It's just too bad that he can't do that if he wanted to right now because he doesn't want to talk to us."

Rodriguez started to speak.

"Nope, you can't talk to us, remember?" Schoonmaker told him. "You can't say anything."

⬦⬦⬦⬦⬦⬦⬦⬦

Rodriguez wouldn't stay behind bars long.

On March 21, 2017, at Rodriguez's first appearance in court, Maderal agreed to a bond of $100,000. Rodriguez was the lowest ranking of the three amigos and had a family tying him to Miami. He had to surrender his passport and agree not to talk to Barrage or Granda. Rodriguez was allowed to live with his family under house arrest.[4]

After the gold dealer paid up and was released, Schoonmaker, not for the first time over the last few days, challenged the prosecutor's tactics. They'd already let Barrage flee the country. Now Rodriguez might run, too.

"How can you let him out?" the agent asked Maderal.

Rodriguez needed to feel the pressure of being locked up, Schoonmaker said. It might force him to flip. Worst of all, the agent added, Maderal hadn't discussed his decision with his team. That wasn't teamwork. That wasn't how things were done.

"He had three weeks to run, Tim," Maderal said. "He didn't do it. I'm not going to hold him if he's not a flight risk."[5]

He'd had his fill of the agent's questioning. He had been feeling vulnerable, without the protection of his bosses, building a new kind of money laundering case founded on illegal gold mining in South America and smuggling the metal to Miami. Now that the first arrests had been made, the last thing he needed was a doubting Thomas on his own team bullying him into doing something he didn't think was right. Maderal picked up the green notebook where he had jotted down all his case notes and threw it against the wall. The spine snapped.

"We're doing what we're doing," Maderal shouted. "Can you help or not?"

Then he stormed out.

Schoonmaker turned to Willis, who was sitting next to him at the conference table.

"Well, that was something," he said.

She nodded.

But the steam-letting was a necessary release.

Maderal and the agents were so close to finishing off the investigation. They had made two arrests and were working their way up the chain to Elemetal and Peter Ferrari.

It felt like they were on the brink of bringing down dirty gold.

∞∞∞∞∞∞∞

The next day, it was Granda's turn to appear in federal court for a detention hearing.

Maderal wasn't willing to cut him a break. He was a flight risk with an Ecuadorian passport, the prosecutor said. His family owned a farm in Ecuador. He had ties there and in Colombia. His colleague Barrage was suspected of having gone on the lam.

The money laundering charge that he faced was serious, carrying potentially twenty years in prison. "The scope of the conspiracy is enormous," Maderal said in court, accusing Granda and his two NTR colleagues of importing a mind-boggling $3.6 billion in illegal gold.

Maderal said the three gold dealers acted as money launderers by promoting Perú's illicit gold trade.

To put it all in perspective, the prosecutor said NTR bought nearly $1 billion worth of gold from Perú in 2013—and one-third of that amount was supplied by five companies linked to a Peruvian man who Maderal identified as "P.F." P. F. had not yet been charged in the United States. But anyone who knew the gold case knew who he was: Peter Ferrari.

Maderal summed up the gravity of Granda's crime, the billions in dirty gold sales and the potential punishment. "The Defendant's [sentencing] guideline is out to life imprisonment," he said, with some exaggeration.

Granda's defense lawyer tried to fight back with tidbits about Granda's formative years in Miami and business degree from Florida State University, but he seemed completely overwhelmed by the allegations of the sprawling multi-billion-dollar scheme and his client's central role in it. He cross-examined FBI special agent Refina Willis on the stand. But it wasn't clear to anybody in the courtroom what he was asking her or why. The magistrate judge eventually cut him off.

Sure, Granda was a Miami guy, the judge reasoned. But he had family in Ecuador and other links to South America, including his colleague Barrage, who might help him flee to avoid prosecution. "He has connections in foreign countries who might not want him to be here in the United States under pressure to testify against them," the magistrate judge said. "I am going to hold him in detention based on risk of flight."

On his way out the door back to the Federal Detention Center in Miami, a deputy US Marshal pulled Granda aside.

"You've got the worst lawyer I've ever seen," the marshal said.

∞∞∞∞∞∞

Maderal and the federal agents had no faith that Samer Barrage would return on his own to Miami, even though he had booked a round-trip ticket. Rather than wait for NTR's top gold dealer to come home, a group of Homeland Security agents flew to Cali, Colombia, to grab him on March 23. Barrage spent a few days in a Colombian jail before arriving in Miami.[6]

At Barrage's detention hearing, Maderal reprised the same persuasive argument that he had made against releasing Granda—topping it off with his deep suspicions about the suspect's hasty nighttime flight to South America.

Barrage's lawyers claimed their client was traveling on a routine, four-day business trip between Miami and Colombia. They said he cut his trip to Colombia short by one day once he knew he was being charged so that he could turn himself in. "He was on his way back, on his way back to deal with this," his defense attorney, Marcos Beaton, told the judge. "He had hired counsel. On his way to confront these charges."

The feds didn't buy that for a second. "He knew he was soon to be arrested himself," Maderal countered.[7]

A magistrate judge refused to grant Barrage a bond before trial. He may have had a wife and two children back in Miami, but he also had extended family in Colombia—plus $2 million in the bank from his NTR gold income.

⚬⚬⚬⚬⚬⚬⚬⚬⚬

Elemetal's Colombian subsidiary was not cited in the criminal case. A lawyer for the subsidiary later said in an email that the company had "no relationship" with NTR's operations in Florida and "has not had and does not currently have any connections" to the case against the US company.[8]

Even after Elemetal directed its subsidiaries to stop buying gold from other South American countries, the company had allowed the Colombian subsidiary to continue operating. Elemetal's internal investigation had found fewer problems with the anti–money laundering vetting process there than in the rest of its Latin American operations. The company ultimately closed its Colombian subsidiary in March 2017, however, citing issues with the vetting process and Barrage's involvement in the operation.[9]

⚬⚬⚬⚬⚬⚬⚬⚬⚬

Despite Schoonmaker's prior agreement with Maderal not to inform Peruvian authorities that customs broker Andrés Tejeda was cooperating with the feds, the DEA agent ultimately decided on his own to do just that. Schoonmaker felt he couldn't withhold crucial information from his counterparts. They were supposed to be partners, after all. But someone on the Peruvian side must have leaked.

On May 3, 2017, more than a month after NTR's three amigos were arrested, a Peruvian newspaper published a story about the massive money laundering case in Miami and noted that Tejeda was a key witness who was cooperating with US authorities—even though he was not identified by name in the federal complaint and prosecutors and agents had not revealed his identity.

Immediately, Tejeda—who had testified against NTR's three amigos, Ferrari, and his Peruvian associates before the grand jury the previous December—began getting threatening phone calls.

"Don't say another word," the voice on the other end would say. "Shut up now."

Panicked, the customs broker called his handler at the DEA, Tim Schoonmaker, who was fast approaching retirement. Tejeda and his family had to get out of Lima. Now.

Schoonmaker dialed Maderal and Almeida. The Homeland Security Investigations agent arranged a hotel room in the United States for Tejeda, his wife, and his children. He got Diplomatic Security to issue them emergency visas.

Tejeda's wife had no idea what was happening. On Schoonmaker's advice, her husband hadn't told her he was cooperating. Now, he was explaining something that would change her life forever.

Schoonmaker sent his team of Peruvian police to surveil Tejeda's home in case there was trouble. The family would need constant security until the flight, which was booked for just a few hours away. The family waited nervously. Schoonmaker called ahead to the airport. When they arrived, Schoonmaker's team would be able to shepherd the Tejedas through security. They were going to the United States.

Almeida and Willis, the FBI agent, met Tejeda and his family at the gate at Miami International Airport.

"We're here to help you," Almeida said. "You're safe now."

∞∞∞∞∞∞

For Juan Pablo Granda, being denied bond and having to endure federal jail may have been a blessing.

When he first arrived at the Federal Detention Center in Miami, Granda told his lawyer he wanted to fight. "Fuck the feds," he said. "They can go to hell. We're going to war. They took the [WhatsApp] text messages illegally. All this is bullshit."

But the other prisoners, veterans of the federal criminal justice system—not to mention the prosecutor, Maderal—gave him a dose of reality: it was all about cutting your losses, or face the grim prospect of a long time in prison.

When the Florida State University business grad tried to review the more than one million pages of documents entered as evidence against him, he had to share a single computer with 160 other inmates. The aging machine wouldn't even let him copy-paste. He had to write down the page numbers of relevant documents and provide them to his lawyer. It was starting to dawn on him, as it does on so many inmates awaiting trial behind bars, that the prosecutors were going to destroy him.

The deck is stacked against criminal defendants in the federal system. Only 2 percent of defendants accused in federal criminal cases go to trial, according to the Pew Research Center. The risks are too great. Sentences are long and defense attorneys are able to win acquittals in only a tiny fraction of trials. It's better to cooperate and plead guilty in exchange for a lesser sentence. In 2018, federal prosecutors attained guilty pleas in 90 percent of all cases, while the remaining 8 percent were dismissed.

One prisoner serving time for white-collar fraud laid it out for Granda: "You either got to make a business decision or an emotional decision." An emotional decision meant fighting the charges and potentially facing years behind bars. A business decision meant pleading guilty and serving as little time as possible. A high-profile inmate detained in the same facility as Granda put it to him bluntly. "You can't beat these people," said the convicted Colombian paramilitary and cocaine trafficker Diego Murillo Bejarano—better known as Don Berna.

Granda hired new lawyers, Daniel Rashbaum and Allison Green, and soon offered to cooperate with the feds. But he felt uncomfortable talking about his old friends. He tried to stay focused on the roles of the NTR dealers in importing billions of dollars of gold from South America. Foremost, he wanted Maderal to promise that his two colleagues would be offered the same deal he was getting. The prosecutor agreed. And so for days, in the jail's cramped visitation area, Granda walked the investigators through how NTR's $3.6 billion illegal gold operation worked. It was difficult talking about his buddies, but it was easy to roll over on Peter Ferrari, who he believed had ripped off $10 million worth of gold from the three amigos. "It would be my pleasure to give you that piece of shit," Granda told Maderal.

Barrage agreed to cooperate, too. He had plenty of information on Ferrari—but little on the Elemetal executives he so often communicated with as NTR's vice president for Latin America. They simply didn't ask, and he didn't tell.

Rodriguez was slower to see the jig was up. He still refused to believe that what he had done was against the law. It would cost him.

On September 5, 2017, nearly six months after their arrests, Granda and Barrage pleaded guilty to one count of conspiracy to commit money laundering. In a "factual proffer" submitted to the court, they admitted to playing key roles in a $3.6 billion scheme that encouraged illegal mining, gold smuggling, bribery of foreign officials, customs fraud, and narcotics trafficking. Granda agreed to give the government $466,422.76, representing the money he had earned while working for NTR Metals and the contents of his Fidelity Investments 401(k) account. Barrage had to pay back $850,000 but was allowed to keep his homes abroad.

For their crimes, they faced a maximum of ten years in prison.[10]

The length of their prison sentence—which would be handed down by a federal judge—depended on how fully they cooperated with Maderal.

CHAPTER 49

Ferrari's Freefall

PETER FERRARI'S SONS–PETER DAVIS PÉREZ GUTIERREZ AND GIAN PIERE Pérez Gutierrez—felt both cursed and blessed by their notorious father.[1] The twins were the first born of his ten children, the product of their father's wild teenage years. They were the reason he'd given up his dreams of being an actor in Hollywood and taken up the family business of buying and selling gold.

The thirty-three-year-old brothers were raised by their mother, far removed from their father's inner circle of wealth and generosity. While he ran around in sports cars and had bodyguards, they grew up in Lima's working-class La Victoria neighborhood and went to public schools. They never went to college because money was tight.

In recent years, however, they had started rebuilding their relationship with their old man. Sometimes they'd swing by his busy gold-buying office on La Paz Avenue to help out with chores and run errands. Gian Piere had even dipped a toe into the family business, starting his own gold-buying company, Minerales Gold MPP, along with his cousin.

But the last several months were trying. The previous January, they had been stunned as they watched their father arrested on live TV. They had sat through Ferrari's grueling pretrial hearing on charges of organized crime, illegal gold mining, and money laundering. And they had been deeply rattled when their father, his bodyguard, and their cousin were sentenced to eighteen months in pretrial detention.

"They got sent to jail, a bad jail, for a long time, and they've never even been put on trial," Gian Piere said.

But the twins thought they were in the clear. Yes, they'd pitched in around their father's business and even cashed some checks for him when he didn't have time to run to the bank. But as far as they were concerned, they'd done nothing wrong.

It was January 9, 2018, just over a year to the day since their father's arrest, but the twins had other things on their mind. It was the birthday of Gian Piere's four-year-old daughter and they were in downtown Lima getting money changed and buying last-minute gifts.

They were just pulling out of a parking lot when the police rushed them, hauled them out of their BMW, and handcuffed them.

They were being detained on charges of conspiracy to commit money laundering. But it wasn't the Peruvians that were after them, it was Uncle Sam. The twin brothers were told they were going to be extradited to face American justice.

On November 16, 2017, Frank Maderal had filed an indictment against them, their father, and Ferrari's longtime driver and associate, José Estuardo Morales.

But there was no way for any of them to have known it. The indictment was under seal, hidden from view. The charge was identical to the one Maderal had filed against Samer Barrage, Juan Pablo Granda, and Renato Rodriguez. Only the names had been changed.

It was only the day after the twins' arrest that the US Justice Department finally announced they'd shut down a "multi-billion dollar, international gold money laundering scheme" spanning two continents and including a widening cast of characters.

It was also the first time the US government had named Barrage, Granda, and Rodriguez in a statement even though they'd been arrested the previous year.

"I couldn't believe what was happening," Gian Piere said. "One minute you're on your way to your daughter's birthday party and the next minute your life is destroyed."

The brothers were hauled into the police station and put in *el hueco*, the hole, a tiny, windowless cell they shared with ten other people. One of their cellmates had an open wound on his leg where he'd been stabbed with a knife covered in feces. After five days they were moved into the larger prison population of Ancón I in Lima, where their father was being held in a separate wing.

The brothers were stuck in a section with three hundred other people, run by an unholy alliance of gangs and corrupt prison guards. It was a place where you had to pay for everything: security, the right to use the showers (there were only two for the entire ward), the right to bring food into the jail.

"Inside there it's no-man's-land," Gian Piere said. "If you didn't have money to pay for things, you'd die."

Despite being told they were facing serious charges, the brothers hadn't seen any documents outlining the allegations against them. And although they were wanted in the United States, no one from the US Embassy visited them in jail or asked for their side of the story.

The twins said it took US and Peruvian authorities more than two months to show them the US grand jury indictment. The document was both frightening and bewildering. In just three and a half pages, the US government was accusing the twins, their father, and Morales of conspiring with NTR's three amigos to commit money laundering.

But it was the language in the document that was so alarming. Maderal's innovative and aggressive legal strategy meant the money laundering charges against the twins had to be based on evidence that their gold business was financing or promoting "specified unlawful activities." And the indictment listed those crimes as illegal mining, smuggling, bribery, and "the manufacture, importation, sale or distribution of a controlled substance."

Maderal's careful legalese left the twins dumbfounded.

"They're accusing us of being drug dealers," Gian Piere said. "It's not true. The United States just made it up."

In many ways the indictment read like a black hole. Except to say that the unlawful activities took place between May 2012 and March 2017, there were no other details. Nothing about what illegal gold they bought or how it was being smuggled. No indication of which officials were being bribed. Not even a mention of what kinds of drugs were theoretically being made, moved, and sold with the money from their gold deals.

Under US-Peruvian law, American courts don't have to turn over evidence, or discovery, until the suspects are present in US court. Although there may be solid legal reasons for that, it put the twins in an impossible bind.

"How are we supposed to defend ourselves if we don't even know what we're being accused of?" Peter Jr. asked. "There is not a single piece of evidence in there, it's just a series of vague statements. And that's enough to send us to the United States?"

It was only months later that they got access to the Peruvian police reports that were the basis of the US case.

According to those documents, Peruvian authorities believed the twins were a key part of their father's subterfuge, that he used them and their other siblings to hide his wealth by buying them luxury cars and other items.

They also focused on Gian Piere's stake in Minerales Gold MPP, the gold-trading company he'd formed on February 15, 2013, with his cousin, Miguel Ángel Rivero, in which his father had power of attorney.

That ownership structure "is the fundamental reason that allows us to demonstrate that both the son and nephew of 'Peter Ferrari' were being used as straw men," one of the police reports stated. Ferrari had also implicated his sons when he asked them to cash checks for him.

Between September and October of 2012, the twins had withdrawn more than half a million dollars.[2] For US authorities this was clear evidence that they were involved in an illicit scheme. To the brothers, these were innocuous acts—the work of two sons giving their busy father a hand.

Just because they cashed some checks didn't mean the money was theirs. It was cash their father needed to make the next round of gold purchases. There was nothing nefarious about it. And it certainly wasn't conspiracy.

As for the cars, they were long overdue.

"He bought us cars during the gold boom because he'd never bought us anything before in our lives, and he was doing well," Peter Jr. explained.

And, they realized, the Peruvian police reports made no mention of drugs. Where were the US prosecutors—the ones who seemed to be so infallible on the American television shows the twins watched—coming up with this stuff?

If their father did anything wrong, the twins said, it was that he was too trusting—that he believed people about the origins of their gold. If a customer told Ferrari they had found the gold in a legal mining area, or that the gold jewelry they were selling had been an inheritance, he wasn't about to call them liars.

"It's possible that he was missing some document or that a miner didn't provide some piece of documentation, but that doesn't make it illegal gold," Peter Jr. said. "In the end it's an act of good faith."

Sitting in a bar in April 2019, still awaiting his father's trial in Perú and his own extradition to the United States, Gian Piere said the experience made him reevaluate his instinct to reconnect with his father.

"I wish I had nothing to do with him," he said. "I should have just called him on Father's Day and Christmas and left it at that."

CHAPTER 50

Way Beyond Money Laundering

ON JANUARY 19, 2018, TEN DAYS AFTER PETER FERRARI'S TWIN SONS WERE arrested in Lima, Juan Pablo Granda and Samer Barrage stood in front of US district judge Robert Scola. They were there to be sentenced to prison. Prosecutor Frank Maderal had been pleased by their cooperation against Peter Ferrari and his partners in Perú. But they were still going away.

"I'm deeply ashamed to be standing here in front of my family and friends," Barrage told the judge as a gaggle of his friends and family looked on. "There is absolutely no excuse for this. . . . Remorse does not even begin to scratch the surface of how I feel."

"The only person I can blame is myself," said Granda, joined in the courtroom by his attorneys, Daniel Rashbaum and Allison Green, and his mother, aunt, sister, and nearly a dozen friends.[1]

Scola sentenced Granda to six years in prison. Barrage received six years and eight months. But in an unusual move the judge went out of his way to deliver a brief lecture to the two defendants about the wider societal toll of their crimes. The massive gold case was not just about money, the deep-voiced judge noted from the bench, like so many crimes in the federal judicial system. Rather, their crimes had driven the devastation of the South American rain forest, the pollution of environmental resources, and the exploitation of poor miners.

"This goes way beyond [money laundering]," the judge said.[2]

Later that month, it was Renato Rodriguez's turn. As the last to come to the table to cooperate and plead guilty, which he had done late the previous year, Rodriguez would be handed a sentence of seven and a half years. Out on bail, unlike his colleagues, he had worked seventy hours per week at his brother's pizza restaurant. Now he would have to surrender. Given the chance to speak, Rodriguez offered the court and his family an apology.

"I just wanted to say how sorry I am for what I've done to my family over the last nine months," he said through tears. "It's been the hardest thing that my family and I have been enduring. I love my family very much and I—I teach my daughters to always do right by everyone. I learned from my father how to be a good man, how to be a good husband, and how to be a good brother and friend. And I just want to say how sorry I am."

His was the longest stint any of the three amigos would have to serve, even though Judge Scola acknowledged Rodriguez played "somewhat of a lesser role in the conspiracy" than Granda and Barrage. If only Rodriguez had cooperated sooner.[3]

Still, the judge reiterated the broader societal cost of the trio's crimes.

"The offense of conviction may be money laundering," Scola said, "but the activities . . . led to the destruction and deforestation of rainforests, the poisoning of rivers and waters [and] the poisoning of workers and people who live in the vicinity."

Rodriguez hung his head and wept.

Epilogue

"They Busted Our Ass"

AFTER BEING SENTENCED, JUAN PABLO GRANDA WAS IMPRISONED AT THE Federal Correctional Institution–Miami, the same place where former Panamanian strongman Manuel Noriega had been held, although Granda lived in a minimum-security camp sectioned off from violent offenders. His mother came to visit him every weekend. The prison was just twenty minutes from their family home in South Miami-Dade. While he was growing up, Granda's mom used to drive him by the prison on the way to and from school and sports games. Looking at the fence from the safety of the car, he always wondered who was on the other side.

Granda was released to a halfway house in Miami's Little Havana neighborhood on August 15, 2019—the result of his sentence being cut substantially because of his assistance to the feds. He started retyping his résumé but wasn't sure what to put for the 883 days he had spent locked up.[1]

Federal rules prohibited NTR's three amigos from being imprisoned in the same facility. Samer Barrage was sent to a prison in Pensacola in Florida's panhandle. In October 2019, his prison term was reduced by two years. He was released in May 2020.

Renato Rodriguez, the last to cooperate, once again drew the short straw, ending up in a South Carolina federal lockup. With the distance and his twin daughters' busy schedules, the family he loved so much could only visit a handful of times. He was later moved to a prison in Tallahassee and then closer to home to FCI-Miami, where Granda had been incarcerated. His bid to serve the remainder of his time in "home confinement" because of the COVID-19 pandemic was denied. He is scheduled for release in January 2022.

∞∞∞∞∞∞∞

On December 26, 2018, confidential informant Andrés Tejeda, the Peruvian customs broker, was arrested by federal agents at Miami International Airport trying to fly home to Lima, where his wife and children had already returned. As a crucial witness against Peter Ferrari—in addition to NTR's three amigos—Tejeda was required to stay in the United States. It is unclear whether he was homesick and worried about his family, as is common for informants trapped in a foreign land, or whether he was trying to dodge potentially testifying against Ferrari at a future trial. Trying to leave the country was a huge mistake, however. By fleeing, he forfeited his right to witness protection—a deal that included help with his immigration status, financial assistance, and housing—and was charged with conspiracy to commit money laundering, just like the three amigos, whom he had betrayed. On Friday, January 21, 2019, in Miami federal court, Tejeda was sentenced to two and a half years in prison.

"He made a bad decision in wanting to return to his country," said defense attorney Armando Rosquete, hinting at his client's "issues" and "pressures" in Perú and suggesting his family was being threatened because of his cooperation.

"If he had continued down the path [of witness protection and cooperation] and not tried to return to his country, he probably would not have been charged," Rosquete added.[2]

While the three amigos and Tejeda did hard time, prosecutor Frank Maderal never charged individual executives at Elemetal. Even with Barrage, the most senior of the three amigos, cooperating, no incriminating evidence emerged that cofounders Steve and John Loftus or CEO Bill LeRoy or general counsel Trey Gum or any other bosses had personal knowledge of the NTR dealers' smuggling scheme and should be held criminally liable. Steve Crogan, Elemetal's former head of compliance, was also not charged. For the bosses, the old saw was true: see no evil, hear no evil, face no charges.

Still, the gold-trading company would not go unpunished. In March 2018, Elemetal pleaded guilty in Miami federal court to failing to maintain an adequate anti–money laundering compliance program under the Bank Secrecy Act, a felony crime. The company's fine: $15 million.

Elemetal had to pay $5 million to the US government. The remaining $10 million was forgiven based on the loss value of NTR's gold shipment that Peruvian authorities had seized from Peter Ferrari at the Lima airport in late 2013. As part of its plea deal, Elemetal gave up its claim to the metal. "Elemetal wholeheartedly condemns the shocking behavior of these former NTR Miami employees in South America," the company said in a statement. "Elemetal, however, also accepts full responsibility for its employees, the employees of its subsidiaries, and the failure of its international anti-money-laundering program to prevent the misdeeds of the employees operating in South America."[3]

Without gold to smelt, Elemetal closed its precious-metals refinery in Ohio. It was barred from trading gold on bullion markets. In effect, it had to return to its humble roots, buying and selling scrap gold in the domestic market.[4] Almost all the remaining workers at the plant in Jackson, Ohio, were let go. The loss of good jobs was a stinging blow for an area that had already suffered so much. And it seemed so pointless. The plant had been doing fine under local ownership before the Texas businessmen swooped in.

"This didn't need to happen," said Walter Luhrman, who founded the refinery as Jackson Precious Metals in 1974 before selling it to Alan Stockmeister three decades later. "The [Elemetal executives] should have questioned where the gold was coming from."

The out-of-towners "busted our ass," said Judge Mark Musick, who oversees a local drug court in Jackson. "And they didn't even know us."

Edward Finley, a former melt room supervisor with a bushy Sam Elliott mustache who worked more than thirty years at the refinery before being laid off in 2017 with dozens of other employees, had a different take. Given how much pain and devastation all that illegal gold flowing into Jackson had caused in South America, Finley said, "maybe it was the right thing we shut down."

Stockmeister stepped down as the chairman of Elemetal but remained on the board of the Ohio State University. The local media barely covered the case.[5]

⬦⬦⬦⬦⬦

After learning about the charges against the three amigos, Jeffrey Himmel hired the law firm of Daniel Gelber, a former federal prosecutor, one-time Florida Senate minority leader, and current mayor of Miami Beach. He had already retained two other high-priced attorneys, Daniel Fridman and Michael Garcia of White & Case, to look into the seizure of MVP's gold and help clear his name. US prosecutors believed Himmel's story that he didn't knowingly buy Peruvian gold smuggled into Ecuador. He was a dupe. In early 2018, he received a letter from Frank Maderal of the US Attorney's Office informing him he was not a "target" of Operation Arch Stanton.[6]

The next year, the American Diabetes Association invited Himmel to serve on its Volunteer Engagement Council. To this day, he still is looking to recapture his position as the organization's board chair.

Paul Borja, Himmel's right-hand man in his Ecuadorian gold venture, was also not charged.

In late 2017, after they had spent a year and a half in pretrial detention, an Ecuadorian court acquitted Alberto and Jordi March—the brothers linked to one of MVP's former gold suppliers—of money laundering charges.[7] Ecuadorian prosecutors appealed, but another court upheld the decision in 2018 and, citing a lack of evidence, acquitted the other businessmen linked to Spartan del Ecuador and Clearprocess, including Javier March. Neither Spartan del Ecuador nor Clearprocess had been charged with a crime, but the Ecuadorian court ordered the removal of any sanctions imposed against the companies.[8]

Later that year, the United Nations Working Group on Arbitrary Detention issued an opinion on the Ecuadorian government's handling of the case against Alberto March. The working group concluded that he had been held in pretrial detention for longer than legally allowed and that the government had violated his right to a fair trial.[9]

Mara Cecilia Gordillo Bedón, the woman Colombian prosecutors allege was known as "the queen of gold," and the legal representatives of Enmanuel Gold, one of NTR Metals Zona Franca's suppliers in Colombia, have not been convicted of any crimes. As of May 2020, they were still awaiting trial. Gordillo has denied any wrongdoing and said she and her business associates were set up by major gold exporters to distract law enforcement from investigating those larger companies.[10] Enmanuel Gold has not been charged with any crimes.

While NTR's gold purchases from Colombia were included in the criminal complaints against the three amigos, they were not mentioned in the factual proffer filed with Elemetal's plea agreement. US court records do not mention NTR Metals Zona Franca's gold purchases from Enmanuel Gold.

Peruvian prosecutors would not provide information on the status of their investigation into Rodolfo Soria, the Peruvian exporter from whom both NTR and Harold Vilches bought gold, including whether it is still ongoing. The existence of an investigation was confirmed during Peruvian court proceedings in 2017.[11] Internal NTR records show that NTR imported gold from an alleged Peruvian front company associated with Soria, who did not respond to multiple requests for comment.[12]

⚬⚬⚬⚬⚬⚬⚬⚬

Prosecutor Frank Maderal had one more big case in him after gold: in the summer of 2018, he unveiled an indictment charging Venezuelan and other foreign nationals with a $1 billion money laundering scheme involving funds looted from Venezuela's state oil company PDVSA. The investigation even targeted Venezuelan president Nicolás Maduro and his three stepsons, though they have not been charged.[13] (Maduro was later charged in a separate drug-trafficking conspiracy case in New York.) On August 31, 2018, Maderal fulfilled his promise to his wife and quit the US Attorney's Office to return to his old law firm in Coral Gables, which specializes in personal injury, class-action, and tort litigation.

Operation Arch Stanton won an award from the Department of Justice's Organized Crime Drug Enforcement Task Force for its innovative, collaborative approach. The photographer needed a wide lens to capture all the agents, analysts, and prosecutors who participated in the sprawling case.

Cole Almeida, the Homeland Security agent, asked for a transfer to the international financial investigations unit, hoping he could take the gold case with him. His bosses refused, saying it was standard practice to leave old cases behind. Losing the gold case cut deep. He had started the investigation and hoped to see it through—and worried that without him not every target in the case would be brought to justice. But he couldn't sway his bosses. He continues to investigate some of Homeland Security's biggest cases of money laundering, foreign kleptocracy, and fraud.

Refina Willis remains at the FBI.

Tim Schoonmaker retired from the DEA and moved with his wife to the United States' Mountain West. Despite a bum knee, he still skis and bikes.

Gold, his last case, was in some ways the biggest of his decorated career—and yet it also broke his heart. No executives from Elemetal or any of the other gold-trading companies in Miami were held liable. None of them had to return the personal wealth they earned.

The only ones to go down were NTR's three amigos.

He's still mad about it.

∞∞∞∞∞∞∞

Operation Arch Stanton rattled Miami's gold industry—and brought it unprecedented public attention.

On January 16, 2018, Senator Marco Rubio (R-FL) released a statement after the publication of a *Miami Herald* series on the NTR Metals case entitled "Dirty Gold, Clean Cash."

"Trade in gold from Latin America, which is largely destined for US consumers, is becoming the preferred way for drug cartels, terrorists and bad regimes to launder their dirty money," Rubio said. "The US Department of Justice's prosecution of illicit gold traders Juan Granda, Samer Barrage and Renato Rodriguez, who pleaded guilty to money laundering involving dirty Latin American gold, is the tip of the iceberg, and should put all bad actors on notice."[14]

That year, Elemetal rival Kaloti Metals & Logistics, which also bought gold from Peter Ferrari, simply closed its doors. The owner of World Precious Metals, another Ferrari customer, said he was looking to get out of the business, too. Gold had become a headache. Other Miami refineries stayed in business. But the volume of the trade through South Florida is falling as the trade shifts to other ports of entry like Atlanta and Salt Lake City. Peruvian gold of murky origin continues to leave the county by the ton—only now it is increasingly heading for India and the United Arab Emirates rather than the United States. The underlying motivation to trade gold remains: the per kilo price, which fell drastically from nearly $57,000 in 2013 to $34,000 three years later, was back on the rise at above $50,000 in 2020.

Republic Metals Corporation, which had been one of Operation Arch Stanton's targets, filed for bankruptcy in 2018 for reasons that were never publicly explained beyond an "accounting error" stemming from the company's inventory practices. Early the next year, the Rubin family sold its business to the Japanese precious-metals giant Asahi for $25.5 million—proceeds that went toward paying off creditors.[15]

Legally speaking, the company fared much better than Elemetal and was never charged. Instead, the US Attorney's Office closed its investigation into Republic by signing a "nonprosecution agreement" with the Miami refinery. Unlike at Elemetal, there was no evidence that anyone at Republic sought to subvert anti–money laundering laws. And although the company had done business with questionable suppliers such as Peter Ferrari, Republic demonstrated that it broke ties with those people when it became aware that the source of their gold was unclear.

Still, according to the agreement with prosecutors, "the nature of [Republic]'s conduct . . . is serious and worthy of investigation." That conduct remains a secret. Details of why federal investigators targeted Republic and what they uncovered were summarized in a so-called statement of facts attached to the agreement. Although the agreement is otherwise public, the US Attorney's Office refuses to release the statement of facts, saying the information is being kept confidential at Republic's request.

Under the agreement, Republic—which prosecutors acknowledged "made significant efforts to create a culture of proper compliance"—agreed to improve its anti–money laundering program, at a cost of $1 million. No formal fine was levied. Republic had "a history of cooperating voluntarily with the federal government" while it was owned by the Rubins, the US Attorney's Office noted. The suspicious transactions first noted by Almeida in 2015—which involved paying third parties for gold—turned out to be routine financing arrangements, unlike NTR Metals' shell game meant to obscure its suppliers.

"We have always applauded efforts to hold wrongdoers accountable and, by the same token, believe it is important and fair that companies like Republic that intend to operate lawfully be recognized as such," a spokesman for the company said.[16]

∞∞∞∞∞∞∞

In his three years as a gold smuggler, Chilean investigators believe, Harold Vilches bought and sold roughly two tons of gold, almost all of which he'd smuggled into the country from Perú and Argentina.[17]

After his arrest, Vilches's life changed dramatically. Chilean authorities seized most of his assets, and he and his wife moved out of their upscale apartment and into a working-class neighborhood.[18] Vilches sold some of his remaining possessions and tried to adapt to a modest lifestyle. He spent months on nighttime house arrest.[19]

Vilches was finally sentenced in Chile on January 30, 2018. Because he had cooperated with prosecutors and testified before a federal grand jury in Miami, he wasn't punished with jail time.[20]

Instead, Vilches was slapped with a $24 million fine—the total amount of the taxes he'd evaded—and five years of probation for money laundering, smuggling gold, forming part of a criminal organization, and presenting false customs declarations.[21] His case was Chile's first money laundering conviction related to gold smuggling.

Vilches's family members and employees were also sentenced to probation for the same crimes: Carlos Rivas and Javier Concha to three years each and Vilches's wife, Scarlett Rivas Cifuentes, who was convicted as an accomplice, to 541 days. Luis Patricio Mella, the stockbroker and currency exchanger, got 320 days of probation, which the court determined was time served, for money laundering.[22] Dagoberto Muñoz, the gold coin broker, pleaded guilty to a tax fraud charge stemming from the case and was sentenced to three years of probation in 2019.[23]

The Vilches case left a black mark on Chile's gold market.

Gold brokers joke that the history of their industry can be divided into "before Harold Vilches" and "after Harold Vilches," and in many ways it's true.[24] Chile has since instituted tough import and export regulations.[25] As one exporter put it, if you tell Chilean customs officials today that you want to export gold, they "put you up against the wall and pat you down."

As for Vilches, he went back to college to finish his business degree, got into real estate, and tried to make a fresh start.[26] But he didn't completely give up on precious metals. After he was released from house arrest, Vilches could sometimes be spotted melting gold in a friend's cramped jewelry stall in the back corner of a shopping mall in downtown Santiago.

For the most part, outside of the gold industry, Vilches's case has receded from public memory. Sometimes, strangers stop Vilches at the grocery store to ask if they've met before. They tell Vilches they remember his face from somewhere, they just can't say exactly where.[27]

∞∞∞∞∞∞

Gone were the cars, the pool, the women, the parties, the wealth.

Perú's Cochamarca maximum security prison is eight hours overland from the capital and holds 1,224 inmates. It has a wing designated for the country's most dangerous criminals—murderers, rapists, escape risks. It was in this "special section," at the end of a dark corridor, that Pedro David Pérez Miranda—aka Peter Ferrari—was spending his days.

Along with the biting cold, the prison sits at 11,325 feet, more than twice the altitude of Denver. Amnesty International has said the prison's mere elevation might constitute "cruel, inhuman and degrading" treatment.[28]

The former gold magnate ended up in this prison in February 2018, after he'd been accused of plotting to break out of his jail in Lima and putting a hit on the judge overseeing his case, Richard Concepción Carhuancho. Ferrari denied both allegations and suggested that shadowy and powerful forces were trying to bury him. Since that initial hearing, he'd been sentenced to an additional eighteen months of detention as the investigation churned on with no clear end in sight. Although he'd never been put on trial, much less convicted, he'd already served three years in some of the nation's worst jails. And he still had a US extradition order hanging over his head, with money laundering charges pending in Miami.[29]

Some believed Ferrari's new jail was designed to isolate him so that he wouldn't divulge what he knew about an industry that has also attracted politicians and other powerbrokers—people who were doing virtually the same thing he was, buying and selling gold they knew very little about.

But even at this maximum security hellhole, the one-time play-boy had managed to build a life of relative luxury. In a compound where visitors and inmates aren't supposed to have shoelaces, belts, or watches, Ferrari was wearing a brand-new pair of Nikes (with laces) and a matching blue sweatsuit. On his wrist was a chunky gold watch.

It was April 2019, and despite being in the crosshairs of two nations and named by a handful of witnesses as the mastermind of a sprawling illegal mining operation, he was convinced that authorities didn't have any proof against him because, he maintained, he hadn't done anything wrong.

Like all his competitors, he bought gold from anyone willing to sell it and didn't always know where it came from. "Jewelry and gold don't have birth certificates," he said, repeating one of his well-worn justifications. "The entire industry is built on trust."

Many of the miners he bought the metal from were so poor and from such rural areas they didn't even have national identification cards required to complete a transaction. Who was he to say their gold didn't come from honest dirt digging? And who was harmed if he made up receipts to back up those gold purchases? Technically, he may have broken some rules, but that didn't make him an illegal miner.

"Look, they can accuse me of doing things informally, maybe some missed paperwork, but that's an administrative fault," he said. "Go ahead and fine me, but don't put me in a prison with murderers and the worst of the worst."

He also denied one of the United States' central contentions: that once his operations were shut down in Perú, he started smuggling gold into neighboring countries to export it from there.

"That never happened," he said. "They can't accuse me of doing anything illegal or criminal because it never happened." Ferrari claimed the true villain in the story was the Peruvian government that had denied him his day in court and the right to exonerate himself.

"I've been kidnapped," an angry and despondent Ferrari told Judge Carhuancho during one of his multiple hearings. "I've been kidnapped by you."[30]

Ferrari saw himself as the heir to a long line of gold merchants stretching back to the time of the Incas, when the kings covered the walls of their temples in sheets of gold and sat on gilded thrones.

Up until several years ago, buying and selling gold was considered an honorable way to make a living, a trade deeply tied to national identity. But then a few bad actors and scandal-loving journalists twisted the industry's image, he said, making it seem like ecological devastation and slavery were synonymous with the shiny metal itself.

"Why is gold so stigmatized?" he asked. "There's so much ignorance. Not all gold comes from Madre de Dios; it's not all as terrible as that."

But he believed his case wasn't really about gold; rather, it was about his overblown ego—his almost pathological need to flaunt his good fortune in a country where there's crushing poverty. Like most prisoners, Ferrari obsessed over his future and said he was determined to change his ways—not because he'd been broken or tamed but for the sake of his children.

Some of his kids, like Gian Piere and Peter Jr., had been dragged into his legal mess. After spending more than eight months in jail, the twins were released in 2018—buried in legal bills and anxiety— but still awaiting trial in Perú and with the US extradition pending.

"I might be forced to leave this world of gold for the sake of my family," Ferrari said. "I've become an embarrassment for them and it's not fair that they have to pay the price."

Gold, he'd come to believe, simply wasn't worth it anymore.

◇◇◇◇◇◇◇◇◇

In May 2020, Ferrari was finally released from prison and placed under house arrest. Peruvian prosecutors asked for a thirty-six-month extension to continue investigating his case.

The respite didn't last long.

Ferrari's release came as the coronavirus pandemic was sweeping the globe, and it hit Peru particularly hard. In late August, just weeks after walking out of prison, he was rushed to an intensive care unit in Lima. The man who had boasted of his eternal youth and never getting sick had contracted the coronavirus. On September 26, 2020, at the age of 60, he died of COVID-19.

The news that Ferrari had, once again, slipped the grip of justice was met with skepticism by many. Online, speculation raged that Ferrari had faked his own death, bribing doctors with a "few bars of pure gold" and then completed his disappearing act with a staged cremation.[31]

This time the truth was more mundane. Ferrari's family and friends said his funeral was delayed several days so that Peruvian and US authorities could collect DNA and make sure it was, indeed, Pedro Pérez Miranda on the coroner's slab. (US officials denied that they requested or pulled his DNA.)

For those entangled in Ferrari's legal mess, his death raised questions about their own fate. José Estuardo Morales, Ferrari's long-time driver and bodyguard, and Ferrari's twin sons, Gian Piere and Peter Jr., still faced charges.

Shortly after his boss's funeral, Morales said it was unclear to him and his lawyers if Perú or the United States would continue to pursue the matter.

"They've been investigating this for so many years and they haven't been able to prove anything," Morales said. "And the man they were really after is dead."

<hr />

In February 2019, Peruvian President Martín Vizcarra launched "Plan Mercury," sending more than fifteen hundred police and military to shut down La Pampa—one of the hemisphere's largest illegal gold mines—once and for all.

Steeped in stories about the murderous thugs who controlled the illegal goldfields, the military was prepared for the worst.

"We knew they had hired killers who were protecting the bosses and that there were gangs in the area," Perú's Defense Minister José Huerta Torres said. "The entire operation was a mystery for us, because we didn't know if we were going to face resistance."[32]

Once again, however, the gold trade corruption machine was in good working order. Most of the miners, the gangs, and the bosses had been tipped off about the raid and scattered.

Some took their equipment with them; others sank their gear in the toxic pits, waiting for the military to leave—as they always had in the past.

As usual, the military went on an orgy of destruction, blowing up almost four hundred dredges and barges and more than three hundred motors used to run the suction pumps. They also arrested more than eighty people in the first phase of the raid.

But then they did something unexpected: they stayed. As the military set up camps inside La Pampa, Vizcarra promised the skeptical nation that the soldiers would be there for at least two years, the vanguard of a longer term project to wean the region off illegal gold and create jobs in agriculture, forestry, and tourism.

Many miners didn't believe him.

"They can't stay there forever," one prospector said four months after the operation began. "When they're gone, we'll go back in."

The raid on La Pampa pulled back the curtain on an area that had been the source of endless speculation and largely off-limits to the police, NGOs, and reporters. But some of the worst rumors— that there were mass graves and torture sites hidden in the dunes— appeared overblown.

Plan Mercury also laid bare exactly how dependent the region was on the illicit gold trade.

The new governor of Madre de Dios, Luis Hidalgo Okimura, was a cheerleader for the military operation, even as he discovered just how painful it was for the community. Though his administration received no tax revenue from the goldfields, he estimated the shutdown at La Pampa had blown a $69 million hole in the local economy.[33] And tens of thousands of miners, mostly young men, were foisted into a community that didn't know how to absorb them.

As unemployment soared, gangs of thieves started preying on the region's other cash cow: tourism. In February, men ambushed a nature lodge and murdered a worker. Two months later, a bus full of tourists heading to an indigenous community called Infierno was robbed at gunpoint. About 40 percent of all the tourism packages scheduled for 2019 were canceled as a result of the spate of violence, the governor said.

And there was still the matter of what to do with the sprawling abandoned mine. Okimura was hoping the international community, which had raised such a stink about the illegal gold trade, might finance timber and agricultural projects, even as he feared the land might not be suitable for agriculture for years, if ever. Others had floated the idea of using the vast empty space to set up solar cells to provide power to the region.

But locals believed the fate of the bare plain had been sealed by God and geology.

Ever since the time of the Incas, Madre de Dios had been valued for its riches. And La Pampa hadn't completely given up hers. Conventional wisdom was that decades of mining by tens of thousands of workers had only scraped away about 40 percent of the available metal.

As Germán Ríos, a local historian, put it, people sacrificed blood and treasure searching for El Paitití—the El Dorado of Madre de Dios.

"El Paitití exists," he said. "And it's there in La Pampa."[34]

At first glance, the military intervention seemed effective. By June 2019, mining operations in the goldfield had come to a virtual halt. The roar of motors and dredges and the hiss of pumps were gone.

Many miners left the region to try their luck elsewhere. But hundreds, if not thousands, had simply moved their equipment to the other side of the Interoceanic Highway connecting Perú to Brazil and kept working. The area is a designated "mining corridor"— a place where mining, in theory, is legal. But in order to work there, operators still need titles and permits and to follow environmental laws. None of that was happening.

Dozens of prospectors had punched into a piece of jungle once owned by Alfredo Vracko, a local businessman who had been murdered in 2015 as he tried to keep illegal gold miners off his property. Now his land is trapped in a family dispute and overrun. A few months after La Pampa was shut down, teams of men were cutting down trees and building a path deep into the property. At the end of the trail was a massive expanse of red earth and mud—a newly opened mine.

Solutions

How to Stop Dirty Gold

IN 2018, THE NONPROFIT AMAZON AID FOUNDATION RELEASED A DOCU-
mentary film titled *River of Gold* that tracked a team of journalists and a biologist who traveled by canoe deep into the ravaged
Amazonian rain forest in Perú. The filmmakers captured haunting
images of illegal miners scorching the earth in the Madre de Dios
region with chainsaws, fire hoses, and toxic mercury, leaving behind
massive pits the size of football fields.

All for a morsel of gold.

"Have you ever seen anything like this?" journalist Donovan
Webster asks Peruvian biologist Enrique Ortiz, as they stand on the
rim of a vast mining hole at dawn.

"No, this is beyond my expectations," Ortiz says. "This is pretty
shocking."

"Is the value of the forest higher than the gold or not?" Webster
asks, as a miner buzz-saws the trunk of a towering tree hundreds of
years old.

"The value of this gold here is a one-time shot," Ortiz says. "The
forest is a long-term provider. So, yes, gold is a faster way to get
cash. . . . You can hear [them say], 'Let's get the gold and go away.'"[1]

Anyone looking for serious solutions to this complex problem
cannot simply blame the miners.

Even environmental activists crying out for the end of deforestation in the Amazon acknowledge these small-scale miners are simply struggling to survive. Many operate under the thumb of criminal

gangs. They use toxic mercury only because it is available, cheap, and easy (although horribly inefficient at isolating gold).

While everyone agrees the world would be a better place if alluvial mining in the Amazon stopped, that is unlikely to happen in the short term. Perú's central government is too weak and the lure of profits is too strong. So if the miners are going to do their work, at least they can be given safer tools.

"Mining is mining. It's always going to be a nasty business, but it can be done with care for the environment," said Susan Keane, a senior director of global programs at the nonprofit Natural Resources Defense Council, one of the largest environmental advocacy groups in the United States. Keane, whose organization focuses on alternatives to the use of mercury and other environmental issues, said the gold-mining crisis in South America's rain forests is not unique to that continent. "It's happening all over the world."

Keane and others believe solutions lie in foreign governments more effectively regulating the gold-mining industry, educating small-scale miners, and financing projects that promote safer technological methods.[2]

The NRDC and other major environmental groups are pushing for less-toxic alternatives to mercury. Today, more than 120 countries have signed the 2013 Minamata Convention on Mercury. One article in the treaty requires countries with small-scale gold mining such as Perú to reduce and, if feasible, eliminate the use of mercury.

The United Nations has poured millions into programs under the Minamata Convention to reduce the use of mercury in mining operations. One organization doing that is the Global Environmental Facility, which is funded by the United Nations, development banks, and international nongovernmental organizations. The group is providing $45 million in financing to help artisanal gold miners eliminate the use of mercury in Perú, Colombia, and six other countries.[3]

Kevin Telmer, executive director of a group called the Artisanal Gold Council, said the foremost challenge to improving the methods of small-scale mining is political. Foreign governments, he said, must recognize artisanal mining is here to stay, decriminalize the work, and help "formalize" the operations. That way the miners can have access to noncriminal financing, safer technologies, and the global "fair-mined" marketplace. It's no easy task. An array of issues bedevil the mining of gold, from land rights to mining titles to environmental permits and workforce conditions.

"We need to put in the structures so the small-scale miners don't have to sell their gold to criminal gangs and drug traffickers," Telmer said. (Perú's government has floated the idea of reopening a state bank to buy gold directly from miners and cut out problematic middlemen like Peter Ferrari and criminal gangs.)[4]

Telmer said the key to improving safety is to show miners they can recover more gold and make more money without mercury. Large-scale industrial mines have stopped using mercury because it is so inefficient. The simplest alternatives for small-scale miners are basic gravity techniques such as panning, shaking tables, and centrifuges that separate gold.

Even more effective, with proper safeguards, is a method called cyanide leaching—though the chemical is highly toxic. If it leaks, cyanide can pose serious environmental dangers and health risks. The leaching process entails miners agitating ore in vats of cyanide, which dissolves the gold into columns. The resulting doré is then extracted. About 90 percent of the gold is recovered from the ore, more than twice the yield in the mercury process.[5]

"Cyanide leaching has its drawbacks, but it's superior to mercury processing," Telmer said.

Small-scale miners are also being pitched on a "two-kilo" proposal in Perú, Africa, and Indonesia. The pitch is that if miners invest just two kilos of gold into mercury-free techniques, they can greatly improve the health and safety of their operations.

⬦⬦⬦⬦⬦⬦⬦⬦⬦

As difficult as it is to wean artisanal miners off using mercury, efforts to revive the lifeless earth in the alluvial mining regions of Madre de Dios are even more of a challenge.

In Perú, the Artisanal Gold Council is collaborating with the government on a test-case remediation project to remove five kilograms of mercury ore from five acres of already mined land in the Madre de Dios region.

In Madre de Dios, where Luis Fernandez, a tropical ecologist at Wake Forest University's Center for Amazonian Scientific Innovation, runs a research laboratory, aerial imagery shows hundreds of thousands of acres have been deforested. Much of the damage is happening in national parks and ecological preserves.

He and a team of researchers are leading efforts to study how to reforest such a devastated ecosystem, including using charcoal-enriched soil to grow vegetation again and testing a mix of forty native plant species for their viability.[6]

◌◌◌◌◌◌◌◌◌

There are two major sources of gold in Latin America: large mines controlled by multinational conglomerates, and gold brokers known as "aggregators," who buy from artisanal miners.

Aggregators offer a riskier business model, experts say, because it's so difficult to trace the origins of their gold. Some buy gold from mines controlled by criminals—and cover it up by falsifying paperwork and bribing officials, as NTR Metals' dealers did.

When dealing with aggregators, "it's impossible to know the original source of the gold," said Mike Riess, a precious-metals consultant who sat on a US Treasury Department anti–money laundering advisory board over the past decade. "It's more likely at this point that you're dealing with a criminal organization."

Despite the risks, many global gold firms seeking to meet endless demand still buy from aggregators. That has historically included two of the world's biggest refineries, Switzerland-based Metalor and Japan-based Asahi, which both have operations in the United States.[7] (Metalor recently said it would stop buying gold from aggregators in Latin America. A spokesman for Asahi said the company sources "material in a legal and responsible manner.")[8]

Before bankruptcy, Republic Metals in Miami had unveiled a "Peace of Mined" plan that saw it drop aggregator suppliers in favor of large mines.

Riess, the precious-metals consultant, said the criminal case against Elemetal and its NTR gold dealers was a wake-up call. "It certainly elevated everyone's sense that consumer due diligence had to be improved," Riess said. "There was always a reasonable level of sensitivity to the regulations and compliance requirements, but [companies] have become more conscious of them."

However, Riess believes the greater responsibility in the gold supply chain lies with the countries exporting the precious metal.

"The origin countries have to do their part," he said. "When you're looking at dysfunctional countries like the Congo or Central African Republic, it's not realistic because they can't get their house in order."

"But in the case of Perú and Colombia, you have responsible governments and they're helping gold buyers in improving the supply chain. If Perú and Colombia step up their efforts to formalize the gold mining industry, that's key."

The standards and regulations for buying and selling gold are growing stricter as governments worldwide, including the United States, adopt tougher mineral supply chain and anti–money laundering policies. For instance, Venezuela is off-limits for American gold buyers because its president, Nicolás Maduro, has taken over the nation's precious-metals industry and is suspected of collaborating with a US-designated terrorist group in Colombia that smuggles Venezuelan gold in exchange for weapons. Not to mention, Maduro was indicted in New York in 2020 on federal charges of playing a central role in a narco-terrorism conspiracy with current and former Venezuelan officials.

Equally significant: consumers have demanded more transparency about the source of gold, while corporations have grown more sensitive to those concerns. Such sweeping reform needed to clean up the gold industry is not without precedent, experts say, citing the scandal over "blood diamonds" that erupted two decades ago. Since 2003, more than seventy-five countries, including the United States, have signed on to a United Nations–backed accord called the Kimberley Process that certifies diamonds as "conflict-free," meaning rebel groups do not profit from their sale. (However, some controversy persists, because critics believe that governments in developing countries are not being held to the same standards as the rebels.)

Major international groups, including the Paris-based Organisation for Economic Co-operation and Development, have promoted new conflict-free standards for buying and selling gold and other minerals that are being adopted by Western nations. At the same time, the United States has enacted a law targeting the purchasing of "conflict minerals" under the Dodd-Frank Act.[9] Passed in 2010, that provision led to an effective boycott of conflict gold sourced in the Congo, Central African Republic, and other nations.

Carly Oboth, a policy adviser at Global Witness, a nonprofit that seeks to expose the links between the exploitation of natural resources and human rights abuses, said US businesses are waking up to the reputational issues posed by dealing in tainted gold. Cleaning up their supply chains is a matter of survival.

"Companies are seeing these provisions as self-preservation measures," Oboth said. "If a company doesn't follow these compliance standards, there could be real financial, legal and reputational harm. Because these supply chains are so fluid and complex, it's in their best interest to trace the origins of their purchases."[10]

The tech industry, including Apple, and some jewelers like Tiffany & Co. have led the way in disclosing their supplier lists and inviting public scrutiny. But ironically, when dirty suppliers like Elemetal are exposed and found to be listed in supply chain disclosures, transparent companies find themselves more vulnerable to criticism than secretive competitors that do not publicize their sources of metal.

Oboth said US refineries and dealers must do a better job of investigating their suppliers' sources of gold and disclosing them honestly when they submit compliance audits to industry groups, such as the London Bullion Market Association. She cited the fact that Elemetal passed audits to make the "good delivery" lists of the LBMA and other groups, despite obvious misrepresentations and fraud by employees and a disastrously ineffective corporate compliance program.

"These industry schemes involving the LBMA [certification] provided a veneer of responsibility when in actuality there was not a lot of work being done to comply with the laws," she said.

If at the end of the day all the audits and laws and treaties don't alter the behavior of corporations and stop the flow of dirty gold, consumers can take matters into their own hands.

To prove it's possible, Oboth points to her own experience when she got engaged in 2017. Her fiancé made a point of seeking out a Philadelphia jeweler that advertised its responsible sourcing methods. The ring he bought had a recycled diamond set atop a band of gold from Colombia and came with a fair-mined certificate. Consumers who want to see the gold industry improve, Oboth said, must change their own habits first.

A Note on Sources

This book began as a series for the *Miami Herald* and grew to encompass a sprawling gold-smuggling case spanning seven countries. We interviewed more than sixty people involved in the case or with knowledge of the secretive US gold industry and reviewed thousands of pages of court records in the United States and South America.

While writing the book, we made reporting trips to Chile, Perú, and Colombia to speak with investigators and gold traders as well as miners in the Madre de Dios region, one of the epicenters of the illegal gold trade. We also interviewed three of the protagonists of this story: Juan Pablo Granda as he was serving his sentence in a US federal prison in Miami; Harold Vilches while he was rebuilding his life in Santiago, Chile; and Pedro David Pérez Miranda, aka Peter Ferrari, during his incarceration in Perú's mountaintop Cochamarca maximum security prison.

Whenever possible we have identified the people we interviewed in the endnotes. However, many people spoke to us on the condition of anonymity, either because they weren't authorized to discuss the case or because they feared for their safety.

The US Attorney's Office in Miami continues to investigate the gold industry, meaning Operation Arch Stanton remains ongoing. As a result, people with direct knowledge of the Elemetal branch of the investigation—which is for all intents and purposes over—proved reluctant to share their stories. In many cases, they were legally prohibited from doing so.

At the end of the day, this book relies on fearless sources who believe readers need to understand the consequences of misconduct in the gold industry.

Quotations from emails, phone tap recordings, and court documents were taken directly from those records. Quotations included in dialogues were reconstructed based on participants' contemporaneous notes and/or their recollections of those conversations. Many of the events described in this book were witnessed by more than one person. Wherever possible, we relied on primary documents and notes to reconstruct those events.

We have made every effort to contact everyone who is named in this book. In one case, we gave a pseudonym to a confidential informant, Andrés Tejeda, in the US criminal case against the three NTR Metals dealers and Pérez Miranda to avoid endangering him and his family in Perú.

The information about ongoing investigations in Perú and Colombia is current through May 2020.

Acknowledgments

Dirty Gold would never have been possible without the support of an army of friends, family, colleagues, and dozens of sources, many of whom spoke to us at great personal risk and on condition of anonymity.

In particular, we're indebted to our colleagues at the *Miami Herald* and McClatchy, who are committed to the type of investigative journalism that made this book possible. They not only urged us to pursue stories about the illegal gold trade but also gave us the leeway and encouragement to write this book at a time when daily newspapers are struggling yet more essential than ever.

Among those who provided support, guidance, and feedback are investigative editor Casey Frank, *Miami Herald* executive editor Aminda Marqués Gonzalez, managing editor Rick Hirsh, editors Amy Driscoll, Curtis Morgan, Marjie Lambert, Dave Wilson, John Yearwood, Jay Ducassi, and Nancy San Martin, and translator Oscar Diaz. We're also incredibly grateful for colleagues like Joey Flechas, Jacqueline Charles, Antonio María Delgado, and others who covered for us while we were on book leave.

In addition, we'd like to thank our editor, Ben Adams, the entire team at Hachette, and our agent, David Patterson, for believing in the project and for their patience with us as we learned the ropes, as well our copy editor, Christina Palaia, who saved us from many an embarrassing mistake, and Carolyn Levin, the attorney who reviewed the manuscript.

The book could not have been written without the help of Juan Granda, one of the three NTR gold dealers, who allowed us to conduct numerous interviews with him while he was in prison and after he was released.

We also would like to thank the US federal law enforcement agencies that followed the dirty gold trail from Miami to South America, many of whom gave us hours of their time.

In Chile, we'd like to thank prosecutors Emiliano Arias Madariaga, Tufit Bufadel Godoy, José Luis Pérez Calaf, Pablo Alonso Godoy, and Nicolás Rodríguez Videla and Chilean federal agents Juan Figueroa and Juan Pablo Sandoval Valencia for taking time out of their busy schedules to talk to us and for answering endless questions once we were back in Miami. We also want to thank Harold Vilches, who patiently sat for long interviews about a period in his life from which he was trying to move on, and Tony Gonzalez, Jose Daniel Freixas, Jonathan David Kane, and Andrew Hevia for facilitating the interviews.

In Perú, we'd like to thank Pedro David Pérez Miranda, who spoke to us from jail at considerable personal risk. We'd also like to thank members of his family, his legal team, and his inner circle, who provided valuable context and guidance. There were numerous Peruvian officials who took the time to give us an inside look at their fight against the illegal gold trade. Many appear in the book, others do not. In particular we'd like to thank the late defense minister José Huerta and Madre de Dios governor Luis Hidalgo Okimura for their time and input.

Kyra Gurney would like to thank her parents, Burke Gurney and Deborah Cornish, and sister, Elise Gurney, for reading a draft of the manuscript and sharing valuable feedback. She would also like to thank her sweet and patient husband, Daniel Hernández Medina, who packed up their entire apartment when they moved a few months before the deadline in order to give her time to finish the book.

Nicholas Nehamas gives all his thanks to his wife, Danielle, who made him laugh when he was stricken by writer's block and made him work when he couldn't laugh anymore. He also sends his love to his parents, Susan Glimcher and Alexander Nehamas, who gave him his first books and told him that one day he would write one of his own; and to Danielle's parents, Patricia McCarthy-Guillette and David Guillette, who have welcomed him into their family with open and loving arms.

Jay Weaver gives heartfelt thanks to his wife, Marta Lavandier, a photo editor with the AP, who never once lost her cool while he was working evenings, weekends, and vacations to help complete this book. He would also like to thank his entire family, who have always supported his journalistic endeavors.

Jim Wyss would like to thank his partner and confidant, Ana Soler, who has been there when it mattered most. He'd also like to thank his mother, Susan Bursey, his brother, John A. Wyss, and his father, John H. Wyss, for their love and support over the years.

Notes

Prologue

1. Juan Pablo Granda, interviews with the authors at Federal Correctional Institution–Miami, June 2019.

2. Mariela Jara, "For the Rural Poor of Peru, the Social Agenda Is Far Away," Inter Press Service News Agency, February 22, 2018, http://www.ipsnews.net/2018/02/rural-poor-peru-social-agenda-far-away/.

3. Leslie E. Sponsel, "The Master Thief: Gold Mining and Mercury Contamination in the Amazon," in *Life and Death Matters: Human Rights, Environment, and Social Justice*, ed. Barbara Rose Johnston (London: Routledge, 2016), 128.

4. Jorge Caballero, Martín Pillaca, Max Messinger, Francisco Román, Miles R. Silman, and Luis E. Fernandez, "Three Decades of Deforestation from Artisanal Gold Mining in the Peruvian Amazon," *Center for Amazonian Scientific Innovation Research Brief* 1 (August 2018), http://cincia.wfu.edu/wp-content/uploads/CINCIA-Research-Brief-No.-1.pdf.

5. Jose Huerta Torres (Peruvian Defense Minister), interview with the authors, April 3, 2019.

6. Analysis of Form SD Specialized Disclosure Reports filed with the Securities Exchange Commission by Fortune 500 companies. Provided to the authors by a confidential source, 2017.

7. Jim Wyss, "Gold Is 'False God' Fueling 'Slavery,' Pope Says. Much of the Metal Ends Up in Miami," *Miami Herald*, January 19, 2018.

Chapter 1: The Party

1. Juan Pablo Granda's biography was described at his detention hearing and in interviews with Granda, his associates, and confidential sources; *United States v. Juan P. Granda*, No. 17-20215, PACER (S.D. Fla., April 3, 2017); interviews with the authors, 2019.

2. Renato Rodriguez's biography was described in the transcript of his detention hearing, his sentencing memo, letters submitted by friends and family to the court, and interviews with confidential sources and his associates; *United States v. Renato Rodriguez*, No. 17-20215, PACER (S.D. Fla., March 27, 2017); interviews with the authors, 2019.

3. Samer Barrage's biography was described in the transcript of his detention hearing, his sentencing memo, and interviews with confidential sources and his associates; *United States v. Samer H. Barrage*, No. 17-20215, PACER (S.D. Fla., April 29, 2017); *United States v. Samer H. Barrage*, No. 17-20215, PACER (S.D. Fla., January 17, 2018); interviews with the authors, 2019.

4. Susanne Barton, "The Perth Mint Has Recast This Gold Bar More Than 65,000 Times," *Bloomberg*, February 15, 2019, https://www.bloomberg.com/news/features/2019-02-15/the-perth-mint-has-recast-this-gold-bar-more-than-65-000-times.

5. Michael W. George, "Gold," in *US Geological Survey, Mineral Commodity Summaries*, US Department of the Interior, February 2019, https://prd-wret.s3-us-west-2.amazonaws.com/assets/palladium/production/s3fs-public/atoms/files/mcs-2019-gold.pdf.

6. Intergovernmental Forum on Mining, Minerals, Metals and Sustainable Development, *Global Trends in Artisanal and Small-Scale Mining (ASM): A Review of Key Numbers and Issues* (Winnipeg: International Institute for Sustainable Development, 2017), https://www.iisd.org/sites/default/files/publications/igf-asm-global-trends.pdf.

7. Federal criminal affidavit against Granda, *United States v. Juan P. Granda*, No. 17-20215, PACER (S.D. Fla., March 15, 2017).

8. Analysis of US Customs data provided to the authors by WorldCity, Inc.

9. *Glengarry Glen Ross*, directed by James Foley (Los Angeles, CA: New Line Cinema, 1992).

10. Miami-Dade County, Department of Planning and Zoning, Planning Research Section, *Residential Foreclosures*, July 2009.

11. Chris Kirkham, "At Kaplan University, 'Guerrilla Registration' Leaves Students Deep in Debt," *HuffPost*, December 22, 2010, https://www.huffpost.com/entry/kaplan-university-guerilla-registration_n_799741.

Chapter 2: Moths to the Flame

1. This description of the Varna necropolis and modern-day archaeological excavations is drawn from Andrew Curry, "Mystery of the Varna Gold: What Caused These Ancient Societies to Disappear?" *Smithsonian Magazine*, April 18, 2016, https://www.smithsonianmag.com/travel/varna-bulgaria-gold-graves-social-hierarchy-prehistoric-archaeology-smithsonian-journeys-travel-quarterly-180958733/.

2. Peter L. Bernstein, *The Power of Gold: The History of an Obsession* (New York: John Wiley & Sons, 2000).

3. University of Bristol, "Where Does All the Gold Come From?" Phys.org, September 7, 2011, https://phys.org/news/2011-09-gold.html.

4. "How Much Gold Has Been Mined?" World Gold Council, accessed 2019, https://www.gold.org/about-gold/gold-supply/gold-mining/how-much-gold.

5. Agustino Fontevecchia, "How Many Olympic-Sized Swimming Pools Can We Fill with Billionaire Gold?" *Forbes*, November 19, 2010, https://www.forbes.com/sites/afontevecchia/2010/11/19/how-many-olympic-sized-swimming-pools-can-we-fill-with-billionaire-gold/#720272c669fl.

6. Samer Barrage's hiring at Elemetal was described in his sentencing memo and by confidential sources. *United States v. Samer H. Barrage*, No. 17-20215, PACER (S.D. Fla., January 17, 2018); interviews with the authors, 2019.

7. Renato Rodriguez's biography and family life was described in his sentencing memo. *United States v. Renato Rodriguez*, No. 17-20215, PACER (S.D. Fla., January 29, 2018).

8. Cecilia Rivas Guerrero, letter to Judge Robert Scola. *United States v. Renato Rodriguez*, No. 17-20215, PACER (S.D. Fla., January 29, 2018).

9. Father Jesus Arias, letter to Judge Scola. *United States v. Renato Rodriguez*, No. 17-20215, PACER (S.D. Fla., January 29, 2018).

Chapter 3: A Gold-Covered Brick

1. Peruvian Supreme Court extradition ruling, No. 59-2018 (Lima, Perú, May 31, 2018).

2. Company registration information for Business Investments was accessed on the Peruvian government's National Customs and Tax Administration Superintendency website. "Consulta RUC," Superintendencia Nacional de Aduanas y de Administración Tributaria (SUNAT), accessed 2018, http://www.sunat.gob.pe/cl-ti-itmrconsruc/jcrS03Alias.

3. Pedro Pérez Miranda, interview with the authors, April 7, 2019.

4. Pedro Pérez Miranda, interview with the authors, April 7, 2019.

5. Panorama, "INPE decide trasladar a 'Peter Ferrari' a penal de Cochamarca por peligro de fuga" (Pedro Pérez Miranda, interview by Panorama TV), YouTube video, 18:05, uploaded February 18, 2018, https://www.youtube.com/watch?v=e0ZlF0IbTQk.

6. Carol Graham, "Peru: The Prison of Poverty Is the Problem," Brookings, January 11, 1997, https://www.brookings.edu/opinions/peru-the-prison-of-poverty-is-the-problem/.

7. "Reporte Final," Commission de la Verdad, accessed May 2020, http://cverdad .org.pe/ifinal/.

8. "En dos meses lavó $18 millones de dólares," *El Comercio*, June 24, 1999.

9. "En dos meses lavó $18 millones de dólares," *El Comercio*, June 24, 1999.

10. "Mafia de Peter Ferrari incluía coroneles," *El Comercio*, June 23, 1999.

11. Lima Superior Court ruling No. 917-0 (Lima, Perú, February 28, 2005).

12. "Peter Ferrari exige al estado devolución de $2.5 millones," *El Comercio*, June 6, 2012.

13. "Interrogan a Carlos Vidal," *El Comercio*, July 1, 1999.

14. "El SIN tenia un grupo especializado en rastreo y extorsion a empresarios," *El Comercio*, July 17, 2005.

15. "Drug War Paradoxes: The U.S. Government and Peru's Vladimiro Montesinos," *Drug War Monitor* (Washington Office on Latin America Briefings series), July 2004, https://www.wola.org/sites/default/files/downloadable/Drug%20Policy/past/ddhr _monte_brief.pdf.

16. Peruvian Supreme Court Sentence No. 917-01 (Lima, Perú, February 28, 2005).

17. Confidential source (former Pérez Miranda employee), interview with the authors, 2018 and 2019.

18. "Peter Ferrari exige al estado devolución de $2.5 millones," *El Comercio*, June 12, 2005.

19. "Peter Ferrari exige al estado devolución de $2.5 millones," *El Comercio*, June 12, 2005.

20. Confidential source (former Pérez Miranda employee), interview with the authors, 2018 and 2019.

Chapter 4: Hand of God

1. Joseph Cesar Leyva Miyashiro, deposition with Peruvian police, September 22, 2014.

2. Confidential source, interview with the authors, November 2018.

3. Confidential source (former lawyer for Pérez Miranda), interview with the authors, 2018.

4. Peruvian Supreme Court extradition ruling, No. 59-2018 (Lima, Perú, May 31, 2018).

5. Steve Crogan, email to Samer Barrage and at least four Elemetal executives, August 2012. Message cited by federal prosecutors in Barrage and Juan Pablo Granda's factual proffer. *United States v. Samer H. Barrage*, No. 17-20215, PACER (S.D. Fla., September 5, 2017).

6. Confidential sources, interviews with the authors, 2019.

7. Charles Forelle, "Metalor Unit Agrees to Plea Deal," *Wall Street Journal*, January 9, 2004, https://www.wsj.com/articles/SB107359164321205900.

8. Crogan email, August 2012. Cited by federal prosecutors in factual proffer. *United States v. Samer H. Barrage*, No. 17-20215, PACER (S.D. Fla., September 5, 2017).

9. Steve Crogan email to Elemetal executives, November 30, 2012. Reviewed by the authors, 2019.

10. Company registration information for Lern United Mines Corp. was accessed on the Peruvian government's National Customs and Tax Administration Superintendency website. "Consulta RUC," Superintendencia Nacional de Aduanas y de Administración Tributaria (SUNAT), accessed 2018, http://www.sunat.gob.pe/cl-ti-itmrconsruc/jcrS03Alias.

11. Peruvian Supreme Court extradition ruling, No. 59-2018 (Lima, Perú, May 31, 2018).

12. While Perú's Supreme Court mentions Lern United, Pérez Miranda's representatives say they had nothing to do with that firm.

13. Peruvian Police Report No. 5805, October 21, 2014.

Chapter 5: Mr. Third Rail

1. Renato Rodriguez email to Steve Crogan, February 15, 2013. The authors reviewed this and all subsequent emails referenced in this chapter.

Chapter 6: The Gold Rush

1. Dante Gallardo, interview with the authors, June 2019.

2. Sara Regina Nicho Tisnado, interview with the authors, April 6, 2019.

3. Luis Hidalgo Okimura (governor of Madre de Dios), interview with the authors, June 1, 2019.

4. Leslie E. Sponsel, "The Master Thief: Gold Mining and Mercury Contamination in the Amazon," in *Life and Death Matters: Human Rights, Environment, and Social Justice*, ed. Barbara Rose Johnston (London: Routledge, 2016), 127–128.

5. Timothy Green, *The Gold Companion* (Geneva: MKS Finance, 1991), 108.

6. Germán Ríos, interview with the authors, June 2019.

7. Miguel Herrera, interview with the authors, June 2019.

8. This section on the effects of mercury comes from interviews conducted in 2018 with several scientists from Wake Forest University's Center for Amazonian Scientific Innovation, or CINCIA, including executive director Luis Fernandez.

9. Jim Wyss, "How U.S. Demand for Gold Jewelry and Bullion Is Poisoning Children in the Amazon," *Miami Herald*, January 26, 2018, https://www.miamiherald.com/news /nation-world/world/americas/article196933579.html.

10. "SNMPE: 'No es un buen momento para tener un banco minero, ni tampoco adecuado,'" *Gestión*, September 20, 2013, https://gestion.pe/economia/snmpe-buen-momento -banco-minero-adecuado-48640-noticia/.

11. Miguel Herrera, interview with the authors, June 2019.

12. "Tambopata National Reserve," Rainforest Expeditions, accessed 2019, https:// www.perunature.com/about-tambopata/tambopata-national-reserve/.

13. Mikaela J. Weisse, "Buffer Zones in the Peruvian Amazon Bring Conservation Benefits Despite Ambiguous Rules and Uncertain Authority" (master's thesis, University of Wisconsin, 2015), https://pdfs.semanticscholar.org/6cb8/39c0d2ebf035d0266a d295e2068073960c04.pdf.

14. Nadia Drake, "Isolated Tribes and Forests Threatened by New Amazon Road," *National Geographic*, March 23, 2018, https://www.nationalgeographic.com /news/2018/03/peruvian-amazon-road-forests-uncontacted-tribes-indigenous-rights/.

15. Jorge Caballero, Martín Pillaca, Max Messinger, Francisco Román, Miles R. Silman, and Luis E. Fernandez, "Three Decades of Deforestation from Artisanal Gold Mining in the Peruvian Amazon," *Center for Amazonian Scientific Innovation Research Brief* 1 (August 2018), http://cincia.wfu.edu/wp-content/uploads/CINCIA-Research-Brief-No.-1.pdf.

16. "Anuario Minero 2017," Perú Ministerio de Energía y Minas, April 30, 2018, https://cdn.www.gob.pe/uploads/document/file/98805/ANUARIO_MINERO_2017 _1_.pdf.

17. Confidential and police sources, interviews with the authors, June 2019.

18. Claudia Ortiz, "Luis Otsuka, dirigente de la mineria ilegal, entrego manifesto al papa francsico," *La Republica*, January 18, 2018, https://larepublica.pe/politica /1172944-luis-otsuka-dirigente-de-la-mineria-ilegal-entrego-manifiesto-al-papa -francisco/.

19. Luis Otsuka, interview with the *Miami Herald*, 2018.

20. Three people in Puerto Maldonado confirmed that Pérez Miranda was a frequent visitor.

21. "Reportan un policía muerto tras una emboscada en Madre de Dios," *RPP Noticias*, September 22, 2017, https://rpp.pe/lima/seguridad/reportan-un-policia -muerto-tras-una-emboscada-en-madre-de-dios-noticia-1078408.

Chapter 7: The Fed

1. This account of Schoonmaker's activities during Operation Arch Stanton comes from the authors' review of certain case files and notes, as well as dozens of interviews with sources familiar with the case.

2. "Foreign Office Locations," United States Drug Enforcement Agency, https:// www.dea.gov/foreign-office-locations.

3. United Nations Office on Drugs and Crime, *World Drug Report, 2019: Global Overview of Drug Demand and Supply* (Vienna: United Nations, June 2019), https://wdr.unodc.org/wdr2019/prelaunch/WDR19_Booklet_2_DRUG_DEMAND.pdf.

4. Stephanie Boyd, "Who's to Blame for Peru's Gold-Mining Troubles?" *The New Yorker*, October 28, 2013, https://www.newyorker.com/business/currency/whos-to-blame-for-perus-gold-mining-troubles.

5. Joel Sartore, "Walrus," National Geographic Photo Ark, https://www.nationalgeographic.com/animals/mammals/w/walrus/; Stefan Ogbac, "20 of the Lightest Cars Sold in the U.S.," *MotorTrend*, October 12, 2015, https://www.motortrend.com/news/20-of-the-lightest-cars-sold-in-the-u-s/.

6. DEA-Perú internal research documents reviewed by the authors.

7. Jim Wyss and Kyra Gurney, "Dirty Gold Is the New Cocaine in Colombia—and It's Just as Bloody," *Miami Herald*, January 16, 2018, https://www.miamiherald.com/news/nation-world/world/americas/colombia/article194188034.html.

8. Analysis of US Customs data provided to the authors by WorldCity, Inc.

Chapter 8: A Well-Oiled Machine

1. Factual proffer submitted by Juan Pablo Granda to the federal court in Miami. *United States v. Juan P. Granda*, No. 17-20215, PACER (S.D. Fla., March 15, 2017).

2. Nicholas Nehamas, "Developer Unveils Car Elevator for Porsche Design Tower," *Miami Herald*, June 15, 2015, https://www.miamiherald.com/news/business/real-estate-news/article24411289.html.

3. James Kelly, "South Florida: Trouble in Paradise," *Time*, November 23, 1981, http://content.time.com/time/magazine/article/0,9171,922693,00.html.

4. June Preston, "New York City, Miami Area Had Record Number of Murders in 1981," United Press International, January 1, 1982, https://www.upi.com/Archives/1982/01/01/New-York-City-Miami-Area-had-record-number-of-murders-in-1981/6756378709200/; Florida Department of Law Enforcement, *Crime in Florida Abstract: Miami-Dade County*, 2018, https://www.fdle.state.fl.us/FSAC/UCR/2018/Counties/Miami-Dade18.aspx; US Census Bureau, "Resident Population in Miami-Dade County, FL [FLMIAM6POP]," FRED Economic Data, Federal Reserve Bank of St. Louis, https://fred.stlouisfed.org/series/FLMIAM6POP, August 28, 2019.

5. Nicholas Nehamas, Kevin G. Hall, and Lily Dobrovolskaya, "This Russian General Fought the Mob. Why Does He Own $38 Million of Florida Real Estate?" *Miami Herald*, October 20, 2017, https://www.miamiherald.com/news/local/community/miami-dade/article179877266.html; Jay Weaver, "Venezuela's Ex-treasurer Sentenced to 10 Years for South Florida Money-Laundering Scheme," *Miami Herald*, November 27, 2018, https://www.miamiherald.com/news/local/article222226225.html; Nicholas Nehamas, "How Secret Offshore Money Helps Fuel Miami's Luxury Real-Estate Boom," *Miami Herald*, April 3, 2016, https://www.miamiherald.com/news/business/real-estate-news/article69248462.html.

6. Jay Weaver, "Spaniard López Tardón Sent to Prison for 150 Years in Miami Money-Laundering Case," *Miami Herald*, September 29, 2014, https://www.miamiherald.com/news/local/crime/article2296479.html?mod=article_inline.

7. "Average Monthly Hours of Sunshine in San Francisco (California)," World Weather and Climate Information, August 30, 2019, https://weather-and-climate.com/average-monthly-hours-Sunshine,San-Francisco,United-States-of-America.

8. "Peru en el Ranking Mundial de la Produccion Minera," Ministerio de Energia y Minas, accessed August 2019, http://www.minem.gob.pe/minem/archivos/file/Mineria /PDAC2017/ESTADISTICA_001.pdf.

9. Confidential source, interview with the authors, June 2018.

10. Confidential source, interview with the authors, 2018.

11. James M. Guthrie, revised August 2012 by Jeffrey R. Ferguson, "Overview of X-Ray Fluorescence," University of Missouri Research Reactor, Archaeometry Laboratory, http://archaeometry.missouri.edu/xrf_overview.html.

12. Ohio Precious Metals, "Notice of Application for Air Permit," submitted to Ohio Environmental Protection Agency, October 1, 2012, http://wwwapp.epa.state.oh.us /pub/county/archive/JACKSON/2012b_pn.html.

13. Timothy Green, *The Gold Companion: The A–Z of Mining, Marketing, Trading and Technology* (London: Rosendale Press Limited, 1991), 91.

14. Henry Sanderson, Neil Hume, and James Fontanella-Khan, "Scotiabank Puts Gold Business up for Sale," *Financial Times*, October 18, 2017, https://www.ft.com/content /4cb73a06-b3dd-11e7-a398-73d59db9e399.

15. Nicholas Nehamas, Jay Weaver, and Jim Wyss, "As Feds Target 'Blood Gold' and Dirty Money, This Miami Refinery Has Bigger Problems," *Miami Herald*, December 21, 2018, https://www.miamiherald.com/news/business/article223213905.html.

16. Nicholas Nehamas, "Family Behind Miami Gold Refinery Raided Coffers to Fund 'Lavish Lifestyle,' Lawsuit Claims," *Miami Herald*, February 7, 2019, https://www .miamiherald.com/news/local/article225917785.html.

17. Peruvian Police Report No. 5805, October 21, 2014.

18. David E. Kaplan, Philip P. Willan, Eleni Dimmler, Carol Salguero, and Mark Madden, "The Golden Age of Crime," *U.S. News & World Report*, November 29, 1999.

19. This account of the collaboration between Juan Pablo Granda and Andrés Tejeda is drawn primarily from the criminal affidavits filed in federal court against Granda and Tejeda, as well as from their factual proffers.

20. Description of Granda's personal life comes from author interviews with Granda at FCI-Miami, June 2019.

21. "El caso de la mineria ilegal en Peru," CooperAcción, http://cooperaccion.org.pe/el -caso-de-la-mineria-ilegal-en-el-peru/.

Chapter 9: Under Ferrari's Hood

1. Joseph Cesar Leyva Miyashiro, deposition with Peruvian police, September 22, 2014; Peruvian Police Report No. 5805, October 21, 2014.

2. Joseph Cesar Leyva Miyashiro, deposition with Peruvian police, September 22, 2014; Peruvian Police Report No. 5805, October 21, 2014; Pedro Pérez Miranda, interview with the authors, April 7, 2019.

3. Luis Rolando Madueño Chocano, deposition with Peruvian police, September 26, 2014; Peruvian Police Report No. 5805, October 21, 2014.

Chapter 10: "Flight of Last Resort"

1. *Elemetal Direct* 1, no. 4 (Spring 2016), https://issuu.com/ntrmetals/docs/samer -barrage-elemetal.

2. "Gold Prices," USA Gold, accessed 2019, http://www.usagold.com/reference/gold prices/2008.html.

3. Hibah Yousuf August, "Gold Tops $1,900, Looking 'a Bit Bubbly,'" *CNN Money*, August 23, 2011, https://money.cnn.com/2011/08/22/markets/gold_prices/index.htm.

4. "Dow Jones—DJIA—100 Year Historical Chart," Macrotrends, accessed 2019, https://www.macrotrends.net/1319/dow-jones-100-year-historical-chart.

5. *Elemetal Direct* 1, no. 4 (Spring 2016), https://issuu.com/ntrmetals/docs/samer-barrage-elemetal.

6. Former Elemetal employees and business associates, interviews with the authors, 2019.

7. Young Turks, "Glenn Beck on God, Blood & Goldline," YouTube video, 9:10, August 25, 2010, https://www.youtube.com/watch?v=g-aBUoO7aSA.

8. Dan Bigman, "Forbes Celebrity Covers: Glenn Beck, April 2010," *Forbes*, June 25, 2013, https://www.forbes.com/sites/danbigman/2013/06/25/forbes-celebrity-covers-glenn-beck-april-2010/#34850c046498.

9. Tim Murphy, "Glenn Beck's Favorite Gold Company Charged with Fraud," *Mother Jones*, November 1, 2011, https://www.motherjones.com/politics/2011/11/glenn-becks-favorite-gold-company-charged-fraud/; Matthew Mosk, "Goldline Agrees to Refund Millions to Customers," *ABC News*, February 22, 2012, https://abcnews.go.com/Blotter/goldline-agrees-refund-millions-customers/story?id=15768897.

10. David Goldman, "Your Dead iPhone Is a Gold Mine—Literally," *CNN*, October 13, 2011, https://money.cnn.com/2011/10/13/technology/iphone_trade_in/index.htm.

11. "Gold Demand Trends Q1 2019," World Gold Council, May 2, 2019, https://www.gold.org/goldhub/research/gold-demand-trends/gold-demand-trends-q1-2019.

12. Carolyn Cui, "High Metals Demand Spurs Merger of Recyclers," *Wall Street Journal*, April 9, 2012, https://www.wsj.com/articles/SB10001424052702304587704577334190440848190.

13. US Census Bureau, 2018; Ohio Department of Jobs and Family Services, *July 2019 Ranking of Ohio County Unemployment Rates*, July, 2019, https://ohiolmi.com/Home/RateMapArchive.

14. Historical background and present-day observations on Jackson, Ohio, come from a reporting trip and author interviews with Megan Malone, director of Jackson's Lillian E. Jones Museum, as well as other locals, 2017.

15. Walter Luhrman (founder of Ohio Precious Metals), interviews with the authors, 2017.

16. John W. Miller, "Gold Rush in Ohio? Small Town Plays Big Role," *Wall Street Journal*, November 18, 2014, https://www.wsj.com/articles/gold-rush-in-ohio-small-town-plays-big-role-1416357910.

17. Stephen Koff, "President Barack Obama Signed the Stimulus Bill Seven Years Ago Today. How Did It Work Out?" *Plain Dealer* (Cleveland), February 17, 2016, https://www.cleveland.com/open/2016/02/president_barack_obama_signed_the_stimulus_bill_seven_years_ago_today_how_did_it_work_out.html.

18. Carolyn Cui, "High Metals Demand Spurs Merger of Recyclers," April 9, 2012, https://www.wsj.com/articles/SB10001424052702304587704577334190440848190.

19. Steve Brown, "Vacant Addison Office Building Sold," *Dallas Morning News*, April 20, 2012.

20. Matthew Kent, "Metals Recycling Company Expanding to Waverly," *Chillicothe Gazette* (Ohio), March 27, 2013.

21. Terry Johnson, "Teamwork Leading to New Jobs for Southern Ohio," *Herald-Dispatch* (Huntington, WV), January 24, 2013.

22. Ohio Precious Metals, "OPM—First US Gold Refiner to Be Conflict Free Compliant" (news release), September 19, 2012, https://www.prnewswire.com/news-releases/opm---first-us-gold-refiner-to-be-conflict-free-compliant-170375546.html.

23. Ohio Precious Metals, "Ohio Precious Metals Achieves Good Delivery Status" (news release), September 14, 2012, https://www.prnewswire.com/news-releases/ohio-precious-metals-achieves-good-delivery-status-169768236.html.

24. Ohio Precious Metals, "OPM Metals LBMA Good Delivery for Gold" (news release), December 27, 2013, https://www.prnewswire.com/news-releases/opm-metals-lbma-good-delivery-for-gold-237500281.html.

25. "Good Delivery," LBMA, http://www.lbma.org.uk/good-delivery.

26. "Good Delivery," LBMA, http://www.lbma.org.uk/good-delivery.

27. Analysis of Form SD specialized disclosure reports filed to the Securities and Exchange Commission by Fortune 500 companies. Provided to the authors by a confidential source, 2017.

Chapter 11: The Crackdown

1. "Decreto legislativo de lucha eficaz contra el lavado de activos y otros delitos relacionados a la minería ilegal y crimen organizado," *El Peruano*, accessed 2019, https://busquedas.elperuano.pe/normaslegales/decreto-legislativo-d0e-lucha-eficaz-contra-el-lavado-activos-decreto-legislativo-n-1106-778570-3/.

2. "Las exportaciones mineras cayeron 12.5% en el 2013, según la SNMPE," *Gestión*, February 24, 2014, https://gestion.pe/economia/Exportaciones-mineras-cayeron-12-5-2013-Snmpe-4867-noticia/.

3. *SUNAT, Peru: Exportación Definitiva*, 2013, http://www.sunat.gob.pe/estad-comExt/modelo_web/informes/anuarios/2013/cdro_30.xls.

4. Jose Morales, interview with the authors, November 2018.

5. Panorama, "INPE decide trasladar a 'Peter Ferrari' a penal de Cochamarca por peligro de fuga" (Pedro Pérez Miranda, interview by Panorama TV), YouTube video, 18:05, uploaded February 18, 2018, https://www.youtube.com/watch?v=e0ZlF0IbTQk.

6. Panorama, "INPE decide trasladar a 'Peter Ferrari' a penal de Cochamarca por peligro de fuga" (Pedro Pérez Miranda, interview by Panorama TV), YouTube video, 18:05, uploaded February 18, 2018, https://www.youtube.com/watch?v=e0ZlF0IbTQk.

7. Miners, a cab driver, and fellow gold buyer in Puerto Maldonado, Madre de Dios, interviews with the authors, June 2019.

Chapter 12: The Raid

1. "Aduanas incautó media tonelada de oro ilegal por US$18 millones," *El Comercio*, January 8, 2014, https://elcomercio.pe/lima/aduanas-incauto-media-tonelada-oro-ilegal-us-18-millones-283672. Information was also obtained from Peruvian police reports.

2. Peruvian Police Report No. 5805, October 21, 2014.

3. James Bargent, "A Seizure, a Lawsuit and Illegal Gold from Peru," InSight Crime, December 16, 2015, https://www.insightcrime.org/news/analysis/seizure-a-lawsuit-and-illegal-gold-from-peru/.

4. Confidential source who was once Pérez Miranda's lawyer, interview with the authors, December 2018.

5. Pedro Pérez Miranda, interview with the authors, April 7, 2019.

6. Confidential police source, interview with the authors, April 5, 2019.

7. Oscar Castilla, "Aduanas incautó media tonelada de oro ilegal por US$18 millones," *El Comercio*, January 8, 2014, https://elcomercio.pe/lima/aduanas-incauto-media-tonelada-oro-ilegal-us-18-millones-283672.

8. James Bargent, "A Seizure, a Lawsuit and Illegal Gold from Peru," InSight Crime, December 16, 2015.

9. Joseph Cesar Leyva Miyashiro, deposition with Peruvian police, September 22, 2014, and Luis Rolando Madueño Chocano, deposition with Peruvian police, September 26, 2014.

10. Pedro Pérez Miranda, Miguel Ángel Rivero Pérez, Alfredo Néstor Egocheaga pretrial detention hearing, Lima, Perú, January 17, 2017.

11. Peruvian Police Report No. 5805, October 21, 2014.

Chapter 13: *La Base*

1. Luis Rolando Madueño Chocano, deposition with Peruvian police, September 26, 2014; International Volleyball Hall of Fame, accessed in 2019, https://www.volleyhall.org/gabriela-perez-del-solar.html.

2. Luis Rolando Madueño Chocano, deposition with Peruvian police, September 26, 2014.

3. Michael W. George, *2013 Minerals Yearbook: Gold [Advance Release]* (US Department of the Interior, US Geological Survey, October 2015), https://s3-us-west-2.amazonaws.com/prd-wret/assets/palladium/production/mineral-pubs/gold/myb1-2013-gold.pdf.

4. George, *2013 Minerals Yearbook*, https://s3-us-west-2.amazonaws.com/prd-wret/assets/palladium/production/mineral-pubs/gold/myb1-2013-gold.pdf.

5. Michael W. George, *2014 Minerals Yearbook: Gold [Advance Release]* (US Department of the Interior, US Geological Survey, November 2016), https://s3-us-west-2.amazonaws.com/prd-wret/assets/palladium/production/mineral-pubs/gold/myb1-2014-gold.pdf; federal criminal affidavit against Granda, *United States v. Juan P. Granda*, No. 17-20215, PACER (S.D. Fla., March 15, 2017).

6. Federal prosecutors cited this email in Elemetal's factual proffer. *United States v. Elemetal*, 18-20173, PACER (S.D. Fla., March 19, 2018).

7. Internal Elemetal emails reviewed by the authors.

8. Several WhatsApp conversations were included in the federal criminal affidavits against Juan Pablo Granda, Renato Rodriguez, and Samer Barrage. *United States v. Juan P. Granda*, No. 17-20215, PACER (S.D. Fla., March 15, 2017).

Chapter 14: The Perfect Patsy

1. Alison Leigh Cowan, "Martin R. Himmel, Who Marketed Dull Brands into Gold, Dies at 66," *New York Times*, November 26, 1991, https://www.nytimes.com/1991/11/26/nyregion/martin-r-himmel-who-marketed-dull-brands-into-gold-dies-at-66.html.

2. Cowan, "Martin R. Himmel, Who Marketed Dull Brands Into Gold, Dies at 66," https://www.nytimes.com/1991/11/26/nyregion/martin-r-himmel-who-marketed-dull-brands-into-gold-dies-at-66.html.

3. "Ovaltine," Himmel Group, https://www.himmelgroup.com/ovaltine.

4. Miami-Dade Property Appraiser, 2019, https://www8.miamidade.gov/Apps/PA/propertysearch/#/.

5. "Violetas Grand Opening," World Red Eye, September 22, 2011, https://worldredeye.com/2011/09/violetas-grand-opening.

6. Emails reviewed by the authors, 2019.

7. Florida Department of State, Division of Corporations, Articles of Organization for Florida Limited Liability Company, MVP Imports, March 1, 2013, http://search.sunbiz.org/Inquiry/CorporationSearch/ConvertTiffToPDF?storagePath=COR%5C2013%5C0308%5C00048632.Tif&documentNumber=L13000032008.

8. George, *2013 Minerals Yearbook*, https://s3-us-west-2.amazonaws.com/prd-wret/assets/palladium/production/mineral-pubs/gold/myb1-2013-gold.pdf.

9. Ecuadorian President Rafael Correa made these remarks in a radio interview. Ecuador Gold and Copper Corp., "Ecuador Gives Mining Industry a Big Wet Kiss" (news release), June 16, 2014, https://www.globenewswire.com/news-release/2014/06/16/644388/10085796/en/Ecuador-Gives-Mining-Industry-a-Big-Wet-Kiss.html.

10. The authors reviewed brochures and presentations prepared to pitch Himmel's pipeline project, which was called Ecosolami, 2019.

11. "La ruta del oro comercializado por Spartan y Clearprocess registra presuntas anomalías," Ecuadorian Prosecutor's Office, August 13, 2016, https://www.fiscalia.gob.ec/la-ruta-del-Oro-comercializado-por-spartan-y-clearprocess-registra-presuntas-anomalias/.

12. Ecuadorian court records, case no. 09286-2016-02579, accessed in 2019, http://consultas.funcionjudicial.gob.ec/informacionjudicial/public/informacion.jsf.

13. Ecuadorian court records, case no. 09286-2016-02579, accessed in 2019, http://consultas.funcionjudicial.gob.ec/informacionjudicial/public/informacion.jsf.

14. Alberto March, email to the authors, September 11, 2019.

15. Alberto March, email to the authors, August 8, 2019.

16. *United States v. Juan P. Granda*, No. 17-20215, PACER (S.D. Fla., March 15, 2017).

17. David Voreacos and Michael Smith, "Florida 'Boutique' Tied by U.S. to Alleged Gold Laundering Plot," Bloomberg, https://www.bloomberg.com/news/articles/2017-04-07/florida-boutique-tied-by-u-s-to-alleged-gold-laundering-plot; Ecuadorian court records, case no. 09286-2016-02579, accessed in 2019, http://consultas.funcionjudicial.gob.ec/informacionjudicial/public/informacion.jsf.

18. Alberto March, emails to the authors, August 8, 2019, and September 11, 2019.

19. The authors reviewed copies of emails between Himmel and Elemetal executives.

Chapter 15: The College Student

1. Harold Vilches, interviews with the authors, June 17–21, 2019. Whenever possible, the information Vilches shared was corroborated using court and business records, phone tap recordings, photographs, and interviews with police, prosecutors, and other people with knowledge of the case.

2. Chilean court records, *Fiscalía de Alta Complejidad Occidente v. Harold Vilches*, case no. 3265-2015.

3. Harold Vilches, interviews with the authors, June 17–21, 2019.

4. Harold Vilches, interviews with the authors, June 17–21, 2019.

5. Harold Vilches, interviews with the authors, June 17–21, 2019.

6. "El lobo de la Plaza de Armas," *El Mercurio*, March 17, 2018, http://www.economiaynegocios.cl/noticias/noticias.asp?id=451656.

7. Harold Vilches, interviews with the authors, June 17–21, 2019.

8. Harold Vilches, interviews with the authors, June 17–21, 2019.

9. Harold Vilches, interviews with the authors, June 17–21, 2019.

10. Chilean tax code, "Ley sobre impuesto a las ventas y servicios," National Congressional Library of Chile, https://www.leychile.cl/Navegar?idNorma=6369.

11. "Ventas y servicios," Internal Tax Service of Chile, http://www.sii.cl/pagina/jurisprudencia/adminis/2000/ventas/julio11.htm.

12. Harold Vilches, interviews with the authors, June 17–21, 2019.

Chapter 16: Moving Up

1. "La trama oculta del mayor contrabando de oro detectado en Chile," *CIPER*, August 19, 2016, https://ciperchile.cl/2016/08/19/la-trama-oculta-del-mayor-contrabando-de-oro-detectado-en-chile/; Michael Smith and Jonathan Franklin, "How to Become an International Gold Smuggler," *Bloomberg*, March 9, 2017, https://www.bloomberg.com/news/features/2017-03-09/how-to-become-an-international-gold-smuggler.

2. Harold Vilches, interviews with the authors, June 17–21, 2019.

3. Harold Vilches, interviews with the authors, June 17–21, 2019.

4. Chilean court records, *Fiscalía de Alta Complejidad Occidente v. Harold Vilches*, case no. 3265-2015.

5. Harold Vilches, interviews with the authors, June 17–21, 2019.

6. Chilean court records, *Fiscalía Adjunto de Las Condes v. Harold Vilches*, case no. 1173-2015.

7. Harold Vilches, interviews with the authors, June 17–21, 2019.

8. Chilean court records, *Fiscalía Adjunto de Las Condes v. Harold Vilches*, case no. 1173-2015.

9. Guiora Kaplan, email to the authors, August 8, 2019.

10. Catherine Lathrop Rossi (lawyer for Fujairah Gold in Chile), interview with the authors, June 18, 2019.

11. Chilean court records, *Fiscalía Adjunto de Las Condes v. Harold Vilches*, case no. 1173-2015.

12. Chilean court records, *Fiscalía Adjunto de Las Condes v. Harold Vilches*, case no. 1173-2015.

13. Chilean court records, *Fiscalía Adjunto de Las Condes v. Harold Vilches*, case no. 1173-2015.

14. Harold Vilches, interviews with the authors, June 17–21, 2019.

15. Smith and Franklin, "How to Become an International Gold Smuggler," https://www.bloomberg.com/news/features/2017-03-09/how-to-become-an-international-gold-smuggler.

16. Harold Vilches, interviews with the authors, June 17–21, 2019.

17. Edgar Mandujano, "Freno a Ferrari," *Caretas*, January 19, 2017.

18. Harold Vilches, interviews with the authors, June 17–21, 2019.

19. "Aduanas decomisa 15 lingotes de oro en aeropuerto de Arica," National Customs Directorate, August 2014, https://www.aduana.cl/aduanas-decomisa-15-lingotes-de-oro-en-aeropuerto-de-arica/aduana/2014-08-18/151429.html.

20. Harold Vilches, interviews with the authors, June 17–21, 2019.

21. *United States v. Juan P. Granda*, No. 17-20215, PACER (S.D. Fla., March 15, 2017). According to this complaint, internal NTR records show that NTR imported gold from an alleged Peruvian front company associated with Soria.

22. *United States v. Juan P. Granda*, No. 17-20215, PACER (S.D. Fla., March 15, 2017); Harold Vilches, interviews with the authors, June 17–21, 2019.

23. Harold Vilches, interviews with the authors, June 17–21, 2019.

24. *United States v. Juan P. Granda*, No. 17-20215, PACER (S.D. Fla., March 15, 2017).

25. Harold Vilches, interviews with the authors, June 17–21, 2019.

26. Juan Figueroa and Juan Pablo Sandoval (Investigations Police of Chile), interview with the authors, February 2, 2019; *United States v. Juan P. Granda*, No. 17-20215, PACER (S.D. Fla., March 15, 2017).

27. Chilean court records, *Fiscalía de Alta Complejidad Occidente v. Harold Vilches*, case no. 3265-2015.

28. "Fiscalía destaca condena por Asociación Ilícita en caso de Contrabando de Oro," Chilean Prosecutor's Office, February 4, 2018, http://www.fiscaliadechile.cl /Fiscalia/sala_prensa/noticias_regional_det.do?id=14166.

29. Harold Vilches, interviews with the authors, June 17–21, 2019.

30. "El lobo de la Plaza de Armas," *El Mercurio*, March 17, 2018, http://www .economiaynegocios.cl/noticias/noticias.asp?id=451656.

31. Juan Figueroa and Juan Pablo Sandoval (Investigations Police of Chile), interview with the authors, February 2, 2019.

32. Rodrigo Pino, "Sujetos huyen con más de $6 mil millones tras asaltar camión Brinks en aeropuerto de Santiago," *BioBioChile*, August 12, 2014, https://www.biobio chile.cl/noticias/2014/08/12/millonario-robo-afecta-camion-de-valores-brinks-en-la -losa-del-aeropuerto-de-santiago.shtml.

33. Harold Vilches, interviews with the authors, June 17–21, 2019.

34. Chilean court records, *Fiscalía de Alta Complejidad Occidente v. Harold Vilches*, case no. 3265-2015.

35. Harold Vilches, interviews with the authors, June 17–21, 2019.

36. Chilean court records, *Fiscalía de Alta Complejidad Occidente v. Harold Vilches*, case no. 3265-2015.

37. Chilean court records, *Fiscalía de Alta Complejidad Occidente v. Harold Vilches*, case no. 3265-2015.

38. Chilean court records, *Fiscalía de Alta Complejidad Occidente v. Harold Vilches*, case no. 3265-2015.

39. Harold Vilches, interviews with the authors, June 17–21, 2019.

40. Chilean court records, *Fiscalía de Alta Complejidad Occidente v. Harold Vilches*, case no. 3265-2015.

41. Harold Vilches, interviews with the authors, June 17–21, 2019.

42. Chilean court records, *Fiscalía de Alta Complejidad Occidente v. Harold Vilches*, case no. 3265-2015.

43. "La trama oculta del mayor contrabando de oro detectado en Chile," *CIPER*, August 19, 2016, https://ciperchile.cl/2016/08/19/la-trama-oculta-del-mayor -contrabando-de-oro-detectado-en-chile/.

44. Chilean court records, *Fiscalía de Alta Complejidad Occidente v. Harold Vilches*, case no. 3265-2015.

45. Catherine Lathrop (lawyer for Fujairah Gold in Chile), interview with the authors, June 18, 2019.

46. Chilean court records, *Fiscalía Adjunto de Las Condes v. Harold Vilches*, case no. 1173-2015.

47. Harold Vilches, interviews with the authors, June 17–21, 2019.

48. Chilean court records, *Fiscalía Adjunto de Las Condes v. Harold Vilches*, case no. 1173-2015.

49. Chilean court records, *Fiscalía Adjunto de Las Condes v. Harold Vilches*, case no. 1173-2015.

50. Chilean court records, *Fiscalía Adjunto de Las Condes v. Harold Vilches*, case no. 1173-2015.

51. Juan Figueroa and Juan Pablo Sandoval (Investigations Police of Chile), interview with the authors, February 2, 2019.

52. *United States v. Juan P. Granda*, No. 17-20215, PACER (S.D. Fla., March 15, 2017).

53. Harold Vilches, interviews with the authors, June 17–21, 2019. Vilches, who no longer has a copy of this message, reconstructed it from his memory of the conversation.

Chapter 17: A Suitcase Full of Gold

1. *United States v. Juan P. Granda*, No. 17-20215, PACER (S.D. Fla., March 15, 2017).

2. Harold Vilches, interviews with the authors, June 17–21, 2019.

3. *United States v. Juan P. Granda*, No. 17-20215, PACER (S.D. Fla., March 15, 2017).

4. Harold Vilches, interviews with the authors, June 17–21, 2019. Vilches provided a receipt, which matches Chilean customs records, showing that he sold gold to NTR in November 2014.

5. *United States v. Juan P. Granda*, No. 17-20215, PACER (S.D. Fla., March 15, 2017); Michael Smith and Jonathan Franklin, "How to Become an International Gold Smuggler," *Bloomberg*, March 9, 2017, https://www.bloomberg.com/news/features /2017-03-09/how-to-become-an-international-gold-smuggler.

6. Smith and Franklin, "How to Become an International Gold Smuggler," https:// www.bloomberg.com/news/features/2017-03-09/how-to-become-an-international -gold-smuggler.

7. *United States v. Juan P. Granda*, No. 17-20215, PACER (S.D. Fla., March 15, 2017).

8. *United States v. Juan P. Granda*, No. 17-20215, PACER (S.D. Fla., March 15, 2017).

9. Harold Vilches, interviews with the authors, June 17–21, 2019.

10. Harold Vilches, interviews with the authors, June 17–21, 2019.

11. Renato Rodriguez, email message to the authors, May 28, 2020.

12. *United States v. Juan P. Granda*, No. 17-20215, PACER (S.D. Fla., March 15, 2017).

13. *United States v. Juan P. Granda*, No. 17-20215, PACER (S.D. Fla., March 15, 2017).

14. *United States v. Juan P. Granda*, No. 17-20215, PACER (S.D. Fla., March 15, 2017).

15. Harold Vilches, interviews with the authors, June 17–21, 2019.

16. *United States v. Juan P. Granda*, No. 17-20215, PACER (S.D. Fla., March 15, 2017).

17. *United States v. Juan P. Granda*, No. 17-20215, PACER (S.D. Fla., March 15, 2017).

18. *United States v. Juan P. Granda*, No. 17-20215, PACER (S.D. Fla., March 15, 2017).

19. *United States v. Juan P. Granda*, No. 17-20215, PACER (S.D. Fla., March 15, 2017).

20. Photographs provided by Harold Vilches.

21. Photograph provided by Harold Vilches.

22. Harold Vilches, interviews with the authors, June 17–21, 2019.

23. *United States v. Juan P. Granda*, No. 17-20215, PACER (S.D. Fla., March 15, 2017); Harold Vilches, interviews with the authors, June 17–21, 2019.

24. Harold Vilches, interviews with the authors, June 17–21, 2019.

25. Chilean court records, *Fiscalía de Alta Complejidad Occidente v. Harold Vilches*, case no. 3265-2015.

26. *United States v. Juan P. Granda*, No. 17-20215, PACER (S.D. Fla., March 15, 2017).

27. Chilean court records, *Fiscalía de Alta Complejidad Occidente v. Harold Vilches*, case no. 3265-2015.

28. Chilean court records, *Fiscalía de Alta Complejidad Occidente v. Harold Vilches*, case no. 3265-2015.

29. Harold Vilches, interviews with the authors, June 17–21, 2019.

30. Juan Figueroa and Juan Pablo Sandoval (Investigations Police of Chile), interview with the authors, February 2, 2019.

31. Juan Figueroa and Juan Pablo Sandoval (Investigations Police of Chile), interview with the authors, February 2, 2019.

32. Harold Vilches, interviews with the authors, June 17–21, 2019; Smith and Franklin, "How to Become an International Gold Smuggler," https://www.bloomberg.com/news/features/2017-03-09/how-to-become-an-international-gold-smuggler.

33. Chilean court records, *Fiscalía de Alta Complejidad Occidente v. Harold Vilches*, case no. 3265-2015.

34. Chilean court records, *Fiscalía de Alta Complejidad Occidente v. Harold Vilches*, case no. 3265-2015.

35. Dagoberto Muñoz, interviews with the authors, January 29 and February 1, 2019.

36. Chilean court records, *Fiscalía de Alta Complejidad Occidente v. Harold Vilches*, case no. 3265-2015.

37. Dagoberto Muñoz, interviews with the authors, January 29 and February 1, 2019.

38. Chilean court records, *Fiscalía de Alta Complejidad Occidente v. Harold Vilches*, case no. 3265-2015.

39. Harold Vilches, interviews with the authors, June 17–21, 2019.

40. Tufit Bufadel, Pablo Alonso, and José Luis Pérez Calaf (prosecutors), interview with the authors, January 31, 2019.

41. Harold Vilches, interviews with the authors, June 17–21, 2019.

42. Chilean court records, *Fiscalía de Alta Complejidad Occidente v. Harold Vilches*, case no. 3265-2015.

43. Harold Vilches, interviews with the authors, June 17–21, 2019.

44. Juan Figueroa and Juan Pablo Sandoval (Investigations Police of Chile), interview with the authors, February 2, 2019.

45. *United States v. Juan P. Granda*, No. 17-20215, PACER (S.D. Fla., March 15, 2017).

46. Chilean court records, *Fiscalía de Alta Complejidad Occidente v. Harold Vilches*, case no. 3265-2015.

47. Chilean court records, *Fiscalía de Alta Complejidad Occidente v. Harold Vilches*, case no. 3265-2015.

48. Harold Vilches, interviews with the authors, June 17–21, 2019.

49. Online advertisement "Hermosa Casa en Condominio Las Brisas de Chicureo," MercadoCasas.Cl, December 4, 2015, http://www.mercadocasas.cl/property/hermosa -casa-en-condominio-las-brisas-de-chicureo; "El Rey del Oro," *Contacto*, Canal 13, August 21, 2016, https://www.t13.cl/videos/programas/contacto-2016/contacto-rey -del-oro.

Chapter 18: *El Patrón del Mal*

1. Several WhatsApp conversations were included in the federal criminal affidavits against Juan Pablo Granda, Renato Rodriguez, and Samer Barrage. *United States v. Juan P. Granda*, No. 17-20215, PACER (S.D. Fla., March 15, 2017).

2. The professions of his friends were described at his detention hearing in federal court. *United States v. Juan P. Granda*, No. 17-20215, PACER (S.D. Fla., April 3, 2017).

3. Miriam Wells, "Peruvian Cocaine Best Value for Traffickers: Bolivia Police," In-Sight Crime, May 21, 2013, https://www.insightcrime.org/news/brief/peruvian-cocaine -best-value-for-traffickers-bolivia-police/.

4. This account of the collaboration between Juan Pablo Granda and Andrés Tejeda is drawn primarily from the criminal affidavits filed in federal court against Granda and Tejeda, as well as from their factual proffers.

5. Oscar Castilla, "Peru: Investigan lavanderia de oro de la mineria ilegal," *Ojo Publico*, August 1, 2018, https://ojo-publico.com/764/estado-eligio-companias -investigadas-por-lavado-de-mineria-ilegal-para-comprar-oro.

6. *United States v. Juan P. Granda*, No.17-20215, PACER (S.D. Fla., March 10, 2017), criminal affidavit, page 12, footnote 11, regarding Minera San Fidel and Los Curas.

Chapter 19: Land of the Jaguar

1. Gilda Mora, El Dorado Colombia website, https://www.eldoradocolombia.com/.

2. "Madre de Dios," Congreso de la República del Perú, accessed 2019, http://www4 .congreso.gob.pe/congresista/2001/esalhuana/Madre_Dios/Historia/madre_d_dios _new.htm.

3. "Madre de Dios," Congreso de la República del Perú, accessed 2019, http://www4 .congreso.gob.pe/congresista/2001/esalhuana/Madre_Dios/Historia/madre_d_dios _new.htm.

4. "Juan Recio de León," El Dorado Colombia, http://arteyarqueologia.com/juan _recio_de_leon.html.

5. Mike Collis, "The History of Fitzcarrald," *Iquitos (Perú) Times*, 2006, http://www .iquitostimes.com/fitzcarrald.htm.

6. Jon Lee Anderson, "An Isolated Tribe Emerges from the Rain Forest," *New Yorker*, August 1, 2016, https://www.newyorker.com/magazine/2016/08/08/an-isolated -tribe-emerges-from-the-rain-forest.

7. Nigel J. H. Smith, J. T. Williams, Donald L. Plucknett, and Jennifer P. Talbot, *Tropical Forests and Their Crops* (Ithaca, NY: Cornell University Press, 1992), 222–223.

Chapter 20: "Major Unwanted Heat"

1. David Lewis, Ryan McNeill, and Zandi Shabala, "Gold Worth Billions Smuggled Out of Africa," Reuters, April 24, 2019, https://www.reuters.com/investigates/special-report/Gold-africa-smuggling/.

2. Global Witness, "US Conflict Minerals Law" (briefing), November 15, 2017, https://www.globalwitness.org/en/campaigns/conflict-minerals/dodd-frank-act-section-1502/.

3. Daniel Flynn, "Gold, Diamonds Fuelling Conflict in Central African Republic: U.N. Panel," Reuters, November 5, 2014, https://www.reuters.com/article/us-central africa-un-panel/gold-diamonds-fuelling-conflict-in-central-african-republic-u-n-panel -idUSKBN0IO21420141105.

4. Barack Obama, "Blocking Property of Certain Persons Contributing to the Conflict in the Central African Republic" (Executive Order 13667 of May 12, 2014), *Federal Register* 79, no. 94 (May 15, 2014), https://www.treasury.gov/resource-center/sanctions/Programs/Documents/car_eo.pdf.

5. The authors reviewed copies of these emails.

6. The authors reviewed copies of these emails.

Chapter 21: Things Fall Apart

1. Oscar Castilla, "Los vuelos secretos del oro ilegal," *OjoPublico*, December 5, 2014, https://ojo-publico.com/12/los-vuelos-secretos-del-oro-ilegal.

2. Several WhatsApp conversations were included in the federal criminal affidavits against Juan Pablo Granda, Renato Rodriguez, and Samer Barrage. *United States v. Juan P. Granda*, No. 17-20215, PACER (S.D. Fla., March 15, 2017).

3. Mitra Taj, "Peru Crackdown on Illegal Gold Leads to New Smuggling Routes," Reuters, November 25, 2014, https://www.reuters.com/article/us-peru-gold/peru-crack down-on-illegal-gold-leads-to-new-smuggling-routes-idUSKCN0J90E720141125.

4. Harold Vilches, interviews with the authors, June 17–21, 2019.

5. *United States v. Juan P. Granda*, No. 17-20215, PACER (S.D. Fla., March 15, 2017).

6. *United States v. Juan P. Granda*, No. 17-20215, PACER (S.D. Fla., March 15, 2017).

7. Harold Vilches, interviews with the authors, June 17–21, 2019.

8. *United States v. Juan P. Granda*, No. 17-20215, PACER (S.D. Fla., March 15, 2017).

9. *United States v. Juan P. Granda*, No. 17-20215, PACER (S.D. Fla., March 15, 2017). Harold Vilches, interviews with the authors, June 17–21, 2019.

10. *United States v. Juan P. Granda*, No. 17-20215, PACER (S.D. Fla., March 15, 2017).

11. Renato Rodriguez, email message to the authors, May 28, 2020; Michael Smith and Jonathan Franklin, "How to Become an International Gold Smuggler," *Bloomberg*, March 9, 2017, https://www.bloomberg.com/news/features/2017-03-09/how-to-become-an-international-gold-smuggler.

12. Harold Vilches, interviews with the authors, June 17–21, 2019.

13. Chilean court records, *Fiscalía de Alta Complejidad Occidente v. Harold Vilches*, case no. 3265-2015.

14. Tufit Bufadel, Pablo Alonso, and José Luis Pérez Calaf (prosecutors), interview with the authors, January 31, 2019.

15. Chilean court records, *Fiscalía de Alta Complejidad Occidente v. Harold Vilches*, case no. 3265-2015.

16. Chilean court records, *Fiscalía de Alta Complejidad Occidente v. Harold Vilches*, case no. 3265-2015.

17. Emiliano Arias (prosecutor), interview with the authors, January 31, 2019.

18. Nicolás Rodríguez Videla (prosecutor), interview with the authors, June 19, 2019.

19. Harold Vilches, interviews with the authors, June 17–21, 2019.

20. Harold Vilches, interviews with the authors, June 17–21, 2019.

21. Several WhatsApp conversations were included in the federal criminal affidavits against Juan Pablo Granda, Renato Rodriguez, and Samer Barrage. *United States v. Juan P. Granda*, No. 17-20215, PACER (S.D. Fla., March 15, 2017).

22. Copies of the following WhatsApp messages were reviewed by the authors.

23. The authors reviewed a copy of this email.

24. The authors reviewed copies of emails between Rodriguez, Crogan, Granda, and Almeida.

25. Armando Salguero, "Dolphins Beat Patriots, 33–20 to Take Opener," *Miami Herald*, September 7, 2014, https://miamiherald.typepad.com/dolphins_in_depth/2014/09/dolphins-beat-patriots-33-20-to-take-opener.html.

Chapter 22: Mama Customs

1. *United States v. Juan P. Granda*, No. 17-20215, PACER (S.D. Fla., March 15, 2017).

2. Harold Vilches, interviews with the authors, June 17–21, 2019; unless otherwise noted, the information in this chapter is based on interviews with Vilches as well as photographs of the trip.

3. Harold Vilches, interviews with the authors, June 17–21, 2019.

4. Harold Vilches, interviews with the authors, June 17–21, 2019.

5. Fumbuka Ng'wanakilala, "Tanzania Sets Up Mineral Trading Centers to Curb Illegal Gold Exports," Reuters, March 18, 2018, https://www.reuters.com/article/us-tanzania-mining/tanzania-sets-up-mineral-trading-centers-to-curb-illegal-gold-exports-idUSKCN1QZ1SD.

6. "Tanzania: Hazardous Life of Child Gold Miners," Human Rights Watch, August 28, 2013, https://www.hrw.org/news/2013/08/28/tanzania-hazardous-life-child-gold-miners.

7. Harold Vilches, interviews with the authors, June 17–21, 2019.

8. Receipt dated February 20, 2015.

9. Harold Vilches, interviews with the authors, June 17–21, 2019.

10. Harold Vilches, interviews with the authors, June 17–21, 2019.

11. Receipt dated February 20, 2015.

12. Harold Vilches, interviews with the authors, June 17–21, 2019.

13. *United States v. Juan P. Granda*, No. 17-20215, PACER (S.D. Fla., March 15, 2017).

14. Renato Rodriguez, email message to the authors, May 28, 2020; Michael Smith and Jonathan Franklin, "How to Become an International Gold Smuggler," *Bloomberg*, March 9, 2017, https://www.bloomberg.com/news/features/2017-03-09/how-to-become-an-international-gold-smuggler.

15. Harold Vilches, interviews with the authors, June 17–21, 2019.

16. Harold Vilches, interviews with the authors, June 17–21, 2019.

17. "El lobo de la Plaza de Armas," *El Mercurio*, March 17, 2018, http://www .economiaynegocios.cl/noticias/noticias.asp?id=451656.

18. Harold Vilches, interviews with the authors, June 17–21, 2019.

19. Harold Vilches, interviews with the authors, June 17–21, 2019.

20. Harold Vilches, interviews with the authors, June 17–21, 2019.

21. Harold Vilches, interviews with the authors, June 17–21, 2019.

22. Harold Vilches, interviews with the authors, June 17–21, 2019; *United States v. Juan P. Granda*, No. 17-20215, PACER (S.D. Fla., March 15, 2017).

Chapter 23: "Jeffrey, We Just Had a Problem"

1. Steve Striffler, *In the Shadows of State and Capital: The United Fruit Company, Popular Struggle and Agrarian Restructuring in Ecuador, 1900–1995* (Durham, NC: Duke University Press, 2002), 11.

2. Ecuador's National Statistics and Census Institute, 2019, https://www.ecua dorencifras.gob.ec/censo-de-poblacion-y-vivienda/.

3. The history of gold mining around the region of Machala is drawn primarily from a report prepared for Ecuadorgoldcorp SA and submitted to the US Securities and Exchange Commission. Wimer Castro, "Geological Report of the Muluncay Deposit of the Portovelo-Zaruma-Ayapamba Area, El Oro Province, Ecuador," February 2008, https:// www.sec.gov/Archives/edgar/data/1378948/000138713109000146/exhibit_10-3.htm.

4. "Anti-Money-Laundering Programs for Dealers in Precious Metals, Precious Stones, or Jewels," §103.140, 31 CFR Ch. I (7–1–10 Edition), Government Printing Office, June 9, 2005, https://www.govinfo.gov/content/pkg/CFR-2010-title31-vol1/pdf /CFR-2010-title31-vol1-sec103-140.pdf.

5. Copies of these emails were reviewed by the authors.

6. Jay Weaver, "More Million-Dollar Gold Bars, Stolen in Gold Heist, May Be in Miami," *Miami Herald*, May 1, 2015. https://www.miamiherald.com/news/local/crime /article20051649.html?Fb_comment_id=957778790907649_957954670890061.

7. Jay Weaver, "Miami Man Gets 3½ Years in Prison for Extortion in Gold-Heist Case," *Miami Herald*, September 21, 2015. https://www.miamiherald.com/news/local /crime/article35949891.html; Jay Weaver, "FBI: Opa-locka Man Directed Daring Gold-Heist Plot," *Miami Herald*, March 4, 2016, https://www.miamiherald.com/news/local /crime/article64111767.html; Jay Weaver, "FBI Cracked the Miami-N.C. Gold Heist, but Where Are Nine Missing Bars?" *Miami Herald*, May 7, 2016 https://www.miami herald.com/news/local/article76177207.html.

8. *United States of America v. Samer H. Barrage*, case no. 20215, PACER (S.D. Fla., January 17, 2018).

Chapter 24: The Golden Chicken

1. Harold Vilches, interviews with the authors, June 17–21, 2019.

2. Harold Vilches, interviews with the authors, June 17–21, 2019.

3. Harold Vilches, interviews with the authors, June 17–21, 2019; Chilean court records, *Fiscalía de Alta Complejidad Occidente v. Harold Vilches*, case no. 3265-2015.

4. Michael Smith and Jonathan Franklin, "How to Become an International Gold Smuggler," *Bloomberg*, March 9, 2017, https://www.bloomberg.com/news/features /2017-03-09/how-to-become-an-international-gold-smuggler.

5. Chilean court records, *Fiscalía de Alta Complejidad Occidente v. Harold Vilches*, case no. 3265-2015.

6. Harold Vilches, interviews with the authors, June 17–21, 2019.

7. Harold Vilches, interviews with the authors, June 17–21, 2019.

8. Harold Vilches, interviews with the authors, June 17–21, 2019.

9. Renato Rodriguez, email to the authors, May 28, 2020.

10. Chilean court records, *Fiscalía de Alta Complejidad Occidente v. Harold Vilches*, case no. 3265-2015.

11. Emiliano Arias (prosecutor), interview with the authors, January 31, 2019.

12. Chilean court records, *Fiscalía de Alta Complejidad Occidente v. Harold Vilches*, case no. 3265-2015.

13. Emiliano Arias (prosecutor), interview with the authors, January 31, 2019.

14. Emiliano Arias (prosecutor), interview with the authors, January 31, 2019.

15. Juan Figueroa and Juan Pablo Sandoval (Investigations Police of Chile), interview with the authors, February 2, 2019.

16. Juan Figueroa and Juan Pablo Sandoval (Investigations Police of Chile), interview with the authors, February 2, 2019.

17. Chilean court records, *Fiscalía de Alta Complejidad Occidente v. Harold Vilches*, case no. 3265-2015.

18. Chilean court records, *Fiscalía de Alta Complejidad Occidente v. Harold Vilches*, case no. 3265-2015.

19. Emiliano Arias (prosecutor), interview with the authors, January 31, 2019.

20. Emiliano Arias (prosecutor), interview with the authors, January 31, 2019.

Chapter 25: The Wire

1. Harold Vilches, interviews with the authors, June 17–21, 2019.

2. Harold Vilches, interviews with the authors, June 17–21, 2019.

3. Chilean court records, *Fiscalía de Alta Complejidad Occidente v. Harold Vilches*, case no. 3265-2015.

4. Nicolás Rodríguez Videla (prosecutor), interview with the authors, June 19, 2019.

5. Nicolás Rodríguez Videla (prosecutor), interview with the authors, June 19, 2019.

6. Nicolás Rodríguez Videla (prosecutor), interview with the authors, June 19, 2019.

7. Emiliano Arias (prosecutor), interview with the authors, January 31, 2019.

8. Chilean court records, *Fiscalía de Alta Complejidad Occidente v. Harold Vilches*, case no. 3265-2015.

9. Nicolás Rodríguez Videla (prosecutor), interview with the authors, June 19, 2019.

10. Nicolás Rodríguez Videla (prosecutor), interview with the authors, June 19, 2019.

11. Chilean court records, *Fiscalía de Alta Complejidad Occidente v. Harold Vilches*, case no. 3265-2015.

12. Chilean court records, *Fiscalía de Alta Complejidad Occidente v. Harold Vilches*, case no. 3265-2015.

13. Nicolás Rodríguez Videla (prosecutor), interview with the authors, June 19, 2019.

14. Nicolás Rodríguez Videla (prosecutor), interview with the authors, June 19, 2019.

15. Juan Figueroa and Juan Pablo Sandoval (Investigations Police of Chile), interview with the authors, February 2, 2019.

16. Chilean court records, *Fiscalía de Alta Complejidad Occidente v. Harold Vilches*, case no. 3265-2015.

17. Juan Figueroa and Juan Pablo Sandoval (Investigations Police of Chile), interview with the authors, February 2, 2019.

18. Chilean court records, *Fiscalía de Alta Complejidad Occidente v. Harold Vilches*, case no. 3265-2015.

19. Nicolás Rodríguez Videla (prosecutor), interview with the authors, June 19, 2019.

20. Chilean court records, *Fiscalía de Alta Complejidad Occidente v. Harold Vilches*, case no. 3265-2015.

21. Chilean court records, *Fiscalía de Alta Complejidad Occidente v. Harold Vilches*, case no. 3265-2015.

22. Chilean court records, *Fiscalía de Alta Complejidad Occidente v. Harold Vilches*, case no. 3265-2015.

23. Juan Figueroa and Juan Pablo Sandoval (Investigations Police of Chile), interview with the authors, February 2, 2019.

24. Juan Figueroa and Juan Pablo Sandoval (Investigations Police of Chile), interview with the authors, February 2, 2019; Michael Smith and Jonathan Franklin, "How to Become an International Gold Smuggler," *Bloomberg*, March 9, 2017, https://www.bloomberg.com/news/features/2017-03-09/how-to-become-an-international-gold-smuggler.

25. Tufit Bufadel, José Luis Pérez Calaf, and Pablo Alonso (prosecutors), interview with the authors, January 31, 2019.

26. Tufit Bufadel, José Luis Pérez Calaf, and Pablo Alonso (prosecutors), interview with the authors, January 31, 2019.

27. Jim Wyss and Kyra Gurney, "Dirty Gold Is the New Cocaine in Colombia—and It's Just as Bloody," *Miami Herald*, January 16, 2018, https://www.miamiherald.com/news/nation-world/world/americas/colombia/article194188034.html.

28. Brenna Hughes Neghaiwi, Mitra Taj, and Peter Hobson, "Special Report: Sleeping Beauty—How Suspect Gold Reached Top Brands," Reuters, March 6, 2020, https://www.reuters.com/article/us-gold-peru-swiss-specialreport/special-report-sleeping-beauty-how-suspect-gold-reached-top-brands-idUSKBN20T0TQ; Wyss and Gurney, "Dirty Gold Is the New Cocaine," https://www.miamiherald.com/news/nation-world/world/americas/colombia/article194188034.html.

29. The transcript of Samer Barrage's detention hearing. *United States v. Samer H. Barrage*, No. 17-20215, PACER (S.D. Fla., April 29, 2017).

30. Receipts and other business records reviewed by the authors show that NTR Metals Zona Franca purchased gold from Enmanuel Gold.

31. Colombia Attorney General's Office, "Capturados 'Los Mercaderes' del oro, señalados de comercializar ilegalmente tres toneladas del mineral en dos años" (news release no. 21184), August 17, 2017, https://www.fiscalia.gov.co/colombia/crimen-organizado/capturados-los-mercaderes-del-oro-senalados-de-comercializar-ilegalmente-tres-toneladas-del-mineral-en-dos-anos/.

32. Colombia Attorney General's Office, "Capturados 'Los Mercaderes' del oro," https://www.fiscalia.gov.co/colombia/crimen-organizado/capturados-los-mercaderes-del-oro-senalados-de-comercializar-ilegalmente-tres-toneladas-del-mineral-en-dos-anos/.

33. *United States v. Samer H. Barrage*, No. 17-20215, PACER (S.D. Fla., January 17, 2018).

Chapter 26: "A Conflict Diamond Is a Conflict Diamond"

1. Jay Weaver, "He Caught the World's Worst Drug Traffickers. Now Dick Gregorie Is Ready to Hang It Up," *Miami Herald*, May 16, 2018, https://www.miamiherald.com /news/local/article211153669.html.

2. Jon Nordheimer, "U.S. Attorney in Miami Guarded After Death Threats Are Reported," *New York Times*, March 17, 1987, https://www.nytimes.com/1987/03/17 /us/us-attorney-in-miami-guarded-after-death-threats-are-reported.html.

3. Peter S. Green, "Cocainenomics: The Ever-Changing Logistics of Drug Smuggling," *Wall Street Journal*, September 2015, https://www.wsj.com/ad/cocainenomics.

Chapter 27: Operation Arch Stanton

1. The authors reviewed documentation of this meeting.

2. Nadege Green, "How I-95 Shattered the World of Miami's Early Overtown Residents," *WLRN*, September 24, 2013, https://www.wlrn.org/post/how-i-95-shattered -world-miamis-early-overtown-residents.

3. Regulatory Studies Center, Columbian College of Arts & Sciences, https:// regulatorystudies.columbian.gwu.edu/reg-stats.

4. *The Good, the Bad and the Ugly*, directed by Sergio Leone (Los Angeles, CA: Metro-Goldwyn-Mayer, 1967).

Chapter 28: The Prosecutor

1. Department of Justice, US Attorney's Office, Southern District of Florida, "Miami-Dade County Resident Sentenced in Stolen Identity Tax Refund Scheme Involving Thousands of Individuals' Personal Identifying Information" (news release), July 29, 2014, https://www.justice.gov/usao-sdfl/pr/miami-dade-county-resident-sentenced -stolen-identity-tax-refund-scheme-involving; Department of Justice, US Attorney's Office, Southern District of Florida, "Eight Individuals Charged in Four Separate Cyber Fraud Schemes" (news release), June 3, 2014, https://www.justice.gov/usao -sdfl/pr/eight-individuals-charged-four-separate-cyber-fraud-schemes; Department of Justice, US Attorney's Office, Southern District of Florida, "Miami Gardens Resident Convicted in Shooting of Miami Gardens Police Officer" (news release), February 20, 2015, https://www.justice.gov/usao-sdfl/pr/miami-gardens-resident-convicted-shooting -miami-gardens-police-officer.

2. A search of the *Miami Herald* archives did not produce a mention of Maderal's name before 2016.

Chapter 29: "Dude, This Is Insanity"

1. "Gold Statistics and Information," USGS, accessed 2019, https://www.usgs.gov /centers/nmic/gold-statistics-and-information.

2. Michael W. George, *2015 Mineral Commodity Summaries: Gold [Advance Release]* (US Department of the Interior, US Geological Survey, October 2017), https:// s3-us-west-2.amazonaws.com/prd-wret/assets/palladium/production/mineral-pubs /gold/myb1-2015-gold.pdf.

3. Federal criminal affidavit against Granda, *United States v. Juan P. Granda*, No. 17-20215, PACER (S.D. Fla., March 15, 2017).

4. *United States v. Juan P. Granda*, No. 17-20215, PACER (S.D. Fla., March 15, 2017).

Chapter 30: Turf War

1. New York State Unified Court System, Attorney search database, accessed 2019.

2. Mark Landler and Michael R. Gordon, "Journey to Reconciliation Visited Worlds of Presidents, Popes and Spies," *New York Times*, December 17, 2014, https://www.nytimes.com/2014/12/18/world/americas/journey-to-rapprochement-visited-worlds-of-presidents-popes-and-spies.html.

3. Jenifer Fenton, "What Happened to Prisoners at Bagram, 'Afghanistan's Guantanamo'?" *Aljazeera*, February 11, 2019, https://www.aljazeera.com/indepth/features/happened-prisoners-bagram-afghanistans-guantanamo-190210222540759.html.

4. The authors reviewed emails between Michael Sherwin, Frank Maderal, and other federal agents and prosecutors involved in the sprawling gold probe led by the US Attorney's Office in Miami.

Chapter 31: *La Vuelta Larga*

1. Harold Vilches, interviews with the authors, June 17–21, 2019.

2. Harold Vilches, interviews with the authors, June 17–21, 2019.

3. Harold Vilches, interviews with the authors, June 17–21, 2019.

4. Chilean court records, *Fiscalía de Alta Complejidad Occidente v. Harold Vilches*, case no. 3265-2015.

5. Chilean court records, *Fiscalía de Alta Complejidad Occidente v. Harold Vilches*, case no. 3265-2015.

6. Chilean court records, *Fiscalía de Alta Complejidad Occidente v. Harold Vilches*, case no. 3265-2015.

7. Chilean court records, *Fiscalía de Alta Complejidad Occidente v. Harold Vilches*, case no. 3265-2015.

8. Chilean court records, *Fiscalía de Alta Complejidad Occidente v. Harold Vilches*, case no. 3265-2015.

9. Harold Vilches, interviews with the authors, June 17–21, 2019; Chilean court records, *Fiscalía de Alta Complejidad Occidente v. Harold Vilches*, case no. 3265-2015.

10. Emiliano Arias (prosecutor), interview with the authors, January 31, 2019.

11. Emiliano Arias (prosecutor), interview with the authors, January 31, 2019.

12. Juan Figueroa and Juan Pablo Sandoval (Investigations Police of Chile), interview with the authors, February 2, 2019; Nicolás Rodríguez Videla (prosecutor), interview with the authors, June 19, 2019.

13. Nicolás Rodríguez Videla (prosecutor), interview with the authors, June 19, 2019.

14. Nicolás Rodríguez Videla (prosecutor), interview with the authors, June 19, 2019.

15. Emiliano Arias (prosecutor), interview with the authors, January 31, 2019.

Chapter 32: The Go-By's

1. Jay Weaver and Nicholas Nehamas, "He Sold Antiques in Florida. Then He Helped 'El Chapo' Launder $100M of Dirty Gold," *Miami Herald*, January 16, 2018, https://www.miamiherald.com/news/local/article194188089.html.

2. Department of Justice, United States Attorney's Office, Southern District of New York, "Manhattan U.S. Attorney Announces Seizure of Over $31 Million in Connection with an International Drug Trafficking and Money Laundering Scheme" (news release no. 12-305), October 10, 2012, https://www.justice.gov/archive/usao/nys/pressreleases /October12/SanchezParedesPR.html.

3. United States Attorney's Office, "Manhattan U.S. Attorney Dismisses Civil Forfeiture Complaint Against Funds Held by Refining Company" (news release no. 12-335), November 6, 2012, https://www.justice.gov/archive/usao/nys/pressreleases/November 12/RepublicMetalsPR.html.

4. *United States v. Cia Minera et al.*, No 12-07530, PACER (S.D. NY, July 1, 2013).

5. "Press article on 'ojopublico,'" Italpreziosi, last updated December 23, 2015, https:// www.italpreziosi.it/en/news-en/italpreziosi-news/147-press-article-on-ojopublico-2.

6. *United States v. Samer H. Barrage*, No. 17-20215, PACER (S.D. Fla., April 29, 2017).

7. Jones Day website, https://www.jonesday.com/en/news?tab=presscontacts.

8. The authors reviewed emails between Michael Sherwin, Frank Maderal, and other federal agents and prosecutors involved in the sprawling gold probe led by the US Attorney's Office in Miami.

9. Jay Weaver, "Miami Developer Greer Sentenced to Three Years in $34 Million Housing Fraud Case," *Miami Herald*, December 1, 2016, https://www.miamiherald .com/news/local/article118344913.html.

Chapter 33: "I'm Finished"

1. Chilean court records, *Fiscalía de Alta Complejidad Occidente v. Harold Vilches*, case no. 3265-2015.

2. Harold Vilches, interviews with the authors, June 17–21, 2019.

3. Chilean court records, *Fiscalía de Alta Complejidad Occidente v. Harold Vilches*, case no. 3265-2015.

4. Harold Vilches, interviews with the authors, June 17–21, 2019.

5. Juan Pablo Sandoval (Investigations Police of Chile), interview with the authors, August 21, 2019.

6. Harold Vilches, interviews with the authors, June 17–21, 2019.

7. Harold Vilches, interviews with the authors, June 17–21, 2019.

8. Juan Figueroa and Juan Pablo Sandoval (Investigations Police of Chile), interview with the authors, February 2, 2019.

9. Juan Figueroa and Juan Pablo Sandoval (Investigations Police of Chile), interview with the authors, February 2, 2019.

10. Emiliano Arias (prosecutor), interview with the authors, January 31, 2019.

11. Emiliano Arias (prosecutor), interview with the authors, January 31, 2019.

12. Chilean court records, *Fiscalía Adjunto de Las Condes v. Harold Vilches*, case no. 1173-2015.

13. Chilean court records, *Fiscalía Adjunto de Las Condes v. Harold Vilches*, case no. 1173-2015.

14. Harold Vilches, interviews with the authors, June 17–21, 2019.

15. Michael Smith and Jonathan Franklin, "How to Become an International Gold Smuggler," *Bloomberg*, March 9, 2017, https://www.bloomberg.com/news /features/2017-03-09/how-to-become-an-international-gold-smuggler.

16. Nicolás Rodríguez Videla (prosecutor), interview with the authors, June 19, 2019.

17. Nicolás Rodríguez Videla (prosecutor), interview with the authors, June 19, 2019.

18. Emiliano Arias (prosecutor), interview with the authors, January 31, 2019.

19. Tufit Bufadel (prosecutor), interview with the authors, January 28, 2019.

20. Tufit Bufadel (prosecutor), interview with the authors, January 28, 2019.

21. Chilean court records, *Fiscalía de Alta Complejidad Occidente v. Harold Vilches*, case no. 3265-2015.

22. Harold Vilches, interviews with the authors, June 17–21, 2019.

23. Tufit Bufadel (prosecutor), interview with the authors, January 28, 2019.

24. Tufit Bufadel, Pablo Alonso, and José Luis Pérez Calaf (prosecutors), interview with the authors, January 31, 2019.

25. Chilean court records, *Fiscalía de Alta Complejidad Occidente v. Harold Vilches*, case no. 3265-2015.

26. Tufit Bufadel, Pablo Alonso, and José Luis Pérez Calaf (prosecutors), interview with the authors, January 31, 2019.

27. Simeon Tegel, "Peru Declares State of Emergency in Its Jungles Due to Rampant Mercury Poisoning," *VICE News*, May 24, 2016, https://www.vice.com/en_us/article /8x37eg/peru-declares-state-of-emergency-in-its-jungles-due-to-rampant-mercury -poisoning.

28. Mitra Taj, "Peru Declares Mining-Related Emergency in Remote Part of Amazon," Reuters, May 23, 2016, https://www.reuters.com/article/us-peru-environment/ peru-declares-mining-related-emergency-in-remote-part-of-amazon-idUSKCN0YE2C5.

29. Several WhatsApp conversations were included in the federal criminal affidavits against Juan Pablo Granda, Renato Rodriguez, and Samer Barrage. *United States v. Juan P. Granda*, No. 17-20215, PACER (S.D. Fla., March 15, 2017).

Chapter 34: The Fellowship of the Ring

1. "'I Don't Regret Expelling the DEA from Bolivia': Evo Morales," *TeleSur English*, June 4, 2017, https://www.telesurenglish.net/news/I-Dont-Regret-Expelling-the-DEA -from-Bolivia-Evo-Morales-20170604-0020.html; "Southern Cone," United States Drug Enforcement Administration, https://www.dea.gov/foreign-offices/southern-cone.

2. 18 US Code §1956, Laundering of monetary instruments, https://www.law .cornell.edu/uscode/text/18/1956.

3. *United States of America v. Samer H. Barrage, Renato J. Rodriguez and Juan P. Granda*, Money-Laundering Conspiracy Indictment, Case No. 17-20215, PACER (S.D. Fla., March 23, 2017).

4. *Extradition: Treaty Between the United States of America and Peru*, US Department of State, July 26, 2001, https://www.state.gov/wp-content/uploads/2019/04/03-825 -Peru-Extradition-Treaty.pdf.

5. TomTom, "The TomTom Traffic Index," 2018, tomtom.com/en_gb/traffic-index/ ranking/.

6. UPI, "U.S. Inaugurates New Embassy in Peru," July 4, 1995, https://www.upi.com/ Archives/1995/07/04/US-inaugurates-new-embassy-in-Peru/7090804830400/.

7. Scott Anderson, "The True Story of Lawrence of Arabia," *Smithsonian Magazine*, July 2014, https://www.smithsonianmag.com/history/true-story-lawrence-arabia -180951857/.

Chapter 35: His Last Case

1. Harry J. Lundy, "Pilot Recounts Being Shot Down and Rescued in Vietnam," *Air Combat Command*, April 21, 2010, https://www.acc.af.mil/News/Features/Display /Article/204306/pilot-recounts-being-shot-down-and-rescued-in-vietnam/.

2. Kevin Grange, "Air Force Pararescue Team Saves Sick Baby 1,000 Miles Out at Sea," *Journal of Emergency Medical Services* 42, no. 3 (March 1, 2017), https:// www.jems.com/articles/print/volume-42/issue-3/features/air-force-pararescue-team -saves-sick-baby-1-000-miles-out-at-sea.html; Mary Synnott, "Injured Behind Enemy Lines, This Guy Is Your Best Friend," *National Geographic*, August 18, 2016, https:// www.nationalgeographic.com/news/2016/08/adventure-rescue-pararescue-mountain -climber-air-force/; Oriana Pawlyk, "For Combat Rescue Units, Space Launch Once Again a Priority," *Military.com*, February 22, 2018, https://www.military.com/daily -news/2018/02/22/combat-rescue-units-space-launch-once-again-priority.html.

3. "The Early Years," Drug Enforcement Administration, https://www.dea.gov/sites /default/files/2018-07/Early%20Years%20p%2012-29%20%281%29.pdf.

4. Norm Stamper, "Prohibition: A Parallel to Modern War on Drugs," *Seattle Times*, September 30, 2011 https://www.seattletimes.com/opinion/prohibition-a-parallel-to -modern-war-on-drugs/.

5. Felipe Puerta, "5 Creative Ways Drug Traffickers Evade Authorities," *Insight Crime*, September 18, 2018, https://www.insightcrime.org/news/analysis/5-creative -ways-drug-traffickers-evade-authorities/; Attila Nagy, "13 Shockingly Creative Ways Drugs Have Crossed the Border," *Gizmodo*, March 19, 2013, https://gizmodo.com /13-shockingly-creative-ways-drugs-have-crossed-the-bord-5988877.

6. A copy of this document was reviewed by the authors.

7. "Peru's Shining Path Militant Group," Stratfor Worldview, May 4, 2012, https:// worldview.stratfor.com/article/perus-shining-path-militant-group.

8. "Peru's Illegal Mining on Verge of Funding Armed Groups—Minister," *Andean Air Mail & Peruvian Times*, May 14, 2013, https://www.peruviantimes.com/14/perus -illegal-mining-on-verge-of-funding-armed-groups-minister/19119/.

9. Michael Smith and Jonathan Franklin, "How to Become an International Gold Smuggler," *Bloomberg*, March 9, 2017, https://www.bloomberg.com/news/features /2017-03-09/how-to-become-an-international-gold-smuggler.

10. "Entidades de control revelan presuntas irregularidades de empresas Spartan y Clearprocess," Ecuadorian Prosecutor's Office, August 9, 2016, https://www.fiscalia .gob.ec/Entidades-de-control-revelan-presuntas-irregularidades-de-empresas-spartan -y-clearprocess; Ecuadorian court records, case no. 09286-2016-02579, accessed 2019, http://consultas.funcionjudicial.gob.ec/informacionjudicial/public/informacion.jsf.

11. Alberto March, email to the authors, August 8, 2019.

12. Casto Ocando, "La ruta criminal del oro ecuatoriano," *Vertice*, June 23, 2016, https://vertice.news/la-ruta-criminal-del-oro-ecuatoriano-b2c9a3fbe412.

Chapter 36: The Secret Weapon

1. Monique O. Madan, "Greyhound Riders Are Being Asked for Immigration Papers at South Florida Bus Terminals," *Miami Herald*, https://www.miamiherald.com/news /local/immigration/article234018497.html; Nick Miroff, "Seeking a Split from ICE, Some Agents Say Trump's Immigration Crackdown Hurts Investigations and Morale,"

Washington Post, June 28, 2018, https://www.washingtonpost.com/world/national-security/seeking-split-from-ice-agents-say-trumps-immigration-crackdown-hurts-investigations-morale/2018/06/28/7bb6995e-7ada-11e8-8df3-007495a78738_story.html?noredirect=on.

Chapter 37: "*Investigaciones!*"

1. Juan Figueroa and Juan Pablo Sandoval (Investigations Police of Chile), interview with the authors, February 2, 2019.

2. Juan Figueroa and Juan Pablo Sandoval (Investigations Police of Chile), interview with the authors, February 2, 2019.

3. Harold Vilches, interviews with the authors, June 17–21, 2019.

4. Juan Figueroa and Juan Pablo Sandoval (Investigations Police of Chile), interview with the authors, February 2, 2019.

5. Juan Figueroa and Juan Pablo Sandoval (Investigations Police of Chile), interview with the authors, February 2, 2019.

6. Harold Vilches, interviews with the authors, June 17–21, 2019.

7. Harold Vilches, interviews with the authors, June 17–21, 2019.

8. Juan Figueroa and Juan Pablo Sandoval (Investigations Police of Chile), interview with the authors, February 2, 2019.

9. Harold Vilches, interviews with the authors, June 17–21, 2019.

10. "El Rey del Oro," *Contacto*, Canal 13, August 21, 2016, https://www.t13.cl/videos/programas/contacto-2016/contacto-rey-del-oro.

11. Tufit Bufadel, Pablo Alonso, and José Luis Pérez Calaf (prosecutors), interview with the authors, January 31, 2019.

12. "El Rey del Oro," *Contacto*, Canal 13, August 21, 2016, https://www.t13.cl/videos/programas/contacto-2016/contacto-rey-del-oro.

13. Harold Vilches, interviews with the authors, June 17–21, 2019.

14. Juan Figueroa and Juan Pablo Sandoval (Investigations Police of Chile), interview with the authors, February 2, 2019.

15. Chilean court records, *Fiscalía de Alta Complejidad Occidente v. Harold Vilches*, case no. 3265-2015.

16. Dagoberto Muñoz, interviews with the authors, January 29 and February 1, 2019.

17. Nicolás Rodríguez Videla (prosecutor), interview with the authors, June 19, 2019.

18. Nicolás Rodríguez Videla (prosecutor), interview with the authors, June 19, 2019.

19. Chilean court records, *Fiscalía de Alta Complejidad Occidente v. Harold Vilches*, case no. 3265-2015.

20. Tufit Bufadel, Pablo Alonso, and José Luis Pérez Calaf (prosecutors), interview with the authors, January 31, 2019.

21. Chilean court records, *Fiscalía de Alta Complejidad Occidente v. Harold Vilches*, case no. 3265-2015.

22. Harold Vilches, interviews with the authors, June 17–21, 2019.

23. Harold Vilches, interviews with the authors, June 17–21, 2019.

24. *United States v. Juan P. Granda*, No. 17-20215, PACER (S.D. Fla., March 15, 2017); Harold Vilches, interviews with the authors, June 17–21, 2019.

25. Harold Vilches, interviews with the authors, June 17–21, 2019.

26. Dagoberto Muñoz, interviews with the authors, January 29 and February 1, 2019.

27. Chilean court records, *Fiscalía de Alta Complejidad Occidente v. Harold Vilches*, case no. 3265-2015.

28. Tufit Bufadel, Pablo Alonso, and José Luis Pérez Calaf (prosecutors), interview with the authors, January 31, 2019.

29. Tufit Bufadel, Pablo Alonso, and José Luis Pérez Calaf (prosecutors), interview with the authors, January 31, 2019.

30. Chilean court records, *Fiscalía de Alta Complejidad Occidente v. Harold Vilches*, case no. 3265-2015.

Chapter 38: "DEA Sucks"

1. Doris Aguirre, "Implicado en el caso Comunicore es acusado de 'lavar' US$47 millones de oro ilegal," *La Republica*, September 15, 2016.

2. Internal Elemetal records reviewed by the authors.

Chapter 39: Inside the War Room

1. Chris Isidore, "35 Bankers Were Sent to Prison for Financial Crisis Crimes," *CNN-Money*, April 28, 2016, https://money.cnn.com/2016/04/28/news/companies/bankers-prison/index.html.

2. James B. Stewart, "In Corporate Crimes, Individual Accountability Is Elusive," *New York Times*, February 19, 2015, https://www.nytimes.com/2015/02/20/business/in-corporate-crimes-individual-accountability-is-elusive.html.

Chapter 40: The Flip

1. "El Rey del Oro," *Contacto*, Canal 13, August 21, 2016, https://www.t13.cl/videos/programas/contacto-2016/contacto-rey-del-oro.

2. Juan Figueroa and Juan Pablo Sandoval (Investigations Police of Chile), interview with the authors, February 2, 2019.

3. Tufit Bufadel, José Luis Pérez Calaf, and Pablo Alonso (prosecutors), interview with the authors, January 31, 2019.

4. Tufit Bufadel (prosecutor), interview with the authors, January 28, 2019.

5. Harold Vilches, interviews with the authors, June 17–21, 2019.

6. Harold Vilches, interviews with the authors, June 17–21, 2019.

7. Harold Vilches, interviews with the authors, June 17–21, 2019; Chilean court records, *Fiscalía de Alta Complejidad Occidente v. Harold Vilches*, case no. 3265-2015.

8. Harold Vilches, interviews with the authors, June 17–21, 2019.

9. Tufit Bufadel (prosecutor), interview with the authors, January 28, 2019.

10. Harold Vilches, interviews with the authors, June 17–21, 2019.

11. Harold Vilches, interviews with the authors, June 17–21, 2019.

12. Juan Figueroa and Juan Pablo Sandoval (Investigations Police of Chile), interview with the authors, February 2, 2019; Michael Smith and Jonathan Franklin, "How to Become an International Gold Smuggler," *Bloomberg*, March 9, 2017, https://www.bloomberg.com/news/features/2017-03-09/how-to-become-an-international-gold-smuggler.

13. Harold Vilches, interviews with the authors, June 17–21, 2019.

14. Harold Vilches, interviews with the authors, June 17–21, 2019.

15. Harold Vilches, interviews with the authors, June 17–21, 2019.

16. Juan Figueroa and Juan Pablo Sandoval (Investigations Police of Chile), interview with the authors, February 2, 2019.

17. Tufit Bufadel (prosecutor), interview with the authors, January 28, 2019; Smith and Franklin, "How to Become an International Gold Smuggler," https://www.bloomberg.com/news/features/2017-03-09/how-to-become-an-international-gold-smuggler.

18. Smith and Franklin, "How to Become an International Gold Smuggler," https://www.bloomberg.com/news/features/2017-03-09/how-to-become-an-international-gold-smuggler.

19. Tufit Bufadel (prosecutor), interview with the authors, January 28, 2019.

20. Juan Figueroa and Juan Pablo Sandoval (Investigations Police of Chile), interview with the authors, February 2, 2019.

21. Tufit Bufadel (prosecutor), interview with the authors, January 28, 2019.

22. Tufit Bufadel (prosecutor), interview with the authors, January 28, 2019.

23. Harold Vilches, interviews with the authors, June 17–21, 2019.

Chapter 41: Jumping All the Way

1. This account of what Andrés Tejeda told DEA agents Tim Schoonmaker and Steve Fischer is based in part on court documents and interviews with people briefed or otherwise familiar with the conversation.

2. Federal criminal affidavit against Granda, *United States v. Juan P. Granda*, No. 17-20215, PACER (S.D. Fla., March 15, 2017).

Chapter 43: "Does Your Wife Know You Went There?"

1. Juan Figueroa and Juan Pablo Sandoval (Investigations Police of Chile), interview with the authors, February 2, 2019.

2. Juan Figueroa and Juan Pablo Sandoval (Investigations Police of Chile), interview with the authors, February 2, 2019.

3. Harold Vilches, interview with the authors, June 17–21, 2019.

4. Harold Vilches, interview with the authors, June 17–21, 2019.

5. Tufit Bufadel (prosecutor), interview with the authors, January 28, 2019; Harold Vilches, interview with the authors, June 17–21, 2019.

6. Harold Vilches, interview with the authors, June 17–21, 2019.

7. Tufit Bufadel, José Luis Pérez Calaf, and Pablo Alonso (prosecutors), interview with the authors, January 31, 2019.

8. Tufit Bufadel, José Luis Pérez Calaf, and Pablo Alonso (prosecutors), interview with the authors, January 31, 2019.

9. Harold Vilches, interview with the authors, June 17–21, 2019.

10. Harold Vilches, interview with the authors, June 17–21, 2019.

11. Juan Figueroa and Juan Pablo Sandoval (Investigations Police of Chile), interview with the authors, February 2, 2019.

12. Tufit Bufadel (prosecutor), interview with the authors, January 28, 2019.

13. Juan Figueroa and Juan Pablo Sandoval (Investigations Police of Chile), interview with the authors, February 2, 2019.

14. Juan Figueroa and Juan Pablo Sandoval (Investigations Police of Chile), interview with the authors, February 2, 2019.

15. Juan Figueroa and Juan Pablo Sandoval (Investigations Police of Chile), interview with the authors, February 2, 2019.

16. Harold Vilches, interview with the authors, June 17–21, 2019.

Chapter 45: *La Venganza*

1. Pedro Pérez Miranda, interview with the authors, April 7, 2019.

2. 24 Horas, "Detienen a 'Peter Ferrari' y allanan 11 inmuebles vinculados a caso de lavado de activos"(on *Panamericana de Televisión*), YouTube video, 4:37, January 3, 2017, https://www.youtube.com/watch?v=nkRCIU2ibaY.

3. Peter Davis Pérez Gutierrez and Gian Piere Pérez Gutierrez, interview with the authors, March 28, 2019.

4. Confidential source, interview with the authors, 2018.

5. Carlos Neira, interview with the authors, October 1, 2018.

6. Justicia TV, "CASO: Fiscalia solicita prison preventiva para empresario 'Peter Ferrari' 12-01-2017-Parte 1," YouTube video, 2:47:20, January 12, 2017, https://www.youtube.com/watch?v=jV-tUXdoP1k.

7. Justicia TV, "CASO: Fiscalia solicita prison preventiva para empresario 'Peter Ferrari' 12-01-2017-Parte 1," YouTube video, 2:47:20, January 12, 2017, https://www.youtube.com/watch?v=jV-tUXdoP1k .

8. Gian Piere Pérez Gutierrez, interview with the authors, March 28, 2019.

9. Peruvian Police Report 5805, October 21, 2014.

10. Peruvian Police Report 5805, October 21, 2014.

Chapter 46: Kings of the World

1. Jay Weaver, "'Oxymonster,' Wearing a Long Beard, Sentenced to 20 Years for Drug Deals on Dark Web," *Miami Herald*, October 9, 2018, https://www.miamiherald.com/news/local/article219698010.html.

2. Several WhatsApp conversations were included in the federal criminal affidavits against Juan Pablo Granda, Renato Rodriguez, and Samer Barrage. *United States v. Juan P. Granda*, No. 17-20215, PACER (S.D. Fla., March 15, 2017).

3. *United States v. Juan P. Granda*, No. 17-20215, PACER (S.D. Fla., March 15, 2017).

4. Owen Daugherty, "Kasich Fills Open Board of Trustees Position with Campaign Donor," *The Lantern*, February 22, 2017, https://www.thelantern.com/2017/02/kasich-fills-open-board-of-trustees-position-with-campaign-donor/.

5. Staff, "Governor Appoints Alan Stockmeister to OSU Board," *Jackson County Times-Journal*, February 9, 2017.

Chapter 47: "You Have Nothing to Worry About"

1. Michael Smith and Jonathan Franklin, "How to Become an International Gold Smuggler," March 9, 2017, https://www.bloomberg.com/news/features/2017-03-09/how-to-become-an-international-gold-smuggler.

2. Federal criminal affidavit against Granda, *United States v. Juan P. Granda*, No. 17-20215, PACER (S.D. Fla., March 15, 2017).

Chapter 48: The Depth of Their Betrayal

1. Federal criminal affidavit against Granda, *United States v. Juan P. Granda*, No. 17-20215, PACER (S.D. Fla., March 15, 2017).

2. David Voreacos and Michael Smith, "Florida 'Boutique' Tied by U.S. to Alleged Gold Laundering Plot," *Bloomberg*, April 7, 2017, https://www.bloomberg.com/news /articles/2017-04-07/florida-boutique-tied-by-u-s-to-alleged-gold-laundering-plot.

3. Detention hearing, *United States of America v. Samer H. Barrage*, No. 17-20215, PACER (S.D. Fla., April 3, 2017).

4. Detention hearing, *United States of America v. Renato J. Rodriguez*, No. 17-20215, PACER (S.D. Fla., March 22, 2017).

5. Detention hearing, *United States v. Juan P. Granda*, No. 17-20215, PACER (S.D. Fla., March 20, 2017).

6. Detention hearing, *United States v. Samer H. Barrage*, No. 17-20215, PACER (S.D. Fla., April 29, 2017).

7. Maderal said in court: detention hearing, *United States of America v. Samer H. Barrage*, No. 17-20215, PACER (S.D. Fla., April 3, 2017).

8. Jaime Granados, email to the authors, December 7, 2018.

9. Internal Elemetal records reviewed by the authors.

10. Plea hearings, *United States v. Juan P. Granda and Samer H. Barrage*, No. 17-20215, PACER (S.D. Fla., September 5, 2017).

Chapter 49: Ferrari's Freefall

1. Peter Davis Pérez Gutierrez and Gian Piere Pérez Gutierrez, interview with the authors, March 28, 2019.

2. Peruvian Police Report No. 5805, October 21, 2014.

Chapter 50: Way Beyond Money Laundering

1. Jay Weaver, "Once at Center of 'Sprawling' Money Laundering Scheme, Miami Gold Dealers Headed to Prison," *Miami Herald*, January 19, 2018, https://www.miami herald.com/news/local/article195552089.html.

2. Weaver, "Once at Center of 'Sprawling' Money Laundering Scheme," https://www .miamiherald.com/news/local/article195552089.html.

3. Sentencing hearing, *United States of America v. Renato J. Rodriguez*, No. 17-20215, PACER (S.D. Fla., January 31, 2018).

Epilogue: "They Busted Our Ass"

1. Sentencing reduction, *United States v. Juan P. Granda*, No. 17-20215, PACER (S.D. Fla., June 18, 2019).

2. Andrés Tejeda court records.

3. Jay Weaver, "Firm Behind Gold-Fueled, Miami-Based Money-Laundering Racket Fined $15 Million," *Miami Herald*, March 16, 2018, https://www.miamiherald.com /news/local/article205503659.html.

4. Jay Weaver, "Firm Behind Gold-Fueled, Miami-Based Money-Laundering Racket Fined $15 Million," *Miami Herald*, March 16, 2018, https://www.miamiherald.com /news/local/article205503659.html.

5. Nicholas Nehamas, "Three Miami Dirty Gold Dealers 'Chewed Up and Spit Out' Hundreds of Ohio Factory Workers," *Miami Herald*, January 16, 2018, https://www .miamiherald.com/news/nation-world/national/article194187909.html.

6. Francisco Maderal (Assistant US Attorney) letter to Himmel's lawyer, Dan Gelber, February 6, 2018.

7. Ecuadorian court records, case no. 09286-2016-02579, accessed in 2019, http:// consultas.funcionjudicial.gob.ec/informacionjudicial/public/informacion.jsf.

8. César Rafael García, message to the authors, August 25, 2020; and Ecuadorian court records, case no. 09286-2016-02579, accessed in 2019, http://consultas .funcionjudicial.gob.ec/informacionjudicial/public/informacion.jsf.

9. "Opinion No. 6/2018 concerning Alberto Javier Antonio March Game (Ecuador)," United Nations Human Rights Council, June 27, 2018, http://daccess-ods.un.org /access.nsf/Get?Open&DS=A/HRC/WGAD/2018/6&Lang=S.

10. Mara Cecilia Gordillo Bedón, messages to the authors, 2019–2020.

11. Justicia TV, "Poder judicial dicta sentencia contra Pedro Pérez Miranda, alias 'Peter Ferrari,'" YouTube video, 2:57, January 13, 2017, https://www.youtube.com /watch?v=Rx4XaBm5cvI.

12. *United States v. Juan P. Granda*, No. 17-20215, PACER (S.D. Fla., March 15, 2017).

13. Jay Weaver and Antonio Maria Delgado, "Ring Plundered $1.2 Billion of Venezuelan Oil Money, Laundered It in South Florida," *Miami Herald*, July 26, 2018, https:// www.miamiherald.com/latest-news/article215493015.html; Department of Justice, US Attorney's Office, Southern District of Florida, "Two Members of Billion-Dollar Money Laundering Scheme Arrested" (news release), July 25, 2018, https://www.justice.gov /usao-sdfl/pr/two-members-billion-dollar-venezuelan-money-laundering-scheme -arrested; Jay Weaver and Antonio Maria Delgado, "Venezuela's Maduro Under Investigation in $1.2 Billion Money-Laundering Case," *Miami Herald*, July 27, 2018, https:// www.miamiherald.com/latest-news/article215663355.html.

14. Marco Rubio, "Rubio Statement on Stopping the Use of Dirty Gold from Latin America in Money Laundering" (press release), Marco Rubio US Senator for Florida, January 16, 2018, https://www.rubio.senate.gov/public/index.cfm/2018/1/rubio-state ment-on-stopping-the-use-of-dirty-gold-from-latin-america-in-money-laundering.

15. Jay Weaver and Nicholas Nehamas, "Federal Investigators Investigating 'Blood' Gold Won't Bring Charges Against Miami Refinery," *Miami Herald*, April 17, 2019, https://www.miamiherald.com/news/local/crime/article229361954.html.

16. Weaver and Nehamas, "Federal Investigators Investigating 'Blood' Gold," https:// www.miamiherald.com/news/local/crime/article229361954.html.

17. Chilean court records, *Fiscalía de Alta Complejidad Occidente v. Harold Vilches*, No. 3265-2015; Michael Smith and Jonathan Franklin, "How to Become an International Gold Smuggler," *Bloomberg*, March 9, 2017, https://www.bloomberg.com/news /features/2017-03-09/how-to-become-an-international-gold-smuggler.

18. Harold Vilches, interviews with the authors, June 17–21, 2019.

19. Tufit Bufadel, Pablo Alonso, and José Luis Pérez Calaf (prosecutors), interview with the authors, January 31, 2019.

20. Juan Figueroa and Juan Pablo Sandoval (Investigations Police of Chile), interview with the authors, February 2, 2019; *United States v. Juan P. Granda*, No. 17-20215, PACER (S.D. Fla., March 15, 2017).

21. "Fiscalía destaca condena por Asociación Ilícita en caso de Contrabando de Oro," Chilean Prosecutor's Office, February 4, 2018, http://www.fiscaliadechile.cl/Fiscalia/sala_prensa/noticias_ regional_det.do?id=14166.

22. "Fiscalía destaca condena por Asociación Ilícita en caso de Contrabando de Oro," Chilean Prosecutor's Office, February 4, 2018, http://www.fiscaliadechile.cl/Fiscalia/sala_prensa/noticias_ regional_det.do?id=14166.

23. Chilean court records, *Fiscalía de Alta Complejidad Occidente v. Dagoberto Muñoz*, No. 3265-2015.

24. Felipe Muñoz (founder of Aurica Metales), interview with the authors, January 29, 2019.

25. Paula Comandari, "El joven que vendía oro," *Qué Pasa*, August 19, 2016, http://www.quepasa.cl/articulo/negocios/2016/08/el-joven-que-vendia-oro.shtml/.

26. Harold Vilches, interviews with the authors, June 17–21, 2019.

27. Harold Vilches, interviews with the authors, June 17–21, 2019.

28. "Peru High Altitude Prisons Put Prisoners' Health at Risk," Amnesty International, February 1998, https://www.amnesty.org/download/Documents/152000/amr460021998en.pdf.

29. Pedro Pérez Miranda, interview with the authors, April 7, 2019.

30. Justicia TV, "Audiencia para determina la instalacion de los grilletes electronicos de Pedro David Perez Miranda," YouTube video, 58:44, January 7, 2020, https://www.youtube.com/watch?v=81PHlBvm9h8&t=3118s.

31. "Peter Ferrari murió a causa del coronavirus a los 60 años," *Canal N*, September 26, 2020.

32. Jose Huerta Torres (Peruvian defense minister), interview with the authors, April 3, 2019.

33. Luis Hidalgo Okimura (governor of Madre de Dios), interview with the authors, June 1, 2019.

34. Germán Ríos, interview with the authors, June 2019.

Solutions: How to Stop Dirty Gold

1. *River of Gold*, documentary film, Amazon Aid Foundation, 2018, https://amazonaid.org/river-of-gold/.

2. Susan Keane, "Time to Roll Up Our Sleeves and Tackle Toxic Mercury Use in Small-Scale Gold Mining," Natural Resources Defense Council, March 16, 2015, https://www.nrdc.org/experts/susan-egan-keane/time-roll-our-sleeves-and-tackle-toxic-mercury-use-small-scale-gold-mining.

3. "Mercury," Global Environment Facility, https://www.thegef.org/topics/mercury.

4. "Peru Proposes State-Owned Bank Buys Gold," Reuters, September 7, 2016, https://www.reuters.com/article/peru-gold/peru-proposes-state-owned-bank-buys-gold-from-artisanal-miners-idUSL1N1BJ1J6.

5. "The Metallurgy of Cyanide Gold Leaching—an Introduction," CORE Resources, https://www.coreresources.com.au/the-metallurgy-of-cyanide-gold-leaching-an-introduction/.

6. Nicholas Nehamas, Jay Weaver, and Kyra Gurney, "Blood Gold in Your Jewelry Is Poisoning Workers in the Rainforest. Here's How to Stop It," *Miami Herald*, January 16, 2018, https://www.miamiherald.com/news/nation-world/world/americas/article 194188459.html.

7. Nehamas, Weaver, and Gurney, "Blood Gold in Your Jewelry," https://www .miamiherald.com/news/nation-world/world/americas/article194188459.html.

8. Nehamas, Weaver, and Gurney, "Blood Gold in Your Jewelry," https://www .miamiherald.com/news/nation-world/world/americas/article194188459.html.

9. Organisation for Economic Co-operation and Development, Paris, France, About page, https://www.oecd.org/about/.

10. Global Witness, https://www.globalwitness.org/en/.

Index

KYRA GURNEY is a journalist based in Washington, DC. She has worked at the International Consortium of Investigative Journalists and at the *Miami Herald*, where she and her coauthors were finalists for the 2019 Pulitzer Prize for explanatory reporting for "Dirty Gold, Clean Cash," a series on the illegal gold trade. Before working at the *Miami Herald*, Kyra was a reporter at InSight Crime, a nonprofit investigative journalism outlet based in Colombia. Kyra has a master's degree in journalism from Columbia University.

NICHOLAS NEHAMAS is an investigative reporter at the *Miami Herald*. He was part of the global team of journalists that broke the Panama Papers and won the 2017 Pulitzer Prize for Explanatory Reporting. His work covering the local real estate industry led him into the dark underbelly of South Florida's shadow economy. He earned a master's degree in journalism from Columbia University.

JAY WEAVER is an award-winning reporter at the *Miami Herald* who has covered the courts, government, and politics in South Florida for more than twenty-five years. He was part of the *Miami Herald* team that won a Pulitzer Prize for breaking news in 2001 for its coverage of the federal seizure of Cuban boy Elián González. He and his *Herald* coauthors were finalists for the 2019 Pulitzer Prize for Explanatory Reporting for "Dirty Gold, Clean Cash," a series on the illegal gold trade. A graduate of UC Berkeley, he has won numerous journalism awards, including for exposing New York Yankees slugger Alex Rodriguez's lies about using performance-enhancing drugs.

JIM WYSS is a prize-winning journalist who has spent most of his career living and working in Latin America for outlets like the *Economist*, the *San Francisco Chronicle*, and *Latin Trade*. From 2011 to 2019, he was the *Miami Herald*'s South America correspondent based in Bogotá, Colombia. He now lives in Puerto Rico and covers the Caribbean for Bloomberg News. He has a master's degree in journalism from Columbia University through the Knight-Bagehot Fellowship and was also part of the reporting team that won the 2017 Pulitzer Prize for Explanatory Reporting for their work on the Panama Papers.

PublicAffairs is a publishing house founded in 1997. It is a tribute to the standards, values, and flair of three persons who have served as mentors to countless reporters, writers, editors, and book people of all kinds, including me.

I. F. STONE, proprietor of *I. F. Stone's Weekly*, combined a commitment to the First Amendment with entrepreneurial zeal and reporting skill and became one of the great independent journalists in American history. At the age of eighty, Izzy published *The Trial of Socrates*, which was a national bestseller. He wrote the book after he taught himself ancient Greek.

BENJAMIN C. BRADLEE was for nearly thirty years the charismatic editorial leader of *The Washington Post*. It was Ben who gave the *Post* the range and courage to pursue such historic issues as Watergate. He supported his reporters with a tenacity that made them fearless and it is no accident that so many became authors of influential, best-selling books.

ROBERT L. BERNSTEIN, the chief executive of Random House for more than a quarter century, guided one of the nation's premier publishing houses. Bob was personally responsible for many books of political dissent and argument that challenged tyranny around the globe. He is also the founder and longtime chair of Human Rights Watch, one of the most respected human rights organizations in the world.

. . .

For fifty years, the banner of Public Affairs Press was carried by its owner Morris B. Schnapper, who published Gandhi, Nasser, Toynbee, Truman, and about 1,500 other authors. In 1983, Schnapper was described by *The Washington Post* as "a redoubtable gadfly." His legacy will endure in the books to come.

Peter Osnos, *Founder*